PENGUIN BOOKS

JOB POWER

David Jenkins is a free-lance journalist and translator. He has written for more than fifty publications, including *The New York Times, Business Week, Fortune,* the *Economist,* and *Business International.* Author of one previous book—*Sweden and the Price of Progress*—Mr. Jenkins spent more than two years researching *Job Power* in Europe and in America. He lives in France.

DAVID JENKINS

JOB POWER

BLUE AND WHITE COLLAR DEMOCRACY

PENGUIN BOOKS INC · *New York* · *Baltimore*

PENGUIN BOOKS INC
72 Fifth Avenue
New York, New York 10011

PENGUIN BOOKS INC
7110 Ambassador Road
Baltimore, Maryland 21207

First published by Doubleday & Company, Inc.,
Garden City, New York, 1973
Published by Penguin Books Inc, 1974
Reprinted, 1974

Printed in the United States of America

CONTENTS

ACKNOWLEDGMENTS

This book could scarcely have been written without the very active assistance of the hundreds of managers, workers, psychologists, sociologists, labor leaders, consultants, government officials, and ideologists in a number of different countries with whom I spoke in gathering material. Many of them are mentioned in the text and my sincere thanks is due to all. A number of them deserve my special gratitude and, needless to say, they should not be blamed for my conclusions, which, for better or worse, are my own. I should first mention Einar Thorsrud of Oslo, whose very outstanding work in Norwegian factories first stimulated my interest in industrial democracy and with whom I have frequently discussed the problems. A number of people active in work-reorganization activities in Sweden have been helpful to me on many occasions, particularly Bertil Gardell, Reine Hansson, and Arne Derefeldt. In Israel, I was very grateful for the assistance provided by R. Peyton of the Government Press Office in Tel Aviv and by Arye Globerson of the University of Tel Aviv. In Yugoslavia, I was greatly aided in my research by Mrs. Vera Bejaković of the Federal Secretariat of Information in Belgrade and by Branko Raić at the Republican Secretariat of Information in Zagreb. In France, I received very valuable guidance and advice from Philippe Heymann, Michel Drancourt, and Henri Lepage of *L'Entreprise*, from sociologist Alfred Willener, and from John

Condon, labor attaché at the American Embassy. In the United States, I have benefited greatly from the opinions and knowledge of Louis Davis, who is without doubt among the most original and advanced thinkers in the field of work reform in America. I also appreciate the very considerable assistance provided by Rensis Likert, Director Emeritus, Institute for Social Research at the University of Michigan; by Harold M. F. Rush, of The Conference Board; and Neal Q. Herrick, of the Department of Labor. Personal acquaintances who have provided important, and morale-building, help include Miss Beth Bogie, Bob Borson, and Rainer Esslen. Finally, I should make special mention of Miss Shirley Dewis of London, who, at various stages of the manuscript, supplied fast and highly professional typing.

PREFACE TO THE PENGUIN EDITION

Since this book was written, it has become increasingly apparent that a democratic work organization fits the human temperament as does no other. It is therefore scarcely surprising not only that democracy is overwhelmingly popular with the average man but also that it "works." When Thomas Jefferson wrote that "the light of science" showed that "a favored few" had not been picked by God to rule "the mass of mankind," he was stating a truth that has since received ample confirmation. It is now clear that the need for control over one's working life is a deep and enduring trait in the human being, and that when no provision is made for meeting this need in the design of a work organization, it is going to be bad news for both the organization and the individuals involved.

Therefore, those—and there are many—who scoff at the application of democracy in industry because it is "only" ideology are missing the point. Ideology and the findings of social psychologists (proved countless times under day-to-day operating conditions in industry) happen to coincide. The choice of terms in which you express the idea is of course open, but in the end it hardly matters. Democracy "works," and a work organization in which people have maximum democratic freedom "works" for the same reason it "works" when employees are not blindfolded, handcuffed, or otherwise prevented from using their inborn capacities.

One point I should perhaps make clear. Many people have maintained—either in praise or condemnation—that industrial democracy is primarily a method of getting higher productivity. That is not the opinion or the message of this book. The only real reason for promoting industrial democracy—and the only reason for writing this volume —stems from the fact that people are being irreparably damaged by current autocratic management methods and that democracy can improve the situation because it is more suited to the real needs of human beings.

It is not realistic, however, to expect that the idea of industrial democracy will be welcomed in countries dominated by conservative business interests unless it is possible to prove that it "works" in conventional terms. Well, it does, and the evidence presented here on that score, which testifies to its practicality, is overwhelming. The fact that democratic methods help profits is no reason to keep the merits of industrial democracy a secret, just because it means that workers demand (as they generally have to) and are given (as they should be given) a share in any increase in productivity.

It is unnecessary to add appreciably to the data contained in this book, but we might note a couple of points that have been brought out in the study of worker attitudes made for the U.S. Department of Labor by the Institute for Social Research at the University of Michigan—probably the most comprehensive such study ever made. One of the findings was that the most highly valued element in work was "control" over the job—and that fact cut across categories of white-collar/blue-collar, male/female, and other classifications. Another interesting point was that when employees were asked about major work "difficulties," they gave first place to problems in getting their work done.

In other words, a general characteristic of workers is that they wish for nothing so much as the chance to do their jobs and to be allowed to use their own skills and knowledge in performing them. Numerous surveys have shown that most people feel they could do much more work than they actually do, but they are held back by tiresome bureaucratic entanglements, self-defeating "scientific management" work procedures, rigidly ceremonial hierarchical patterns, and company policies based, roughly, on the idea that all employees are morons and should be treated accordingly. There is among employees, however, a great reservoir of know-how waiting to be tapped and a willingness to use it. Unfortunately, this know-how is usually ignored. So is anyone surprised that most employees are scarcely "working" at all—that they are merely "sleepwalking"?

Note that we are speaking of "employees"—not only "workers." In recent months a modicum of attention in the United States has been focused on problems of work, but there is a general impression that the problems are experienced by only blue-collar and assembly-line workers. It is easy to conclude that the problems of these workers are not worthy of so much attention. This is a tragic fallacy. The advertising copywriter, the draftsman, the chemist, the accountant, the securities analyst, and the junior executive can suffer as much from heavily bureaucratized authoritarianism as the man on the assembly line. The existence of shiny, fast-moving machinery may make an alienating environment more frighteningly visible, but it is equally present among the rosewood desks and filing cabinets as it is among the turret lathes and riveting guns.

Our prevalent ideas about work—and thus our work organizations—have been primarily shaped by such theoreticians as Frederick W. Taylor, who was more of a philosopher than an engineer. His methods were based not on a knowledge of machinery but on his view of the human being. "Most of us remain," he wrote, "grown-up children"—and need to be treated as such. This basic philosophy can, of course, be applied anywhere, and out of it has grown Taylorism, time and motion study, scientific management, and the assembly line—as well as bureaucratized office routines, ultrafragmented jobs, heavy amounts of unnecessary supervision, and other widespread illnesses.

Interest in industrial democracy is—as it was when this book was written—at a high level in Europe and is constantly becoming more intense. The most striking developments in recent months have occurred in Britain and France.

For some years there had existed in Britain a gradual growth of sympathy for industrial democracy, but neither the labor unions nor any of the political parties had given the principles any official support. It was thus a major turning point when, in mid-1973, both the Labour Party and the Trade Union Confederation announced that they would henceforth push for legislation to give more power to lower-level employees, primarily through representation on boards of directors. As this is written, it is rumored that the Conservative government (partly in order to steal the fire from the opposition) will present its own program for industrial democracy.

In France the Communist-Socialist coalition formed prior to the March 1973 parliamentary elections included a measure of "worker control" in its program (despite the obvious reluctance of the Communist Party and the Confédération Générale du Travail, the Communist-dominated union, to accept such wild ideas). President Georges Pompidou therefore included promises for more "participation" in *his* program, and having won the election, is now in the process of delivering on these promises. At this moment legislation is being prepared to give employees board representation, decision-making power over working conditions, the chance to purchase shares of their companies, and other forms of increased power.

If the picture of the rather conservative Pompidou government straining itself to meet worker demands for more power seems bewildering, it is hardly avoidable in the present French climate of opinion. This climate was most forcefully expressed in the summer of 1973, when the Lip watch factory in Besançon, scheduled for a shutdown due to severe financial difficulties, was seized by the workers, who announced that they would henceforth manage the factory themselves. This drama has not now run its course, but the key point is that employees in France—when faced with a crisis—now regard such "self-management" action as perfectly natural, and so do the French people, who according to opinion polls, overwhelmingly approved of the Lip workers' decision.

The situation is more or less the same in almost every European country, and governments are scrambling to push legislation to satisfy widespread and quite articulate demands from the people to gain more control over their lives. There has been much new legislation in various European countries in recent months in this area, and more is on the way.

It should be pointed out that industrial democracy does *not* mean merely representation on the board of directors, more interesting jobs, or any other single element. It *is* a concept that includes various forms of control. It often covers a more meaningful job with more responsibility, but it also includes freedom from arbitrary and unjust decisions by one's superiors. For example, one piece of legislation passed in France in 1973 grants workers protection against unjustified dismissal. Similar legislation is in the works in Sweden as well. Not surprisingly, democracy is a large subject.

Sad to say, however, interest in industrial democracy is still at a low level in the United States. There is little understanding of or sympathy for the basic principles. As a result, there is little public discussion of the question.

To be sure, there is some progress. In negotiating new contracts with the auto companies in the fall of 1973, the United Automobile Workers stated firmly that such issues as voluntary overtime and "humanization of work" should take precedence over money issues. What the ultimate outcome of these demands will be is not clear at this moment, but the important point is that they have been raised for the first time in a major U.S. contract negotiation. (On September 17, 1973, the United Automobile Workers reached a settlement with the Chrysler Corporation that Leonard Woodcock, the union president, described as "precedent-setting" and "a breakthrough." The agreement includes provisions restricting compulsory overtime as a result of which no worker may be forced to work more than nine hours a day or to work on Sunday or on more than two consecutive Saturdays. It also calls for the establishment of machinery through which union and management will work jointly to improve health and safety conditions in the factories. The union hopes that this settlement will set the pattern for new contracts with Ford and General Motors as well.)

Otherwise, discussion of the problems of work has centered very much on "job enrichment," a topic that covers various methods of rearranging jobs. Although such measures are admirable as far as they go, they usually do not go far enough, and they do not strike at the root of the problem, which is the lack of control exercised by employees over their jobs. Even more distressing, surveys by the American Management Association and other groups show that only a small minority of companies have displayed much interest in such limited-goal procedures, despite their well-documented success.

It would appear unlikely that any great interest in industrial democracy will develop in America until politicians, labor leaders, and other molders of public opinion turn their attention to the subject. The U.S. Department of Health, Education and Welfare published an excellent report, *Work in America*, documenting the problems of work and giving some suggestions for improvement, but it has aroused no perceptible interest in the Nixon administration, which commissioned it, or in any other influential quarter.

How can we explain this odd lack of interest in industrial democracy in the United States, which, after all, is a center of democratic ideology? Perhaps this is a measure of the overall atmosphere in America just now. Perhaps we have lost—only temporarily, let us hope—faith in our own basic ideas. While prime ministers in Europe are energetically trying to find ways to give people more control over their lives, the President of the United States has been saying that the average American is like the "child in the family" who has to be told what to do. Can the concept of industrial democracy (or indeed of any form of democracy) flourish in such an environment?

The most widely discussed subject in America during recent months, of course, has been the Watergate affair. Whatever may be the ultimate disposition of this matter, it is clear that there is a parallel between the "Watergate mentality" and the problems of work we are discussing here. That is, a central failing in the Watergate matter was the blind loyalty shared by a large group of people to the goals of their superiors. An astoundingly large number of those involved were good "organization men," slogging along in their narrow grooves, faithful to their immediate superiors and their immediate goals, never questioning, nor encouraged to question, the rightness of the short-term goals set before them. We can now see how disastrous this blind emphasis on short-term goals has been.

In the business world this short-term attitude is known as bottom-line thinking—an emphasis on what appears at the bottom of the profit-and-loss statement, regardless of what damage might be done to the organization as a whole in order to achieve that result (see page 237). Such mistakes in business are rarely exposed to the merciless glow of publicity that has surrounded the Watergate affair, but companies and parts of companies are being wrecked every day by overzealous managers suffering from a "bottom-line" obsession who unduly restrict the freedom of their subordinates.

Part of the problem, of course, is that managers have been trained to believe that the exercise of power over other people is one of the perquisites of success. The tradition that success must carry the privilege of telling other people what to do—including the corollary principles that everyone is interested in this kind of success and that it is worth having—is one of our more enduring myths, but it is a myth nonetheless. There is every evidence that this kind of "power" hierarchy is unnecessary and counterproductive. What we need is a hierarchy of competence, based on the recognition that people farther down in the hierarchy have much more to contribute than they have even been given an opportunity to contribute—and that they are eager to do so.

In short, what we need is more democracy.

Paris
September 1973

I. INTRODUCTION: INDUSTRIAL DEMOCRACY

This book is about industrial democracy.

The idea of transferring power to employees in a business enterprise can seem a drastic notion, particularly in America.

It is more than that; it is an entirely new stage of industrialism—the abolition of petty office and shop-floor autocrats, management dictators, and meaningless work rules, the transformation of work from a kind of punishment into a source of genuine human satisfaction. It can turn industrial capitalism—which too often has been a fountain of boredom and restriction—into an instrument of liberation and human development.

It is a revolution that works. Experience throughout Europe and America suggests that it is not only feasible but essential in solving some of the pressing problems now faced by industrial capitalism. Its further rapid growth is not only desirable and necessary, but very probably inevitable.

The central feature of industrial democracy, as this book uses the term, is the possession of real decision-making power over substantial matters by the employees of an enterprise. This is a radical change from the traditional rigid, pyramidal, authoritarian management structures that are virtually universally accepted. At the very least, democracy means a firm check on the issuance of dictatorial management ukases from the airy reaches of the pyramidal peaks. It means an end to the assumption that "managers" and "employees" are somehow fundamentally different, the former endowed with vastly superior thinking powers, the latter totally incapable of formulating decisions of their own, able only to follow instructions, and at that only under threat of punishment. It means that the intelligence and knowledge of employees —assets often underutilized or nonutilized—can be put into action, to the benefit of both employees and organization. Mindless jobs consisting of subdivided and subsubdivided tasks, and/or of blind obedience to arbitrary rules, can be remolded into reasonable occupations worthy of the attention of dignified human beings.

An agreeable but impractical concept? No—not any longer, at least.

To be sure, the evils of regimented work processes under industrial capitalism have long been recognized. Adam Smith noted two hundred years ago—during the very birth pangs of the system—that under the strictly disciplined work processes necessary for the proper functioning of capitalism the individual "generally becomes as stupid and ignorant as it is possible for a human creature to become."[1] That this is true, and that it has been leading to increasing distaste for work and work environments in the industrial-capitalist world, is by now painfully obvious. But Adam Smith's answer was the same as those customarily given, explicitly or implicitly, down to our own times: The vast benefits of the capitalist system make all the suffering worthwhile. Indeed, the full dimensions of the problem are rarely discussed or even much noticed, the situation having been thoroughly accepted, like tornadoes, boll weevils, and acne, as just one more of the many unavoidable and incurable miseries of life.

And neither is industrial democracy a new idea. Some fifty years ago, G. D. H. Cole, the British guild socialist, one of the earliest and most articulate proponents of democratic worker control, could write: "Political democracy must be completed with democracy in the workshop."[2] But he couldn't show what good, if any, that might do anyone, and he couldn't prove it was a practical idea.

The new element today is that these two notions—the brutalizing effects of work under capitalism and the democratization of work organizations—are shown to be firmly, clearly, and intimately connected, and that the latter can be remarkably powerful in alleviating or eliminating the former. A fortuitous connection, and one of not immediately apparent logic? Perhaps. But it exists nonetheless, and by now there is a massive accumulation of evidence that may be of critical importance in the future of industrial capitalism.

There are numbers of reasons why the evidence has been, until recently, neglected. It has come to light in widely scattered locations, the full force of its meaning has only gradually emerged over the past two or three decades, and—perhaps most important —it is in direct conflict with orthodox thinking on how a business should be managed.

Nevertheless the basic situation, the problems, and the solutions are all concrete, tangible, hard-boiled realities. The subject is as solid and real as the barrels of ten thousand bolts each rolling down the assembly line (see Chapter IV).

It should be made clear that there are a number of things industrial democracy is *not*:

• It is not merely a profit-sharing arrangement, or plan for distribution of shares to employees, or an incentive-payment program —although such measures have sometimes been included in systems that can be classed as democratic. The central idea of industrial democracy is the re-distribution of power, not money, in an organization. Money may (and perhaps should) be included, but the key is power over decisions.

• It is not a program for the appointment of "public" or "consumer" representatives to company boards of directors. Such notions may or may not be worthwhile, but that is not the subject of this book. To oversimplify somewhat, we are discussing here methods of reducing the power of companies to abuse their employees. The regulation of company abuse of society as a whole is another, and doubtless more complex, question.

• It is not trade unionism. Unions are necessary institutions, but they are not instruments of industrial democracy as that term is used here (though it has sometimes been applied to unionism), because unions do not exercise decision-making power. They do carry out aggressive invasions into management's decision-making territory, but only to fix limits within which management may operate. Unions do not decide anything—decisions are still made by management. Unions in some parts of the world are now agitating for more democracy in companies, but this is clearly an activity outside and quite separate from their normal function.

• It does not refer only to "industrial"—that is, manufacturing—operations. The term "industrial democracy" is used here only because, despite some ambiguities, it is the best available in the United States. As we shall see, the basic problems are fully as serious in commercial and service organizations as in manufacturing—if not more so.

• It is not simply a permissive environment in which everyone does as he pleases without regard to the goals of the enterprise.

• It is not just another management "trick" to induce employees, in the illusory belief that they are in control, to give more to the company, to work harder, and to complain less—although some of the principles described in the coming pages have, regrettably, been and still are being used in that way. There is a crucial difference between having the "feeling" of having control and actually having control.

• It is not simply a matter of everybody being "nice" to each other, as indicated by, for example, friendly habits of addressing one's employers and fellow workers on a first-name basis. Surely there can be nothing wrong with being nice to one's fellow man, but industrial democracy is more than that.

• It has nothing to do with what, in the United States, has been called "corporate democracy," meaning the exercise by shareholders of their legal right to supervise a company's management. It can reasonably be assumed that, after many decades during which shareholders have remained contentedly apathetic despite repeated admonitions to seize the power that they in fact already have, shareholders neither need nor want that power.

• It is not, unfortunately, a ready-made system that can be installed in a company on order, like a new time clock or machine tool. The abolition of traditional authoritarian patterns and the creation of new forms of control can be a delicate and complicated process, and the benefits can be slow in materializing. We are still in the early stages of a movement that calls for breaking down psychological and organizational barriers built up over hundreds of years.

• It is not merely a rearrangement of tasks to make jobs more "interesting." In recent discussions of worker discontent in the United States, it has been assumed that problems can be solved by replacing a "dumb" job, in which the worker is forbidden to exercise his autonomy, with a "smart" job, in which the worker is forbidden to exercise his autonomy. The supposition is that an omniscient management, by fiddling with the job, can eliminate its defects; but the worker is still presumed to be incapable of doing the fiddling himself. This has come to be known as "job enrichment," and while such an approach is a worthwhile starting point, it is only a first step in eliminating the basic ills, which arise from excessive authoritarianism. Industrial democracy, in the true sense of this expression, is not merely the enrichment of jobs, it is the enrichment of life.

As to what industrial democracy *is*, it is not possible to give a single brief description; some of the more interesting and instructive forms that have been tried at various times and in various places are discussed in later chapters. The purpose of this survey is not to present any all-inclusive encyclopedia of experience in industrial democracy. The objective is rather to point up some of the phenomena that appear to be significant for future development. The different systems can seem, at least superficially, to vary widely—the kibbutzim in Israel, self-management in Yugoslavia, codetermination in West Germany, participative management in the United States, and the wide-ranging democratization of enterprises in Norway. Yet, upon closer examination, the different approaches are part of the same trend, which appears throughout the industrialized world. A key common factor is the deep-seated desire of human beings to exercise control over their own work lives, and this has led, in one way or another, to the creation of organizations designed to satisfy that desire.

By examining briefly some of the problems of modern work organizations and some of the systems of industrial democracy that have been tried, we will see how the latter can serve to alleviate the former, and how all this can help in constructing a practical system of industrial democracy for the future.

It must be said that some of the systems are badly thought-out and quite "wrong." But even some of the "wrong" systems are, in many respects, more "right" than orthodox management structures, characterized by rigid hierarchies in which authority is highly centralized and filtered down through multiple layers of command.

It is relevant to ask, as many people do ask: "Is it not dangerous to give power to employees—might they not run the company into ruin through their lack of management ability?" Some observers might object to the assumption in the question—that somehow managers are all geniuses and lower-level employees are all imbeciles. Naturally, nobody would wish that the imbeciles be put in charge of running the companies. In the past few years, we have seen some of the world's great enterprises come to grief— Penn Central, Ling-Temco-Vought, Lockheed, Rolls-Royce, Investors Overseas Services, Goodbody & Co., and dozens of other Wall Street firms. If any of these companies had been managed partly or wholly through democratic systems, that fact would certainly inspire grave doubts about the value of industrial democracy. Yet all of them were solidly capitalistic companies under orthodox genius-managers. Clearly, there is something wrong with the assumption that the customary principles are correct and the other approaches must be wrong. The painful fact is that some companies are so badly managed that neither democratic management nor any other kind of nontraditional approach could be worse.

When we come to examine the financial consequences of industrial democracy in some detail—as we will do a bit later—we do not find that democracy is inferior to orthodox management methods. Though the evidence is not always clear-cut, such evidence as is available suggests that even the somewhat primitive democratic systems—among which we might class the Israeli kibbutzim, the Yugoslavian self-management arrangement, and the West German codetermination structure—function as well as or better than conventional management systems. When we move to the companies in Britain, Scandinavia, and the United States where more scientific methods have been used to introduce "democracy" (whether or not that term is used), the superior efficiency of democracy is usually clear-cut and often astoundingly so. As knowledge of organizations has increased, so has the effectiveness of democracy become ever clearer, and so have techniques been developed to place unusually great decision-making power in the hands of employees while improving an organization's efficiency.

This point should not be particularly startling. To look at it on the simplest possible level, if organizations are arranged so that employees are using their intelligence and powers of judgment, should not the use of these additional assets alone logically produce better results?

One might say that a central problem in developing workable democratic structures is the cultivation of responsible attitudes among employees to accompany the increased freedom of action granted them. A common belief is that, while most employees will welcome more freedom, they are unwilling and/or unable to accept responsibility for the constructive use of that freedom, and that, therefore, tight discipline is needed in any organization that is to function efficiently. This is a rather bleak, but remarkably widespread, view of man's basic nature. Experience shows, however, that large reserves of responsible behavior lie waiting to be tapped, if only the effort is made to uncover and to utilize them. The average person is, to a much larger extent than is recognized in the business world, capable of making decisions for himself. The rigid discipline, the constant watching by "big brother," the ever-present threats of punishment for contravention of the rules—it is all quite unnecessary.

As a matter of fact, what is astonishing is not that anyone should have the curious idea of democratizing business enterprises, but that frankly authoritarian managements should still be surviving on so widespread a scale in our supposedly open and free society. The unquestioned authority of any employer, the dangers of sudden and arbitrary management decisions, the lack of any appeal against those decisions for most employees—all these factors are in obvious and direct conflict with the stated values of our society.

Nevertheless, it is not necessary to refer to such philosophical and sentimental ideas to justify democracy. Company democracy is both an end and a means. Ideally, it is both a method of efficient operation and an efficient means of establishing an efficient method of operation. A democratic company is not a better company because democracy is a conceptually elegant and socially acceptable value, but because it works better.

Many people, of course, dislike authority, but not everyone realizes that it can be not only useless, but quite harmful. When I was very young, I was sent for a time to a "military school," which was run along lines of strict discipline and which was for that reason supposed to be good for you. The inflexible rules and the regimentation of life were extremely tiresome. However, it was quite clear that the system had no real sense in itself; nobody thought for a moment that enemy troops were going to attack the gymnasiums and lecture halls we guarded so zealously with our wooden rifles—the whole thing was an obvious sham but theoretically possessed some educational value.

In modern industrial capitalism, we find many authoritarian methods on approximately the same level of pointlessness, and they serve no useful purpose at all; they interfere with efficiency, they create unhealthy conditions for both managers and employees, but they endure because they have only recently begun to be questioned. The indications are that they must be changed, because they are an integral part of the immense troubles now afflicting industrial capitalism.

II. WHAT'S WRONG WITH EVERYBODY?

The impression has begun to get about that the Industrial Revolution is not going to work out after all.

It seems only a few short years ago that modern capitalism—the prime creation of the Industrial Revolution—was being eulogized in books with cheerful titles like *The Triumph of American Capitalism* and *The Twentieth Century Capitalist Revolution*, while today there is a constant flow of pronouncements certifying to the rottenness, the emptiness, the inner weaknesses, the frailty, the utter dispensability, the need even for an immediate dismantling of the whole gigantic structure—that monstrous creation, the strangulation apparatus, the instrument of oppression, industrial capitalism, the "system." Michael Harrington writes: "Practically every ethical, moral, and cultural justification for the capitalist system has now been destroyed by capitalism."[1] Armas Lappalainen, a prominent leftist ideologue, writes in Sweden's largest-circulation morning paper: "Society, in the not-too-distant future, will, because of the inherent contradictions between workers and capitalists, be struck by a crisis . . . and a revolutionary situation will arise."[2] Daniel Cohn-Bendit, the German-French activist, avers (redundantly, though succinctly): "We totally reject the entire system."[3] Such inflammatory sentiments are by no means confined to eccentrics and extreme leftists. As the mildly liberal critic Irving Howe has pointed out: "Even among those who play the game and accept the social masks necessary for gaining success, there is a widespread disenchantment."[4]

So widespread is the disenchantment that we see today a considerable industry devoted to the production of anticapitalism, antiestablishment, and anti-"system" screeds, documenting industrial capitalism's undesirable features: manipulation of consumers, destruction of the environment, debasement of cultural life, unjust distribution of wealth, disproportionate privileges enjoyed by the wealthy, the corrupting pursuit of profit, and the promotion of militarism.

Rather little attention has been paid in recent years to another phenomenon created concomitant with capitalism and, indeed, the very kernel of the system, the thing that makes it go at all—the worker. But many of the harshest critiques of capitalism—from Marx onward—have taken as a starting point the drab and dissatisfying nature of work under capitalism, and it is quite possible that this is the system's most central, most significant, and most terrifying defect. Roger Masters, cultural attaché at the U.S. Embassy in Paris, has noted: "There's every reason to believe that industrial society, a relative innovation, is simply unnatural from a biological point of view. Man got along for 2,000 years in an agricultural society. Then he was following a natural cycle. Now he just works himself to death, breaks it periodically with a vacation and the rest of the time gets bored and has the impression of never getting anywhere."[5]

Moreover, increasing quantities of social conflict, bitterness, and strife have been swirling up around problems of work, and much of it is connected with employer ideas of authority and worker reluctance to accept these ideas. Some years ago, a poll conducted among businessmen elicited comments like these: "The problem is to get people to work; they're just lazy." "People don't want to work; they have to be pushed." "People tend to take the lazy way." "Fifteen years ago, a man was hungrier; he'd finish the job in half the time it takes now—and he gets three times the money."[6] The problems have been brought suddenly and clearly into focus by the United States' sagging world trade position that has developed at the beginning of the 1970s. One report points out: "A prime reason for the U.S. troubles is that all too many American workers . . . no longer give a damn."[7]

And, when given the opportunity, workers themselves eagerly supply solid confirmation of their suspected disgruntlement. A dramatic event of this type in the United States was the breakdown at the General Motors auto assembly plant at Lordstown, Ohio, where the engineering values of a hypermodern and superautomated assembly line experienced a head-on collision with the values of a hypermodern and unusually young workforce in early 1972. Expressing dislike and disgust for GM's hard-driving, high-speed (101 cars an hour) production philosophy, the workers responded with soaring absentee rates, sabotage, and finally a bitter twenty-two-day strike. A good bit of attention was given to these surprising events, and some public concern about work in general was stimulated by this "nightmare for General Motors."[8] But the basics of the situation and the dangers therein were not news. In 1970, two years before Lordstown, a personnel research specialist at GM told me the crisis of work was already painfully apparent. As an example, he told me of the company's well-meaning attempts to help members of minority groups and other disadvantaged persons to obtain well-paid employment of a dignified nature. "One thing we learned about hard-core unemployment," he said, "is that we do not have so much to offer these people after all. Blacks accustomed to making a living after a fashion by 'hustling' [that is, engaging in various illegal and semilegal pursuits] would come in and we would give them instructions on how to find a bus to get to the plant and so on; but when they found out what kind of work they were going to do, they just vanished. There was more opportunity to develop self-respect in hustling."

The growing distaste for rigidly disciplined work environments is not confined to blue-collar workers. One 1968 study showed that 56 percent of college students "did not mind being bossed around on the job," but the percentage dropped to 36 percent in 1971.[9] Neither is the condition unique to the United States. In France, in 1968, the "events of May"—the revolt largely powered by resentment against the excessively authoritarian system in that country—highlighted the widespread bitterness felt by workers. And the "fear of May" returns to haunt the populace each spring —apprehension that the explosion may occur again. Disgust with work is so rife in France that, according to a Paris municipal official, "the cause of our most grave social conflict, a conflict which nobody discusses, is the refusal of young people to accept manual work."[10] In Sweden, a class of schoolchildren, when asked whether they wanted to become industrial workers, "unanimously burst into laughter."[11] In Britain, the "middle classes are developing an allergy to total job involvement, the fight for promotion and all the other trappings of the rat-race."[12] And the symptoms are not peculiar to the West. One report on conditions in Eastern Europe noted: "Slacking and absenteeism are endemic to these workers' states."[13] And *Pravda* has complained that "most" young Soviet citizens "felt that their lives were ruined if they had to become workers."[14]

What's more, there is a good deal of feeling that all this anti-work sentiment is thoroughly justified—that it is the fault of the work, not the workers. Historian Staughton Lynd writes: "Work for most Americans may no longer be dirty, but it is still boring, humiliating, and unworthy of what a man can be. The young are right to rebel against an adulthood which insults them."[15] W. N. Penzer, a personnel expert, says: "It is becoming increasingly clear that the employees entering the world of business are unwilling to accept the system of unanswered questions, half-baked opportunities, and half-assed jobs. . . . They will no longer unquestioningly accept the organizational party line and will no longer stand idly by while their business lives are controlled and manipulated from above."[16]

Though this ferment of discontent has obviously been building for some time, only very recently have the problems of work gained much notice in the United States. The press has devoted a modicum of attention to the issue, especially in the wake of the Lordstown disaster, and it is no longer a novelty to observe that most jobs are stupefyingly boring. A U. S. Army recruiting poster, reflecting the increased awareness of the question, perceptively coaxes: "If your job puts you to sleep, try one of ours."

At this writing, however, the new concern about work is still embryonic and has scarcely manifested itself in any widespread understanding of the problems or intensive search for solutions. That the situation could build to an explosive level while being scarcely noticed is no doubt partly due to the general neglect—

developed over the years among social thinkers, intellectuals, and others in charge of our collective conscience—of any troubles that might be afflicting the blue-collar worker.

The blue-collar worker was once an object of cold analysis as well as warm compassion on the part of social thinkers interested in improving (or abolishing, or replacing) the system. In the 1930s, liberal social thinkers and other intellectuals actively supported the ordinary worker in his struggle for justice, and the "liberal-labor" coalition, as a political force no less than an idealistic-ideological unity, once upon a time seemed indissoluble.

By now, all that has faded into the mists of the past along with such dimly remembered phenomena as Elinor Glyn, Edgar Guest, and Fred Waring. Brendan Sexton, a union official, points out: "Not since the early and dramatic days of the CIO have liberals and intellectuals (with some honorable exceptions) shown much sympathetic interest in workers or unions."[17]

Not only has the sympathy evaporated, but it has been replaced with distrust and outright contempt. There is now a tendency to think of the worker as having achieved all his goals (union recognition, high pay, job security), possessing no further problems, and having adopted a position of stanch, racist conservatism, antiprogress, and an exceptionally narrow outlook. Examples of this somewhat elitist contempt are not hard to find. Herbert Marcuse charges that the working classes "have become a prop to the established way of life."[18] Theodore Roszak, prominent prophet of the "counterculture," echoes this view: "The working class sits tight and plays safe: the stoutest prop of the established order."[19]

As it began to be evident in the early 1970s that something was up with blue-collar workers, one common reaction was wonderment that they should persist in stirring up so much difficulty. In examining this line of reasoning, prominent economist Leonard Silk formulated the reaction thus: "What is at the heart of the blue-collar blues—the discontent, even anger, of blue-collar workers over current trends in the American society and economy?"[20]

Gradually, the picture of the worker as a man with problems has been replaced by the image of a man creating problems. Even when, with the blue-collar worker's gradual emergence into the limelight, he is given some sympathetic attention by American social thinkers, it has most often been with a kind of halfway view of the full complex of problems. For example, Senator Abraham Ribicoff, in a friendly analysis of the "alienation" of workers, rightly points out that "we have ignored their increasing difficulties and needs," but discusses these difficulties primarily in economic terms.[21] For most of our social thinkers, the problems workers have with their work still do not merit close examination.

To a great extent, this neglect of the blue-collar worker and his worries is understandable. Under the curious American class structure, students, intellectuals, and others who are responsible for social criticism and who might have been expected to direct public attention to the very serious underlying problems, tend to be rather isolated from society as a whole and thus have little opportunity to notice problems of this nature until they reach a high level of flammability. Walker and Guest, in their pioneering study *The Man on the Assembly Line*, drily define an intellectual as "the man who thinks about machines . . . without having any personal or professional experience with them."[22] American students, who generally come from the elite classes, have little experience with menial work, either personally or through their fathers. The report on U.S. universities prepared by Dr. Harold Hodgkinson for the Carnegie Commission on Higher Education noted the increasing isolation of university student bodies from the worker classes: "Institutions have become less open to social classes than they have to races," the report stated, in referring to the effective near-elimination of children of blue-collar workers from the university system.[23]

In fact, many social critics, restricted to a narrowly limited area by experience and inclination, bluntly proclaim the elitist nature of their commentary. Mark Gerzon, a renowned explainer of youth feelings, meticulously states that his analysis applies only to "one who comes from a middle- or upper-class background; who is white; who attends college or is capable of doing so. . . ."[24] Theodore Roszak delimits his field of vision even farther, explaining that the group which "desperately requires" attention "excludes our more conservative young . . . our more liberal youth . . . the scattering of old-line Marxist youth groups . . . in large measure the black young. . . ."[25] (One wonders how the remaining few can have such awesome .powers as to be able to provide "the saving vision our endangered civilization requires.")

It should be emphasized that the situation is very different in Europe. As we have seen, the surface manifestations of the problems are roughly the same in Europe as in America. The difference, however, is that in Europe there is—and has been for some years —a widespread awareness that the work-connected problems must be dealt with. Specifically, there is considerable understanding that the problems all point to the necessity to modify or abolish the traditional authoritarianism in industry and commerce, and to replace it by some form of genuine democracy. Although the reforms being promoted vary from country to country, they have one point in common: the transfer of real decision-making power to employees. In almost every West European country, student groups, political factions, independent organizations, social thinkers, intellectuals, writers, and labor leaders are actively urging democratic reform of business enterprises, and anyone in these countries drawing up a list of social issues requiring attention would surely put near the top of the list some form of industrial democracy, worker control, *Mitbestimmungsrecht, cogestion* or *autogestion, företagsdemokrati, bedriftsdemokrati, medbestemmelseret,* or whatever. By contrast, the virtual vacuum in this area in the United States is startling, confusing, and not altogether understandable. (In this respect, Mark Gerzon, the youth specialist, is badly off balance when he confidently asserts: "Already it is clear to American young people who have been in Europe that they have much in common with their European counterparts."[26]) Even though the U.S. is at the moment rather backward in this field, there are definite signs—as we shall see—that democratization of companies is fully as feasible in America as it is in Europe—if not more so. Indeed, some of the very radical democratization moves made by major American companies go well beyond anything so far achieved in Europe. Nevertheless, the general awareness of, or interest in, these facts among Americans is at an appallingly low level.

The consciousness of the problems among European students, intellectuals, and other opinion molders is not wholly a matter of altruism. There is a great realization that the work-connected dangers of the industrial-capitalist behemoth are of intimate concern not only to men in blue collars, but to almost everybody. In describing the student-worker alliance forged during the May 1968 revolt in France, Daniel Cohn-Bendit notes that the students were aware that they were all in the same boat: "Most students will end up as managers and administrators, toiling away amid millions of other workers at their narrow little tasks, without any chance of deciding their place in society, their work, in short the pattern of their lives."[27]

This grim fact of life should surely be apparent in the United States as well. It was in his discussion of white-collar workers that C. Wright Mills gloomily described work thus: "Underneath virtually all experience of work today, there is a fatalistic feeling that work *per se* is unpleasant."[28] And is not the "organization man," the very epitome of the mindless, empty, passive victim of industrial capitalism, the brother-under-the-skin of the blue-collar worker? As William H. Whyte, Jr., the chronicler of this suffering creature, points out, the organization men "are not the workers, nor are they the white-collar people in the usual clerk sense of the word. These people only work for The Organization. . . . and most are destined to live poised in a middle area. . . ."[29]

There is no question that work, and the image of work, has sunk badly—for blue-collar workers, for organization men, for contemptuous young people, for almost everyone. Such a shambles has work, as a product of industrial capitalism, become that one can almost conclude that the only force keeping anyone at it is the mythology of the nobility of the thing, however distasteful it might be. W. H. Auden puts his finger on this unhappy reality: "The Greeks were harder-hearted than we but clearer-headed; they knew that labor as such is slavery, and . . . in our society . . . practically all workers have been reduced to laborers."[30]

And yet . . . and yet, there is a nagging feeling that work is not only desirable for an individual to function satisfactorily, but that it is an indispensable element in a full life. Frank Lloyd Wright once observed: "This new American liberty is of the sort that declares man free only when he has found his work and effective means to achieve a life of his own."[31] Freud classed work, along with sex, as one of the basic creative forces in society: "The life of human beings . . . had a twofold foundation, i.e., the compulsion to work, created by external necessity, and the power of love, causing the male to wish to keep his sexual object, the female, near him. . . ."[32] But Freud also took note of the ambiguous attitudes toward work: "The daily work of earning a livelihood affords a particular satisfaction when it has been selected by free choice, i.e., when through sublimation it enables use to be made of existing inclinations. . . . And yet as a path to happiness work is not valued very highly by men. They do not run after it as they do after other opportunities for gratification."[33]

What happened to work over the centuries, and how did it get into its present troubles?

III. EVOLUTION OF THE ANTIWORK SYNDROME

The crisis of work, and of our ideas about work, has materialized relatively recently, as one stage in the progress (if that's the right word) of industrial civilization. Obviously, the nature of work has changed over the centuries; somewhat less obviously, attitudes toward work have also changed. Indeed, one might say that a central problem today is the large gap between prevailing attitudes toward work and the realities. It was not always so.

In primitive societies, as far as can be learned, the difference was minor. The notion of work itself, as a separate activity, scarcely existed. "If contemporary hunting and gathering societies provide any clue to man's distant past," writes Walter Neff, a historian of the subject, "it is that the earliest meaning attached to work is hardly a distinctive meaning at all. It also seems likely that no distinction existed between work and non-work, between labor and leisure. . . ."[1]

In ancient Greece and Rome, a radical transformation in ideas about work took place. The separation between "work" and "life" was complete. French historian Claude Mossé points out that, for men in antiquity, "labor . . . appeared as a sentence to which no redeeming value was attached," while "idleness was . . . an ideal to which every gentleman aspired."[2] Labor was deemed fit only for slaves and barbarians, but this attitude was subject to some subtle, and peculiarly modern, qualifications. For one thing, work on the land was not considered demeaning. Moreover, in general, it was the humiliating conditions under which work was carried out that were so reprehensible rather than work itself: "It is not the actual activity of work which makes labor despised. . . . But to work for another man, in return for a wage of any kind, is degrading."[3] And the definitions of work in force at the time were somewhat different from our modern ideas. Xenophon has Socrates condemn the work of artisans who must "sit still and live indoors" because of the damage to the spirit: "The softening of the body involves a serious weakening of the mind." Yet Xenophon was a prolific writer and, today, writers, who also must "sit still and live indoors," are normally thought to be engaged in "work."[4]

During the Middle Ages, under the influence of the Church, work regained a measure of respectability and was even felt to serve a moderately useful purpose. Benedict proclaimed that all monks must work to avoid the unhealthy effects of idleness. Work was fully honorable and even a "gateway to spirituality." Paul's stern admonition, "If any would not work, neither should he eat,"[5] was interpreted by Thomas Aquinas as meaning exactly what it says—work is thoroughly acceptable and admirable, but only to the extent that it is necessary.

During the Renaissance, a new view of work arose: the idea that work, as an activity separate and distinct from the rest of life, could not only be meritorious but a positive source of joy and creative fulfillment. C. Wright Mills wrote: "By his own activity, man could accomplish anything; through work, man became creator. How better could he fill his hours? Leonardo rejoiced in creative labor; Bruno glorified work. . . ."[6] As we saw in some opinions quoted earlier, this noble idea lingers on today, though for most of the population it is only a remote and pleasant abstraction, with little connection with reality. A British factory worker considers this attitude in connection with his own employment: "Nothing is gained from the work itself—it has nothing to offer. . . . People who speak grandiosely of the 'meaning of work' should spend a year or two in a factory."[7]

Unhappily, our modern ideas about work have been primarily shaped by more powerful, more destructive, and more lasting influences than the joy expressed by Leonardo. One of the most significant was Protestantism, which greatly aided the development of capitalism through its benevolent view of commercial activity in general and the money-making side of it in particular. Catholicism had taken (officially, at least) a dim view of excessive profit. As Max Weber pointed out, even in Florence in the fourteenth and fifteenth centuries, "the most highly capitalistic centre of that time," a favorable view of profit "was considered ethically unjustifiable, or at best to be tolerated."[8] R. H. Tawney, a British historian, gives the official doctrine: "Craftsmen and merchants must receive what will maintain them in their calling, and no more."[9] This was to change sharply.

Martin Luther was somewhat uneasy when confronted with harshly materialistic ideas, and he continued, at first, the official disapproval of the acquisition of wealth. (The Bible, of course, provides handy support for such disapproval, inasmuch as it contains numerous passages of the "woe unto you that are rich"[10] variety.) But he increasingly leaned toward the opinion that worldly duties were a necessity in the eyes of God, thus coming ever closer to an outright commercial opinion.

Building on the base created by Luther, Calvin added a vital link: asceticism. With this key connection, work *and* money-making could be fully legitimatized—as long as you were careful not to enjoy either. Like Thomas Aquinas before him, Calvin quoted Paul's statement regarding the necessity of work for those who would eat, but he gave these utterances a reverse interpretation, classifying work as a burden to be carried throughout life, a kind of necessary suffering.[11] This was no doubt a more accurate —if not especially cheerful—reading; Paul, in his letters to the hippie-like Thessalonians ("we hear that there are some which walk among you disorderly, working not at all, but are busybodies"[12]), put his exhortations to "work with your hands" in the same category of disciplinary unpleasantnesses as his orders "to be quiet . . . to do your own business" and "to abstain from fornication."[13] In developing the severe Pauline doctrines, Calvin supplied an important philosophical basis to the idea that work was holy and unpleasant and that, ideally, it should be both. The Calvinist ideal, Tawney wrote, "is a society which seeks wealth with the sober gravity of men who are conscious at once of disciplining their own characters by patient labor, and of devoting themselves to a service acceptable to God."[14]

The concept of work as explicitly unenjoyable drudgery was refined further by the English Puritans. "The real moral objection," according to Weber, "is to relaxation in the security of possession, the enjoyment of wealth with the consequence of idleness and the temptations of the flesh, above all of distraction from the pursuit of a righteous life."[15] The Puritan writings are "dominated by the continually repeated, often almost passionate preaching of hard, continuous bodily or mental labor."[16] The acquisition of wealth now became not just permissible if it were carried out in the right spirit, but a positive imperative. "If God show you a way in which you may lawfully get more than in another way," wrote one publicist, "if you refuse this, and choose the less gainful way, you cross one of the ends of your calling, and you refuse to be God's steward. . . ."[17] Still, it was clearly spelled out that such remunerative pursuits should not involve any pleasure or lead to idleness.

There is room to question how much real significance these preachments had at the time they were first formulated; attitudes toward making money, and the relationship between making money and the work involved, could not be terribly relevant in a relatively undeveloped economic structure. But they proved to be a powerful ideological accompaniment of capitalism and helped in the construction of its central principle: "the earning of more and more money, combined with the strict avoidance of all spontaneous enjoyment of life."[18]

For one of the great creations of industrial capitalism was the idea of work as a purely monetary activity completely separate from sentimental considerations of its suitability or desirability, in human terms, for the people involved in it. The religious content in all this has, needless to say, faded almost entirely by now. But capitalism has not, and neither have the Calvinistic-capitalistic ideas of work. The Calvinistic ideas fitted in marvelously well with the type of work that was created by industrial capitalism.

The Industrial Revolution began in Britain in the late eighteenth century with the confluence of a number of forces—technological advances, population growth, and the appearance of large-scale markets. Phyllis Deane, an economic historian, points out that the critical elements were "organizational changes," of which a major one was "the change from the largely self-subsistent family unit of production to the capitalistic market-oriented forms of enterprise employing specialized labor and costly capital equipment."[19] This shift toward specialization was motivated by economic efficiency. The worker who tends a single phase of the mechanical process is able to produce far more than the worker who has to stop and start again for every operation in a chain of production steps.

For the first time, the worker became a detail in a mechanical complex of a strictly authoritarian nature, where his own freedom of movement is limited by the demands of a mechanized and thoroughly planned production process; his exercise of independent thinking, creative abilities, and personal involvement in the work is reduced to approximately zero. To be sure, an authoritarian work atmosphere was not first invented at the time of the Industrial Revolution, but it was then that it became an essential part of the process and a completely *mechanical* authoritarianism: the subordination of man to the requirements of the machine.

Adam Smith's famous description of the pin factory gives the basic idea: "In the way in which this business is now carried on, not only the whole work is a peculiar trade, but it is divided into a number of branches, of which the greater part are likewise peculiar trades. One man draws out the wire, another straights it, a third cuts it, a fourth points it, a fifth grinds it at the top for receiving the head; to make the head requires two or three distinct operations; to put it on is a peculiar business, to whiten the pins is another; it is even a trade by itself to put them into the paper; and the important business of making a pin is, in this manner, divided into about eighteen distinct operations. . . ."[20] Adam Smith made the very conservative calculation that, by splitting up the work in this way, the workers were able to produce 240 times as many pins as they could have if each man were trying to produce the entire pin.

This superb mechanical complex has its advantages, but it also has its drawbacks, both human and economic. Miss Deane notes: "One effect of a high degree of specialization is to increase the number of routine tasks in an economy. This has important implications for the attitude to work which could outweigh some of the productivity gains. . . . As an economy becomes more industrialized, moreover, the disutility of labor tends to increase for most workers, partly because the social satisfactions of work diminish."[21]

Even Adam Smith—the prophet of capitalism and unquestionably much impressed by the conceptual advance embodied in the pin factory—was extremely conscious of the defects in the system. "The man whose life is spent in performing a few simple operations . . . has no occasion to exert his understanding or to exercise his invention in finding out expedients for removing difficulties which never occur . . . and generally becomes as stupid and ignorant as it is possible for a human creature to become." When such work is extremely widespread, Smith added, "all the nobler parts of the human character may be, in a great measure, obliterated and extinguished in the great body of the people."[22]

The damaging effects of this mindless, repetitive work may have been more obvious in the eighteenth century, when such work was still a novelty, than they are today. But very much the same criticisms have often been enunciated in the nearly two centuries that have elapsed since, and the implicit answer of society has been the same as it was for Adam Smith—that the supposed overpowering economic advantages of the system ruled out any possibility of alteration. At the present time, these deforming effects of the system are noted only occasionally by the general public—even though the effects are becoming increasingly troublesome—and almost no attempt is being made to bring about any change.

In Adam Smith's time, the prevailing *idées reçues* about the Calvinistic disagreeableness of work undoubtedly facilitated the acceptance of the new manufacturing methods. Was it not in the order of things that work should be performed for money alone, regardless of its unpleasantness (and, indeed, that it *ought* to be unpleasant)?

Adam Smith was not, however, primarily concerned with making value judgments implied in such considerations, but with merely describing tne capitalistic system as he saw it. And he saw that, for every element in the system, the driving force—indeed, the *only* force—was money, and that the division of labor and all the rest followed naturally. "It is not," he wrote, "from the benevolence of the butcher, the brewer, or the baker that we expect our dinner, but from their regard to their own interest."[23] The same principle applied to workers, and so important was money presumed to be for them that Smith recommended, as the only possible motivation, the payment of high wages: "Where wages are high . . . we shall always find the workmen more active, diligent, and expeditious than where they are low."[24]

This is the basic view sometimes referred to as the "money-instrumental" attitude toward work: the worker is only an instrument purchased by the employer for a certain task, just as the work is only an instrument for the achievement of the worker's economic goals. There is no question of the worker's being interested or involved in his work, neither is there any possibility that he would perform it at all if it were not for the money. Since money is the single motivation, it is generally accepted that few people like their work, and that most people in fact are quite lazy. So thoroughly indoctrinated have modern workers become with this view that work disputes are generally thought of in money terms, discontented employees feel that most of their complaints can be handily solved by higher pay, and employers usually assume that high pay is a sufficient guarantee that valuable employees will not be lured away by competitors. Despite obvious and overwhelming evidence of the shakiness of these assumptions, they are rarely questioned because work is rarely discussed, on a practical level, in any terms other than money. Individuals have little choice but to suppress any doubts they may have about the universal applicability of the instrumental attitude and unfortunately are therefore rarely aware that it might be possible to consider their own work situation from any other viewpoint. As Jean-Luc Godard once remarked, "In modern industrial society, prostitution is the normal condition."[25]

The initial degradation of work noted by Adam Smith under industrial capitalism was only the beginning. Later, the social chaos created by the Industrial Revolution, the urban slums, and the economic oppression of the masses helped push the status of work even lower. Reinhard Bendix observes that in England in the early nineteenth century, because "employers used the system of poor relief to recruit pauper labor at lower wages, the distinction between work and punishment for poverty became blurred."[26] In some ways, things have improved since, but one cannot say that this blurred distinction has gotten completely unblurred.

Adam Smith foresaw with great perceptivity the potentials of the new system. On at least one point, however, he was wrong: It was not at that early stage of industrial capitalism that the worker became "as stupid and ignorant as it is possible for a human creature to become." A later step forward (or backward) would not only bring work closer to being a punishment but would call forth even greater resources of stupidity and ignorance. This invention was to be known as "scientific management" and was without doubt the most significant method of dehumanizing work ever devised. It is impossible to exaggerate the importance of this discovery, the effects of which have been felt throughout the world—not only with respect to the details of the system itself, but from the reinforcement it has given to the money-instrumental view of work, and thus to the further degradation of work, work environments, and workers.

The proud father of scientific management was Frederick W. Taylor, who stumbled upon his ideas in 1883. As chief engineer for a Philadelphia steel company, he was trying (without much success) to persuade his workers to produce as much as he knew they could (he had started his own career as an ordinary worker). He soon concluded that both management and workers were wrong in the attitudes they held at the time.

The workers were wrong because they were deliberately underproducing. "The natural laziness of men is serious," he later wrote, "but by far the greatest evil from which both workmen and employers are suffering is the systematic soldiering which is almost universal"—that is, working at the slowest possible production rate.[27]

Management was wrong because it didn't know how to stop the subtle sabotage. At the time, "the men and the management had about equal weight in deciding how fast the work should be done."[28] Beyond that, a manager who wanted to increase production could only seek to persuade, induce, bully, or otherwise get the worker to "use his best endeavors, his hardest work, all his traditional knowledge, his skill, his ingenuity, and his goodwill—in a word, his 'initiative.'"[29] In doing this, management could hold out the promise of "rapid promotion . . . higher wages . . . shorter hours . . . better surroundings and working conditions. . . ."[30] But Taylor saw that these attempts failed more often than not.

With this observation as a starting point, Taylor worked out his own solutions, which he called "scientific management." The central rule was that a single "one best way" for performing every job could be scientifically established and that every worker could most efficiently do his job by adhering to the rigid, pre-established pattern.

Taylor used a number of approaches in establishing the one best way. Most importantly, he discovered the use of the stopwatch. He selected a group of ten to fifteen men who were doing a particular job and recorded the precise sequence of movements each man made and the time required for each. He then could establish the best sequence and, by cutting out all useless and repetitive movements, produce the one best way—an exact program of what motions should be made and how much time each should take. Thus was born "time and motion study," which has become a vital part of industrial operations throughout the world and, in theory at least, a major element in raising production efficiency.

For jobs involving physical strength, he calculated the maximum physical demands a man could stand without tiring to the point of unacceptably low productivity. One of his more famous achievements was in "the science of shoveling." He found that some shovels take so large a load that workers tire rapidly and productivity declines. Others take so little that, however fast they are moved, it is impossible to do a proper amount of work. Through careful experimentation, he found that the optimum weight was twenty-one pounds—shovels that took above or below this amount resulted in a productivity drop. The weight, of course, depends on the material being shoveled, and for that reason Taylor scientifically designed a variety of sizes of scientific shovels for his clients.[31]

Both these approaches were combined in the tale of the Pennsylvania Dutch pig-iron handler, Schmidt, who worked at Bethlehem Steel around 1900. Taylor and his colleagues had carefully analyzed the loading of pig iron in the company's yard, which at the time was proceeding at the rate of 12½ tons per man per day. They were sure they could raise that figure to between 47 and 48 tons.

To test their calculations, Taylor first picked a dim-witted immigrant ("Vell, I don't know vat you mean," as Taylor wittily reported his reaction when invited to participate), and enlisted his cooperation with the promise of a substantial premium in pay. The only condition was that all instructions be followed precisely: "You will do exactly as this man tells you tomorrow, from morning till night. When he tells you to pick up a pig and walk, you pick it up and you walk, and when he tells you to sit down and rest, you sit down. You do that straight through the day. And what's more, no back talk. . . . Do you understand that? When this man tells you to walk, you walk; when he tells you to sit down, you sit down, and you don't talk back at him." The happy ending is that the worker did exactly as he was told, loaded 47½ tons during the day, and received a substantial money premium.[32]

The "rather rough talk" used in the instructions is part of the method, Taylor points out, and is intimately connected with a major ingredient in "scientific management"—a high degree of stupidity. "With a man of the mentally sluggish type of Schmidt it is . . . effective in fixing his attention on the high wages which he wants. . . ." Without the element of stupidity, Taylor says, the method would never work. A pig-iron handler, he says, "shall be so stupid and phlegmatic that he more resembles the ox than any other type." He adds: "The man who is mentally alert is entirely unsuited to what would, for him, be the grinding monotony of work of this character."[33] In fact, the careful screening of workers for each job was one of the most important parts of the method; in this case, "seven men out of eight" would not do. The eighth was "difficult to find and therefore highly prized . . . a man so stupid that he was unfitted to do most kinds of laboring work, even."[34]

Although Taylor used expressions like "brotherly cooperation" and "pulling together" to describe his methods, he constantly stressed their grueling, mind-deadening, authoritarian character. First, the calculations were set at the absolute physical limit of a strong man: "The tasks were all purposely made so severe that not more than one out of five laborers (perhaps even a smaller percentage than this) could keep up."[35] Moreover, all decisions are to be made by an iron-willed (and presumably omniscient) management: "It is only through *enforced* standardization of methods, *enforced* adoption of the best implements and working conditions, and *enforced* cooperation that this faster work can be assured. And the duty of enforcing . . . rests with management alone."[36] The worker must be completely deprived of his thinking powers: "All possible brain work should be removed from the shop and centered in the planning or laying-out department."[37] The reason for this is simple: "The time during which the man stops to think is part of the time that he is not productive."[38]

One might assume that jobs such as pig-iron handling, which Taylor said "an intelligent gorilla"[39] could probably be trained to do, are exceptional cases. Surely there are jobs of such a nature, and workers of such a nature, that the worker can apply his own intelligence to advantage? Definitely not. In its ultimate stage of development, scientific management could and should control everything: "While there are millions and millions of different operations that take place, yet these millions of complicated or composite operations can be analyzed intelligently and readily resolved into a comparatively small number of simple elementary operations. . . . Under scientific management there is nothing too small to become a subject of scientific investigation."[40] And one cannot escape the Taylorist net by climbing to higher-level jobs, because everyone needs to be told exactly what to do in order to work efficiently: "This inability of the man who is fit to do the work to understand the science of doing his work becomes more and more evident as the work becomes more complicated, all the way up the scale. . . . The law is almost universal . . . that the man who is fit to work at any particular trade is unable to understand the science of that trade without the kindly help and cooperation of men of a totally different type of education."[41] Taylor's claim for the universal applicability of his methods was total, and he even said that he had "seen a time study made of the speed of an average and first-class boy in solving problems in mathematics."[42]

Workers at all levels are thus, in Taylor's ideal universe, to be irretrievably imprisoned in mechanical systems over which they have no control whatever—a truly Kafkaesque vision. Indeed, Kafka once spoke with horror of how the "taylorized life is a terrible curse, out of which only hunger and misery can grow."[43]

Taylor emphasized his love for workers, and his system did include premium payments for workers who could meet the norms. (Those who could not, as Taylor delicately put it, would "find that they have no place in the new organization."[44]) The premiums ranged from 30 percent to 100 percent, depending on the type of work. Taylor proudly and repeatedly proclaimed that the system's something-for-everybody success rested on both high wages *and* low labor cost. However, as he explained, the premiums were not the result of generous impulses on the part of management, but were calculated as the minimum bribe that would make workers accept the new and obviously unpleasant way of doing things.

The working-out of the premiums, in fact, offered rather embarrassing evidence that workers did not much like Taylor's system. He warned that, if too-low premiums should be set, "most" workers "will prefer their old rate of speed with the lower pay."[45] Not surprisingly, the more intelligent workers at higher levels resisted most; this fact accounts for the variation in premium rates—the 30 percent premiums are for the "mentally sluggish" types doing low-grade work, and the higher premiums are for jobs requiring a high order of skill, intelligence, and judgment (and generally filled by workers sufficiently aware of things to demand a high price for their submission to a mechanical routine).

The system of scientific management grew directly out of Taylor's rather gloomy view of the human being. If Adam Smith thought of man as primarily selfish and motivated by his selfish instincts, Taylor thought of man as innately and incurably stupid: "No school teacher would think of telling children in a general way to study a certain book or subject. It is practically universal to assign each day a definite lesson beginning on one specified page and line and ending on another; and the best progress is made when . . . a definite study hour or period can be assigned in which the lesson must be learned. Most of us remain, through a great part of our lives, in this respect, grown-up children, and do our best only under pressure of a task of comparatively short duration."[46]

Taylor's discoveries have had a massive impact throughout the industrialized world, and much of it can well be classed as harmful. The time-and-motion-study engineers now troop by the thousands along production lines, carrying their clipboards and stopwatches and making their silent calculations, aimed at improving production and deadening the workers' intelligence.

The tightly authoritarian work environments of the original Industrial Revolution were to some extent a fortuitous occurrence, inasmuch as they were a technological necessity. Adam Smith could admire the system while deploring the brutalizing effects on workers. Scientific management strengthened the authoritarian structure further, raised the principle of unthinking obedience to the status of an iron law, restricted even further the worker's freedom to "exert his understanding," and tightly locked him into a process in which his every movement was controlled. As Taylor explains, the only type of worker suited to such a system was of the "mentally sluggish" type, the less intelligent the better. More alert workers could be expected to rebel against the "idiot work" the system produced. Originally, "stupidity and ignorance" were merely unfortunate side effects of industrial capitalism; now they become positive, creative forces.

One of Taylor's achievements was in matching the behavior of workers to the classical capitalist view of workers; as expressed by Henry Ford, it runs like this: "The average worker wants a job in which he does not have to put much physical effort. Above all, he wants a job in which he does not have to think."[47]

Taylorism has been widely and heavily criticized. Many experts feel that its discovery was a major disaster, and that in any case it has outlived its usefulness. Robert Ford, a personnel expert who has for some years been restructuring jobs at American Telephone & Telegraph in order to make them more complicated and to prevent the employees from dying of boredom, told me that Taylor had done great harm: "He took us in the wrong direction.

Well, it may have been all right at that time, when he was dealing with uneducated immigrants, but it is certainly wrong for the last half of this century."

Scientific management is no longer being promoted with reference to mentally sluggish types and intelligent gorillas, but it is by no means dead. Quite the contrary, virtually all manufacturing operations in the industrialized world are based on a more or less strict application of scientific management rules. Moreover, the principles have become more and more adopted in white-collar work and in other areas.

The most serious consequences have not been in the actual application of the details of Taylorism, but in the impetus given to the increasing distortion of attitudes toward work. It has lent additional force to the notion that employees, and not only low-level production employees, need to be told precisely what to do and how to do it; that independent thinking is dangerous and unpermissible; that the planning of the work needs to be separated from its actual execution; and that the only motivation is money. These ideas have become so widespread and so widely accepted as to be considered almost truisms in a great many work organizations—to the great detriment of the employees as well as the organizations.

It can be conceded that Taylor, despite everything, did have his good points. He did discover the previously unnoticed fact that a worker's output was not a constant, but could vary under varying circumstances, which proved an important beginning to later research. Moreover, even though his premium pay system had its vicious side, it at least recognized a worker's right to obtain more money in return for producing more. This was progress relative to the standard practices of the early capitalists. As Miss Deane points out: "When they wanted higher output they drove their workers harder."[48] And finally hrough his tactless zeal in promoting his ideas, Taylor doubtless stimulated the growth of trade unions.

In addition to the transformation of work and of ideas about work, industrial capitalism helped create another phenomenon that intensified the pressures on workers: bureaucracy. Mechanization of production, larger industrial units, and increasing emphasis on uniformity and precision led to a petrification of lines of authority in strict patterns, affecting everyone caught up in the machinery.

The classical bureaucratic pattern, as described by its first and best-known theoretician, Max Weber, is a rigid and stable body of rules, sanctions, and offices that govern the entire organization. Responsibility is specifically assigned to certain officials, and duties are carried out according to fixed regulations. There is a multi-level gradation of authority: "The organization of offices follows the principle of hierarchy; that is, each lower office is under the control and supervision of a higher one." Weber believed that this type of construction was a product of extremely advanced social trends and thus an object of admiration: "Experience tends to show that this purely bureaucratic type of administrative organization . . . is . . . formally the most rational known means of carrying out imperative control over human beings." He also noted that it was an essential element in industrial capitalism: "Indeed, without it capitalistic production could not continue. . . ."[49]

Just as the division of labor, which restricted the worker's freedom, was necessary to the functioning of the system, so bureaucratic management, which restricted his freedom further, was also necessary. Thus the unfortunate worker found himself squeezed on the one hand by an autocracy of men and on the other by an autocracy of machines. On both sides, the movement was the same—toward the reduction of the individual to a non-thinking accessory in the industrial-capitalist apparatus.

Moreover, the evolution of the pyramidal bureaucratic structure helped strengthen the idea that, since all the decisions had to be made at the tops of the interlocking layers, only the persons situated in those positions had the intelligence necessary to make the decisions. The absurd idea that all workers were or should be idiots, refined under Taylorism, found its counterweight in the equally absurd idea that all managers were geniuses and that organizations could not function without an unquestioned source of intelligence at the top.

Seemingly irreversible trends sometimes reverse themselves, at least to a minor degree, and the tendencies we have been discussing were no exception. As early as the 1920s management voices began to be raised questioning whether all this authoritarianism was such a good thing after all, whether the primary interest of workers was indeed money, and whether the talents of managers were always so outstanding as to justify so lopsided a division of authority as was frequently the case. Reinhard Bendix points out: "Managers and their personnel specialists began to engage in speculations concerning the 'real' desires of their employees. Some said that workers demanded recognition for themselves in terms of an equality of worth with their employers; they wanted to take pride in their work." The discovery was made that workers, regardless of their menial status in the organization, did not think of themselves as mere appendages to machines, but as real human beings, and that perhaps managers should attempt to look at it from that angle as well. Says Bendix: "By the 1930's this awareness of workers as 'human beings' was widespread among American employers. Failure to treat workers as human beings came to be regarded as the cause of low morale, poor craftsmanship, unresponsiveness, and confusion."[50] This had some effect on the way in which managers saw their own roles: "adaptability and skill in human relations were praised rather than effort and competitive drive in the struggle for survival."[51]

The most influential ideas of this type emerged from the work of Elton Mayo and his associates. In 1924, Mayo, an industrial psychologist, launched a series of experiments aimed at refining some of the Taylor concepts. The testing field was the Western Electric plant at Hawthorne, Illinois, a manufacturer of telephone equipment and other products for its parent company, AT&T. Employee morale was at a low level, and Mayo and his associates wanted (with the enthusiastic cooperation of management) to find out why, and how improvements could be brought about.

The researchers began by accepting the general viewpoint established by Taylor: that certain changes in work rules or working conditions should have predictable changes in the work. It was a kind of "push-button" theory: If the buttons marked "movements" or "good lighting" or "adequate heating" were pushed, certain clearly predictable changes in productivity would result— if, that is, the workings of all conceivable push-buttons could be exhaustively studied.

In one phase of the experiment, a group of women employees was selected for study, and a number of changes in working conditions were put into effect for a number of weeks. The starting point was a forty-eight-hour week consisting of six eight-hour days and a fixed wage for all. Successively, piece-work rates were introduced, two rest pauses per day were allowed, the rest pauses were lengthened, more rest pauses were allowed, the number of rest pauses was reduced, the company provided free hot meals, the workday was cut by thirty minutes, then by another thirty minutes, and finally the original conditions were re-established just as they had been at the outset.

The puzzling thing about all this was that almost every one of the changes was followed by a rise in output. The net result at the end of the experiment was that, with working conditions identical to those at the start, production was up some 20 percent.

Upon analyzing this mysterious result, the experts discovered that the physical working conditions themselves were of little importance: The women had become more involved in their work and were working more efficiently because, for the first time in their working lives, someone was paying attention to them. They felt important, and this had a positive effect on their work. The experiments became justly famous. (One result was that, when industrial psychologists now want to test new methods or forms of organization, they take care not to inform the workers of their intentions or that there is anything unusual about the way they are being treated—to avoid the so-called "Hawthorne effect" of illusive production increases when workers know they have been singled out for a special assignment.)

On the basis of these and other experiments, Mayo formulated a new interpretation of work in which a job's social aspects were considered to be more important than the physical working conditions, that worker needs for recognition and satisfaction can be decisive, and that informal groups shaped by the workers themselves can be more significant than a formal organization chart. The needs of the worker, Mayo concluded, were easy to understand: "What he wants is . . . first, a method of living in social relationship with other people and, second, as part of this an economic function for and value to the group."[52]

The ideas of Mayo and his many followers are sometimes referred to as the "human relations school" of management. To put it briefly, the principle was that there was a clear connection between "work satisfaction," which was largely determined by a satisfying social experience on the job, and productivity.

In a way, this development was unfortunate. To be sure, it added a badly needed element of human kindness to Taylorism and it performed a valuable service in modifying the picture of the worker as influenced by the single motivating factor of money. But the flurry of activity, in companies whose managements felt that the secret to success was to give employees a "feeling" of importance, had many unfortunate results. For one thing, further research showed that sometimes "happy" workers or "satisfied" workers were more productive and sometimes they weren't. Perhaps the indications contained in Mayo's experience needed more study. In any case, the uses to which "human relations" were put were of questionable merit, to say nothing of their doubtful ethical acceptability. There was for some years (and to some extent, there still is) the belief among managers that the creation of a spurious feeling of camaraderie in a company is of prime importance—however little reality there might be in the creation. Industrial relations expert Adolf Sturmthal notes: "For some 20 years or more the 'human relations' approach, with its emphasis on the ability of the manager to manipulate men, has dominated management training and selection in the United States."[53]

As a matter of fact, "human relations" thinking did not move all that far from Taylorism. The assumption that the individual —if he is treated in a "nice" way, with well-planned communications and other human-relations equipment—can be fitted neatly into the organization is not questioned. The authoritarian structure of industry and the tight control on the thinking of individuals remain in force. Eventually, these defects were to lead to other advances, but basically the "human relations" work organization was still an industrial-capitalist, Taylorist system with a thin (albeit welcome) veneer of "niceness."

And that is about where we are at today.

IV. WORK—IT WILL MAKE YOU UGLY

If we seek more precise information on just what is wrong with work under industrial capitalism, there is an abundance of discouraging data provided by critics.

The most penetrating commentary is still that of Karl Marx. His special contribution was the concept of "alienation" of the worker under industrial capitalism.

It should be emphasized that the notion of alienation need not merely be a vague and indefinable feeling of discontent (a "rather general *Weltschmerz*," as one Marxist philosopher derisively describes some writings on the subject). There is a good deal of discussion about the alienation of various groups in society, as if it were a kind of mysterious epidemic that might strike at any time and for which there is no known cure, but the alienation of the worker is quite tangible.

According to Marx, the capitalist "appropriates" the result of the worker's labor, and therefore "the worker is related to the *product* of his labor as to an alien object." The worker is also, in part because of the division of labor under industrialism, alienated from the work and, eventually, from life: "In his work . . . he does not affirm himself but denies himself, does not feel content but unhappy, does not develop freely his physical and mental energy but mortifies his body and ruins his mind. The worker . . . is at home when he is not working, and when he is working he is not at home. His labor is therefore not voluntary, but coerced; it is *forced labor*. It is therefore not the satisfaction of a need; it is merely a *means* to satisfy needs external to it. Its alien character emerges clearly in the face that as soon as no physical or other compulsion exists, labor is shunned like the plague."[1]

Marx believed that alienation derived directly from the existence of private property, and that "the emancipation of the workers" could only occur with "the emancipation of society from private property."[2] The logical connection was so tight, he argued, that "the overthrow of the existing state of society by the communist revolution . . . and the abolition of private property" would automatically bring about "the liberation of each single individual."[3]

Marx's analysis breaks down at this critical point: the importance of ownership. Numerous studies have shown that the average employee is relatively untroubled by the fact that his company may or may not be owned by absentee landlords (and is largely uninterested in the question). Moreover, experience in both the East and the West indicates that a shift in ownership from private to state (or vice versa) or even to a labor union has no automatic connection with a decrease in alienation. Some of the most spectacular labor disputes in, for example, France, Britain, and Sweden have occurred at state-owned enterprises. This does not mean that ownership cannot have, under special circumstances, an importance to the workers, but the connection is by no means necessary.

Nevertheless, Marx's recognition of the basic problem, and many of his observations were, and still are, perceptive. For example, he considered the possibility of combating alienation through raising workers' wages. He erred in thinking that this was impossible under capitalism (an "anomaly," he said), but he was correct in predicting that, if by some chance it could occur, it would not alone restore to the worker his "human status and dignity"—a view that has been amply confirmed by the premium-priced but nonetheless dehumanizing methods of scientific management.[4]

Modern investigations of alienation support in part the outlines of Marx's thought. Robert Blauner, in his book *Alienation*

and Freedom, offers a definition based on recent sociological
studies: "Alienation exists when workers are unable to control
their immediate work processes, to develop a sense of purpose
and function which connects their jobs to the over-all organization
of production, to belong to integrated industrial communities,
and when they fail to become involved in the activity of work
as a mode of personal self-expression." He isolates four ingredients of alienation: (1) powerlessness (regarding ownership of
the enterprise, general management policies, employment conditions, and the immediate work process); (2) meaninglessness
(with respect to the character of the product worked on as well
as the scope of the product or the production process); (3) isolation (the social aspect of work); and (4) self-estrangement ("depersonalized detachment," including boredom, which can lead
to "absence of personal growth").[5]

As thus broken down, alienation is inherent in industrial
capitalism and its customary concomitants—pyramidal, bureaucratic management patterns and advanced, Taylorized technology, which divide and subdivide work into minute, monotonous elements.

This breaking up of work into tiny subtasks is more or less involved in all of Blauner's categories of alienation and has received
considerable attention by other students of the subject. French
social philosopher Georges Friedmann's aptly titled book *Le Travail en Miettes* (literally, "work in crumbs") analyzed in detail
the effects of such work.[6] Adam Smith saw quite early the "stupidity and ignorance" produced in workers by the first efforts along
this line; Marx, in turn, attacked the "stupidity, cretinism" generated by the system.[7]

As Friedmann shows, the progress of compartmentalization of
work has been steady, and has long since reached alarming proportions. He cites, as a rather tame example, but all the more appalling for that, a wine-bottling facility where one worker "whose
job is, all day long, all week long, all year long, to place on the
bottle a label. . . . But she only places it on the neck. It is
one of her colleagues, her neighbor on the line, who glues it
down." As he points out, such work is designed for "mental crip-
ples."[8]

It is not only philosophers and sociologists who have noticed the grimness of this type of work; workers themselves are painfully aware of the problems. The context most famous for its creation of alienating work conditions is the assembly line—and especially the automobile assembly line. Its fame is understandable, since it contains all the worst and most degrading aspects of modern work. It is completely authoritarian; few of the jobs require any intelligence whatever; the average worker has virtually no freedom to make even the smallest decision of his own; most see only a small part of the total production process (in many assembly-line operations, workers have scarcely any idea of what they are working on); the work is deadening because it is split up into tiny elements and because the worker is completely subjected to the machine. It is in automobile plants that the money-instrumental attitude to work has reached its highest refinement (it is no accident that auto workers are, in most countries, among the highest paid of any group possessing comparable low-level skills).

No doubt few auto workers have read Marx, and thus might not be supposed to know that they are alienated, but the overwhelming majority of them dislike intensely the repetitive, boring nature of their jobs—in the Walker and Guest study, *The Man on the Assembly Line*, about 90 percent—and the relatively high wages, though welcome, do not make the work any easier to bear.[9] Moreover, their spontaneous comments confirm their alertness to the defects of their Sisyphus-like work: "The assembly line is no place to work, I can tell you. There is nothing more discouraging than having a barrel beside you with 10,000 bolts in it and using them all up. Then you get another barrel with another 10,000 bolts, and you know that every one of those 10,000 bolts has to be picked up and put in exactly the same place as the last 10,000 bolts." "It's not a matter of pace. It's the monotony. It's not good for you to get so bored. I do the same thing day after day; it's just an everlasting grind." "The job gets so sickening—day in and day out plugging in ignition wires. I get through with one motor, turn around, and there's another motor staring me in the face. It's sickening."[10] Almost all the workers interviewed in the Walker and Guest study wanted to transfer to other jobs, not to improve their "economic or social status," but to "get away from the line."[11] The most sought-after jobs were those involving chal-

lenge, variety, and some intelligence, such as those of maintenance man and "utility man" (a worker who fills in wherever
needed and who thus must learn a multitude of jobs).

But for most workers, there are few chances for escape. Despite
the pleasant Horatio Alger mythology in American business, the
average worker's chances of rising into management ranks are almost nil. There is a widespread dream of setting up one's own
business, but there is also a widespread consciousness that it is only
a dream: "If I could be my own boss," remarked one worker, "or
work myself up to that position, I'd leave. Otherwise, I might as
well stay where I am."[12] Walker and Guest stress the all-pervasive
character of the line: "This is one of the most important effects
of mass production methods of industrial organization. . . . The
immediate world of the auto assembler is the factory. It is still
becoming possible to rise in that world and even out of it, but
each year it is becoming more difficult."[13]

Or, as the French philosopher Simone Weil described the impact on a worker: "From one day to the next, he becomes a mere
supplement to the machine, a little less than a 'thing.' . . . Most
workers at this moment in their lives experience the feeling of no
longer existing."[14]

One critical fact in all this is often overlooked: Rigidly authoritarian work environments not only affect an individual's attitude
toward his job; they can also poison his entire life. As a student
poster displayed in Paris during the 1968 revolt put it with admirable conciseness: "Work—It Will Make You Ugly."

Work is by far the dominant activity in most people's lives, and
it would be surprising if it did not have a profound influence on
one's entire existence. Workers subjected to the modern industrial-capitalist world tend to become "stupid and ignorant" not
only on the job, but off it as well.

Various aspects of this situation have been apparent for some
time. In 1927, B. Zeigarnik investigated the deleterious effects of
the subdivision of work into small units, where each worker per-
forms only a part of the task and none has an over-all view of the
whole. Zeigarnik compared reactions of workers to jobs that they
carried through to fulfillment with others on which they per-

formed only a part. He found that, when asked to describe the tasks, the workers remembered the interrupted jobs about twice as fast as the others. Friedmann comments: "When a task is completed, it is easy to forget. On the other hand, when it is not completed, it weighs on the mind and can even derange one's mentality."[15] A Swedish survey on the subject concludes: "Work which gives limited opportunities for independent control, meaningfulness, and self-actualization tend to lead to weaker and more passive behavior in other contexts of life as well—such as social relations, involvement in social activities, and the like."[16]

Further light is shed by Arthur Kornhauser's study in the 1950s of the mental health of auto workers. Mental health, as defined by Kornhauser, is "an overall balanced relationship to the world which permits a person to maintain realistic, positive belief in himself and his purposeful activities," which he breaks down into six components: manifest anxiety, self-esteem, hostility, sociability and friendship, over-all satisfaction with life, and personal morale.[17]

Kornhauser found a striking correlation between the type of job held and the individual's mental health. The impact of repetitive, nonskilled jobs is unmistakable. When the jobs are classified in a descending scale, ranging from highly skilled to unskilled, the workers holding these jobs tend to rank on a downward-sloping mental health pattern.[18] The lowest-grade workers rate lowest on the scale of mental health, and they have fewer friends and have less satisfactory family relationships.[19] On the other hand, those with higher mental health "resort less to passive, 'escapist' activities like television . . . and drinking at bars; and they devote more time to reading."[20]

This poisonous character of low-grade work was observed some years ago by Georges Friedmann, who noted that assembly line work tended to disorient workers outside of work, "to stimulate aggressive impulses, through which the personality seeks to assert itself in a brutal manner in the use of stimulants of all sorts—gambling, alcohol, habits of conspicuous consumption, brutal amusements such as 'stock cars' and mass spectacles of so-called 'sports' such as boxing, wrestling, and horror and crime films."[21] Stanley Parker, a British sociologist, found that persons more involved in their jobs, as shown by their opportunities to use many of their abilities in their work, were more likely to belong to outside organizations than those who used few of their abilities (78 percent against 57 percent) and also were more apt to spend free time reading or studying (25 percent against 9 percent). He concludes: "Non-involvement in work seems more likely to discourage than to facilitate involvement in leisure."[22]

It is not only personal life and social relationships that suffer from dehumanizing work patterns, but also workers' views of society as a whole, which become warped and degraded. Among Kornhauser's more disturbing findings was a general antisocial attitude among industrial workers. They were seen to possess markedly primitive attitudes toward racial integration and to harbor great admiration for strict authority. And workers in low-grade jobs tended to be especially outstanding on these points.[23]

In today's world, we have been so thoroughly indoctrinated with the money-instrumental attitude toward work—that an adequate wage has top priority and that the work itself is not supposed to make any real sense—that there is a constant, automatic effort to repress any feelings that might conflict with these principles. It scarcely ever occurs to us to question the mind-killing nature of monotonous, authoritarian work environments. That does not mean the feelings do not exist; they are there, just below the surface. In probing to learn workers' real attitudes, Kornhauser (and other researchers) found that by far the most important aspect of a job for most workers was the opportunity it provided to use one's thinking powers. Despite everything, a deeply rooted anti-authoritarianism survives throughout long years of repression in a harshly authoritarian structure. The brainwashing is so complete that workers almost never voluntarily mentioned this subject in discussing their jobs, yet many showed immediate enthusiasm when it was brought to their attention.[24] Other job characteristics—pay, job security, and physical working conditions (which have traditionally received, and still do receive, the main attention of both management and labor)— were outranked by the opportunity the work offers for "use of the worker's abilities and for associated feelings of interest, sense of accomplishment, personal growth, and self-respect."[25] The chance for the worker to use his own abilities is precisely the feature that has been carefully filtered out of most jobs.

It is worth pointing out that there are parallels between the alienation suffered by industrial workers and mental states that are generally considered to be more alarming. The detachment of the worker from his work is similar to the detachment in the schizoid condition described by R. D. Laing. The individual subjected to the strain of "a threatening experience from which there is no physical escape" develops an elaborate protective mechanism, "he becomes a mental observer, who looks on, detached and impassive, at what his body is doing or what is being done to his body." For that person, "the world is a prison without bars, a concentration camp without barbed wire."[26] Instead of experiencing reality directly, he develops a "false" self as a buffer for the real world, while the real self retires to an "inner" position of unexposed safety. All of life seems full of "futility, meaninglessness, and purposelessness," since it is not, in fact, being directly experienced. The real self is completely blocked, barred from any spontaneous expressions or real freedom of action, and totally sterile. "In the absence of a spontaneous natural, creative relationship with the world which is free from anxiety, the 'inner self' thus develops an overall sense of inner impoverishment, which is expressed in complaints of the emptiness, deadness, coldness, dryness, impotence, desolation, worthlessness, of the inner life."[27]

Laing's description of the depths of the schizoid state at its worst are remarkably similar to the descriptions of industrial capitalist work at its worst.

Though we have been discussing the authoritarian work atmosphere under capitalism, it should be made clear that it is also present in that "other" system, the one in force in the Soviet Union—which the French businessman-philosopher Marcel Loichot terms "monocapitalism," as contrasted to the Western "oligocapitalism."

That is to say, it is present insofar as one is able to judge. According to the original Marxist dogma, alienation was to disappear with the abolition of private ownership of the means of production. This principle has been a bit modified by more recent

Soviet Marxists, though the official line still holds that the type of subhuman work we have been discussing is somehow different under the Soviet system. Foreign researchers are not exactly welcome to see for themselves how this works out, and most reports by the Soviets themselves seem suspiciously one-sided. For example, the abolition of the division between intellectual and manual labor is not only claimed to have taken place, but it is even written into law, and official spokesmen are not anxious to dispute the law. E. Kapustin, director of the Moscow Scientific Research Institute for Labor, at a congress on workers' participation held in Geneva in 1970, revealed that workers are not only vigorously participating in management, but his scientific studies "prove the advantages of socialism over capitalism."[28]

Nevertheless, there are grounds for suspecting that work alienation in the Soviet Union is roughly as severe as it is in the West. It could scarcely be otherwise, since the Soviet industrial apparatus has been largely copied from the Western model.

This was not the original idea. In 1917, Lenin said: "It is perfectly possible . . . immediately, within 24 hours after the overthrow of the capitalists and the bureaucrats, to replace them in control of production and distribution, in the business of control of labor and products by the armed workers, by whole people in arms."[29] A central weapon in Lenin's seizure of power was the slogan "all power to the Workers' and Soldiers' Councils," and workers' councils were in fact given full control of factories by a decree shortly after the revolution of November 1917.[30] This did not last long.

Even though the period of "workers' control" was rather brief, many historians argue, as does Olga A. Narkiewicz, that the workers were "in many cases . . . running the nationalized factories quite efficiently."[31] There are a number of documented case histories of factories that prospered under the management of the workers' councils. It is true that over-all industrial production fell, but this was in large part due to the chaos caused by the civil war, raw material shortages, disruption of communications, and deliberate sabotage by the former capitalist owners. Nevertheless, Lenin quickly turned his attention to the liquidation of workers' control. His official reasoning was the claimed inefficiency of the councils, but he was doubtless also conscious of the possible threat to the centralized state if the councils should grow too strong. In any case, there was no real chance to judge the effectiveness of the councils, since they lasted only about a year. By early 1919 "workers' control" was being replaced by "workers' management," which, in practice, turned out to be only a euphemism for a tightly disciplined militaristic management system.

There was obviously, perhaps because of the general admiration of Western production methods and eagerness to imitate these methods, a "capitalistic" disinclination to believe that workers could accept responsibility or could make any worthwhile contributions in industry. Mrs. Narkiewicz regards the ending of workers' control as a grievous failure to capitalize on the workers' good will, and avers that this failure created lasting antagonism among workers and "contributed in a great measure to the many ills from which Soviet industry suffers even today."[32] By 1918, Lenin was developing a fulsome admiration for Frederick Taylor. Though he described Taylor's scientific management as an example of "the refined brutality of bourgeois exploitation," he also saw it as one of the "up-to-date achievements of capitalism," and urged: "We must organise in Russia the study and teaching of the Taylor system and systematically try it out and adapt it to our own ends."[33] A management "class" was soon under development, differing in no great respect from that in the West.[34]

The mythology has been carefully maintained, however. By the 1930s, according to Friedmann, work that was identical to that done in capitalist countries somehow "took on an entirely different significance and psychological coloration for the Soviet worker, influenced by 'socialist emulation,' working in an enterprise belonging to the collectivity and whose profits he knows go to the collectivity."[35]

But even though it is different, it is the same. A fascinating collection of essays by Soviet work experts illuminates the point. A study by Zdravomyslov and Yadov on attitudes to work produces very much the same results as similar studies made in the West. By far the most important aspect of a job is the degree to which it offers an opportunity to use one's abilities, exercise one's thinking powers, and make one's own decisions. The authors note: "The employment of one's intellectual facilities in the course of work, regardless of vocational distinctions, was shown

to be the prime incentive for the young workers interviewed."
So influential is this factor, say the authors, that the main target in
education of young workers "should be to give greater play to the
workers' initiative." But nowhere is there any indication that this
type of work is any more common in the Soviet Union than in
capitalist countries, nor that less inspiring types of work have been
eliminated in the USSR.[36]

Other essays in the same anthology suggest that a principal concern of work specialists in the USSR is very much the same as
those in the West—that is, to further refine authoritarian work
environments along Tayloristic lines. D. A. Oshanin, an enthusiastic admirer of Pavlov, calls for more efforts to control the worker's movements and reactions in detail, and thus make him a
more efficient appendage to the machine, through carefully controlled stimuli: "The effectiveness of various mental functions,
such as perception of signal stimuli of different modalities and
sensory characteristics, loudness, brightness, color, shape, etc.,
could then be taken directly into account by designers of automatic systems."[37]

Scattered evidence indicate that this process is causing troubles
very similar to those in the West. One report described a group of
highly educated young people in a Krasnoyarsk engine repair
shop. They were complaining about, among other things, the
petty autocracy of the foreman, who refused to give them any
scope for developing new ideas. Because of the rapid growth in
the numbers of trained people planned for the future, the report
observes: "Situations like this are likely to become more and more
typical," and it cites an ominous warning from *Izvestia* that the
managers were "clashing with the spirit of the times, and this
spirit you can neither sack nor remove to another job."[38]

At the moment, the USSR would seem to be marked by an
extremely authoritarian work philosophy. Work historian Reinhard
Bendix wrote a few years ago regarding the head of an enterprise:
"The authority of the Director is absolute within the enterprise.
He is charged with responsibility for the fulfillment of the plan
and he is given the powers necessary to accomplish that end."[39]

And developments do not seem to be for the better. A new labor law put into effect in the USSR in July 1970 (replacing the

one from 1922) spells out in great detail the autocratic structure that is to prevail.[40] It lays down as a central principle an admonition lifted from St. Paul: "He who does not work, neither shall he eat."

The main objective of work, according to the law, is "promoting labor productivity, efficiency in social production." The means for achieving this end is "strengthening labor discipline, gradually transforming labor for the common weal into the prime vital need of each able-bodied citizen." One of the fifteen chapters of the law is devoted to this subject, specifying, among other things, "it is the duty of the factory workers and office employees to work honestly and conscientiously to observe labor discipline, to carry out the orders of the administration promptly and accurately, to raise labor productivity, to improve the quality of the products, observe the requirements of the production techniques. . . ." Although workers who follow these strict rules stand a chance of getting a bonus or even a "listing in the Book of Honor or the Roll of Honor," there is nothing in the law about efforts to eliminate alienation or the promotion of employee participation in management. It may be true, as E. Kapustin claims, that working conditions in the USSR "prove the advantages of socialism over capitalism," but the evidence is not especially convincing.

Despite all the gloomy evidence of the effects of work under modern conditions, it is important to realize that not all jobs in a single industry are alike and that not all industries are alike. In this respect, Robert Blauner's analysis of conditions in four different industries is illuminating. The industries are: printing (a close cousin to traditional crafts), textiles (a highly mechanized, "machine-tending" industry), automobiles (the hard-driving, fast-paced assembly line), and chemicals (representing the newer, highly automated process industries).

Printing is characterized by a "nonalienating relation" to work, largely because the workers have a large degree of control over their own work. They use their skills and their intelligence to a high degree, make many of their own decisions, and they suffer to a minimum from interference by petty superiors. Interestingly enough, this unusual state of affairs is in large part the creation of a powerful union, which has taken care to preserve the almost "medieval" freedom of the workers. Blauner comments: "When work provides opportunities for control, meaning, and self-expression, it becomes an end in itself, rather than simply a means to live. For printers . . . satisfactions are largely intrinsic, related to the nature of the work itself, rather than extrinsic, or concerned with aspects of the job beyond the actual work."[41]

In the textile industry, the situation is precisely the opposite. Despite the obvious presence of "objectively alienating conditions" in an industry marked by "organizational backwardness," the actual presence of alienation is minimal. This is strictly attributable to extrinsic factors—a low educational level, a high percentage of women workers (whose main interest is outside work), and tightly knit social patterns connecting the community to the work place. Moreover, Blauner observes: "The traditional-oriented workers in the industry have few aspirations for work with control, challenge, and growth potential, and are therefore not greatly frustrated by the absence of these qualities."[42]

The worker in the automobile industry, as is apparent from other studies, suffers greatly from alienation—perhaps more so than in any other industry.

When we look at the worker in the chemicals industry, we are confronted with an entirely new phenomenon. The further automatization of production does not lead to a further rise in alienation—quite the contrary. The number of workers employed in a chemical plant is small relative to the capital employed. Their work is neither physically demanding nor precisely paced, and consists primarily of keeping watch on a rather large number of controls. It is thus varied and flexible. In an emergency, it places high demands on quick thinking and ability to react. These workers are mostly nonalienated, and they enjoy a high degree of satisfaction and pride in their work.

The appearance of this type of work—and this type of worker— in the latest phase of industrial capitalism might be regarded as the sure cure for all the ills of alienation.

Indeed, Blauner suggests that the direction of industrial development is to some extent taking care of the problem. He argues that, as the character of industry moves from (1) a traditional craft structure to (2) a medium degree of mechanization to (3) a high degree of automation, the extent of worker alienation traces "a course that could be charted on a graph by means of an inverted U-curve"—that is, through a bleak stage of "deskillization" in mechanization and then to a phase of higher demands on intelligence and responsibility in fully automated processes. This type of work, Blauner says, should increase steadily in importance.

But as we veer along this U-curve, a change is taking place. The worker in the chemicals process industry is not the craft worker who is engaged in a free, creative activity. What is required "in place of the *able workman*," Blauner notes, is a "*reliable employee*." Because this worker tends to be "luke-warm to unions and loyal to his employer, the blue-collar employee in the continuous-process industries may be a worker 'organization man' in the making."[43] Many observers would object that this is scarcely progress, the "organization man" being a prominent example of the crushed, conformist individual under industrial capitalism.

And many experts do not agree that this evolution toward non-alienating jobs is at all inevitable as more production processes are automated. Some newly created jobs do call for more alertness and sharper skills, but in many cases the "deskilling" process continues. Paul Blumberg, after examining the evidence, observes: "Those who believe that complex automated machinery demands increased skill of the machine operator have simply not thought the matter through thoroughly."[44]

A major effect of the automating of industry is, of course, the gradual reduction in the percentage of the workforce accounted for by manufacturing employees, and a corresponding growth in the importance of white-collar and other commercial and clerical jobs. It might be thought that such jobs are immune to alienation; this is not so, and it is becoming steadily less so. Traditionally, office work is thought of as more elegant and prestigious than blue-collar work, but this belief is largely based on rather hollow status considerations. C. Wright Mills writes: "The alienating conditions of modern work now include the salaried employees as well as the wage-workers. There are few, if any, features of wage-work . . . that do not also characterize at least some white-collar work."[45] Anyone who has ever worked in an office can recognize the familiar gloom described by Theodore Roethke's lines:

> I have known the inexorable sadness of pencils,
> Neat in their boxes, dolor of pad and paperweight. . . .
> Ritual of multigraph, paper-clip, comma,
> Endless duplication of lives and objects. . . .[46]

Indeed, some of the most poignant descriptions of work in an overpoweringly authoritative atmosphere have been of office work —ranging from Gogol's timid civil servants and Melville's "Bartleby the Scrivener" to more recent tales of executive suites and gray flannel suits and *New Yorker*-type tales of middle executives in a state of despair.

White-collar and service work environments have been steadily degraded, with the growth of importance of these sectors and the refinement of management techniques, developed primarily for use in manufacturing, applied to other types of work. One report points out: "The scientific management theory has been successful in the entire industrialized world and is being applied today by most managers and industrial engineers, more or less to the letter. It would be a gross error to assume that this management philosophy has become obsolete. . . . Quite the contrary, it appears that scientific management principles, which were originally developed for industrial organizations, are now spreading to all other areas, such as offices, hospitals, and government administrations."[47] One consultant firm active in applying precise work-measurement and work-planning techniques to office work claims to be able to break down office work to their minutest details with the help of "massive tables prepared over the years to calculate 'target times' for performing clerical jobs." Among other things, the tables show "the time it takes to prepare a first-class mailing label (24 seconds) or make a phone call (slightly over 25 seconds to notify someone that a duplicating order is ready) to the time required for a telephone-company draftsman to draw up a street conduit system 1,220 feet long (one hour)."[48]

As a result of the refinements of dehumanizing management techniques, white-collar workers have been rapidly catching up with blue-collar workers in terms of alienation. In a 1969 survey of worker attitudes made by the Survey Research Center at the University of Michigan for the Department of Labor, 13 percent of white-collar workers expressed negative attitudes toward work, not a great deal under the 17 percent figure for blue-collar workers. More significantly, in the under-thirty age groups, the percentage of those in the two groups harboring negative feelings toward work was identical: 24 percent.[49]

And white-collar alienation does not know any upper limits. P. C. Jersild, a Swedish novelist and psychiatrist, has written: "Even a white-collar worker who is pressured to the point of a bleeding ulcer by his boss can feel the threat to his existence—even if the process takes place on a wall-to-wall carpet."[50] Erich Fromm notes: "The managerial elite . . . are just as much appendages of the machines as those whom they command. They are just as alienated, or perhaps more so, just as anxious, or perhaps more so, as the worker in one of their factories."[51] This has, in fact, been empirically confirmed. An astonishing report on "management discontent" published by the American Management Association pinpointed "an increasing condition of alienation" among executives, and three out of four managers polled believed the situation was getting worse. The reasons are identical to those behind the blue-collar discontent: "a decreasing sense of personal reward and personal achievement" arising from "the highly bureaucratic and authoritarian structure" of the modern corporation, preventing the average executive from "making the decisions he feels his position entitles him to make; they are made for him. . . ." So deeply unhappy are managers that 18 percent would consider joining a "managers' union," and this figure rises to 50 percent in the under-thirty groups. The authors warn of "the possibility of a revolt in the ranks of supervisory and middle management."[52]

Regardless of the fact that many jobs, if not most, are "objectively alienating," according to studies of sociologists and other scientists, the large majority of workers, when asked directly, profess themselves to be satisfied with their work. Is not this fact, observed in numerous studies, rather embarrassing for anyone seeking to stress the importance of alienation?

No.

In the first place, the existence of deep discontent among a sizable minority of the population would seem in itself adequate justification for attacking the problems. In the 1969 study made for the Department of Labor, some 15 percent of workers were found to express "negative attitudes toward work," and the percentage was far higher for some groups; for black workers under thirty it was 37 percent. Though this is a minority of all workers, it would seem a minority of sizable proportions.

In addition, the situation is deteriorating under the pressures of rising education and other influences that work to increase worker aspirations. Einar Thorsrud, a Norwegian work psychologist, explained to me that this was a powerful impetus behind the Norwegian drive for industrial democracy: "We saw that people were getting more and more general education, but 'scientific management' was making jobs more and more simple. Why were we taking the trouble to educate people? It was apparent that something was wrong."

Obviously, the effects of brain-numbing work on a worker without much brains is not especially noticeable. But as the basics change, so do the consequences. This is clearly shown in Blauner's studies. "The more education a person has received," he writes, "the greater the need for control and creativity."[53] He shows that alienation in southern textile mills tends to be lower than one might expect, due to factors of education and other characteristics affecting aspirations: "Because of their relative lack of education and aspiration, southerners are less likely to find routine work monotonous than northerners . . . the question of aspiration is paramount."[54]

This is a critical point in the United States. Though the U.S. educational system is frequently attacked, a larger number of Americans get a good education than is the case in Europe. One British analysis of OECD data concluded that "the really striking difference between the United States and the rest of the world is that more people are better educated on their side of the Atlantic than on ours," and offered this as one reason for the higher U.S. standard of living.[55] In 1965, there were 28.6 university students per 1000 population in the United States—two to three times the figures in European countries.

These rising standards of education are colliding head-on with jobs that are less and less demanding, in increasingly authoritarian climates. Workers are acquiring more and more brainpower and less and less opportunity to use it.

And what might happen to aspirations if the general population should become aware of the fact that work need not be so alienating, that job atmospheres need not be so uniformly poisonous, that there are viable alternatives to strict authoritarianism in work organizations? Up to now, workers have been generally willing to accept the conventional wisdoms about work without too much question. The person who cannot adapt and who suffers every minute of his job in more or less dignified silence is often apt to blame himself for his shortcomings. That work could be, or should be, something other than mere punishment or drudgery is not a possibility that most workers have ever been confronted with, even on the most theoretical level. It would thus hardly ever occur to the average worker to question the natural painfulness of work. But a low level of aspirations does not mean that work is not having its under-the-surface paralyzing effects. It also does not mean that aspirations will not rise—as they almost certainly will. If and when there appears a general awareness of the tragic wrongs being perpetrated in contemporary work organizations, and of the readily available means for righting the wrongs, the effects could be explosive.

Economic progress is also transforming worker expectations. In the early days of the Industrial Revolution, the money-instrumental view of work was not all that unreasonable, since the desire to stay alive was paramount, and the role of work in helping to achieve that desire outranked any other characteristics it might have had. Obviously, this is no longer true in industrialized countries, and it will doubtless have an increasingly great effect on worker expectations.

The distaste for work is so grave and so widespread that one intriguing question arises quite naturally: is work necessary?

In examining the average man's disdain for work, Freud wrote about the fortunate man who "knows how to heighten sufficiently his capacity for obtaining pleasure from mental and intellectual work. . . . The weak point of this method, however, is that it is not generally applicable; it is only available to the few."[56] Proceeding from this point of view, theorists sometimes speak of a future utopia in which the business of work would be handled by a handful of individuals, while the remainder could be free to enjoy "life"—meaning an absence of work.

But it will very likely be more practical to reform work than to do away with it, as work appears to be a "natural" and, indeed, essential part of life. Peter Drucker has written: "Individual dignity and fulfillment in an industrial society can only be given in and through work."[57] But this does not apply only to industrial societies. A report on the Abkhasians in the USSR, who make up a society only slightly industrialized, and who commonly live to 120 years and more, notes the great emphasis this culture places on work: "An Abkhasian is never 'retired,' a status unknown in Abkhasian thinking. From the beginning of life until its end, he does what he is capable of doing because both he and those around him consider work vital to life." Evidently, the efforts to provide useful work geared to the physical capacities of individuals is of great benefit: "Both the Soviet medical profession and the Abkhasians agree that their work habits have a great deal to do with their longevity." And, obviously, Americans compare poorly in this respect: "Even as adults, only a small percentage of Americans have the privilege of feeling that their work is essential or important."[58]

Even in other societies, opportunities to work are frequently seized by people who are generally supposed to be not interested in work at all. Philips Lamp in the Netherlands has built production facilities especially designed to provide work to retired persons who do not want to remain idle. In Florence, after the 1966 flood, hundreds of young people, usually assumed to be interested only in pop music and other such amusements, turned up as volunteers to wade through the mud to help repair the damage. In Denmark, in summer "free communities" provided for young people to "do their thing," the authorities take care to provide opportunities for satisfying work, such as restoring Viking towers, which the young people themselves manage.

The most important human need satisfied by work is the need for the creative accomplishment of some task in a relatively free atmosphere, together with some recognition of the accomplishment. As Antoine de St.-Exupéry wrote: "One becomes a man by challenging an obstacle."[59] Or as Adam Smith put it, the worker yearns "to exert his understanding or to exercise his invention in finding out expedients for removing difficulties."[60] In more scientific descriptions, researchers differ somewhat on details, but they agree on the general outlines. For example, the work psychologists Lawler and Hackman specify four elements in jobs which, if all are present, will positively affect job satisfaction as well as quality of performance: variety, autonomy, task identity (the execution of a "whole" piece of work), and feedback (a return of information to the individual on his performance).[61]

These characteristics are not so very different from those of many other human activities. We noted earlier that, in primitive societies, there is no real division between work and leisure, and the perception of work as a separate phenomenon is a relatively recent innovation. If it is practicable to reorganize work to accord more closely with man's needs, it should be possible to break down the sharp division between work and leisure and to see the two as existing along a continuum, both presenting similar, though not necessarily precisely identical, characteristics. Stanley Parker observes that "whether these two spheres need to be as separate as they are for most people today is debatable."[62]

Studied from this point of view, work can be seen to be a more "natural" activity than is sometimes believed. The child psychologist Erik Erikson speaks of "a sense of industry" as a key stage in a child's development: "His ego boundaries include his tools and skills: the work principle teaches him the pleasure of work completion by steady attention and persevering diligence."[63] "Pleasure" may seem an odd word to apply to work, considering work's low repute today, but it is not, in its essentials, all that different from play. The Dutch thinker Huizinga, in his study of play, lists the need to "accomplish" as a central element in play: "all want to achieve something difficult, to succeed, to end a tension."[64] The work-play relation is distorted and obscured, of course, by the grotesque ways in which work is organized. Scott Myers gives a provocative illustration of the distortion in considering the consequences of reorganizing a game of bowling: "Hiding the pins from the bowler by hanging a drape halfway down the alley. . . . Having a 'supervisor' give the bowler an opinion of how well he is doing—along with some 'constructive criticism.'

... Changing the rules of the game ... without involving the
bowler in the change process, or even telling him why the changes
were made. ... Preventing social interaction among bowlers.
... Giving most of the credit and recognition to the supervisor
for performance of the bowlers under his supervision. ... Keeping bowlers on the job by threat of job security or by paying
them enough money to make the 'time' in the bowling alley
worth their while."[65] It would be surprising if a bowling establishment restructured along such lines would enjoy much business,
yet this is precisely the way most work organizations are set up
—and managers frequently wonder why the interest of employees
is at a low level.

The key point would seem to be the way an activity is organized,
rather than the type of activity. In the eighteenth century, Elector
Max Emanuel of Bavaria, who entertained a strong feeling for
the common man, ordered a small lathe constructed for himself,
so that he might learn to operate it and thereby acquire an in-
sight into the thought-processes and problems of the ordinary
worker. He did in fact develop some facility with the thing, and
in time was able to turn out candlesticks and the like with fair
skill. But he neglected to realize that his voluntary toil in the
sumptuous rococo surroundings of his Nymphenburg Palace could
scarcely tell him much about the average worker's feelings. Artistic
creation is generally considered to be in its nature nonalienating,
but one wonders if the employees of the Douven factory at
Leopoldsburg, Belgium—which turns out six thousand hand-
painted pictures a week on an assembly-line basis—are any less
alienated than workers in any other kind of factory.[66] And even
the most creative work contains traces of drudgery. Bertrand Russell's *Principia Mathematica* is considered to be one of the great
intellectual achievements of all time, yet he recalled that, once he
got the basic theories worked out in his head, writing the book
was a purely "mechanical job" at which he labored "ten to twelve
hours a day for about eight months."[67] And on the other side,
washroom attendants and such workers are sometimes found to
be astonishingly pleased with their jobs. British industrial psychologist J. A. C. Brown cited the case of a lavatory cleaner who
became highly insulted when she was asked to clean ovens—it
seems that the lavatory cleaner's job in that particular factory

carried especially high status, since the occupant enjoyed a great deal of autonomy and freedom, "had charge of certain materials such as soap and toilet rolls, and had the authority to move out other workers when she considered that they had been talking or smoking too long."[68]

This fact is all the more striking if we consider the automobile industry. There is scarcely an activity more engrossing and attractive to young men than tinkering with automobiles; yet the designers of auto plants have performed the considerable achievement of transforming this fascinating activity into the world's most hated work place. The mother of one of the young rebels at the Lordstown GM plant explained her son's reaction: "One thing, Tony is not lazy. He'll take your car apart and put it together any day. Ever since he's been in high school we haven't had to worry about car trouble. . . . And I'm not lazy either. I love to cook. But supposing they gave me a job just cracking eggs with bowls moving past on a line. Pretty soon I'd get to the point where I'd wish the next egg was rotten just to spoil their whole cake."[69]

One large difficulty with insisting on a terminological division between work and leisure is that they cannot be separated in real life. As we have seen, there is a powerful interaction between the two, and experience in work—both positive and negative—will inevitably and powerfully affect other spheres of a person's life. This central importance of work is increasingly recognized. David Riesman, when he wrote The Lonely Crowd in 1951, theorized that, so rapid was the advance of automation and so hopeless the situation of work, that "the meaning of life" should best be "sought in the creative use of leisure." But he later (1965) changed his mind and declared that work was so central to man's life that it could not be neglected. But neither could it be left in its present state: "What I am asking for now is hardly less than reorganizing work itself so that man can live humanely on as well as off the job."[70]

It thus appears certain that, for better or worse, work is here to stay—and that we had better make our peace with it.

What, then, should be done about work?

The most obvious answer and the most popular is: nothing.

There is a widespread feeling that the problems, if ignored with sufficient intensity, will somehow disappear; that the classes of society involved are not worthy of all that much attention; or that it would be generally fruitless to try to work on such problems. There is a surprisingly common belief that life is inevitably and unavoidably full of suffering—as Sophocles put it: "Not to be born, is past all prizing, best."[71]

Moreover, so immense do the problems appear that some of those observers who have studied them most closely have the most pessimistic views of their susceptibility to cure. Arthur Kornhauser concludes his depressing study of the mental dangers of modern industrial processes with the very frank opinion that, from a practical point of view, nothing much can be done about it. He offers, as his best suggestion, that workers might get more "zest" out of their lives if they were "to join with their fellows in efforts to build a better world."[72]

As it happens, there do exist solutions, and there is overwhelming evidence that they work. And they revolve around a rather simple equation: If the problems arise mainly from an excessively authoritarian structure, which leads to endless division and subdivision of tasks and deprives the worker of his decision-making abilities, then the obvious cure is to reverse the process, abolish the authoritarian patterns, and give the worker's intelligence back to him—that is, the replacement of autocracy by democracy.

This is, of course, an oversimplification. Working out the actual equation can be quite complicated. But the general principle would seem demonstrably valid, as most of the rest of this book will strive to make clear.

That does not mean that there are not enormous difficulties involved. One of the most serious is the existence of long-established thinking patterns, the strength of which no sane person would underestimate. The most obvious barrier of this type is the resistance of management to change in the established power relationships (about which we will have more to say later), but it is worth noting that another hindrance to democracy—and linked, in a way, to the first—is the fear of freedom among more subordinate persons. This seemingly odd phenomenon was noticed by Rousseau, who pointed out: "Man is born free, and everywhere he is in chains." Unfreedom, he said, becomes a habit: "Slaves lose everything in their chains, even including the desire to be rid of them; they love their servitude. . . ."[73]

That people should enjoy servitude, especially in a world full of fervent defense of freedom at all points along the political-economic spectrum, can appear peculiar, but there is a great deal of *willingness* in the acceptance of degrading work conditions—even if the process is a largely unconscious one.

It is likely that this is one of the strengths of the modern work system. Individuals can be seen to cling to an outmoded authoritarian system in order to protect themselves from the unknown dangers that freedom might hold. Erich Fromm, in *Escape from Freedom*, holds that this situation arose with industrial capitalism, which, supported by the work-oriented philosophies of Luther and Calvin, succeeded in giving the human being all the necessary elements needed for freedom—except freedom itself. Having failed to master the new set of circumstances, man instead acquired a "feeling of individual insignificance and powerlessness."[74]

In attempting to resolve the problems thus created, one escape is to "fuse one's self with somebody or something outside oneself in order to acquire the strength which the individual self is lacking."[75] This masochism is connected with a "desire to get rid of the individual self" and thereby to rid oneself of gnawing doubts about oneself. By seeking pain, the individual attempts to get rid of everything that is involved with his real self. But he never thereby overcomes his isolation and powerlessness—indeed, they only increase—and he thus never gets what he has been trying "to pay for: inner peace and tranquility."[76]

To come back to the other side of the authoritarian pattern— the managers—we see that it is only a variation on the same theme. Fromm notes that the sadist and the masochist are victims of the same basic disease, and they attempt to combat it through basically similar approaches: gaining power over another, or submitting to another's power, and thus merging with the other and escaping from one's insignificant self. "Both the masochistic and sadistic strivings tend to help the individual to escape his unbearable feelings of aloneness and powerlessness."[77] These methods are ultimately unsatisfactory, but they do accomplish one thing:

They get rid of "the burden of freedom." This leads to "the authoritarian character"—the admiration for and love of involvement with power, on both sides of the equation; such a person "admires authority and tends to submit to it, but at the same time he wants to be an authority himself and have others submit to him."[78]

This argument helps illuminate a paradox: Why should workers so often support the myths of the authoritarian structure in which they are enmeshed—that is to say, the ideology of industrial capitalism, the superiority of the profit motive, and the virtues of ambition and hard work—even though they do not stand the slightest chance of ever benefiting from such abstractions? One can gain a kind of inner strength by submitting to the system, however apparent its injustices.

Nevertheless, the desire for democracy remains strong. Says Fromm: "The drive for freedom inherent in human nature, while it can be corrupted and suppressed, tends to assert itself again and again."[79]

As noted earlier, it is surprising that industrial democracy has made so little progress in America, which possesses a democratic ideology. Yet the principles involved are, basically, the same as those applying in the political field. Thomas Jefferson wrote: "The general spread of the light of science has already laid open to every view the palpable truth, that the mass of mankind has not been born with saddles on their backs, nor a favored few booted and spurred, ready to ride them legitimately, by the grace of God."[80]

Despite the obvious parallels, the connection between industrial democracy and political democracy is rarely discussed. One of the few political thinkers to insist on it was G. D. H. Cole, the British democratic socialist, who attacked the idea of collectivist-bureaucratic control along with capitalist-bureaucratic control. Democracy in industry, was, he argued, an essential element of full citizenship democracy in society as a whole, and he spoke of "giving to the workers responsibility and control, in short freedom to express their personality in the work is their way of serving the community. . . . Political democracy must be completed by democracy in the workshop."[81] More recently, Carole Pateman, a political science thinker, has made very much the same point in a theory of "participatory democracy." The exclusion of so important a sphere as industry from an over-all democratic system is scarcely logical, she says, and most probably damaging to the efficient functioning of the system. All important elements of a society must be included in a democratic whole. "The most important area is industry," she writes. "If individuals are to exercise the maximum amount of control over their own lives and environment then authority structures in these areas must be so organized that they can participate in decision making."[82] She concludes that the "authority structure" of a person's work environment can have a deciding influence on his political opinions, and she suggests that increased democracy in industry could have a larger social impact: "Experience of a participatory authority structure might also be effective in diminishing tendencies toward nondemocratic attitudes in the individual."[83]

This observation accords with findings regarding the disturbingly antisocial attitudes among blue-collar workers engaged in assembly-line jobs, which can very probably help to explain the puzzling surge of antidemocratic views among workers in the United States in recent years.

Many theories of industrial democracy have been advanced, and many forms have been tried—some good, some not so good. But the efforts made so far have great lessons for the future. Elements of various systems can prove worthwhile in constructing even more satisfactory systems—or, as one should more democratically put it, in creating conditions under which individuals involved in systems can themselves construct them. Even the failures can be instructive. There is no intention here to make an exhaustive survey of this area, but we can usefully look at some of the attempts that have been made to satisfy what in our modern world is a basic human feeling—the desire for democracy.

V. THE DESIRE FOR DEMOCRACY

The authoritarian management machinery built up under industrial capitalism has never been wholeheartedly accepted by those subjected to it. From the very birth of capitalism, there have been endless attempts to soften the hierarchical structure and restore to the individual freedom in work. Many of these attempts have failed completely or fallen well short of the goal.

It can be useful to glance briefly at two manifestations of this impulse for freedom—very different in nature and appearing at different stages in history.

One of the more concrete expressions of dissatisfaction with industrial capitalism was the wave of utopian communities established in the United States during the nineteenth century. The moral attack of the communities was carefully aimed: in contrast to the harshness and greed already clear-cut in the burgeoning capitalist society, these communities stressed democracy and equality. Despite their varied peculiarities, they shared a deep distaste for the society around them.

One of the more successful utopian movements was the Shaker crusade, which came to the New World from France in the late eighteenth century and which was guided by stern religious principles—including a prohibition of all sexual activity. However, the religious element was combined with a primitive communism and equality among members of the same community. The first Shaker community was established in 1787 in New Lebanon, New York, and at one time eighteen communities flourished from Maine to Indiana. The economic side of Shakerism was only an incidental necessity, but the blend of austere religion and democratic agriculture and crafts proved a winning combination. Stow Persons, a historian of the movement, noted: "As an economic enterprise Shaker communitarianism was an unqualified success."[1]

Its durability was unfortunately critically weakened by the ban on sex. The Shaker communities were dependent on constant recruitment of converts, and when the supply of such ran out in the late nineteenth century, the movement died.

The anticapitalistic spirit was even more marked in the movement created by Robert Owen, who was combating the evils of capitalism as he had learned them from the inside. Born in a poor family in Wales in 1771, he was able to exercise his natural gifts in the newly formed capitalistic framework, and before he was thirty he had amassed a considerable fortune in a Scottish cotton-mill empire. But, as historian Albert Fried has noted, he became increasingly distressed by "the paradox of 'progress': as wealth grew, thanks to the introduction of labor-saving machinery, the lot of labor worsened."[2] In his own factories, he met the problem by a precocious paternalistic system of housing, education, and welfare for his employees.

For more general use, he developed a program for "Villages of Cooperation," which would gather together relatively small groups (five hundred to fifteen hundred persons) in cooperative communities containing agriculture, industry, and social life, all combined in a smoothly functioning whole. He had little luck with his ideas in England, and embarked for America in 1824, where he addressed Congress, met enthusiastic crowds of admirers, and bought a village called Harmony, Indiana, for $135,000, which was to serve as the testing ground for his ideas. He renamed the village New Harmony, where the basic principles were to be the reverse of capitalism: "The whole of this country is ready to commence a new empire upon the principle of public property and to discard private property." In view of that fact, he conceded that his timing was extraordinarily precise: "For years past everything seems to have been prepared in an unaccountable and most remarkable manner for my arrival."[3]

Tested against the brutalities of everyday life, Owen's ideas failed to hold up. New Harmony, plagued by disorganization and amateurism, lasted only two years, and of the handful of other Owenite communities, only one endured for as long as three years.

A similar pattern of communist living was developed in the "associationist" movement, dominated by the ideas of the French utopist Charles Fourier, who had been much admired by Owen. Fourier was promoted in America by Albert Brisbane, who published a book on his teacher's ideas in 1840. Fourierism was explicitly an answer to the degrading living and working conditions created by the nascent capitalism. In fact, Brisbane discovered Fourier's philosophy while he was traveling throughout Europe in search of remedies for the appalling conditions he saw around him. When he met Fourier—first the writings and later the man—he knew that he had discovered the answer to the problems that had been troubling him. "Now for the first time," he wrote, "I had come across an idea which I had never met before—the idea of *dignifying* and *rendering attractive* the manual labor of mankind; labor hitherto regarded as divine punishment inflicted on man."[4] Primarily as a result of Brisbane's efforts, Fourier gathered a large American following, especially among intellectuals.

The central feature of Fourierism was the "Phalanx," consisting of about two thousand persons in which, despite a detailed set of ordinances regarding organization, education, housing, and work, a natural environment would be created for the uninhibited flowering of human instincts. In his observations of industrial capitalism, Fourier was horrified by "the great attention given to the dead machinery, and the neglect and disregard of the living machinery." He accordingly placed a transformation of work as a primary goal of a Fourierist society: "Dignify work and render it attractive."[5] Specifically, he intended to remedy the aspect of capitalistic work that was most detested—its uninteresting quality. Edmund Wilson points out that this was to be changed under Fourierism: "It was not . . . necessary that people should bore or fatigue themselves by working continually at one task."[6] They would thus shift from one to another.

One notable "associationist" community that eventually converted to Fourierism was the Brook Farm Institute of Agriculture and Education, founded in 1841 in Massachusetts by intellectuals such as George Ripley and William Henry Channing and visited by Hawthorne and Emerson. The central position of work, and the harmonious spirit of the community, as contrasted with the rough-and-tumble American capitalism of the day, was clearly spelled out in a statement of principles: to promote "a more natural union between intellectual and manual labor than now exists; to combine the thinker and the worker, as far as possible in the same individual" and thus to bring about "a more wholesome and simple life than can be led amidst the pressure of our competitive institutions."[7] At first, the principles served admirably: Life was pleasant, equality was practiced, membership rose from thirty to seventy persons, the members indulged in intellectual pursuits in their spare time and achieved the goal of more human working conditions. As Fried notes, "the duties were varied and interesting." But after a series of mishaps, including a fire, membership fell off, and Brook Farm disbanded after six years of existence. And none of the other Fourierist communities—there are known to have been at least twenty-eight—lasted that long.

Without doubt the most stunning success of all the utopian communities was registered by, in some ways, the most curious— the "Bible Communist" society in Oneida, New York, founded by John Humphrey Noyes, ex-Yale divinity student, prophet of the Perfectionist religion, and discoverer of "complex marriage." This last item, which dictated that all the male members of the community were engaged in sexual marriage with all the female members, led to some notoriety for the community among its more conformist neighbors—so much so that Noyes had been forced to abandon his original site in Putney, Vermont, after only two years, but when he moved to Oneida, New York, in 1848, the settlement proved surprisingly (considering its unconventionality) durable.

Despite the "free love" label that outsiders happily pinned on Oneida, the Perfectionists were intensely serious, deeply moral, and well disciplined in Noyes' rules of propriety (e.g., all sexual advances had to be formally pursued through the offices of a third party). And the "complex marriage" idea was not merely a titillating frill on an otherwise rather plain religion; it was an integral part of Perfectionist communism, which was intimately connected with the nature of work. In his religious studies, Noyes had become increasingly convinced that the existing "Marriage System" was just as wrong as the existing "Work System," and he was determined to end both at once. Among other evils, he averred that conventional marriage led to "the sexual and economic domination of men over women." He regarded economic possessiveness in the same light as sexual possessiveness. "The grand distinction between the Christian and the unbeliever," he wrote, "is that in one reigns the We-spirit and the other the I-spirit. From *I* comes *mine*, and from the I-spirit comes exclusive appropriation of money, women, etc. From *we* comes *ours*, and from the We-spirit comes universal community of interests."[8] Not surprisingly, this was all closely involved with the abolition of the inhuman work environment common under industrial capitalism. "In vital society," he explained, "labor will become attractive. Loving companionship in labor, and especially the mingling of the sexes, makes labor attractive." In actual practice, the Perfectionists also avoided some of the more dreadful accepted practices of industrial capitalism. They avoided specialization, shifted from job to job to avoid monotony, and worked relatively short hours.

Astoundingly, Oneida defied conventional sexual morality as well as conventional capitalist morality—and prospered. The population rose to about three hundred persons, and agriculture was supplemented by a brisk export trade in steel traps, sewing silk, preserved fruit, and silverware. Outside pressures forced the abandonment of complex marriage in 1879, and the community was converted into an ordinary share company. Thus gradually the eccentric community faded back into the society from which it had come.

Dozens of other similar communities were established in the mid-nineteenth century—Rappite villages, Icaria, Modern Times, Fruitland, Hopedale—and even though some of them lingered on for decades (Icaria lasted, after a fashion, for forty-eight years), they all failed in the end. But, as Stewart Holbrook states, every one of these eccentric innovators "was working, even in his maddest moments, to improve and embellish the United States."[9] And, in virtually all the communities, a key element was a distaste for industrial capitalism as it was developing at the time, and most particularly, the character of work under industrial capitalism.

Why did these honest efforts fail? Probably the single most important defect was the insistence on fighting "the system" by abandoning it altogether—a fatal weakness. Edmund Wilson noted that the idea was that "self-contained societies should be organized inside the larger society."[10] Marx wrote contemptuously of the founders' dreams "of experimental realization of their social utopias, of founding isolated *phalanstères*, of establishing 'home colonies' or setting up a 'Little Icaria'—pocket editions of the New Jerusalem," in ways that made them dependent on the "bourgeois" classes at the same time they were trying to check out of bourgeois society.[11]

Most subsequent attacks on the dehumanizing elements of industrial capitalism have been either more violent—e.g., the Russian Revolution—or have been much more mild, and completely within the framework of the system.

In any case, one of the major creations of industrial capitalism was a desire for more democracy in the autocratic enterprises that arose. This desire found for many years its main expression in the battle for union rights, a battle which, in most industrialized countries, has now been won.

We need not concern ourselves with the well-known development of unionism, except to point out that it was not a total solution. It was perhaps logical to believe that it should have been— if workers should acquire a powerful instrument to promote their interests, then they should be able to formulate their demands in any way they want—and perhaps it would have been, if, in the early days of unionism, wages had not been such a clear-cut issue and if there had been more precise knowledge of the other problems. As it has worked out, unions have concentrated on wages and a narrow range of other issues which, like wages, can be precisely described in a demand or a contract and which can be a subject of conflict. In few countries, and only recently, have unions turned their attention to other, less precisely calculable issues, despite increasingly clear evidence that questions relating to the dehumanization of work are becoming more important. Unions have, because of their original preoccupation with a narrow range of subjects and because they have by now become bureaucratized, developed a certain rigidity and an incapacity in dealing with new problems that require more flexible thinking. The rigid authoritarianism of the enterprise is thus counterbalanced by rigid thinking patterns of the unions. Increasingly, the realization has spread that, if any real degree of democracy is to be realized, more flexible institutions are needed. During the past few decades, this realization has manifested itself in a number of European countries through the establishment, either independently of or parallel with unions, of "workers' councils" intended to deal with matters of concern to workers in a looser, more informal atmosphere than is generally possible in a monolithic union-management confrontation. Though these councils differ in character from country to country and have arisen under varying circumstances over the past several decades, they appear to answer a deeply felt need among workers and are therefore closely connected with the larger problems of industrial democracy.

Essentially, the "workers' councils" are management-labor joint bodies in which problems of mutual interest may be discussed. Worker representatives are elected by the workers, either directly or through their unions. The councils are supposed to receive certain information from management and to meet at frequent intervals. However, the councils are only of a "consultative" nature—they have no power to decide anything of importance, though in some countries they may make decisions regarding "welfare" or "social" issues and even supervise the disposition of funds in this area.

Most of the "council" systems were established sometime between the end of World War II and the early 1950s (i.e., in 1945 in Norway, in 1946 in Sweden, in 1945 in France, in 1950 in Holland, in 1952 in Germany), meaning that they have had twenty years or so to prove their worth. Therefore, it is not a snap judgment to aver that they have been largely failures.

The critical weakness has been their lack of decision-making power. If they cannot do anything, managements have too often felt that it was useless even to deal with them. At best, they have been used as manipulative instruments, whereby workers could be given a "feeling" of participation while management was pushing through its own ideas anyway.

As it happens, I was present at a meeting of one of these councils in Sweden a few years ago, in one of Sweden's largest companies and one known for its well-developed councils. The meeting included about thirty-five workers and a handful of top executives, and it went on for hours. It was, as they say, a "free and frank exchange of views." The workers were outspoken in making their proposals and the executives were firm and forthright in discussing (and mostly rejecting) them. Later, I spoke to the president of the company, who thought it was a marvelous system for getting the workers to accept management's views. I asked him if management had ever been influenced by worker suggestions. He thought a moment and said: "Well, yes. We were going to build a new plant and we showed the workers the plans at one of the meetings. They objected very much to the fact that the plant had no windows." He shrugged. "So we changed the plans and had some windows put in. It doesn't cost much more and actually the building looks better. And the workers feel better."

This, however, is, for all its triviality, an unusually bright picture. In Sweden, one study showed that a third of the councils were receiving insufficient information from management even to discuss important subjects. The central Swedish trade union confederation conducts schools to teach council members the rudiments of corporate finance and other intricate matters that are supposed to be discussed at the meetings, but union officials have bitterly concluded that this is rather useless if the basic material from management is not forthcoming.

The situation has been much the same in other countries. In France, I have been told that managements frequently blandly inform the councils that certain information that they are required by law to reveal is simply not available. Adolf Sturmthal, an authority on this subject, says that the workers "are usually not given information of any significance." And if it is, it is muddled to the maximum extent: "Company reports are infrequent, and they are usually presented in such a fashion that the uninitiated will learn little from them."[12] Managements react to the councils as to a threat: "Sometimes when they had important suggestions to make, employers refused to take them seriously, out of fear of losing their authority."[13]

Studies in The Netherlands show similarly depressing results. More than half of worker councils members feel their knowledge and training insufficient to discuss the matters at hand. Moreover, the average worker has very little contact with the council and little knowledge about what is taking place there. Management feels that the workers are not really interested in the councils' work, while the employees complain that they are not given enough information on subjects in which they are interested. One report concludes that the councils are of little help in promoting democracy, and that "real democracy within the firm" calls for other approaches.[14]

Experience in West Germany is somewhat more positive than in most other countries—perhaps because the tradition stretches back farther (the first councils were established in 1920, only to be abolished in 1933), because they are supported more vigorously by the unions, and because they are supplemented by other forms of labor-management cooperation. Sturmthal says: "The institution of works councils has undoubtedly helped to reduce the domineering attitude of management which was in any case difficult to maintain in the stormy days after World War II."[15] And W. Schwartz has written that the system "has functioned satisfactorily and without disturbances. . . . In the great majority of enterprises, it has brought about a climate of cooperation which has contributed heavily to the maintenance of social peace. . . ."[16]

Poland, the one country in the Soviet bloc with some experience of workers' councils roughly comparable to those in the West, shows similarly discouraging results. Originally organized spontaneously during the troubles of 1956, the councils were regarded by the workers as true representative bodies, in contrast to the unions, which, according to Sturmthal, were regarded with "disdain" and contemptuously referred to as "the second government."[17] Wladyslaw Gomulka recognized the workers' demands, and the councils were officially recognized as "self-governing" bodies in the factories, with wide-ranging management rights and authority over a small profit-sharing fund.

But the councils as genuine management bodies did not last long. In less than a year, their powers were being restricted by the regime, and they eventually wound up as little more than arid discussion groups. Sturmthal pointed to "a striking parallel" between the evolution of Polish and French councils, toward decreasingly viable entities.[18]

Such criticism by outsiders is in fact confirmed by Polish sources. A report prepared by Z. Rybicki of the University of Warsaw in 1967 took a dim view of the councils' effectiveness, putting most of the blame on the workers themselves. The great majority of proposals made by the councils were not put into effect, Rybicki said, largely because the councils "took too little interest in the fate of their own proposals."[19] Pointing to the "workers' need to learn the difficult art of industrial management," Rybicki cites Lenin's insistence that "the masses must gradually be prepared for their role as master of the economy." In this respect, the Polish establishment joins hands with Western businessmen in their dim view of workers' intelligence.

By the time the riots of the 1970–71 winter came, the Polish councils had become virtually paralyzed. According to an official report, only a minority of council members were actually workers (varying from 20 percent to 45 percent), and the councils met an average of only two to three times a year.[20] Reacting swiftly to workers' demands, the new Secretary General of the United Workers' (Communist) Party, Edward Gierek, like Gomulka before him, promised the workers at Gdansk and Szczecin to establish "workers' power" in the factories, which, as one reporter pointed out, "poses an even graver problem for the party."[21]

Though circumstances differ in the East and in the West, most observers would agree that the workers' councils have been approximately equally disappointing everywhere. Rather than a step toward greater participation, they have proved to be a dead end. An OECD report bluntly notes that the councils have been "a failure"[22]—so much so that "workers' reactions to the councils are overwhelmingly negative," and they even tend to suspect anyone cooperating with them. Studies have shown that, in Germany, 40 percent of workers distrust union members in the councils, as do more than half of workers in The Netherlands.

What does all this prove?

Most importantly, both the utopian communities and the workers' councils show, in their very different ways, that resistance to the overly autocratic organization of industrial capitalism runs deep—it did in the early days and it still does. Though both these forms of attack on the problem have failed in the end (for different reasons), they provide ample evidence that the desire for democratic organization, for control over one's own existence, and against dictatorial styles of life, are extremely persistent.

The utopian communities failed largely because they were overly isolated from the society around them. The enormous pressures of industrial capitalism were too much for these weak little islands. A refusal to face the harsh realities of society may be a noble gesture, but in the end it is only a gesture.

The saga of the utopian settlements is being re-enacted today in the numerous "communes" established here and there in the United States. It is entirely possible that at least some of these—helped by greater over-all prosperity—may show better durability than did the utopias of the last century. But they retain the most severe defect of those settlements—a total isolation from, and lack of, integration with the outside environment.

The workers' councils have failed because they have no power to do anything. Even as morale-building discussion clubs, they seem to have fallen far short of any reasonable goals. Too often, managements have regarded them as tiresomely transparent shams that could be irritating but that need not be taken seriously.

Nevertheless, disappointing as these efforts have been, their experience can be instructive in the search for more productive ideas.

VI. ISRAEL: THE SPIRIT OF THE KIBBUTZ

In many ways, the kibbutzim of Israel resemble the American utopian communities of the nineteenth century; since they have lasted longer than any of those unfortunate settlements, are still thriving today, and have survived wars, economic turbulence, and their own "mini" industrial revolution, they are well worth a look for what light they may shed on the workings of democracy in a coldly economic context.

The first kibbutz—the word means "group" in Hebrew—was established in 1909. Today, there are some 230 kibbutzim in Israel with about 90,000 members, equal to about 3.5 percent of the Jewish population of Israel. All the kibbutzim are owned and operated by the members themselves, with little outside help or interference.

Like the American utopian communities, the kibbutzim represent a reaction to the merciless industrial-capitalist world, and they have always put heavy stress on work as a dignifying and liberating force. Melford Spiro, an American sociologist and student of kibbutz life, notes: "Probably the single most important ideal upon which the entire kibbutz culture is based is what might be termed the moral value of labor." The principle seems suspiciously close to the Calvinistic-puritanical ideas, but there are some sharp differences. For one thing, work is regarded not as a form of suffering or punishment, but as a source of joy and a sustaining force in life. Second, even though work was regarded as a necessity, its materialistic aspects—and thus the money-instrumental view of work—were clearly rejected from the very beginning: "Labor was not merely a means for the satisfaction of human needs; rather, labor itself was viewed as a need—probably man's most important need—the satisfaction of which became an end in itself." A. D. Gordon, one of the founders of the Zionist movement, developed the idea of "the religion of labor," which held that, through work, "man became one with himself, society, and nature."[1]

Moreover, the reaction to industrial capitalism was from a special Jewish point of view. In Europe, Jews had been traditionally barred from agriculture, and the kibbutzim were, not coincidentally, based on agriculture. Manual work was more worthy than intellectual pursuits, and the noblest form of manual labor was agricultural.

But the kibbutzim differed sharply from the American utopias. Even though based on important philosophical principles, the kibbutzim were mostly nonreligious (and often vehemently antireligious). More importantly, they were not in conflict with the society around them. They were heavily involved in building the nation of Israel—indeed, it would be only a slight exaggeration to say that the nation grew up around the kibbutzim— and contributed significant numbers of soldiers, politicians, and labor leaders to the new country. At present, despite their minuscule size relative to the country's population, they are a source of great pride to the people. Even the casual visitor to Israel finds himself being constantly informed of the great achievements of the kibbutzim, and one gets the impression that the members are regarded as a kind of pioneering elite.

Most of the early kibbutzim were founded on rather doctrinaire socialist principles, but there was hardly any possibility of conflict with capitalism in the early days. Moshe Kerem, a kibbutz historian, points out: "There was no point in socialism launching a campaign against capitalists. There were no capitalists to speak of."[2] Even today, the socialist kibbutzim are not a disturbing element. Even although the Israeli economy is largely capitalist-oriented, deviations from capitalism are accepted as a matter of course. A fifth of industry is owned by the state and another fifth

by the labor unions, and some two hundred cooperative enterprises are owned and managed by the employees—including
Egged, the leading interurban bus company which, with its more
than seven thousand employees, is said to be the largest such
enterprise in the world.

Not all kibbutzim are identical. They are divided into five
groups, according to political philosophy, and each group has a
central headquarters dispensing management advice, financial
aid, and cooperative support. But each kibbutz is free to go its
own way, even to violate the principles of its own group if it
wishes.

All kibbutzim are thoroughly democratic and have been from
the beginning. Every major decision is approved by a general
meeting in which each member has a vote. Members are given
jobs, to the extent possible, according to their own wishes and
capabilities. Members are rotated in all jobs, including supervisory posts. Nobody receives any real "salary," and everyone receives equal treatment regarding his basic needs—housing, food,
clothing, and a minimal allotment of pocket money. Private
property is, strictly speaking, a violation of the kibbutz principles,
and for many years even such simple personal possessions as radios
and tea-making equipment were frowned upon by more traditionally minded members. Children are raised in common, and all
decisions regarding their education are made by the collective.

As noted earlier, work is, in all kibbutzim, a central concern
and a source of great satisfaction in different ways. Spiro notes
that kibbutz members are motivated not only by "personal economic improvement" (in a collective sense) but also by intrinsic
satisfactions from the work itself, competitive pride in achievement, and the prestige among fellow members of carrying out
hard, physical labor.[3] Moreover, intellectual and bureaucratic positions are rated low. Teachers tend to be looked down on, and those
nominated for important administrative positions customarily
make it clear that they do not want such jobs and will accept them
only reluctantly.

It is a very special kind of life, and it places severe demands on
those who would follow it. Bjørg Aase Sørensen, a Norwegian
sociologist who lived on a kibbutz, wrote: "The first Hebrew word
I learned was 'we.'"[4] She adds: "Like monks in a monastery,

kibbutz members have little opportunity for truly private life . . .
it is obvious that being raised in a traditional family does not
qualify one for the kibbutz life."[5] New recruits have been mainly
drawn from new immigrants who have undergone lengthy educational courses abroad.

Nevertheless, for the first several decades of kibbutz history, the
principles held up well: Communistic agricultural communities,
hard physical labor, austerity, and devotion to ideals of brother-
hood and equality proved a winning combination. Since nobody
was ever forced to remain on a kibbutz if he didn't want to stay,
the mere fact that they survived and even steadily grew in numbers is adequate evidence that the principles worked well. From
an economic point of view, the agricultural kibbutzim were
clearly successful. Joseph E. Shatil, in an economic survey of
kibbutz results, observes: "In adjustment to normal conditions of
modern agriculture, the kibbutz proved adaptability and ability to
find new solutions. . . . In technological efficiency, the kibbutz
development shows an uninterrupted high rate of growth."[6]
Whatever the difficulties, the ideology and the abundant other
satisfactions were adequate to maintain the kibbutzim as living
institutions.

But as to all things, change must come, and change came to
the kibbutzim in the form of their own little industrial revolution.
During World War II, the British Army, as well as the kibbutzim
themselves, needed various processed food items and manufac-
tured products, and a number of the kibbutzim established industrial production facilities alongside the agricultural operations. At first, this was a temporary exigency, but as time passed,
industrialism made further gains for different reasons. Advances
in agricultural productivity rapidly reduced the need for workers
and, since the amount of additional land available was limited,
agricultural expansion was impossible. Under kibbutz ideology, it
was unthinkable to expel surplus workers—jobs must be created
for them, as well as for older workers who could no longer do
heavy farm work anyway, but nevertheless had a need to work
(in accordance not only with the ideology but with sound psychological principles). Finally, the country needed to be developed economically, and the kibbutzim could scarcely refuse to
participate in this urgent task.

At present, some two-thirds of the kibbutzim have industrial operations employing a total of about eight thousand persons. Many have several factories each, and in a few cases two or more kibbutzim have combined to form relatively large industrial units. They represent a wide range of specialties: canning, metalworking, plastics, furniture, chemicals, and building materials. Growth in industrial production is easily outpacing that in agriculture, and more plants are steadily being added.

Industrialization was often greeted with suspicion and even hostility by kibbutz members, but it was not a clear-cut conflict with the ideology. In any case, the practical forces were compelling. Dan Giladi, Professor of Labor Relations at the University of Tel Aviv, remarked to me: "The realities were stronger than the principles."

Industrialization brought in its wake a less welcome innovation: the hiring of outside workers on a regular wage basis. This practice was begun originally because kibbutz members alone were insufficient to build up the factories to a scale required for efficient operation, and was thought to be temporary. It has continued, because of a continuing shortage of kibbutz members (the kibbutzim's industrial operations are growing far faster than new members can be recruited) and because of the need for highly trained persons. Today, almost all the kibbutz industrial operations have outside workers—some only a handful, others several hundred. The largest kibbutz factory is a plywood operation at Afikim, employing 40 kibbutz members along with 320 outside workers.

This trend is seen as an obvious disruption of kibbutz principles. Dan Giladi remarked to me: "The kibbutz members realize it is against their principles, and they would like to get rid of the outside workers. It undermines the basis of kibbutz life—the kibbutz member becomes an exploiter." Some observers feel that the continuation of the practice has produced something of a crisis in kibbutz life. As Yair Levi, project director of the International Research Center on Rural Cooperative Communities, sadly told me: "The problem of hired labor is very acute."

Most seriously, the use of outside labor has gravely impaired the democratic spirit in many kibbutzim. One might assume that, with all the decades of accumulated experience with democratic organization, it would be a relatively simple matter to include the hired workers in a democratic system adapted to the new era. For the most part, this has not happened. Whereas the traditional pattern was for all workers to join in free discussions regarding management matters, organizing the work, work assignments, and other important matters, most of the kibbutz industries tend to function much as any other industrial plant, with a pyramidal hierarchy and an autocratic power system. Such democratic practices as job rotation and group discussions tend to diminish or disappear entirely. Avraham Ben-David, head of the industrial division of Hakibutz Ha'artzi Hashomer Hatzair (one of the central kibbutz organizations), told me: "I'm afraid we are not such good managers."

To be sure, the pattern varies. Peter Jordan, technical manager of the Arad water-meter factory operated at the kibbutz Dahlia, which has fifteen hired employees among its one hundred workers, is not overly disturbed by the trend. "It's against our principles," he concedes. "There is not the same kind of contact as there is between people who live together all the time." But he says that the outsiders have not caused any conflicts, and that, besides, the plant would be severely crippled without its outsiders, one of whom is the chief engineer. "If we didn't use them," he said, "we would have to turn down some export deals, and that would damage Israeli industry."

Bjørg Sørensen concludes that the kibbutz she studied, which employs a fair number of technicians and other outside workers in its plastics factory, has nevertheless maintained a high level of democracy in its operation, though she notes that the kibbutz in question (which she does not name) is regarded as a "model" kibbutz.[7] Job rotation has been continued despite the difficulties caused by the need for specialization and the presence of hired workers. Certain jobs, especially the boring, monotonous, or otherwise undesirable ones, are passed around for fixed periods. In some cases, the practice is more informal: "Some of the rotation occurs spontaneously, according to the wishes of the workers to learn more or to experience a change."[8] For the most part, the work is carried out by small, self-governing groups; on one occasion, Mrs. Sørensen asked where the "foreman" was: "The reaction was immediate—'There is no foreman here.'"[9] At one point, a particularly highly qualified technician had built up a strong position of authority in one section, but a group of younger members organized a debate around his position, with the final result that a "real decentralization of that department took place, and the man in question was prevailed upon to share some of his authority."[10] Great emphasis continued to be placed on the democratically organized general meetings, and 92 percent of those who expressed themselves reported that they had the feeling their opinions were listened to.[11]

An example of a kibbutz that has accepted the drastic alterations of the principles is Netzer Sereni, which owns a furniture factory and a plant producing heavy-duty trailers, refrigerators, and other products. The latter employs about 30 of the 300 kibbutz members and 150 hired workers and is managed along hard-headed business lines by Aron Bacia, who is managing director and a kibbutz member. "We have long ago left the basic ideology of the movement," he explained to me. "Of course it would be better if we could have only members working here. But it is impossible. You can either have an industry with hired workers or have no industry at all." One relevant fact is the company's rapid expansion, due to production for export, which had risen by more than 100 percent in one year (total sales were at that time running at around four million dollars annually).

At this plant, as at many other industrial establishments, the principles of job rotation have had to be modified. Bacia said: "You can't rotate people in this kind of position in this kind of company. It's O.K. in a small shop, but not here." As for efforts to build a democratic system in which the ordinary worker could share, he laughs: "You mean I should have him sitting here and making decisions?" Ideas of industrial democracy in general, he feels, are bound to fail. Bacia (who explains that, as an ordinary kibbutz member, he has a budget for his family "which is less than that of the janitor of this factory") says there is only one key to improving worker involvement: "The one way to make workers happy is to let them make more money." His plant has a bonus system which, he says, functions very efficiently.

Some—probably most—kibbutz people are quite appalled by the necessity to employ paid workers. Nissan Shiran, who has a degree in business administration and is "economic adviser" at Givat Brener kibbutz, which operates a furniture factory and juice cannery, is one such. Shiran believes that the hired workers, while necessary, cause major problems. "They are not responsible," he says. "The members do everything they can to improve the work. The hired workers don't care. They have no motivation to work hard." Moreover, the hired workers tend to damage the whole atmosphere. "This half-and-half system—we know it's no good. All hired workers would be better than this." He explains that conditions are much better in the agricultural operation, where only members work and where everyone participates in discussions on organizing the work. I asked why the same procedure couldn't be followed in the factory; he shook his head and answered: "It's the problem with the hired workers. It doesn't matter to them."

Shiran spoke enviously of one kibbutz that came up with a highly successful solution to the problem—Gan Shmuel, which produces canned fruit juice, olives, and citrus oil, and which invested heavily in advanced machinery to raise productivity, making it possible to fire all the outside workers. Previously, there were 50 workers in the factory, about two-thirds of them hired from outside. Today, there are about 40 workers, all of them recruited from among the approximately 460 members of the kibbutz.

Aron Hadar, a keenly intelligent young economics graduate who runs the business side of Gan Shmuel, says that the expulsion of hired workers in 1964 was a major economic and psychological triumph. He explains that Gan Shmuel is one of the five richest kibbutzim in Israel, that productivity of capital employed is about three to four times the average in Israeli industry as a whole, and that the unusually high quality of production has meant success in toughly competitive export markets (90 percent of output is exported).

The success is partly due to the capital investments (capital employed per worker is nearly double that of the average in Israeli industry). But the improvement in the atmosphere also had an impact. Previously, the factory was organized along the traditional lines, with fixed lines of authority. "The members of the kibbutz were always in a higher position than the hired workers," says Hadar. "They became a kind of elite. And they didn't like their

work. Even though they were the bosses, they didn't feel any
involvement. Even if you are the boss you can still be detached."
Because of this split, it was difficult to promote participation:
"There was only a management committee, which made all the
decisions without even consulting the workers. What would have
been the use?"

After the hired workers left, the spirit improved sharply. The
fixed hierarchy was abolished. "We are not against specialization," explains Hadar, "but we are against putting people in the
same job and leaving them there until they die. In each section,
the foreman is changed each year. People move from job to job in
the factory. The disadvantage is that people are not specialized
to the highest degree. But the workers get a better over-all view of
the factory, and they feel more involved." All policy decisions are
discussed openly: "Every Monday evening, all the workers get
together and talk about the problems of the factory. Theoretically,
all problems pass through this meeting, which is very democratic.
Everybody has one vote."

Significantly, the members' feelings toward work in the factory
have changed. Romeck Rotem, general manager of the whole
kibbutz, told me: "After the hired workers left, there was an immediate revival of interest in the factory. A much higher percentage of members wanted to work there than before."

The attempt to absorb the hired workers into the democratic
organization can unquestionably be rated a thorough failure.
This is all the more surprising when one considers how successful
the kibbutz industrialization has been in other respects. For one
thing, they have smoothly met, and conquered, the usual problems arising from a shift away from agriculture—but with one
important difference. Yair Levi remarked to me: "They have carried out the perfect rural exodus without even changing their
residence."

Moreover, the kibbutzim have shown themselves to be as efficient in industry as in agriculture, and the indications are that
their democratic management is an important key to this success.
A study by Seymour Melman, Professor of Industrial Engineering at Columbia University, made a comparative study of Israeli
industrial establishments in six different fields, six at kibbutzim

and six privately owned.[12] The results were striking: On every count, the kibbutzim outperformed the privately owned companies—in productivity of labor (22 percent higher in the kibbutz companies), productivity of capital (40 percent when stated as profit on investment and 38 percent when stated as sales per unit of fixed assets), and net profit per production worker (38 percent higher). And administrative costs were, on average, 8 percent lower on the kibbutzim. (Significantly, this study included kibbutz factories where not more than 10 percent of the workforce was hired labor.)

Another measure of success is the growth of the kibbutz industries, which compete on equal terms with private industry, pay normal taxes, and receive no subsidies. In 1969, total sales volume of the 160 enterprises that are members of the Kibbutz Industries Association rose 25 percent, and exports jumped nearly 35 percent.[13]

As noted, the success can be probably attributed at least in part to the democratic management principles; in any case, these principles do not seem to be barriers, As Mrs. Sørensen notes, kibbutzim are managed according to methods that "capitalistic management ideologies claim are both impossible and unprofitable."[14]

Their most important departure from normal capitalistic thinking is that profitability is by no means the first consideration. The orthodox capitalist establishes a business when market studies, intuition, or other methods of analysis lead him to believe there is a market for his product or service sufficient to return an adequate profit on his investment. Many of the kibbutz businesses are established with the primary aim of providing jobs for members, and jobs specifically adapted to their needs, a procedure that is profoundly democratic. This had become increasingly true in recent years, with the failure of hired labor solutions and as the central kibbutz organizations have tried to discourage kibbutzim from establishing factories unless they can recruit the entire needed workforce from among kibbutz members. Yair Levi remarked to me that a main goal was to avoid the "hierarchical nature" of most industrial organization, meaning that the fields must be selected carefully. Shlomo Stanger, head of the Kibbutz Industries Association when I visited Israel (the occupant of that post is changed periodically), told me of the evolution at his own kibbutz, called Maaian Zvi: "We cannot develop our agriculture any further, but we have lots of sons returning from the army and we have members fifty or sixty years old who are no longer able to work in agriculture. So we must expand, but in fields where the right kind of jobs will be provided. Some years ago we started a garage service for diesel trucks, employing twenty-five to thirty people. Then we opened a small supermarket employing five or six members, because not everybody was able to work in the garage. We've also recently acquired some thirty-ton diesel trucks, which we use in a transport service from the Haifa harbor to Sinai. Now we're starting a polyester factory to make ornamental goods, where we employ about twenty members. But it's not enough to seek new projects—each project has to employ a special type of member. Each member has to be happy in his work. If he's not happy it's no good."

If the average capitalist manager might balk at the idea of placing "worker happiness" as a prime criterion for new investments, he would surely be turned off permanently by the sharp limitations on the power of a manager in a kibbutz: He has no formal power at all. Naphtali Golomb, a kibbutznik who has written widely on the sociology of kibbutz organization, writes of the manager's peculiar position: "Informal power, the degree of influence on members and the ability to win their cooperation and acceptance of his decisions, is fluid, and he must work at all times to earn it."[15] He cannot fire anyone or apply salary penalties; he cannot hold out the promise of a promotion or a raise in pay; he cannot even tell anyone what to do. And as regards himself, he cannot hope to gain higher pay, promotions, stock options, or status symbols.

The "power structure" in the kibbutz is vastly different from the normal pattern in industrial capitalism. Menachem Rosner, a kibbutz authority, has pointed to some of the contrasts between kibbutz organization and the classical industrial-capitalist bureaucratic structure, as described by Max Weber. Whereas that bureaucracy rests on centralized power, the kibbutz is decentralized. And a number of other characteristics of the Weberian bureaucracy are completely opposite to the kibbutz: permanency of office (impermanency of office in the kibbutz); fixed privileges and duties related to an office (a flexible definition of the office) hierarchy expressed in authority (equal value of all functions); nomination of officials on formal objective qualifications (election of officials, which can be based on personal or other considerations).[16]

These same peculiarities have their advantages. One is an openness to new ideas. Naphtali Golomb explained to me that this is one of the great strengths: "The idea of taking risks is built into the system. If the manager makes a mistake in investment—well, everybody had to approve it. And you can't be fired. There is usually a resistance to change, because of fear of unemployment. Not in a kibbutz." There is thus no resistance to installing new machinery in a kibbutz, and the pressure on fast workers to slow down is of course unknown. Mrs. Sørensen relates that one worker left the kibbutz and took a job in the same kind of factory in a city. He came back and explained that he had been "frozen out" by the other workers "because he had continued to work as he had done in the kibbutz (i.e., with maximum effort)."[17]

In analyzing the reasons for the kibbutzim's oddly successful results, the most obvious answer is that the members feel far more involved than workers in an ordinary capitalist company. These are the reasons one repeatedly hears from kibbutz members themselves: "We know we're working for ourselves." "It's the feeling of achievement." "We know it's our own." (There is undoubtedly some difference here between the agricultural operations, where the members find fulfillment in the nature of the work itself, in line with the original ideology, that is, in *intrinsic* factors, and in the factories, where the work is most often organized as in any other factory and where the satisfaction arises from factors *extrinsic* to the work—such as the feeling of involvement, the integration in a cohesive group, and the like.)

But the most powerful factor may well be that the organization is set up in a way that brings out the best efforts in human beings. Mrs. Sørensen maintains that the secret for the kibbutzim's success is in good organization structure, which is most effective when it allows maximum scope for individual decision-making to function.[18] Certainly the idea of adapting the organization to individuals, rather than setting up an organization and then squeezing individuals into it, as in the classical industrial pattern, is fully in line with the most sophisticated work in the functioning of organizations—however horrifying a thought it may be to the average executive in the capitalist system.

The kibbutzim can appear, from many points of view, backward, archaic, and unprogressive: Kibbutzniks frequently stubbornly argue that the kibbutzim must not change, that they must be rural, that they must be based on agriculture, that industry must not upset the traditional patterns, that adapting kibbutz ideas to city living (which has occasionally been tried) is impossible, and that everything must be kept as much as possible as it always was. Bruno Bettelheim, who expresses admiration for the kibbutz principles but is harshly critical of some of the results, sums up his feelings: "Somehow these dynamic people managed to create a static society."[19] Since kibbutz population growth has been slow in recent years (and few new recruits come from Israel), one can easily conclude that this institution is doomed because of its conservatism and refusal to keep up with the times.

All that may, in a sense, be true. But in another sense, the kibbutz can be seen as a dynamic institution much in advance of the rest of the world. Golomb and Katz have noted that a critical problem today "in the highly developed bureaucratic systems" is finding a way "to break down its formalization and to involve people in its operation and management." In this connection, "the kibbutzim, instead of being a conservative force holding over from a pre-state period, may be ahead of the present trends. . . ."[20] Even Bettelheim observes that the kibbutz spirit could be a valuable counterweight to some of the anxiety and alienation in today's world: "I am not sure that it wouldn't be nice to have a few kibbutzim around for those who long to escape the anonymity, selfishness, competitiveness, social disorganization and widespread feeling of purposelessness which are so often found in modern mass society."[21]

The kibbutz system was not, of course, set up according to a well-worked-out theory; if it functions as modern organization theory says a successful organization should function, it is more or less a happy accident. Nevertheless, it would seem logical that the kibbutz principles of democratic management could prove useful to a world in great need of such principles. If the kibbutz experience has any meaning at all, it should lie in the answer to the question: What lessons can the kibbutz offer?

There is a strong sentimental feeling, especially among kibbutz-niks themselves, that a way should be found to extend the benefits of kibbutz life to others. Shlomo Stanger observed: "If we could close the circle, give the same kind of life to people in cities, I'm sure they would be very happy."

But, as we have seen, the kibbutzim have been notably un-successful in extending the full benefits of their democratic methods even within their own borders—that is, to the hired workers. And possibilities of profiting from the kibbutz experi-ence do not always seem bright. Mrs. Sørensen, after analyzing at great length the advantages of kibbutz decentralization, democ-racy, and equality, rather incongruously concludes that the same benefits can perhaps be best reached in other countries through "central planning."[22] Joseph Klatzmann, in a book entitled *The Lessons of the Israel Experience*, is bluntly pessimistic about creating kibbutzim elsewhere: "It is even probable that none could be created anywhere with the same success as in Israel."[23]

As it happens, at least one large-scale effort has been made to transfer the kibbutz spirit to the more prosaic environment of ordinary industry. This effort was launched by Histadrut, the central Israeli labor organization, which not only represents work-ers in their struggles with management, but which *is* management in a vast variety of enterprises it owns, accounting together for about 20 percent of Israel's gross national product. At Histadrut's tenth national convention, in January 1966, a resolution was adopted "to arrange within a fixed period for the workers to participate in the management of Histadrut undertakings, as well as to share in their profits and in the responsibility for achieving them."

Yehuda Yudin, chairman of the Department of Workers' Par-ticipation in Management at Histadrut, told me that the back-ground for this move was strongly ideological: "We are trying to restore a bit of the kibbutz spirit in Israeli industry. And our ex-perience with the kibbutz makes us confident that ordinary workers can make valuable contributions to management." On the face of it, everything should favor the development of genuinely democratic methods in enterprises owned by the workers, especially in such a country as Israel, where, as Yudin has pointed out: "The kibbutz, the cooperative in agriculture and industry, the cooperative passenger transport, all play an important role in the development of Israel's national economy, and in many cases—especially in the kibbutzim—have achieved the highest degree of productivity combined with the fullest equality among its members."[24] Moreover, there had been many years of experience with semidemocratic bodies in industry—Joint Productivity Councils and workers' councils in Histadrut companies. Both of these previous institutions, in fact, share a common characteristic with the newer management-labor bodies which aim to bring about true democracy: None of them work.

Initially, the management-labor bodies were set up on an experimental basis in about a dozen companies. The matters they were to deal with, the frequency of their meetings, and their composition were firmly established in directives issued by the Histadrut headquarters in Tel Aviv. This was undoubtedly a first mistake; whereas one of the great strengths of the kibbutzim is their flexible and informal character, the Histadrut effort at promoting democracy was to be accomplished (even though workers in the factories affected voted on whether to participate in the experiments) through the handing down of rigid statutes from above, much like any other directive in a traditional authoritarian management structure.

The Histadrut plan called for the establishment of "joint managements" in the companies, with a body consisting of top executives of the company involved, representatives of Histadrut (appointed by Histadrut), and workers (elected by the workers). Meetings of the joint management were to be held regularly and it was supposed to make decisions, though the areas in which it could operate were only vaguely defined.

Uri Gazit, manager of the Histadrut-owned Merkavin Metal Works Ltd., a maker of trucks and buses just outside Tel Aviv, told me that the joint management had theoretically been in operation at his company (which he had only recently joined) for about a year, but: "I see that no actual progress has been obtained. There was a lot of argument originally—the workers thought they were going to run the plant." When I spoke to him, Gazit was trying to improve matters, but problems remained. "It was decided that one worker would occupy himself with financial matters," he said. "But what's he going to do—sit on the neck of the chief accountant? Even if he wanted to, he doesn't have the training. So we had to drop that idea."

The workers themselves, though interested in the project, appeared discouraged about the lack of results. Haim Schicker, a welder who is in the joint management, explained that it had set up a worker-management subcommittee that had drawn up a new production plan to improve productivity. "It hasn't been put into operation," he explained to me, "because it is not certain the joint management has the authority to make this kind of decision." Of the other workers' viewpoints, he says: "They do think it's important, and would like it to work. But they are suspicious." Svi Vikelman, a foreman, remarked: "So far, we don't know what participation means. We want to see the results."

An exception to the mostly rather dismal results of the program has been produced at the Hamashir Paper Products Ltd., in Jerusalem, which has about a hundred employees. When I visited the company, Zalmon Klionsky had been manager for about fifteen months. Finding that the joint management project theoretically in operation was "nearly stagnant," he studied the whole question thoroughly and held some trial meetings with the workers. "I rapidly came to the conclusion that the workers did not have enough training for this work. They had no ability to evaluate economic questions. I wanted to get to the point where I could present a budget to the workers and not have to explain the difference between a liability and an asset." He therefore asked Histadrut to organize some courses in basic management matters for the workers.

"After only six months," he said, "we began to see the fruit of this." One example was a chronic loss situation in paper bag production, a problem that had never been thoroughly analyzed. "The joint management decided to trace where this loss was buried. They analyzed the situation from A to Z. They found that a single customer, who was purchasing about half the output, was responsible for nearly all the loss. So the joint management decided to stop selling to that customer, even though it would reduce turnover."

Klionsky said that the joint management was still at "trainee level" and that substantial progress would take about three to four years. "The first year you teach them," he said, "the second year they have to see for themselves if what you taught them was true, and in the third year you begin to see some results." But he felt that the program had already been worthwhile: "We have got to the stage where people feel they are more involved in the firm —they have a sense of identification." Reuven Klepatz, a press mechanic who is one of the workers in the joint management, confirms this view: "There have been some changes, both on the managerial level and between workers and management. The workers have made many proposals. Very slowly, they are getting the idea that things can change, that they can be involved, and that they can be involved more and more."

This experience suggests that democratization *can* succeed, with the help of some imagination. On the whole, however, the Histadrut push for participation—in productivity councils, workers' councils, and joint management—has shown few results. Jay Tabb, a Professor of Industrial Relations at Haifa Technical University, has written: "In spite of 12 years of intentions, declarations and decisions . . . workers' participation in management has still not been introduced in all Histadrut undertakings, and in the few undertakings where joint managements have been established it is doubtful whether they will last and succeed."[25]

Part of the problem is undoubtedly the overly formalistic nature of the program itself and the manner of imposing it on the enterprises from above. Yehuda Yudin at the Histadrut headquarters told me he was certain his approach was the right one: "I believe this will answer the psychological and sociological needs of the workers—even if they are not aware of it." But the basis for this, and for the wish to transfer the kibbutz spirit to ordinary enterprises, would seem to be shaky. Professor Tabb remarked to me: "Yudin believes in this very honestly. He wants to extend the kibbutz principles into industry. Did he ever stop to analyze what the conditions are for the kibbutz success? Can it even be done?"

No doubt an even more fatal weakness is the resistance of managers to democracy. Even though Histadrut managers are essentially noncapitalist, they share many of the archaic views on work and workers cherished by capitalist managers. Professor Tabb surveyed the attitudes of both workers and managers in some of the Histadrut enterprises, and concluded: "A high percentage of the workforce declared itself in favor of participation, whereas the majority of the managers thought that the workers either opposed or were indifferent to participation."[26]

The largest company in the Histadrut galaxy—indeed, the largest company in Israel—is Koor Industries, a conglomerate with about thirty factories producing a wide variety of industrial goods and with 1970 sales of about 250 million dollars. Its labor ownership does not affect its method of operation. Roman Flohr, general secretary, told me: "We are not particularly democratic. The whole thing is run on a profit basis." Meir Amit, the dynamic former head of Israeli Intelligence who is president of the company, has some emphatic views on participation in decision-making by workers. "I am against it," he said bluntly. "When I took this job, one major principle I was very firm on was that management should be very practical. The management people here are experts. They are the best people I can get. I don't want rotation and I don't want workers in management. Yudin can do it in other Histadrut companies, but not here. It's nonsense. It's a harebrained scheme. Why does he only have it in a few factories? It proves even the workers don't want it."

In principle, Histadrut wanted to push democratic management in privately owned companies as well as in their own enterprises, but circumstances have not been favorable. Professor Arye Globerson at the University of Tel Aviv pointed out to me: "The fact that Histadrut did not show spectacular results in participation in their own companies prevented the unions from pressing private industry. As they didn't show good results, there is no pressure on private managements."

Is the experience of the kibbutz of any value to the industrialized world? Yes, I believe it is. Even though one might argue that the very special kibbutz ideology, the relatively small size of kibbutz enterprises, the general failure to include their own hired workers in democratic systems, and the enormous difficulties of transplanting the kibbutz spirit in other industries all pretty well disqualify the kibbutzim from serving as models. However, the kibbutzim do show that thoroughly democratic systems are possible in an economic context, that the barriers between "work" and "life" can be effectively broken down, and that people can be deeply involved in their work to the profit of themselves as well as the enterprise in which they work. Moreover, they suggest that many of the most cherished myths of normal industrial-capitalist systems—that there must be a rigid hierarchy, that there must be one man at the top who makes most of the decisions, and that the opinions of lower-level employees are worthless—need not be universally true.

In addition, the failure of the attempt to transfer the "spirit of the kibbutz" to industry in the Histadrut companies is highly instructive. It shows that good will and a burning desire for democracy are not enough to achieve the goal. The conditions for Histadrut could scarcely have been more favorable; since the union had connections with both management and workers, the power conflicts were minimal. Moreover, the basic social climate in Israel is highly compatible to such programs. The lesson of the Histadrut project is that the introduction of genuine, workable democracy in a company can be a delicate and difficult task.

Prying loose the secrets of the kibbutzim may not be easy, but it would be difficult to deny that it would be worth the effort. An American sociological report on the kibbutzim concludes: "When we understand the kibbutz we will have learned much about how to attain high productivity with mentally healthy individuals who are integrated into their society rather than alienated from it."[27]

VII. YUGOSLAVIA: TITOIST
SELF-MANAGEMENT

In 1948, when Josip Broz Tito, Yugoslavia's president, quarreled with Stalin, culminating in his country's expulsion from the Communist international association, Cominform, one consequence was the creation of an ingenious and still unique system of industrial organization known as "self-management." The imaginativeness of the system is all the more remarkable in view of the primitive state of the Yugoslavian economy at the time.

It must be said, however, that this curious invention evolved more out of a reaction against certain philosophies in disfavor rather than as the product of a vigorous analysis of the society and its needs. Whatever knowledge the Yugoslavian leaders may have lacked regarding industrial management, they were emphatically certain that they did not want to follow (1) the Western capitalist model or (2) the Stalinist Communist model. Dr. Dušan Bilandžić, director of the Center for Social Science Research of the Central Committee of the League of Communists, explained to me that the country was "waging a war" against two trends: "The resistance to the East was because of the events of 1948. The resistance to capitalism was because capitalism had been in existence here for nearly a hundred years and had never done much for the country. Now we are trying to find our own way."

The shock of being brutally read out of the world Communist movement (in 1949, the Cominform asserted that Yugoslavia was "in the hands of spies and murderers") was such that the Stalinist system could be subjected to a searching and detached examination—and found wanting. As Bilandžić has written, it had been assumed that, in view of the ravages of war and Yugoslavia's primitive stage of development in any case, that rapid economic progress would be impossible "without state ownership and a strong centralized government apparatus."[1] Thus, following proclamation of the Federal People's Republic of Yugoslavia on November 29, 1945, the reins of power were placed firmly in the hands of the central government.

All things considered, the arrangement did not work out so badly. From 1945 to 1948, production rose at a satisfying 15 percent annual rate. Moreover, the people appear to have supported the system. According to Bilandžić, this only meant that the wartime revolutionary enthusiasm was still providing a useful impetus: "The bureaucratic system had not yet manifested two of its basic features: the suppression of creative enterprise and the obstruction of democratic social relations."[2] But the negative features of centralism were in fact already appearing: "Democratic methods of work and management were gradually replaced by bureaucratic methods of 'commanding' from above, while persuasion and explaining gradually gave way to coercion."[3]

The Yugoslav view of these autocratic management methods accords closely with the picture of modern industry we have been discussing in earlier chapters—a rather bleak one, which state ownership does nothing to brighten. Tito has described the situation: "Under state ownership . . . the worker's attitude toward his job was that of a wage laborer and he was not directly interested in higher efficiency or better performance by his enterprise. He continued to be alienated from the means of production and could not change the conditions of production."[4]

If centralism was the main poison, then decentralism must be the main cure. It might be thought that Marxism, the supposed basis of the centralized Soviet system and a philosophy to which the Yugoslavs were stanchly committed, could have proved a barrier. Not at all; ample references could be found in that sprawling body of doctrine not only to support decentralization but also to prove that it was the Soviets who were wrong. Najdan

Pašić, a Yugoslav ideologist, has pointed out: "Marx criticised those bourgeois writers who were not capable of grasping social unity other than in terms of state centralism, and explained that the Paris Commune did not lead to disruption of the unity of the nation but rather to its organization on a fresh basis."[5]

Gradually, central bureaucracies were broken up, and a start was made in transferring political power to the six republics and, further, down to the municipalities. The keys to the new system were decentralization and an opposition to bureaucracy, and the idea was to apply both in industry and political life alike. In industry, a cautious beginning was made in the direction of passing control to workers, and workers' councils were established in various factories in late 1949. In June 1950, the first formal step was made with the enactment of a federal law on "management by collectives" applying to virtually all economic enterprises.

Formalization of the new principles was considered to be urgent. It was felt that the "withering away of the state" that is supposed to happen under communism should be rushed along as rapidly as possible. The Communist Party was to be "helped" by a sharp reduction of its centralized power and thus protected from developing into a petrified state apparatus. And the best way to guard against the manifold dangers of state ownership was to abolish state ownership; ownership of economic enterprises have thus been since 1950 vested, not in the state, and not quite in the workers either, but in society as a whole.

Article 6 of the Constitution describes the new system as follows:

"The basis of the social-economic system of Yugoslavia is free, associated work with socially-owned means of labor and self-management of the working people in production and in the distribution of the social product in the working organization and social community."[6]

The distinctions between state ownership and "social" ownership may seem rather fine. Yugoslavs themselves sometimes refer to the "nationalization" of industry, and in practice the difference is almost meaningless. What is not meaningless is management control, which has been put more and more into the hands of the workers.

At the same time, there has occurred a movement away from Soviet-type centralized control of the economy and a substantial increase in political freedom. This has been due partly to an interest in freedom for its own sake and partly to a hard-headed recognition of the merits of a Western-style free economy. Yugoslav ideologists are not always happy about borrowing ideas from capitalism, and do it only when they work better. "We certainly do not idealize the market economy," Tito has said, "but accept it as a necessity at the present level of development."[7]

The conditions for introducing social innovations in Yugoslavia could hardly have been more discouraging. At the end of the war, the country was in a shambles (about 10 percent of the population had been killed in the war). Approximately 75 percent of the population was engaged in agriculture, and most of the rudimentary industry that existed was foreign-owned. The country was not only one of the least developed in Europe economically but also intellectually—as late as 1961 (the most recent available statistics) the illiteracy rate was still nearly 20 percent. Uniting for progress was even more difficult in view of the jungle of different republics and ethnic, religious, and cultural groups (many of them fiercely antagonistic to each other), a variety of languages, and even two alphabets. To add to the troubles, the country was faced with hostility both in the Soviet bloc and in the capitalist West. Building up a new social system under such conditions is a bit like designing and constructing a high-performance racing car while actually engaged in a grand prix race against tough competition.

There have been numerous swings of the pendulum between more freedom and less freedom as the system has been tinkered with to (1) improve its workings or (2) grapple with the grave economic crises that have arisen periodically. For example, in the early 1950s, workers were given rather complete control over wages, but in 1956, when it was discovered that they were being a bit too generous to themselves, this freedom was restricted for some years. As late as 1962, Tito described the funds over which workers had control as only "pocket money."[8] In the years since then, however, the workers' freedom of action has been steadily enlarged.

The key instrument of worker control is the workers' council, one of which must exist in every enterprise. In companies employing less than 30 persons, all employees are members; in larger companies, there are from 15 to 120 members, directly elected by the employees on a one-man-one-vote principle. The council holds all the formal power; it approves all important management decisions, appoints management personnel, sets salary scales, decides on hiring and firing, establishes capital investment programs, carries out long-term planning, and in general runs the company. The members of the council are elected to two-year terms, serve without extra compensation, and continue in their regular jobs while they are serving on the council.

There also is a managing board, consisting of from three to ten members selected by the workers' council, which maintains closer contact with management personnel and which takes a more active role in the company's day-to-day operations.

Over the years, the workers' power has been considerably strengthened, partly through increasing the scope of their operations and partly through weakening other entities. The role of the municipalities has been sharply curtailed. Formerly, general managers were appointed directly by the municipalities, which in practice meant that many general managers were politically agile but weak on business knowledge. In the great "economic reform" of 1965—when a currency devaluation, abolition of price controls on many goods, and a number of other far-reaching social and economic measures were carried out—the duty of appointing the general manager was transferred to the workers' council.

The independence of the enterprises, and thus the power of the workers, has also been increased by further weakening of the federal government, particularly as a consequence of the 1965 reform. Formerly, enterprises were more heavily dependent on the central government for financing assistance than was felt desirable. Therefore, activities of the central government in this area have been cut back, and greater responsibilities have been given to the banks—which, in addition, have become less dependent on the government and more closely linked to the enterprises. According to a report by the OECD, the central government controlled less than a third of investment funds in socially owned enterprises in 1969, compared with more than half in 1963. The banks, which before the 1965 reform supplied only about a tenth of investment funds, were the source of about half in 1970. Moreover, the banks were appreciably less dependent on the central bank for their own short-term funds; it was the source of only about a fifth of these funds in 1970, against more than half before the reforms. The enterprises have also been given an increased role in managing the banks.[9]

The diminishing role of the central government also shows up in its impact on the over-all economy. According to the OECD study, its current receipts represented 8 percent of gross national product in 1969, against 13 percent in 1964. By now, the federal government's activities are almost exclusively confined to three areas: central administration, national defense, and regional development.[10]

Another change of somewhat more subtle nature has also meant more freedom for the worker-powered enterprises: reduced influence of the League of Communists. As is well known, there are no political parties in Yugoslavia, and the former Communist Party is now known as the League of Communists. For some time, its power—at the federal level, in municipalities, and in companies—was considerable. But Tito has been devoting a fair amount of effort to wiping out the "remnants of bureaucratism" in this organization and converting it from a "factor of power" to, as he delicately puts it, "a factor of ideological-political guidance."[11] The most recent step in this process was a "reorganization" of the LC in 1967, to accord it a more modest position in society, at which time Tito pointed out: "The League of Communists must overcome any form of its own monopoly."[12] He added that "the present organizational structure . . . is of a rather closed, static, and rigid character."[13] At the League's 1969 congress, he made some further helpful comments: that the Communists should be drawn out "from their shell of seclusion,"[14] that they "must fight resolutely against bureaucratic and technocratic tendencies,"[15] that the League "has been too preoccupied with itself,"[16] and that Communists must "suppress growing statism."[17]

The significance of this unremitting attack on the League, as far as industry is concerned, has been to curtail the activities of political bureaucrats and give more real power to workers and to their representative organizations, particularly to the trade unions. Tito himself, among his other suggestions, urged the League to "struggle against all tendencies to minimize the importance of organizing workers in the trade unions."[18] Trade unions may well seem a superfluity where the workers are, in effect, already making all the decisions in the form of their representatives on the workers' councils. But power relationships are never quite that simple. League members, organized in tightly knit and highly effective groups, tended to assume unwarranted power in enterprises in earlier years, but have been curbed considerably. Peter Neersø, a Danish observer, notes: "While the labor movement could earlier be regarded as an extended arm of the League, it now has great freedom of action; it has recently, in several important questions—e.g., with respect to wage increases—been able to take positions in direct conflict with those of the League of Communists and the government. This development . . . has strengthened the position of the enterprises . . . and significantly increased their independence."[19]

A very significant step to increase the workers' power in the companies was the creation, in 1961, of "economic units" in parts of large companies—which are, in effect, miniature workers' councils—in enterprises where that is felt to be possible and desirable. The rationale was, in line with the well-known principles of decentralization, that such units could increase worker participation in the self-management system and reduce the feeling of remoteness from the seat of power in larger enterprises. Osman Zubović, secretary of the central board of the Confederation of Trade Unions, explained to me: "The system is being atomized—so that each economic unit within a factory is run by its own workers' council, which decides everything. A factory might have ten or more such units." A unit can be formed in any department or section that can be considered independent, economically and technologically, from the factory's other departments.

The original design of the workers' councils was to create a power link reaching from the middle and bottom portions of the standard "pyramid," connecting externally to the topmost seat of power. Thus one could accurately say that power was disseminated equally throughout the pyramid—but only in the formal sense. On a more practical level, the structure can be seen to be defective; the external power link, however firmly established legally, is obviously artificial. The creation of the economic units is an attempt to overcome this disadvantage and to get the worker more firmly involved in the power network. This has, in fact, tended to happen where economic units have been introduced, but they still do not seem to be numerous, even many years after the legislation that made them possible. In practice, the range of matters they handle has varied widely. In some cases, they discuss only a limited range of subjects, and in others they act as full-fledged workers' councils, handling wage scales, capital investments, and other top-level questions for their parts of the companies.

Whatever advantages or disadvantages the Yugoslavian self-management system may contain, there is no question that it is highly unusual. Even a casual visitor to a company cannot fail to be impressed as he is greeted in a conference room by trimly dressed executives, in appearance much like executives in any other country, along with blue-collar workers, who look like workers in any other country, and calmly informed by the former that they are told what to do by the latter. Zdenko Krstulović, general manager of Jedinstvo, a maker of chemical equipment near Zagreb, explained to me: "I don't make the decisions—I only make suggestions to the workers' council. Most of the time they are accepted. But they have to be explained in great detail so that the workers can understand them. If the council decides differently and I don't accept the decision, they can make me resign." Conflicts can and do arise. "When I was a candidate for the job," Krstulović says, "I made several proposals for changes. One was that a certain company division should have its own sales department. The workers' council objected, but I made this a condition of my acceptance of the position. The meeting lasted for a few hours. But in the end the proposal was accepted."

On another occasion, there was a disagreement over purchase of some new equipment: "I had one proposal, the workers another— but theirs was acceptable to me, so it carried."

Understandably, the workers' lack of training in the more eso- teric areas of management can be a handicap. At some com- panies, I was shown massive documents containing detailed ex- planations of financial statements prepared in order that the workers' council could, first, understand them and, second, ap- prove them. Stanko Pavlović, financial director of Ikarus, a di- versified producer of buses, radiators, machine tools, and other metal-working items in Belgrade, explained to me: "The financial plans are only proposals until they are accepted by the workers' council. In addition to the written material, they get extensive oral explanations. Also, they are constantly being informed throughout the year, so the annual plan doesn't come as a com- plete surprise." Nevertheless, the workers' councils can be rather easily led by the management experts. Josip Rožić, head of or- ganizational and economic planning at Jedinstvo, told me: "My unit makes an over-all plan for the company and plans for each economic unit. But all the plans have to be connected. The units usually accept the plans, though they may modify some details. If there are large conflicts the question can be put up to the central workers' council." Can the workers unravel all these technical details in any useful way? "Even though we are specialists," Rožić said, "we can make some mistakes, which the workers' council can sometimes notice. And there is an ef- fort to get people on the workers' council who can understand these questions." Possibly, but it doesn't always work. At Duga, a chemical company in Belgrade, I asked some of the members of the workers' council about how they went about evaluating management's proposals on depreciation policies—an area in which there is always ample room for variation and, consequently, disagreement. After a few minutes, I realized that they found the whole subject completely bewildering and not one they would ever be likely to delve into in great detail.

This question of the management experts' manipulation of the workers' councils, who are thus diverted from important ques- tions to relatively trivial matters, is one of the most-discussed aspects of the system. Miša Jezernik, Professor of Sociology at the

University of Ljubljana, remarked to me: "It's very easy to manipulate the workers' council. How is the ordinary worker supposed to understand all these complex questions? They spend hours discussing whether the night watchman should get a free cup of coffee and approve a hundred-million-dollar investment program in five minutes."

In the opinion of some observers, the exercise of worker judgments on large corporate questions is not the idea anyway. Bilandžić writes of corporate "policy" issues: "Who is qualified to discuss these matters at the session of the workers' council? The worker at his lathe? Very little. The laboratory technician? Obviously not." Such matters must be left to specialist experts: "There is no other alternative for the workers' council."[20] Surprisingly enough, Bilandžić puts forward a kind of semi-Tayloristic view that nothing much matters if the paycheck is large enough: "The present system of economic relations tends to unite the working people . . . on the basis of their common objective—the acquisition of the biggest possible income."[21]

As a matter of fact, the division of the company's income has always been a matter of intense interest for the workers' councils. Companies are required to set aside certain proportions of profits in reserve funds, funds for development of depressed areas, housing construction funds, and other specified purposes, and the workers' councils can dispose of the remainder as they choose. As noted, in the early days of self-management they tended to be rather overliberal in allocations to wages, and the councils' liberty of action in this area has expanded and contracted periodically. Since the 1965 reform, the philosophy has been to give maximum freedom to the enterprises. Salaries are calculated on an enormously complicated formula involving a "base" pay plus a premium if the company's profits exceed the budgeted amount. The premiums are calculated on the basis of results recorded every month or every quarter. The "base" is simply a list in which each job is given a rating that determines its share of the total basic income, the ratings varying according to the worth each job is judged to possess. The highest-paid position (the general manager) is generally rated about four or five times that of the lowest-paid job. Obviously, there is potential here for much conflict, but in fact this matter is one on which the workers are often able to make a most valuable contribution. At the metal-working company Ikarus, the assessment of the different jobs had been prepared by the management experts, in which each job was given a rating in points—the wage "base." The workers' council rejected it out of hand and demanded that it be revised. It was, and everybody felt that the revised version was much improved. Since this was a relatively important matter, yet one that concerned only the workers (the analysis had nothing to do with the *amounts* of wages, only their relative magnitude), it can be assumed that the workers' intimate knowledge of the different jobs did in fact allow them to improve on the experts' work.

In writings about the Yugoslav system, a much-discussed danger in this wage-setting freedom is that workers will sacrifice more important priorities in order to give themselves higher wages. Albert Meister, a French social thinker who has written extensively (and very critically) on the Yugoslav system, asserts that this fact can have damaging long-term effects on the economy: "To the extent that the enterprises are able to freely fix their wages and other distributions, there is always a danger of a too-rapid increase of income relative to the rise in productivity."[22] This danger is more apparent than actual, however, and derives partly from a misunderstanding of the principles of corporate finance. It is not absolutely necessary for companies, whether in Communist or capitalist systems, to have to choose between wage increases and capital investments. Many capital-intensive companies (such as, for example, U.S. electric utilities) habitually make heavy capital investments year after year, which in a narrow sense they cannot afford, while at the same time raising wages as well as dividend payments to stockholders—covering the ever-yawning gap by sinking further into debt each year. Such practices are fully acceptable and respectable. To be sure, in a relatively poor country such as Yugoslavia, borrowed capital cannot always be had for the asking, and the choice between wages and investment *can* arise. Thus the workers at Ikarus told me they had put through an average 45 percent wage increase for themselves in 1968—but only as a result of higher productivity resulting from heavy investments made while wages were held steady during a number of years. Zika Isajlović, a toolmaker and secretary of the local League of Communists group, explained: "We had to do that—otherwise the workers would have felt we were cheating them when we had told them they were sacrificing for the future."

In any case, there is no evidence in the statistics that wage increases have been, on the whole, excessive, or that investment has suffered. Immediately following the 1965 reform, wages did jump sharply while investments dropped, but this was part of the intention (to compensate consumers for anticipated price rises).[23] The situation has since stabilized: During the 1966–69 period, according to OECD figures, gross fixed investments rose at an average annual rate of 4.9 percent, only slightly less than the 5.2 percent growth in over-all social product, while private consumption rose at an annual rate of 5.4 percent, only slightly above the social product growth rate. For 1969, gross capital formation rose 9.2 percent, while private consumption rose 7.2 percent.

Within these outer limits, there are wide variations and a very conscious acceptance of inequality among workers in the same company and among different companies and different regions. Some Communist purists express some regret about this, but they realize that it is an integral part of the system. At the Trade Union Confederation, Osman Zubović bluntly declared to me: "We are very much against equal wages in this country. Every enterprise has to find its own road to prosperity." A worker at Ikarus, which happens to be a rather successful company, shrugged and said: "There have to be wage differences because we have a market economy."

There is the generally accepted principle that workers should be rewarded according to the value of their work. Though the principle is rather vague, there appears not to be any widespread wish to exploit the situation. Dr. Djordje Ležimirac, a suave and sophisticated manager of General Export, whose office bears a Goodyear calendar on one wall and pictures of Lenin and Tito on another, explained to me that though his firm, a dynamic holding and trading company with annual turnover of 380 million dollars and only 500 employees, could well pay higher wages: "Our profits are sufficient that we could buy every employee a new automobile every month, but we don't. The central government sets a certain goal every year on the expected increase in wages, and we take that as the average wage increase for the company."

The key question regarding the Yugoslav system is, of course, not how it operates, or is supposed to operate, but: Does it work? Whatever aspect that question might refer to, an essential counter-question is: Compared with what? It is not possible to compare one group of Yugoslavian companies under self-management with a control group (as was done with kibbutz factories and nonkibbutz Israeli factories in the study referred to earlier), because *all* companies in Yugoslavia are under self-management. Sturmthal points to other difficulties of forming a judgment: "It is not easy . . . to distinguish between the restrictions on workers' self-government which the dictatorship inevitably involves, purely technical shortcomings of the system, problems created by poverty and lack of industrial tradition, and, finally, the congenital difficulties of any system of workers' management."[24]

Nevertheless, it is possible to make some general assessments. An obvious central flaw is the artificial, formalistic structure of the power relationships. If the goal is to give workers power, placing them in the top levels of management would seem logical, but the formal restructuring of an organization—the redrawing of lines of influence on a chart—does not necessarily change the real situation. And the traditional lines of authority have not been, in fact, decisively altered with the introduction of workers' councils. The workers at one plant explained to me that even the president of the workers' council is, outside the council meetings, just like any other worker: "He has his regular job and must do as his foreman tells him." The traditional industrial organization remains: "These two lines of management are fixed and separate."

This formalistic approach has been the target of much criticism, because of the workers' supposed lack of interest in the subjects discussed at top levels and of competence to contribute anything of value, as well as the remoteness of the power machinery from the worker who does not happen to be a member of the workers' council. All these points are made with great effect by Jiri Kolaja, an American social scientist who observed the inner workings of two Yugoslav factories over a period of several weeks. At meetings of workers' councils and managing boards, he found the workers hopelessly overpowered by the management explanation of business matters, and that they become interested only when personnel questions, wages, and the like were discussed. On the whole, he concludes, "the vast majority of the workers were only lukewarm, though not antagonistic, in their attitudes towards factory organization and management, and displayed a low degree of interest in management participation."[25]

Although the Kolaja studies were made in 1959, and the situation has definitely improved since, Yugoslavs themselves concede the validity of the criticism. Josip Županov, professor on the faculty of economics at the University of Zagreb and one of the leading authorities on self-management, told me: "Unfortunately there is some truth in this. The workers don't have very much power when business policies are considered. I have studied many different firms, and the patterns were quite similar. Obviously, the managers are the most important group. In wages and working conditions, the influence of the workers is greater. But where matters of broad policy are concerned they are in a poor position to judge." Županov added that a more effective approach might have been to give the worker power over his immediate work environment, where he might have more knowledge and more interest: "Perhaps we were wrong in giving the workers a decisive say in higher-level power. Perhaps we unjustly neglected the other aspect." The introduction of economic units, which are aimed at moving the lines of power closer to the worker, are a step in this direction.

Other studies also suggest that the system falls short of the ideal. One made in the mid-1960s by Županov and Arnold S. Tannenbaum of the Institute of Social Research at the University of Michigan is an interesting example. A group of relatively highly skilled workers attending courses at the Workers' University of Zagreb were queried on the sources of power regarding various questions—actual and ideal. The results showed that the managers *actually* had more power than any other group—slightly more than the workers' councils and much more than the workers as a whole—but that the *ideal* situation was the opposite. It is a rather bleak picture, but the workers at least had firm ideas on what was desirable. As the authors commented: "These high positive ideals expressed in the data reflect new social values emerging in con-

temporary Yugoslavia."[26] When I met Tannenbaum in the
United States, I asked him whether he thought the Yugoslavian
system could be said to work. He replied: "If you mean in relation
to the past and in relation to other European countries, the answer is 'Yes.'"

Another report that reveals some shortcomings was made by
Jezernik at the University of Ljubljana, who asked twelve hundred workers from fifteen factories in Slovenia to rank self-management and five other characteristics of their jobs (the work itself, wages, supervisors, coworkers, education) in order of relative
importance. However the respondents were grouped—by age, by
type of worker, by degree of satisfaction with wages, and and so
on—self-management invariably was ranked lowest in importance.
Jezernik concludes: "Workers were either satisfied with the present state of affairs in self-management (which we know is far
from the ideal) . . . or they simply did not care about it. . . .
An alternative explanation is that self-management has been given
low priority because it does not work."[27] The study was conducted in the 1960–64 period. Jezernik told me his impression was
that the system still has its shortcomings, but that the situation
had been improving steadily since the study was made: "We see
that in recent years the perceived situation and the ideal are drawing closer together."

Gradual improvement is also indicated by other evidence. Živan Tanić, a researcher at the Institute for Social Sciences in
Belgrade, carried out a study of the minutes of workers' councils
covering a ten-year period. He found that, over the years, the
number of subjects discussed increased, as did the members' business sophistication. The discussions of important question of
company policy rose, while the discussions of more trivial and
personal questions dropped. Obviously, the more knowledgeable
the workers, the more fully they are able to participate in the
discussions. "There is a positive correlation," Tanić told me,
"between the level of education and participation in management
activities. But the level of education is only one variable—knowledge increases with experience in self-management, and thus
there are some people with only medium-level education who
have a high level of participation."

A large problem here is the sizable proportion of ill-educated peasants working in Yugoslav enterprises. Although they welcome the opportunity to raise their incomes, they often still cultivate their farms and think of themselves as farmers first and industrial workers only incidentally. As one expert told me, "Their jobs mean nothing to them, and neither does self-management." Such workers show a below-average willingness to participate in self-management, and therefore the better-educated and higher-level workers have consistently carried the major responsibilities in the system. The tendency of relatively small groups to become a kind of "aristocracy" within the enterprises has been criticized as a weakness, but it is difficult to see how the system could have functioned at all otherwise. As time goes on, the situation is changing, partly because of efforts to rotate the membership of the workers' councils and managing boards as much as possible. And willingness to participate in the self-management machinery is rising as the general educational level rises, as the country becomes more urbanized, and as familiarity with the system increases. The creation of the economic units, and years of experience with the philosophy of self-management have brought democracy closer to the shop floor. The business of managing has tended to get done at the lower levels, and in many cases workers have begun electing their own foremen—so that there is democracy in a real, day-to-day sense as well as in the formal sense. Moreover, reforms have given more and more real power to workers and curbed the influence of municipal officials, officers of the League of Communists, and the central government.

Just as the self-management system has been criticized because it has not given real power to the workers, it has also been criticized because it has taken away too much power from managers. There is no question, of course, that some of the management prerogatives common in other countries—the right to make autocratic decisions, to create dictatorial work climates, to take action of keen interest to workers without their consent or even knowledge, to exercise a neurotic drive for power—scarcely exist in Yugoslavia, and this is no doubt one of the admirable achievements of the system.

But some critics maintain that curbing managers' freedom of action is wrong and somehow unnatural. One American account of a highly successful Yugoslav company praised the company's record, yet admonished the Yugoslavs for haplessly violating an iron rule of good management: "A diligent, stern manager who improves productivity and profitability is obviously doing more for his workers than an easygoing one. . . ." The report implied that it was too bad that, in Yugoslavia, "a diligent, stern manager might antagonize workers. . . ."[28]

Zdenko Krstulović, director of Jedinstvo, pointed out to me that bitter conflicts between managers and workers' councils are not all that common ("You must understand that management and the workers' council are not at opposite poles"), but that in some cases they can become very bitter indeed: "In that case, there are two things the manager can do—he can accept the workers' council's decision, in which case he is still responsible, or he can just resign. In the past few years, that has been happening all over Yugoslavia. It is better to quit altogether than to stay around when you are convinced things are going badly."

According to Ichak Adizes, an Israeli sociologist who has studied the system in some depth, a great many managers have been quietly suffering rather than resigning, even though they feel they are being "constrained by the self-management structure." The executive, says Adizes, is put in the uncomfortable position of having to have managerial abilities, yet being frustrated in their exercise, of being "unnoticed, yet able to lead."[29] Managers have tried to resolve this conflict by avoiding workers' council meetings or, where that was impossible, by paying as little attention as possible. It would seem that this is the mirror image of worker sabotage in an organization where workers are dissatisfied: "As the workers would 'get back at the system' by slowdowns in production . . . the frustrated Yugoslav executives seemed to get back at the system by not making decisions which were within their authority, or by slowing down communications, not answering letters, confusing data, etc."[30]

This matter of persecuted management is often mentioned in Western discussions of the Yugoslav system—particularly, not surprisingly, by management people or management-oriented people —as if it were a crippling defect. It is, no doubt, regrettable, but surely no more so than the alienation from which ordinary workers normally suffer in more orthodox management structures. Indeed, it would seem to be only a variation of the type of frustration experienced by numerous middle-range executives in the traditional Western pyramid, as we saw earlier. Obviously, the desire to exercise one's decision-making powers with a minimum of bureaucratic interference exists in management people as well as in workers, and it would seem desirable to combat that interference wherever it exists. It is not clear how widespread such behavior is (Adizes says it was not characteristic of all Yugoslav enterprises he observed), but it is difficult to believe it is of catastrophic proportions. Where it exists, it is a sign that the usually exaggeratedly pyramidal structure has been exaggeratedly flattened out; neither tendency is fortunate, but it is surprising that some Western (and especially American) observers can become so disturbed over the restrictions on management in Yugoslavia and so little disturbed over the undoubtedly more grave restrictions on workers in the West. As Adizes remarks, neither extreme is desirable.

"The crucial question," Živan Tanić remarked to me, "which we cannot answer in a statistical sense, is the correlation between the system and its efficiency, because efficiency depends on so many variables."

That is unquestionably true. A number of brave attempts have been made nevertheless. One of these, by Jakov Sirotković, points out that Yugoslavia had an annual average growth rate of gross national product of 7.75 percent in the 1952–65 period, which put it just after Japan among major countries, and concludes that the Yugoslav system "is developing into a more progressive, more humane, and more profitable economic system than any of the preceding systems."[31] This is something of a non sequitur, but the fact remains that Yugoslavia has—despite periodic financial crises and a chronic high unemployment rate—made good economic progress, including a growth in industrial production of more than 400 percent in the 1953–69 period. One cannot, of course, tell how things might have worked out had self-management never come into being at all. One study suggests that the system is quite economically sound. An American research project divided twenty Yugoslav companies into two groups, "more successful" and "less successful" (i.e., in financial terms), and studied the power relationships in each.[32] The main point of the project was to test the validity of the Likert organizational theory (which asserts that more democratically run companies are more successful), but, among other things, the status of the workers' council was investigated. It was discovered that, in the "more successful" companies, the workers' council was perceived to be exercising more control than in the "less successful"—which suggests that the existence of the workers' council does in fact contribute to economic efficiency.

Mitja Kamušič, a Yugoslav expert, concludes a coldly objective study of self-management principles by asserting that they "do not ensure the greatest economic efficiency . . . but they do not oppose it"; he even concedes that self-management "does not differ essentially from the capitalist model." However, he does claim a certain edge for self-management, because "it is possible to improve our system . . . preserving at the same time all the psychological and moral advantages lacking in the capitalistic system."[33]

Even if we cannot prove that the self-management system is more efficient than some other system, we can certainly make the minimum claim that it does not *interfere* with satisfactory economic performance. And we can also draw the corollary conclusion that some of the criticisms of the Yugoslav system, and about workers and management in general, are wrong. It is widely believed, not only with reference to Yugoslavia but as regards business enterprises anywhere, that workers are not interested in being bothered with management decisions and that, even if they were, their lack of knowledge would be disastrous for the enterprises. Professor Tomislav Tomeković, of the Department of Psychology at the University of Belgrade, told me: "These are psychological traits, you know. Some people unconsciously feel that only they are able to make decisions and that workers are only supposed to work and not to think." Yugoslavian evidence would appear to contradict that belief. Just as kibbutz industrial management in Israel seems to lead to acceptable economic results, so companies under self-management in Yugoslavia seem to survive in a satisfactory fashion—even though neither of these peculiar ways of running companies quite fits in with traditional beliefs about the omniscience of the men at the top of the pyramid.

The system—by plunging the unprepared and uneducated worker into immediate contact with questions far beyond his customary sphere of understanding—may have been wrongly designed. In that way, it suffers from the same overformalistic approach afflicting the Histadrut experiments with industrial democracy in Israel. With the assistance of knowledge of the workings of organizations now available (though not, unfortunately, when the Yugoslav system was first established), one can point to obvious and serious flaws in the design.

But even if the Yugoslav system is all wrong, it may be more "right" than the traditional Western organizational structure—in which, to be sure, the worker is shielded against contact with issues beyond his immediate concerns, but in which he is treated as though he were totally lacking in intelligence. Which system is the more distorted?

Mileta Đokić, personnel director of Industrija, a large tractor company near Belgrade, conceded that the workers' council members could not be experts in all areas and therefore had to lean heavily on specialist opinions on various questions. "But," he added, "it's unavoidable. It's the same as in a parliament or any other representative body. The experts prepare proposals and the members pass on the proposals. It can't be otherwise. The workers' council here is like a parliament." Carole Pateman, the British political thinker, addresses herself to the same kind of criticism: "If this is what makes industrial democracy 'impossible' then, since a similar problem is faced by any elected democratic body . . . political democracy is impossible too—and the theorists who claim that industrial democracy is impossible do not wish to say that."[34]

Whatever criticisms may be lodged against the self-management system, it appears securely implanted in Yugoslav society. The balanced judgment of *The Economist* seems extremely accurate: "One thing is clear: workers' self-management cannot be pronounced an economic failure, as its many critics in communist countries shrilly insist. The best that can be said is that it has quite a few uses, from the workers' and managers' point of view, and that certainly from the workers' angle it is preferable to a centralized system of state management."[35] The spirit of freedom and decentralization appears to be spreading more and more. When strikes first began to appear about 1958, the country was shaken by this most unexpected phenomenon, but strikes are now accepted as a normal instrument of worker self-expression and even a point of some pride. By 1969, Nebojša Popov, a Yugoslav theorist, could write of the necessity of strikes in a socialist economy, noting that "the autonomy of the spontaneous labor movement, not being absorbed into the political apparatus, can therefore lead to constant breakthroughs in the area of socialist policy."[36] Some fifteen hundred strikes occurred in the 1958–70 period (mostly lasting a day or two), but their legality was not clear, even though nobody had ever been prosecuted for participating in a strike. In early 1971, the point was cleared up when strikes were made fully permissible.

Inevitably, the spirit of self-reliance fostered by self-management has had political repercussions. Adizes writes: "People learned to be open, to question, to challenge. In industrial organizations they were free to speak up . . . yet in the Party or government ruling bodies, they were restricted in the expression of their opinions. The discrepancies in the system developed to a point where one side had to yield. It was Tito who tipped the balance toward further democratization of the Party in order to bring the political institutions in line with the industrial management developments."[37]

The system seems fully acceptable even to Western capitalists. In 1967, legislation was passed permitting foreign investment in Yugoslavia on a joint-venture basis and provided Yugoslav interests retained majority control of the ventures—and that the workers' councils would have their customary authority. Although this last requirement has acted as something of a deterrent, a number of major companies from the United States, Italy, Japan, West Germany, and other countries have contentedly signed up to invest in Yugoslavia. In 1971, the rules were changed to permit foreign majority ownership. At times, the Yugoslavs seem to be outpacing the Western capitalists in freeing the economy from restraints. The rigorously capitalistic OECD, commenting on the

Yugoslav "plan" for 1971–75 (which is only a set of rough guide-lines), pleaded for a bit less laissez-faire: "There would seem to be a certain risk that the process of decentralization might be pushed to such a point that coordinating development efforts satisfactorily might be hampered."[38]

For their part, the workers appear, on the whole, happy with the system. It seems unquestionable that a better work atmosphere exists in Yugoslav factories today than would have been the case without the self-management system. In great part, this is due to the fact that, if nothing else, it assures that adequate channels of communication are created between management and workers, since the former must explain everything in detail to get the approval of the latter. Kolaja says: "'The principle of publicity' is probably unique, in most cases providing more information to employees in Yugoslavia than is supplied to their counterparts in Britain or the United States, or the Soviet Union."[39]

Even Albert Meister, the French observer of Yugoslavia, who is intensely critical of almost every aspect of the system, avers that it "has, in only 15 years, managed to bring about the basic industrialization of the country, while it took us nearly a century in our own country. And, despite some abuses, Yugoslavia attained this result in a much more human fashion."[40]

Ichak Adizes, also critical of the system, still concludes that it has worked well economically and in other respects: "With all the dysfunctional behavior . . . it should be borne in mind that self-management generally yielded amazing functional results in the long run. . . . If a hierarchical organization had existed . . . the erratic environment would have led to destructive polarization. . . ."[41]

There is a kind of recurring pattern in writings about Yugoslavia. Following comments on the system's appalling defects, its frequent need of revisions, its outrageous unorthodoxy, particularly the high priority given to human values, mention must inevitably be made of the thoroughly creditable results the country has shown. If the system is wrong, it is surely wrong in a way that many other more conventionally managed countries would willingly emulate. As Jan Tinbergen, a Dutch observer, notes: "A rate of growth of per capita real income of about 6 percent, together

with a considerable degree of democracy in the everyday environment of the mass of producers, is not easily found elsewhere."[42]

Almost nobody in Yugoslavia cares to contemplate shifting to
another system—either the Western capitalistic model, which
would be unthinkable, or the Soviet centralized statist model,
which would be more thinkable, but not especially attractive. Sava
Bebić, a machine technician and president of the workers' council at Ikarus, told me: "This system really means something to
the workers. I've been working here for twenty-two years, and
the workers feel very differently now. Before, it was run like a
military factory and the workers had no chance to express themselves." Even a slight restriction of the system would seem to be
remote. Mileta Đokić at Industrija remarked to me: "Although
there is a lot of criticism of the system, it would be impossible
to introduce the old methods. We tried to simplify things here
by eliminating some consultation, but it didn't work. The workers
wanted more consultation, not less. They are always demanding
more rights." Indeed, in one opinion survey, workers "rejected
categorically and in the great majority of 85 percent the possibility
of abolishment of the workers' council."[43]

There often appears to be a tendency for Yugoslavs to pay a
kind of dutiful respect to self-management principles in public
pronouncements, suggesting that the ideas could become a kind of
ideological symbol without any content. However, so far the
Yugoslav leaders have repeatedly shown themselves ready to admit
past mistakes and alter the system in the direction of more
freedom for workers. In 1968, Tito, observing, "I am being critical of myself and of all of us who have been responsible," avowed
that the student disturbances had been a beneficial "blow on the
head for all of us, that we should wake up."[44] Nobody claims that
the system is completely satisfactory, and it will doubtless continue
to be tinkered with. Zdenko Krstulović, director of Jedinstvo,
pointed out to me: "You must understand that self-management
is a completely new thing. Twenty years is not enough to make it
perfect. We are still in the development stage and there still is a
lot to be done."

VIII. WEST GERMANY: SOCIAL REFORM THROUGH CODETERMINATION

The first Western institutionalized system of industrial democracy —that is, which gives employees genuine decision-making power on a meaningful level—is the system of *Mitbestimmung*, or co-determination, or joint management, introduced in the West German steel and coal mining industries in 1951. At that time, employees were given one-half the places in the supreme body of authority in the companies, which thus places in their hands a real measure of decision-making power.

This can be seen as somehow appropriate, in view of the long tradition in Germany of radical unionist agitation. The fact is, however, that the steel and coal codetermination system was established independently of the country's other labor legislation and for quite different reasons. Originally, it had very little to do with the problems of industrial-capitalism discussed in earlier chapters and was not regarded as a cure for alienation or other problems of intimate concern to workers. Nevertheless, it is of great interest, partly because it is the only system of the kind ever tried on a large scale in the West and partly because it appears to be evolving, slowly but surely, into a structure more suited to meeting the real needs of employees.

At the end of World War II, it had been agreed at the Potsdam Conference among the conquering powers that the steel and coal industries—which were especially symbolic of Germany's industrial and military power and which had especially close relations with Hitler—were to be broken up, reduced in size, and weakened in every possible way as one safeguard against their resurgence in their former role. The execution of this decision fell, initially, to the British, whose occupation zone included the Ruhr Valley, center of these industries. In connection with this program, Hans Böckler, head of the newly established postwar labor movement, suggested to the British occupation authorities that a system of worker comanagement would fit in nicely with the goals, since the workers could help keep an eye on the managements. Britain at the time was under the rule of a Labour government, which among other things was nationalizing the coal mines at home, and the British occupation authorities accepted the proposal. Workers were granted, in the companies grouped under the "North German Iron and Steel Control" established in 1946 by the British, rights of comanagement. At the time, the unions viewed this as a first step in the nationalization of these industries; but with time both the unions and the occupying authorities cooled in their attitude toward nationalization.

The managers of the companies in question, which had helped finance Hitler and were among his stanchest supporters, were in a delicate position. Bent Akjær, a Danish student of the question, notes that "they could not expect much sympathy for their interests among the British occupation authorities" and therefore "several prominent industry leaders addressed themselves to the German labor union leaders."[1] Karl Jarres von Klöckner, chairman of Klöckner Werke, wrote that his company, "with the intention of adapting to changing times," was prepared for a "realization of a practical equalization between capital and labor" through an expansion of the board to reach a balance between representatives of capital and labor. Günter Henle, Haspe AG, urged the creation of "a new social structure . . . economic democracy," meaning that "employees shall participate fully in management of the company."[2]

The basic idea of industrial democracy won considerable initial support. Konard Adenauer, head of the Christian Democratic Union (CDU) and first postwar Chancellor, proclaimed at the inauguration of the federal state in 1949 the necessity of "a new order in owner relationships in the basic industries" in favor of more employee influence. The Social Democratic Party (SPD) also supported the call for worker comanagement.

Times change. The German "economic wonder" strengthened capitalist sentiments, the increasingly chilly Cold War reduced the appeal of leftist solutions to industrial problems, the spirit of friendly collaboration between capital and industry during the early postwar reconstruction was forgotten, and the CDU—among others—rather quickly changed its mind. The demand of the Deutscher Gewerkschaftsbund (German Labor Federation—DGB) for the extension of worker codetermination to other fields was rejected. It was installed permanently (by only a small parliamentary majority) in the iron, steel, and coal-mining industries through legislation passed in May 1951.

The following year, more comprehensive legislation was enacted—the "workers constitution act"—establishing workers' councils in virtually all companies of any size and giving workers influence in other ways. One very significant element was a provision giving workers' representatives a minority of the places—and thus only a "consultative" position—on the governing bodies of virtually all German companies. In Germany itself, all these features, along with the steel and coal codetermination, are seen as a single network of labor-management relations. But the steel and coal codetermination is the only part of the system that gives workers a clear-cut position of power, since they have an equal position with shareholders on the boards, and it is therefore this part of the machinery that is of special interest to us.

The 1951 legislation has two central features. First, it gives equal representation to workers and shareholders on the *Aufsichtsrat*, usually translated as "supervisory board" and in some ways equivalent to the American or British board of directors; the supervisory board appoints the *Vorstand* or management board (which actually runs the company on a day-to-day basis), but it is prohibited by law from interfering with management. The supervisory board consists of eleven, fifteen, or twenty-one members (depending on the size of the company), and its composition is determined by a complex and precise formula. In an eleven-member board, four members are named by the shareholders and four by labor (two are elected by the workers' council and two are named by the labor union). Each side then appoints one "additional" member from outside (though he is presumably sympathetic to the side that appoints him), and the entire board then elects a "neutral" member, who must receive a majority of votes from each of the two sides. At least two of the members from labor's side must be employed in the company, and there must be at least one blue-collar worker and one white-collar worker.

The second provision is the creation of a "labor director" appointed by the supervisory board—and with the approval of the employees' side of the board—who is a full member of management and who occupies himself with social, personnel, and other matters of direct interest to employees. The labor director has an extremely powerful legal position within the company, but he is also obviously in a very delicate role, considering his status as a member of management but at the same time a defender of worker interests.

The structure thus imposed on the steel and coal industries is a beautiful architectural creation with rather obvious faults. Like other structures we have examined, it attempts to give workers power by creating an external line of influence, starting at the base of the traditional pyramid and running directly from there to the top level of power. It is thus an artificial channel of authority existing side by side with the orthodox authority structure, and it possesses the defects characteristic of all such designs. The authority exists in a formal sense but not necessarily in any real sense. Moreover, the German model is even more abstract than, say, those in Yugoslavia or in the Israeli Histadrut experiments, since the worker is removed from the real center of power through multiple layers of formal patterns. The ordinary worker has no direct connection with management and even no direct connection with the body that does have a direct connection with management. He participates in electing members of the workers' councils, who in turn appoint some of the supervisory board members, who in their turn participate in appointing the management board, which then runs the company. It is therefore understandable if the worker feels that the power machinery is a bit remote from his concerns and that his opportunities of influencing his company are not large. Gerhard Leminsky, head of the industrial relations section of the DGB-affiliated Labor Institute for Social and Economic Research in Düsseldorf, remarked to me: "It is not really joint management —it is more a kind of check on management."

But as it happened, that was one thing that was needed in these particular industries. Dominated by an industrial aristocracy, the companies had been for decades run along paternalistic, semi-militaristic lines in which the lines of authority were rigid, concentrated, and unquestioned. Werner Willutzki, a union official at Hoesch AG, a major steel producer, told me: "Those authoritarian conditions were especially typical of the steel and coal industries. But since codetermination was introduced, it has changed very much. And today the situation is much harder in other industries." Hoesch managers with whom I spoke generally agreed with this assessment. Burkart Lutz, head of the Institute of Social Science in Munich, described to me one particularly strong institution in the coal industry—the position of *Bergassessor*: "This was a kind of executive training for periods of two to three years. There was very little pay, so those who held the jobs had to be wealthy to be able to afford the time. They believed that God himself had appointed them to administer the wealth and grandeur of the German Reich."

Most observers agree that the mood has shifted. Forced to deal with workers and worker representatives at frequent intervals and on various levels, management people have found it possible to modify their harshly authoritarian attitudes. A presentation of the merits of codetermination by DGB stresses that the system has, at the very least, established "improved communication within the enterprise," broken down the "often oppressive anonymity of the administration process," and made it apparent that "the interests of employees are taken into consideration by elected representatives in all decisions taken by management of the plant."[3] All things considered, this may be regarded as a rather modest achievement, but that is not to say it is worthless.

Some studies suggest that the atmosphere is still not all that happy in the steel and coal industries. A study made in 1966, sponsored by the Confederation of Employers' Associations, compared worker attitudes in the steel and coal industries, subject to

codetermination legislation, with those in other industries, subject
to the Works' Constitution Act, passed in 1952.[4] Although the
study did not specifically examine attitudes toward the different
systems, the assumption was that their impact on the workers
would be reflected in their attitudes toward the companies and in
their general level of satisfaction. The results showed that, in the
coal and steel industries, only 48 percent of employees considered the information they received from management "good"
or "very good," compared with 57 percent in other industries;
28 percent thought they would be "dismissed immediately" if
their companies ran into difficulties, compared with only 11
percent in other industries; a disappointing 32 percent would
defend their companies if criticized by acquaintances, compared
with 56 percent in other industries. Over-all, only 45 percent of
employees in the codetermination industries were rated as "very
satisfied" or "rather satisfied," compared with 71 percent in other
industries.

It is perhaps only a coincidence that the results of the study
parallel so closely the views of the Employers' Confederation,
which commissioned the study and which accepts the Works'
Constitution Act and opposes codetermination of the steel and
coal industry variety. Wilhelm Kaltenborn, an official in the Department of Social Relations at DGB, told me: "The methods
used in that study have been criticized very severely by sociologists.
It did not meet the standards of objective scientific research, in
terms of the structure of the questionnaire and the way the
questions were put. Besides, as everybody knows, working conditions in these industries have always been very hard, and there
has always been a high degree of dissatisfaction there. It is hardly
reasonable to blame that on codetermination."

However, the DGB has not been able to marshal any very
solid evidence that the system, even though it has *eliminated*
some unpleasant features of management in the industries affected, has actually *added* anything substantial to the ordinary
worker's daily life. One study commissioned by the DGB in
1966 to study the social benefits desired by the public in general,
by organized workers, and by nonorganized workers showed that,
though the three groups differed somewhat in their views, they

all placed "reinforcement of codetermination" in last place among eight choices. Another study commissioned by the DGB in 1968–69 is only somewhat more positive. Persons interviewed ranked nine wants connected with work in order of importance. On average, organized workers placed "more codetermination" second (after job security), nonorganized workers placed it third (after job security and better pensions), and professional employees ranked it fifth (after job security, better pensions, higher wages, and better distribution of wealth). Thus, the codetermination system can be considered of some real importance to employees, but not a matter of overwhelming value.[5]

Because of the system's excruciatingly abstract nature, the worker is not only infrequently reminded of its existence, but he also has no particular reason to keep up with the type of high-level questions with which it deals. Some studies made in the early years suggests that workers were hardly even aware of the system. Summarizing these, Professor Friederich Fürstenberg of the Institute of Sociology at Linz, Austria, points out: "About three-quarters of the workers knew that co-determination had been introduced within their undertakings. . . . Not more than one worker in ten had some knowledge of the actual composition of the supervisory board."[6]

However, even though the system's merits may show up only infrequently and on a limited range of questions, it can in those cases be of inestimable value. One of its unquestioned accomplishments is its usefulness in rare times of crisis. The coal mining industry has gone through a painful restructuring in the postwar era, during which mines have been shut down, companies merged, and a large portion of the labor force put out of work. Yet this was all conducted without major social upheavals, and there is general agreement that the codetermination system—which required management to discuss every move with the workers and listen to their opinions, and which involved the labor directors directly in the cutbacks of workforces—helped achieve this. As Burkart Lutz remarked to me: "Codetermination helped to do things smoothly which had to be done anyway." The same type of relatively harmonious action has helped in introducing technological changes in factories, improving vocational training, and maintaining a relatively strike-free record, and in all these areas, the machinery of codetermination has undoubtedly been of benefit, albeit rather indirect, as far as the average worker is concerned. Maria Walther, a psychologist at the Frankfurt Management and Productivity Association (RKW) and one of Germany's most sophisticated work experts, pointed out to me: "The individual does not directly benefit very much from codetermination. But it becomes important when, for example, a coal mine has to be closed—it can assure that retraining measures are introduced, and so on. So in times of crisis it can be extremely useful."

Codetermination has remained, during the more than twenty years of its life, a subject of hot controversy, in great part because the DGB has never dropped its desire, frustrated in 1951, to extend the system to all of German industry. In recent years, the controversy has become even more heated. As long as the stiffly conservative CDU—which began by warmly endorsing codetermination but rapidly shifted its position—was in power, the question could remain at least partly on an academic level. If an expanded codetermination were to be put through at all, it would have to be done by the SPD, which has traditionally close ties with the DGB, which depends heavily on the labor movement for support, and which has long listed an enlargement of codetermination among its goals. Unfortunately, when the SPD at long last did come to power it was, first, in coalition with the CDU (where there was, of course, no question of pushing codetermination), and most recently, in 1969, in coalition with the Free Democrats (FDP). The FDP, which is roughly comparable to the Liberal Party in Britain, favors traditional free-enterprise capitalism, meaning a heavy emphasis on property rights and therefore a position against codetermination. Indeed, the FDP demanded, and got, an agreement from the SPD that the codetermination issue would be dropped as a condition for forming the 1969 coalition.

The SPD, under Willy Brandt, was happy to agree to the condition in order to form a coalition in which it was the dominant partner. But it has not been, contrary to expectations, possible to bury the codetermination issue. It continues to pop up, again and again, suggesting that despite its obvious faults it does have considerable appeal after all.

The most important new element in the controversy during the past few years was the publication, in January 1970, of the report of the Biedenkopf Commission. This Commission, consisting of nine prestigious and respected academic experts and a large research staff under the chairmanship of Professor Kurt Hans Biedenkopf, had been appointed in 1967 to study the history and results of codetermination in the steel and coal industries, as a help in planning the future, if any, of the democratization of industry. There are grounds for suspicion that the government that appointed the Commission—at the time under the CDU —was hoping to kill off the issue or at least to cripple it for some time to come, since at most three of the members of the Commission were firmly in favor of codetermination, the others being neutral, lukewarm, or clearly hostile. It was assumed when the commission began its work that, so disparate were the views among the members, two or more reports accommodating diverging viewpoints would be published when the commission finished its assignment.

That was not, however, what happened. After studying the question for more than two years, the commission issued a unanimous report warmly praising the functioning of the codetermination system, both in general industry (where labor representatives have a third of the places on the boards) and in the steel and coal industries (where labor representatives have equality with capital). It concluded: "Even though conflicts of interest remain . . . the representatives of shareholders and workers, after some initial difficulties, have cooperated in the supervisory boards in the steel and coal industries as well as in the industries where the Works' Constitution Act applies. The integration which was intended when worker representatives were given places on the boards has, in fact, taken place."[7] The commission not only clearly pronounced the system a success, it maintained that it had not been able to find any knowledgeable observer in the industry who was against it. Nor was it able to find evidence supporting the main arguments that have been raised by critics—

that unions were manipulating companies by "remote control" through their inside position, that workers were exercising unhealthy influence on the companies' capital-investment policies, and that "irrelevant" influence on the board was being exercised through making "deals" with the other members.

The commission's recommendations were less positive, however. It strongly opposed the extension of "parity" between capital and labor to other industries, as the DGB had been demanding, and suggested that the existing Works' Constitution Act be tinkered with slightly, to give labor a small amount of additional influence.

Professor Fritz Voigt, head of the Industrial Research Institute in Bonn, who was a member of the commission and who had been the first, as he explained it to me, to make a "scientific study" of the system—for a book published in 1962—told me that the commission had gone through more or less the same process of evolution he had experienced when he had first researched his book: "I started by making certain assumptions— that damage was being done to the economic system, wages were too high, profits were too low, that on the whole the effects were negative. But I came around more and more to a different view, that there had been many positive effects. In particular, I saw how tensions between employers and employees had been lowered. There had appeared a certain 'objectivization' between labor and management—they no longer throw things at each other, partly because they have no secrets from each other. In the work of the Biedenkopf Commission, we used research methods somewhat different from those I used in making my original research. But we came to very much the same result. I wouldn't change one sentence in my first book on the subject."

Voigt emphasizes, as others have, that one of the principal contributions of the system had been its help in avoiding social unrest during sensitive periods, and he cited the wide-ranging structural changes that had taken place in the coal-mining industry as an example: "If the codetermination system had not existed we would have had great problems, because more than half the workers had to shift to other industries. But thanks to this system, labor's side was presented. Previously, profits were the only consideration, but now the social aspects are also looked at. Always before, authority was very strong in these industries.

There was a semimilitaristic organization and no possibility whatever of any influence from the workers."

The workers have, he explained, shown commendable understanding for their heavy responsibility in exercising their influence, and have not attempted to exploit their massive potential economic power: "If they had taken advantage of their opportunities to influence business policies, they could have destroyed the whole economy of the industries."

Is this abstract and remote system of any real interest to the employees? Voigt maintained it definitely was. "If you ask workers directly about what they think of codetermination," he said, "then they will tell you they don't care much. But if you ask them about taking it away, they say they would strike if anybody tried." Professor Voigt told me the system had worked so well, in fact, that he was sure the United States could learn much from it. "In our European view," he said, "there is very little integration between capital and labor in the United States, and very much tension. The codetermination system could be of very great help in lowering tensions in American society."

Considering the fulsome praise given to the system as it had worked out so far, the Biedenkopf Commission's refusal to recommend its extension seems a bit of a non sequitur. One reason given in the report was that managers who did not wish to work under such a system should have the option of looking for work in other industries not subject to the same kind of system. Another was that the unions had very possibly been extra careful to behave themselves so as not to jeopardize the chances of extending the system to other industries. If the system were to be made universal, the unions might exercise their strength to the fullest, stressing short-term benefits at the expense of long-term economic growth and causing damage in other ways.

Nevertheless, the commission did recommend that the workers' one-third membership on supervisory boards of most companies be slightly strengthened through a rather complicated formula and other minor concessions made to the DGB's demands for more worker power. None of the recommended changes would, in fact, bring about much change. Karl Fitting, vice minister of labor, remarked drily to me: "It's a typical German document. When you boil it all down all it amounts to is changing the labor representatives on the supervisory boards from four out of twelve to five out of twelve. That's progress—if you have a mathematical mind."

The DGB didn't see it that way. In fact, the report pleased very few people. The DGB was unhappy because their demand for parity on the supervisory boards was rejected. The Employers' Confederation was unhappy because the recommendation was for an extension, however slight, of the previous system, and it had taken a strong stand on preservation of the status quo.

The system's true nature, its merits and faults, have been unduly obscured by the storms of controversy that have swirled around it. This is reflected in much of the writings about the system in other countries. In America, for instance, it has been described in heavily negative terms. One rather hysterical American report painted the system in uniformly dark colors: The "rank-and-file German worker wants no part of" codetermination, labor representatives on supervisory boards block "management's efforts to counter losses with more efficient production methods" and, in general, the system "has proved to be a dismal failure."[8]

Unquestionably, the DGB has contributed to the controversy by insisting that codetermination be shaped to give power not to workers directly, but primarily through the intermediary of the unions. Such a structure seems not only unnecessarily cumbersome, but also against the true interests of the workers, who would probably prefer—if the choice were offered—to be more personally involved in the bureaucracy, not subjected to yet another bureaucracy over which they have little control. Defenders of the DGB view explain that such attitudes derive from the DGB's relatively weak position. Only some 30 percent of its potential membership is actually organized and it has, in fact, been gradually losing ground during the past decade or so. Therefore, there is the feeling that the DGB's first task is to strengthen its own power base, which will enable it to better protect the workers' interests.

In any case, critics of the system, and of proposed extensions of the system, have focused on the central role the DGB envisages for itself in their attacks. Numerous pamphlets and brochures published by the Employers' Confederation attacking extension of codetermination stress the central position of the trade unions. Codetermination "benefits only the trade unions," says one such leaflet, and adds that, if the system were to cover the entire economy, it "would make the trade unions the strongest power in the State." The Employers' Confederation also points to the considerable influence the unions already wield in various ways, as well as to their weakness, measured in terms of their total membership (which should make them less entitled to such massive power).

Other points made by the Employers' Confederation include both the meaninglessness of the system (it "brings no advantage to the workers" and "does not guarantee employment") as well as its excessive meaningfulness (it "is harmful to the economy," "isolates us with the EEC, and restricts us in markets abroad"). Moreover, it "upsets the social equilibrium" and "undermines private property."[9]

It is difficult to get any precise grip on these criticisms. If the system threatens to damage the economy, then it ought to be possible to track down the damage that has been done by codetermination in the steel industry. When I visited the Employers' Confederation in Cologne, I asked Helmüth Kissler, an adviser on codetermination questions, for some details about this. "It is difficult to show proof," he answered, "because the subjects treated in the supervisory board must remain secret." He added, however, that the industry had been hurt by excessive wage demands: "Collective agreements show that wages are higher in this industry." When I asked for some documentation on that point, it was not forthcoming.

One can suspect that the Employers' Confederation is exaggerating. Helmut Latta, personnel director of Hoesch AG, told me: "Codetermination has had no impact whatever on wage policies. It is subject to a free play of power between employers and employees. It all depends on special factors in special industries." A brief glance at the figures suggests that, in this case as in many other cases of comparisons of figures, there is little precision, but that there is nothing to indicate that wage increases in the West German steel industry have been particularly notable. According to the highly respected compilations published by the Swedish Employers' Confederation, steel industry wages (including fringe benefits) increased by 92 percent in the 1958–67 decade in West Germany, which was more than in Britain (62 percent) or France (56 percent), but about the same as in Finland (91 percent) and less than in Sweden (117 percent), and, in fact, less than in West German manufacturing industries generally (113 percent). Moreover, wages in 1967 were lower than in Germany's EEC partners Belgium and The Netherlands.[10] Since it is clear that Germany is still doing a robust export business in steel, it is not easy to see how the industry has been damaged economically by codetermination.

Burkart Lutz, who in general takes a dim view of codetermination, also dismisses the contention that it has damaged the industry. "The German steel industry," he remarked to me, "is in no better shape than, say, the Italians or the Japanese—and in Italy it is partly nationalized and in Japan it is very capitalistic. You can't prove anything. But you *can* say that, first, it hasn't *harmed* the German steel industry and, second, that it may have been of help during the critical years in the coal industry."

A recorded discussion of codetermination in 1969 brought out similar viewpoints. Ludwig Rosenberg, chairman of DGB at the time (now retired), said: "There is no question . . . that expansion and development in the postwar era has in no other country been carried out so successfully and so smoothly as in Germany. The German steel industry has without doubt attained a strength and a capacity that nobody had expected." Rosenberg attributes this in some measure to the codetermination system. Walter Scheel, then chairman of the FDP (now Foreign Minister), disputed this point: "If your opinion were correct, how in the world has the German chemical industry developed even more rapidly than the steel industry? Another comparison: The Japanese steel industry can show an even better development than we even though they have not a trace of codetermination.[11]

There is no sure proof in past experience of the merits of codetermination, but there also is no proof that it has been harmful.

Those who have had the most intimate experience with codetermination—that is, the companies where it has been in force for some years—seem far less upset about it than is the Employers' Confederation. Günther Nordhues, head of the Legal Department of Hoesch AG, told me: "Codetermination in our company has been successful. The employees are aware that the system means power, but also means responsibility." Helmut Latta, the personnel chief, noted that the frequently voiced complaint that workers were incompetent to serve on boards was unfounded, at least at Hoesch: "There might have been some difficulties in the beginning, but they now have the capacity to participate in decision-making. This complaint is a complaint of the past." The Hoesch executives added that these positive views, if not completely representative of the industry, were most probably "nearly typical."

At the Krupp works, Count Georg-Volkmar Zedtwitz-Arnim, head of the information department, gave me a somewhat different view. The traditional strongly paternalistic pattern at Krupp is proudly maintained today, and Count Zedtwitz-Arnim insisted on showing me a large number of the houses owned by Krupp for the workers. It is obvious that an aristocratic atmosphere still prevails. Nevertheless, he said the company had no strong complaints about the system: "Codetermination is not a menace either to labor or to management, as long as it works. The important point is to stop just before we reach the point where it no longer works. The idea that a worker is too stupid to become a manager is just silly." However, he added: "Of course in public we have to agree with the Employers' Confederation." And he is firmly opposed to the system's extension to other industries.

Lutz told me that he believed the system has, relatively, been a disappointment. "In comparison with what was expected twenty years ago, codetermination has been a complete failure," he said. "People thought it would change everything, create a new society, abolish contradictions between the interests of workers and capital, but it didn't turn out that way. I am against codetermination because I think the trade unions have a role which they find it difficult to fulfill if they are involved in codetermination."

On the other hand, he thought that employers were being shortsighted in not seeing the benefits for themselves: "If I were an industrialist," he remarked, "I would be in favor of codetermination. It gives management a higher sensitivity to what is going on and also better opportunities to manipulate the workers. Grievances can be taken care of and suppressed simultaneously."

This may be an unusually cynical view, but the central idea is unquestionably correct. Most of the opposition to codetermination appears to be poorly documented and highly emotional—such as the Employers' Confederation's simultaneous assurances that the system means nothing and that it means so much that it is damaging the economy.

The controversy surrounding the system probably seems more bitter than it really is, due to the uncomfortable tactical positions occupied by the principal antagonists. The Employers' Confederation has become locked in one unsound position and the DGB has become locked in a different position that is also unsound—and for tactical reasons neither can gracefully slide out of its position. One is tempted to suggest that both sides would be better off to switch sides than to remain in these uncomfortable positions—that is, employers might well be the prime beneficiaries of an extension of codetermination, and workers would probably benefit from a less dominant involvement of their union in the issue. Such are the contradictions of power politics.

The truth would seem to be that, while codetermination has not revolutionized anything, it has been of undeniable social value and has given some benefits both to workers and to management. As Eric Jacobs, British labor writer, points out, the rules regarding representation on the boards "seem to have worked remarkably well." He attributes this primarily to "something less easily definable in the feeling of confidence it spreads, the sense that workers' interests are not going to be ignored and that even if the trade unions cannot hold back the flood of economic change . . . they can at least be informed well in advance. . . ."[12] Even Professor Fürstenberg, who is highly critical of the system as a whole (primarily because it has "relatively little direct bearing upon the individual worker's situation at his workplace"), avers that "the great majority of workers showed a positive attitude towards these institutional changes."[13] In a larger economic and social context, it has aided in industrial development; it has helped the steel industry expand, which was surely desirable; and it has helped ease the suffering of the coal industry's decline, which was inevitable anyway. Moreover, the system furnishes further proof that workers and their representatives *can* participate in decision-making on the highest levels within an enterprise in a competent and responsible manner. Moreover—if the polemics swirling around the question could somehow be quieted—it has created a framework within which more satisfying progress in democracy may eventually be made.

The first requirement for an improved system might be a strong desire to get rid of some of the paralyzing rigidity in the present one and include more flexibility to adapt to true human needs rather than to the patterns of a neatly designed "model." When I asked Karl Fitting about this, he threw up his hands in mock horror: "More flexible? Oh, no. The Germans want laws—fixed, inflexible laws."

Unfortunately, for the time being at least, this seems to be true. The experts on the Biedenkopf Commission, for example, were all legal experts and economists. Although the commission worked with a rather large research apparatus, there was not a single psychologist or sociologist included in the team, or indeed anyone interested in probing the value of the codetermination system—or any other system in any other country—in human terms, or even any interest in looking at the research done on such questions in other countries. The approach was strictly legalistic, formal, and rigidly limited in scope.

A more logical and humane orientation on the question of employee power would be in great part connected with the basic problems of work, work alienation, tediousness, monotony, the human damage resulting from such work and the basic waste of the whole thing for both employee and employer. Naturally, it is not enough to be interested only in the problem—one should also be interested in solutions. There is in West Germany a rather widespread, fatalistic acceptance of the inevitable unpleasantness of work. Karl Fitting remarked to me: "Under any system— whether governed by the thoughts of Mao or Nixon or Brandt— the worker has to do what he's told and perform his tasks. It doesn't matter whether he has codetermination or not, the factory won't change." I asked Werner Willutzki, the union representative at Hoesch, about alienation; he shrugged and brusquely replied: "It's only a philosophical question." Lutz casually remarked to me: "It's impossible to be a worker and to be satisfied. The worker's condition is fundamentally a condition of resignation. You can make improvements, but they do not last." Lutz was surprised that anyone would question this basic truth, which he said had been proven and was "one of the rare things sociology has ever proven." He referred especially to the research done by Ludwig von Friedeburg, now Minister of Education in Essen.

Maria Walther explained to me that this was a common belief among many German sociologists: "They feel that it is an unchangeable fact of life and must be accepted. You see, they are very 'problem-oriented'—they aren't interested in solutions." As for the type of theories advanced by von Friedeburg, she did not agree with the conclusions, but regarded their appearance (in the mid-1960s) as an encouraging sign nevertheless: "He defines the problem more clearly than had ever been done before—so that perhaps others can now go further in finding solutions."

One approach might be to conduct research on the social psychology of organizations in order to learn what makes them function and prevents them from functioning, with a view to solving some of the problems attached to work organizations. But it is obviously not going to happen soon. This is partly because behavioral science, branded a "Jewish science" during the Hitler era, had to start more or less from scratch after the war. More importantly, the DGB, which might logically push for action of this kind, is not anxious to get involved. In 1965, the slogan "codetermination at the work place"—implying a movement of the decision-making machinery nearer to the worker—was originated by DGB, but so far no effort has been made to achieve anything on that level. Maria Walther explains that the DGB has several reasons for caution. For one thing, some of the worst aspects of the manipulative "human relations school" were hastily imported from the United States after the war and clumsily applied to give workers the "feeling" they were being well treated. Now, anything that resembles such doctrines is regarded with suspicion. Further, she noted that other techniques might divert attention from codetermination: "The DGB is afraid they might work and it would lose power."

I asked Wilhem Kaltenborn at DGB about this. He said: "It might mean that the workers would be satisfied on that level and lose interest in codetermination." Does that mean that the DGB wants to keep workers dissatisfied? Well, that was not quite what he meant, of course. But he didn't feel that any large changes could be made in alienation: "I don't think the situation can be changed. I don't know of any models in any country." However, his mind is not closed: "Perhaps we should try to develop a model—a utopia, without worrying about whether it can be attained."

There is, in fact, a growing interest in bringing the system closer to the worker. Gerhard Leminsky, at the research institute affiliated with DGB, remarked to me: "There is a lot of sterility in the discussions on this question. They don't really have any connection with the real problems." He, however, is extremely interested in attacking the problem from a different angle: "We should take every opportunity to come closer to the worker on the shop floor." In this connection, he is impressed by research done in other countries, particularly in Scandinavia, on organizations and how they can be changed to adapt to human needs. "This is a very new element on the German scene," he remarked.

So far, however, the discussion has not come close to that point.

Indeed, the latest significant change in West German labor legislation did represent an attempt to come to grips with problems that are of immediate concern to the worker and did bring democracy closer to his work situation—though not by altering the *Mitbestimmung* system. In 1972, the powers of the workers' councils were considerably broadened to give workers a voice in hiring, firing, promotion, and other personnel questions. In addition, the workers will have a say in deciding disputes in a number of areas. The position of the unions was also strengthened by forbidding employers to interfere with union organizing or other activities within companies.

After the parliamentary elections of 1972, when the FDP scored surprisingly large gains, that party concluded that it had greater potential appeal than had been realized. Thus, as part of a drive to widen its circle of supporters, it dropped its opposition to "equality" *Mitbestimmung* throughout industry. Though the FDP and the SPD have had trouble arriving at a mutually satisfactory formula, the plan is that "equality" legislation will eventually be passed.

IX. FRANCE: THE ELUSIVE "PARTICIPATION"

Without doubt, the country most closely connected—at least in the view of the casual observer—with ideas of worker participation in management is France, in part because of de Gaulle's well-known and long-standing devotion to the idea, but mostly because of the explosive worker-student revolt in May 1968, in which angry demands for "participation" and "worker control" were basic ingredients. So resounding were the shock waves from the "events of May" that they are often seen in other countries as a warning of the social breakdown that may occur if workers' problems are not attended to.

Equally without doubt, there are few other European countries where real progress toward industrial democracy has been slower. Only a few short months after the whirlwinds of social protest swept the country, during which many sober citizens were convinced that sweeping changes were under way, the movement seemed all but dead.

The "movement of May" lives, however. Worry and apprehension of a repeat performance are a source of constant concern and are a steady subject of discussion in the press—particularly in the spring, when a new malaise born of that 1968 disturbance, *la peur de mai* ("the fear of May"), is at its height. The events of May are not yet finished. The explosion created a consciousness of the basic ills, and some efforts to concoct remedies are quietly being made. Whether peaceful changes can be brought about quickly enough before the pressure of dissatisfaction pass another crisis point—well, nobody knows.

May 1, 1968, was a bright, sunny spring day, bringing out bumper crowds for the normal exuberant chaos of the workers' parades, colorful banners demanding justice and revolution, and overwrought speeches filled with leftist rhetoric.[1] It was the customary workers' holiday and, if it had been up to the workers alone, the subsequent events would never have developed. Pressures had been mounting for quite some time among students in France, quite the same as in other countries (one chronology of the events of May begins in 1964, with the first massive "sit-in" at the University of California at Berkeley[2]). A center of agitation was the red-brick University of Nanterre, in a suburb of Paris. The university had been shut down temporarily and a leader of the student activists questioned by the police—Daniel ("Red Danny") Cohn-Bendit, a bright, charismic French-German student of sociology.

May 1 that year lasted a little longer than usual. On May 2, demonstrations were continuing at Nanterre, the university was again shut down, and eight students were ordered to appear before an inquiry being held by the university authorities.

On May 3, the scene shifted to Paris and the uprising into high gear. Angry students filled the courtyard of the Sorbonne. The authorities, with uncanny misjudgment, had them summarily evicted by the police.

The students and police began with a few minor skirmishes; the subsequent battles, which continued around the clock, grew increasingly grim—the students using bricks pulled up from the streets, and the police using their nightsticks. Within a week, the streets of the Latin Quarter resembled a blood-spattered junkyard, littered with bricks, iron grills, debris of all kinds, barricades made of shattered billboards, and overturned, burned-out automobiles. Hundreds of students and police were wounded, and hundreds of students were arrested. But the workers were still not involved.

On May 13, a massive demonstration, ostensibly against the Vietnam War, somehow attracted united student-worker support. The next day, the first factory was "occupied" by the workers, that of the state-owned Sud-Aviation at Bougenais. Occupations spread rapidly across the country. Within a few days, the country was almost entirely paralyzed—there were virtually no factories, shops, trains, or banks in operation, no garbage collections, or anything else. Nobody knows exactly how many people were on strike, because there was nobody around to do the tabulations. But it appears that the only factories functioning were small and in remote provincial areas. As far as anyone could tell, France had stopped running.

At the beginning, the government paid little attention. De Gaulle, haughty and self-assured, flew to make a state visit to Romania the day the strike began and was being entertained by folk-singers as his country was slowly grinding to a stop. By May 24, even de Gaulle realized that something was up, and he addressed the nation, offering prime samples of his incomparable rhetoric and promising a referendum to solve the problems of social unrest. It had little effect. On May 27, negotiations between representatives of the state, the employers' associations, and the workers resulted in concrete proposals, which were rejected by every body of workers to which they were offered. De Gaulle tried once more on May 31, this time making vague promises of increased "participation," dissolving parliament, and ordering new elections. Negotiations were started again, this time with more success. The workers were not overwhelmingly enchanted with the meager wage increases offered them, but there was a widespread realization that, no matter what, the strike had to end. During the early part of June, workers began resignedly taking up their jobs, and factories were reopened. In a few weeks, France was back to normal.

An isolated student incident that became a nationwide student rebellion that touched off a nearly total general strike, paralyzing the nation for weeks. What was it all about?

To some extent, it was not about anything. Raymond Aron derisively referred to it as a "psychodrama." Sociologist Alfred Willener, who gathered material for a sociological study of the events while they were happening, compared it to the Dada movement in the arts and quoted one student who exclaimed, "It was an explosion of joy and liberty,"[3] and another who blandly avowed, "The movement has no political program, no political plans for the future, it has only, for the next three or four days, a certain presence. . . ."[4]

But beyond the "spirit of Kermesse" and superficial pointlessness, the movement was profoundly serious, a culmination of decades of development, containing a spontaneously generated, and perhaps unsystematically presented, but nonetheless remarkably perceptive critique of society and even a program for reform. The movement was, in its essence, nothing less than a broadranging attack on the very bases of French society. As Alain Touraine, a prominent sociologist, wrote: "The creative force of the movement is manifested, not in the abstractions of its proclamations, but in its capacity to put into question the forms of authority."[5] This, then, was the main subject matter of the "movement of May": the stiff, authoritarian structures that were, and still are, characteristic of modern France.

In order to grasp the very peculiar nature of the movement of May, we should glance briefly at the very peculiar nature of French society. Almost alone among Western European countries, France has stubbornly clung to a nineteenth-century system of precisely patterned, unyielding institutions, which determine the direction and extent of social development. In an earlier chapter, the stratification of authority in modern organizations, as examined by Max Weber in his classical description of bureaucracy, was noted as one of the key elements in the dehumanization of modern work relationships. Bureaucracy exists to a greater or lesser extent in all countries, but it is particularly entrenched and powerful in France. Michel Crozier, in his brilliant analysis of "the bureaucratic phenomenon," describes the all-encompassing, rigid bureaucratic framework which, to an unusually great degree, is dominant throughout France, in industry as well as in education and in government. It is important to remember that bureaucracy is not all bad. Indeed, for Max Weber and his contemporaries, bureaucratic organization was considered, despite some obvious but relatively minor drawbacks, to be by far the most efficient form of organization. And Crozier points out the bureaucratization of social relations in France has been of great utility—particularly in maintaining "order and stability" and thus avoiding the chaos that could well accompany social development.

"Progress," he writes, "has certainly been welcomed, but on the terms imposed by the French society; it has had to be established in an orderly manner, by respecting the fundamental arrangement of statutes and privileges and by perpetuating a conservative social structure. Centralization in the French manner has thus allowed France to progress while at the same time conserving completely archaic social structures."[6] The progress, measured in economic terms, is undeniable. Despite such anomalies as the famous abominable telephone system, France is, in gross national product per capita, an extremely wealthy country.

Bureaucratization in relationships between management and labor would scarcely seem to be the right word, in view of the ramshackle labor organizations and the fact that the two sides are hardly on speaking terms. But Crozier argues that the key to the situation is the position of the government, which intervenes at numerous points in the relations between the two, in establishing certain aspects of working conditions and social security measures, as well as in direct participation in negotiations and in its own considerable role as an employer. This arrangement has certain advantages—notably, it skirts "the emotional difficulty which direct contact would constitute"[7]—but its cumbersomeness also carries obvious disadvantages. Though both parties have the theoretical possibility of influencing the other through pressuring for state action of some sort, this is not very efficient. As a consequence, both sides get increasingly locked into their rigid positions. The unions remain weak because whatever influence they are able or willing to apply on management is all but invisible to the potential dues-paying member. Management remains aristocratically backward because the resentment of the state's interference in company affairs "reinforces a complex of reactionary attitudes and an anachronistic attachment to prerogatives which, in fact, are largely outmoded."[8]

The backwardness of management in France cannot be denied. One post-mortem of the 1968 revolt points to one of the underlying causes: "The typical enterprise in France presents a structure not found in any other country: a sort of centralized dictatorship in which the president manages not only the business, but also the bodies which are supposed to act as a check on him, the board of directors and even the general assembly of share-holders."[9] A generally accepted attitude is that the president of the company is alone capable of making decisions, that pressures from workers and/or unions are to be resisted under all circumstances, and that maximum efficiency can be attained by exerting maximum severity of authority. The money-instrumental idea of workers and work is accepted without question: No worker would do anything at all if he were not forced to by threats, bribes, or fear of starvation, and workers are incapable of taking any real interest in their work or of accepting responsibility. Lucien Rioux, a journalist specializing in such matters, described the typical French manager: "Any power apart from his own is unthinkable. His attitude to his workers is that of some headmasters in lycées toward their pupils: Workers are grown-up children who are incapable of appreciating their own interests."[10] The family-controlled company remains an extremely important feature of the industrial scene, and this fact contributes to the parochialism and the narrow-mindedness of French managers. In this autocratic context, there is almost a paranoid concern for secrecy, and even so mundane a step as providing minimal information to employees or the public is regarded as exceptionally radical. Jean Neidinger, secretary general of the social department of Le Conseil National du Patronat Français, the very powerful French Employers' Association, remarked to me with great pride, as an indication of the progressiveness of French employers: "There are some companies which are now publishing newspapers for their personnel" —a practice which, even in other European countries, is no longer considered especially noteworthy. As Roger Priouret has written of the typical French manager's attitude: "It is no different from that of an absolute hereditary monarch."[11]

If French employers tend to be strong and inflexible, labor unions tend to be weak and inflexible. The French unions are numerically insignificant, protected by few legal guarantees, split into various rival factions, and often are more eager to further their ideological aims than to promote the real interests of the workers. There are no reliable figures on union membership, because many workers who are nominally members do not bother to pay their dues, and might or might not pay attention to their leaders. Lucien Rioux estimates that the six largest unions, which claim a total membership of more than 5 million, have actual memberships of 3.3 to 3.7 million.[12] The unions have few rights, and there are no elaborate bargaining procedures, as there are in other countries—for the most part, there is no bargaining at all. Employers prefer to bargain on a regional basis, partly because the subject of bargaining becomes, as one expert explained to me, "not real wages at all, but on the minimum wages paid in marginal firms." In general, managers are bluntly hostile to the very idea of unions. A "militant" is simply a worker trying to organize a viable union, and if he is so careless as to allow his employer to discover that fact before he has drummed up some strengthening sympathy among his fellows, he is likely to find himself fired.

The unions themselves are, it must be said, in great part responsible for their precarious position. By far the largest union (with about 1.5 million members), and therefore something of a pace-setter, is the Confédération Générale du Travail (CGT), which has a long, fiery, and ragged history and which has been, since the early postwar period, dominated by the Communist Party. The CGT has never thought of itself as an instrument of such trivial matters as wages or working conditions, but as a revolutionary force working for the overthrow of the entire capitalist system. "A union based on the class struggle can never limit its goals to immediate demands," writes Henri Krasucki, a CGT thinker. "The CGT's fundamental objective has been since its founding the suppression of capitalist oppression." And the only method of ending that oppression is "the complete transformation of society, that is, the disappearance of capitalism and its replacement by socialism."[13] I asked Livio Mascarello, a top official of the CGT, if it would not be possible for workers to cooperate with management so that the company could pay higher wages while awaiting the final revolution. He said it was totally impossible. "These two elements," he explained, "are diametrically opposed. The workers want to get the highest possible pay, because it is they who are creating the wealth. The employers want to limit their expenses as much as possible. We will not be dragged into any collaboration with the capitalists. We have nothing in common with the capitalists—absolutely nothing."

In view of this rigidly uncompromising view, it is not altogether astonishing that so many workers remain outside the unions.

When the CGT is not promoting its ideological views, it spends a lot of time squabbling with the other unions, particularly with the CGT-Force Ouvrière (about seven hundred thousand members), which broke off from the CGT after World War II. It is said to have been established partly with the help of financial assistance from America; in any case, anticommunism remains one of its main principles. Other important unions are the Confédération Française Démocratique du Travail (CFDT), which formerly was a Catholic union; a splinter group remains Catholic, the Confédération Française des Travailleurs Chrétiens (CFTC) —the former has about seven hundred thousand members, the latter about seventy thousand. None of these unions is especially friendly with the others, and they have often competed with each other in the rigidity of their antimanagement views in order to gain worker favor. As the futility of this custom became apparent to their potential recruits, they have slowly been forced to modify their mutual hostilities and even to cooperate with each other in some areas. But progress has been very slow, and the inflexible position adopted by the CGT has been a major block to evolution toward more positive policies.

The unions have not been completely powerless, however, since they have some ability to promote legislation favoring workers and low-income groups by exerting pressure on the state. The power definitely exists, but it is a clumsy system, and the results are uneven. Moreover, the worker himself is far removed from the levers of power. Crozier writes, "It is impossible for the worker to understand the connection that can exist between the expression of his grievances within the union framework and the bureaucratic results which, one day, will be imposed on his employer."[14]

This was the situation that existed for many years during the postwar period in French industry and, despite occasional breakdowns (such as the semirevolutionary situation in 1958, which brought de Gaulle to power), it worked, in many ways, quite well. The inflexibilities on both sides tended to maintain a kind of dynamic stagnation—there could be a great deal of movement and development within each position, but the positions themselves remained in place and helped immensely in maintaining stability and therefore in promoting economic growth. But pressures for changes were building up in a situation that could not change and that could not adapt to the needs of a modern society and a modern economy. Crozier wrote in 1962: "It now seems . . . that the system has reached the limit of its development and that it lacks resources to solve the increasingly difficult problems created by the environment."[15] He added that the situation was leading to a "very profound upheaval."[16]

There were, in the balmy Gaullist 1960s, a very few other voices warning both management and labor that times were changing and that modern conditions required a modern approach.

One critic of the status quo was Serge Mallet, a sociologist and journalist who, in detailed studies of "the new working class," showed that workers in modern industry were undergoing a rapid transformation. But the traditional putative defenders of workers' interests were choosing to ignore this very significant development. "The 'official Marxists,'" he wrote in 1963, "have curiously discovered empirical processes of 'statistical' American sociology to prove that these new technical conditions concern only a tiny portion of the working class."[17] His recommendations for change, however, were largely limited to restyling the labor unions.

A considerably more bold, and extremely perceptive, set of proposals was put forward by leftist journalist André Gorz. He had a completely new approach to the formulation of union demands adapted to modern conditions—an extremely brash move, as the unions had scarcely accepted the idea of making traditional demands, much less attempted to acquire the strength to do so effectively. The goal was to modify radically the alienating conditions in which the modern worker found himself and thereby to abolish a basic conflict: "The enterprise demands imagination in the execution of his task and, at the same time, a passive, disciplined submission to the orders and the norms issued by management."[18] In order to improve conditions for the "lobotomized proletarians," the conditions and the nature itself of the work, where "the most direct alienation of the worker" exists, would have to be radically altered. Workers would therefore have to "unite indissolubly their demands for wages, demands for management control, and demands for self-determination—over working conditions." Specifically, the workers would control vocational training ("to insure they are educating, not robots, but professional workers . . . capable of progressing in their profession"), the organization of work and the assignment of jobs (to make sure they lead to "the development of the faculties and the autonomy of the worker and not to their shrinkage"), the division of labor, and the pace of the work.[19] In other words, what the modern worker wanted and needed was "to participate in the formulation of decisions and to assure their application."[20] In urging the unions to push for such reforms, Gorz conceded that it would mean compromising with the capitalists, but he hopefully cited Lenin's view that "there are good and bad compromises."[21] The CGT was not impressed.

The best-known proposal for change was a detailed program for reforming French companies, their legal and tax status, their relationship with shareholders and the state, and their treatment of workers; it was written in 1963, primarily for the benefit of business executives, by Marcel Bloch-Lainé, an eminently respectable career civil servant in the Ministry of Finance. He recommended that a measure of "industrial democracy" be introduced into companies and bluntly asserted that current company structures had too many "empty rituals and manifest abuses" to last long.[22] Concerning employees, he recommended greater union rights, some consultation with management on decisions, and more information. Basically, he, like Gorz, felt that what the workers needed was more "participation."

Reform was urgent, he said, and he very perceptively warned that the absence of social disruptions in the tranquil early 1960s did not mean that the situation was satisfactory. "The state of calm is misleading," he wrote. "It conceals many particular dissatisfactions, ready to be ignited at the slightest tremor of the business cycle."[23]

None of these Cassandras had any effect whatever. The rigidity, the stagnation, the refusal to accept change, prevailed in all the major institutional arrangements in Gaullist France. That there was a new type of worker, that he had a need to exercise his intelligence in a human environment, that "participation" might be a valid notion—all this remained hardly better than a curiosity.

The unions were not interested, managements were not interested, the state was not interested. The only parties to be interested at all were a few (mostly obscure) intellectuals—and the workers themselves.

Thus whatever confusion and inconclusiveness that may exist about the 1968 workers' revolt, one thing is certain: The workers were expressing their own deeply felt grievances with complete honesty and spontaneity. They were not being led, manipulated, or used by anyone. Since the revolt happened, it has become customary for commentators to remark on the pre-1968 obviousness of the impending crisis, but the raw fact of the matter is that few people noticed the changes that were taking place under the sleepy surface, and fewer still realized that worker resentments could cause a major social disturbance. Even the most percipient of social critics often tended toward skepticism that the bitterness was so serious as to result in any real disruption of society. André Gorz tempered his analysis with this comment: "The dissatisfaction of the workers . . . has never *spontaneously* resulted in a questioning of what, in the general order of society, was rendering their condition insufferable."[24] And François Bloch-Lainé conceded that the situation, however serious, "is not explosive."[25]

But it was. As soon as the workers perceived the opening created by the students, they responded, spontaneously, accurately, and massively. The students' main objects of attack were the government's neglect of the dilapidated university system, police repression of students' efforts to call attention to their plight, as well as the Gaullist regime as a whole.

The students and workers had, however, plenty in common—primarily, their distaste for the archaic French authoritarian structures in which they were enmeshed and their eagerness to participate in the operation of the system. Alain Touraine noted: "The stake in the struggle is the control of the authority to decide." Both students and workers were setting forth, in opposition to the cozy bourgeois utopia that had developed under de Gaulle, "a counter-utopia, libertarian and anti-authoritarian, communitarian and spontaneous."[26]

It was easy for the students to feel a natural sympathy for the workers, because they knew that they themselves would soon be locked in the same hopelessly autocratic system. One student explained: "The student movement is truly a movement of young workers, of people who need their studies in order to live and who, at the same time, are conscious of the role that they are expected to play in this society, who know very well that they will end up being used just like the others."[27] Young "organization men" in industry, who had been through the same process themselves, knew the students were correct in their assessment. "The new technicians and experts," Touraine wrote, "know, especially if they are young, that the majority of students will never reach positions in management but only in organization, communication, and technical execution, with no participation in decision-making power."[28]

Just as the students could empathize with the workers, the workers harbored some of the students' feelings about the shabbiness of their educational system; one of the workers' primary demands was for an expansion of educational opportunities in industry and thus of the chance to develop personally. The complaints of the workers and the complaints of the students thus fused together and formed an unbroken continuum.

The industrial conflict itself was unlike any in French history —in the type of worker most heavily involved, in the nature of the demands, and in the behavior of the workers during the strike period. It was an extremely instructive manifestation of the feelings of "the new working class."

Though almost all workers were striking, the most important initiatives were those provided, not by the traditional low-skilled workers with doctrinaire socialist or antimanagement views, but by a new generation of highly skilled workers, technicians, and high-level white-collar workers. As Touraine noted, "it is the workers closest to the students, in age as well as profession, who participated most creatively in the movement."[29] It was no accident that the first shutdown occurred at an advanced technology company, Sud-Aviation. Moreover, some of the most significant strike actions were conducted in electronics, atomic power, and other such sophisticated industries.

The aims of the strikers were also sharply different from the traditional ones. They were protesting against organization structures, management methods, and management attitudes, all of which were developed in, and were perhaps well suited to, an earlier stage of capitalism, but that were incompatible with the well-educated employees in modern industry, who were supposed to be sufficiently intelligent to make modern technology function properly and stupid enough to submit passively to the despotic environment in which they found themselves. The normal bread-and-butter issues were largely forgotten. "As a theme of the crisis," Touraine noted, "pauperization was replaced by growth and alienation." And the major demand was no longer for a "redistribution of wealth," but for "self-management."[30]

The unusual nature of the industrial revolt is pointed up in a sociological study of conditions in some 120 enterprises. The employees in revolt were found to be "occupying positions of relatively low qualifications, refusing to be mere instruments in the hands of the hierarchy, and in general rejecting the bureaucratic and technocratic manner of decision-making in their work." They were seeking principally to fulfill their needs for "achievement, dignity in work and freedom (freedom of expression, freedom to control the norms and results of their work)."[31] A recurrent strain in the testimony given by workers was criticism of managements. Demands for "participation," "democratization of the enterprise," "cogestion" (comanagement), and "autogestion" (self-management), were common, and for many strikers, "the strike meant 'there are no more bosses.' "[32] Some of the most frequently voiced wishes of the workers were: consultation with, and information on, changes of job assignments; employee participation in establishing promotion policies; better information on company financial conditions; permanent training policies adapted to the employees' career needs; and rational definition of policies of capital investment and research.[33]

Perhaps the most innovative feature of the revolt was the behavior of the strikers. Far from trying to wreck the hated capitalist physical equipment, the workers took great pains to maintain the machinery, in order to show that "we cared as much about it as the boss and we could run it by ourselves." Many hoped to "get back into production 'without waiting for management.' "[34] In a few cases the workers did in fact resume production, under their own management, especially to fill urgent orders, while they continued to strike "part-time." The radio-TV division of Thomson-Houston at Gennevilliers agreed to produce a transmitter for a foreign TV station.[35] Similarly, a plant of Rhone-Poulenc delivered some hospital equipment in order to meet a need created by an emergency operation, and a worker-management structure was put into place at a plant of the chemicals company Pechiney; these "workers' management" arrangements were based on democratic principles, where the rule was "collective decisions, as often as possible."[36]

The point of all this was to show that workers had sufficient interest, sense of responsibility, and intelligence to be trusted with some of the decision-making power hitherto monopolized by management. This was no far-away thought, since many workers and other observers were convinced that the day of workers' management was not on the horizon, but just around the corner. The show of responsible behavior had its comic aspects—as when strike committees solemnly informed the boss that they were taking over the plant but that he had been selected to continue in his job—but it did demonstrate that both the unions and managements had been wrong in their long-held assumption that workers did not want to share in management decisions.

Despite the obviously nonmonetary nature of the demands behind the strike, it was settled, as strikes are generally settled, primarily with money. The framework agreements worked out by the employers, the leading unions, and the state served as patterns for individual companies. The sizable minorities—perhaps a third or so of the total number of workers—who felt deeply about the necessary organizational changes opposed the settlement in this way; as one worker put it, "We didn't go out on strike for three weeks just to get paid for the days we were out on strike."[37] But they couldn't hold out against the majority who had money worries, had less strong convictions, or were just tired of the strike.

Nevertheless, it was generally thought that the workers had somehow gained an important victory and that a permanent transformation had taken place that would leave a heavy mark on the country's industrial structure. The above-mentioned sociological report concluded: "May 1968 will force an enterprise to be considered not only as a machine of production but a community of human beings who, demanding rights of information, democ-

ratization of decisions, and even worker power, assert the value
of their personal contribution."[38] And *Le Monde,* in considering
whether the feeling for change would remain a "dead letter,"
averred that it would be impossible to "fall back into lethargy."[39]

On the surface, however, that is precisely what happened. The
revolutionary changes that were thought to be, if not already in
place, at least on the way, never arrived. The strike committees
disbanded, the worker-managements handed the factories back
to the owners, and the familiar rigid positions were reassumed as
rapidly as possible. A series of conversations organized by the
parliamentary Commission of Cultural Affairs, in late 1968, shows
this with painful clarity. One of the subjects under discussion
was whether a plant union, that is, a union organization at the
level of a single plant, should be permitted—surely a rather mild
measure, and far from constituting workers' control. Yet Leon
Gingembre, representative of an association of smaller businesses,
showed that his membership had learned nothing from the lessons
of May. In response to a query on the subject, he bluntly replied:
"We are against the plant union."[40] He also avowed that any
change in traditional management methods would be disastrous.
"Democracy within the enterprise," he stated, "means a confusion
of tasks and bad management methods. The specialization of
tasks and the hierchization of responsibilities are phenomena of
the modern world."[41] François Ceyrac, vice president of the Employers' Association, coolly noted that "participation" might take
three forms—"information, consultation, and participation in results"—thereby smoothly skipping over most of the issues the workers had raised.[42] Even so, he made it clear that no great progress
was to be expected in his modest trio of subjects. The release of
information is difficult in France "because of our individualistic
traditions which are opposed to the diffusion of this information."[43] And if managements should consent to "consult" with
workers, it would not be with the aim of listening to their opinions: "The final objective is to obtain support for the necessary
decisions."[44] Labor was scarcely more accommodating. Livio Mascarello of the CGT said: "We believe the workers can only genuinely participate in management through nationalization of the

means of production."[45] At about the same time, Henri Krasucki was writing, regarding suggestions for comanagement: "What would we comanage *with them?* The exploitation of workers?"[46]

The basic mood of those most capable of bringing about change had not altered. De Gaulle had for many years spoken of the necessity of widening participation in enterprises, and he was in fact responsible for the creation of the workers' councils at the end of World War II. But in the 1960s the only result of his feelings on the subject was the "Vallon amendment" (named after its nominal sponsor, Louis Vallon), passed in 1967. This disappointingly feeble move provided for distribution of a share of profits to employees, calculated according to a complicated formula—existing at all only if profits pass a certain minimum and in any case paid out only after five years. In the first year of the program's operation, 1970, only about one out of seven workers got anything at all, and the average amount for those who were lucky enough to be included was 353 francs (about 70 dollars).[47]

Part of de Gaulle's strategy for ending the strike had been a promise that the demands for "participation" would be met. He declared: "It is necessary that, in all of our activities, in a company or in a university, all of the members be directly associated in the manner in which it is operated, in the results that it achieves, and in the services it renders to the nation. In short, participation must become the rule and the dynamism of a rejuvenated France."[48] As a matter of fact, de Gaulle did have a keen understanding of the basic problems, as when he attributed the troubles of May to "the depressing and irritating feeling that modern man feels, of being caught and dragged along in an economic and social machinery over which he has no control and in which he is transformed into a mere instrument."[49] De Gaulle was reportedly preparing legislation designed to give employees a role in decision-making, and had actually gone over, and rejected, several outlines, but his resignation in 1969 put an end to participation. Georges Pompidou, de Gaulle's successor, has displayed minimal interest in the subject. The late René Capitant, a member of de Gaulle's cabinet, resigned the day de Gaulle left office. In a bitter article in *Le Monde,* he charged that Pompidou was not only "preparing to bury the reforms" de Gaulle had favored, but had, while a member of de Gaulle's government, actually prevented de Gaulle from carrying through his ideas on participation.[50]

Nevertheless, some small and unspectacular developments show that the revolt has had an effect. In 1970, unions received for the first time the right to organize at the plant level. Also in 1970, an agreement was reached in negotiations involving the state, the unions, and the employers on a shift from hourly to monthly pay for most production workers, thus putting them on an equal footing with white-collar workers—a move that Michel Drancourt, the well-known business journalist, called "the most important social measure in 20 years."[51] Negotiations between the unions and the employers (nudged along by the state) have resulted in expansion of vocational training opportunities. A much-noticed move was the distribution, in 1970, of common shares to workers in the state-owned Renault automobile works.

On the union front, the powerful CGT has retained its aloofness, but the other organizations have been more flexible. The CGT-Force Ouvrière, while skeptical of being overly involved with the enemy (management), has nevertheless expressed cautious willingness to "consult before decisions are taken" and "to be associated in checking on the execution as well as the results of the decisions."[52] The CFTC affirmed at its 1969 congress that "the right of workers to participate effectively in the formulation of decisions constitutes an indispensable element of economic life."

The boldest initiative of any union was taken by the CFDT, which, at its 1970 congress, reshaped its entire program around the idea of "democratization of the enterprise" and placed "self-management" as its primary ideological goal. The basic reason is the alienating conditions under which the modern worker suffers: "The worker spends his entire life squeezed in the machinery of a hierarchy over which he has no control, in a state of anonymous subordination."[53] The answer, says the CFDT, is self-management, by which it means total workers' control of enterprises. Though the CFDT program insists that socialism must accompany worker control, it nevertheless recognizes that the key to efficient functioning of companies is not political action but sound organizational principles, and that it is useless to talk about worker control without also reworking organization structures. In calling for "replacement of the present hierarchical structures with new types of organization which will promote self-management," it also includes a demand for "research into organizational and management structures" as an integral part of the process.[54] Apart from the demand for socialism, much of the program is, as we shall see, very much in line with the thinking of modern organizational studies.

There has even been some hesitant interest in management circles in participation. Probably the best-known "participation" program advanced from the management side has been the "pancapitalism" of Marcel Loichot—distinguished from Western "oligocapitalism" and Eastern "monocapitalism"—which he has described in great detail. The basic ill he seeks to combat is familiar: "The economic alienation of the worker is at the root of all the essential evils of the world." This could be altered in a system where, with only minor changes, "the worker would become *ipso facto* capitalists by receiving shares in their enterprise."[55] As he explained it to me, the reasoning is childishly simple. "About a million years ago," he said, "man appeared on the earth as a maker of tools. The tool—it was his capital, and that is man's distinguishing mark. During 90 percent of his history, man has been pancapitalist." Under industrialism, however, man no longer owned his own tools, and alienation developed; what is needed is a return to primitive conditions: "If everyone who works in factories can own shares, you will end alienation." Specifically, this would be done by limiting the equity of shareholders in profits and converting the remainder into shares for employees. Otherwise, the increase in wealth among capitalists will be frightening: "It is impossible that oligocapitalism will survive. In fifty years, the United States will be either Stalinist or pancapitalist."

Another well-known philosopher is François Sommer, who has actually installed his "participation" system in Sommer SA, a maker of floor coverings. Basically, the Sommer system is a profit-sharing arrangement where employees receive an annual bonus depending on a complex calculation of results. In recent years, employees have received amounts equal to three to four months' salary—generally totaling more than was paid out to shareholders.

Sales and profits have grown sharply since the system was introduced in 1961, a fact that the company attributes to participation.
Gilbert Collet, secretary of the company, told me: "We have the
idea that if everybody works more intelligently, results will be
better."

The "participation" question has also become a common
topic of discussion in other contexts. Various groups of management people, such as the Center of Young Managers (Centre des
Jeunes Dirigeants d'Entreprise), have taken positions more or less
favoring employee participation in decison-making.[56] Jean-
Jacques Servan-Schreiber, author of The American Challenge, took,
in a manifesto issued in connection with his entry into politics, an
unusually liberal stance on the matter, especially regarding moves
"which effectively disassociate property from power." Management power, in his system, would be held by an "electoral college" representing shareholders, employees, and managers.[57] Another treatise on "participation," published in 1968, was notable, not for the boldness of its ideas (which were decidedly vague
and unoriginal), but because it was written by two prominent
industrialists, Marcel Demonque and J. Y. Eichenberger, and because it dared to regard the notion of "democracy" in an enterprise with some favor.[58]

Although all this activity suggests an increasingly widespread
support for the idea of participation, most of it does not go very
far, and little of it has had any concrete significance. And, notably, there is hardly any interest in matching the content of the
various manifestos, programs, and abstract philosophies to the real
needs of the workers. When I asked Marcel Loichot if he had
looked into the psychological bases of alienation, he replied, "Yes,
but they are only jokes." One reason for this is the relatively undeveloped state of psychology and sociology in France. J. D. Rey-
naud, a professor of work sociology, explained to me: "There are
practically no consultants in this area in France, and they are
mostly concentrating on outmoded technical aspects of management." Denis Cepède, of the National Information Center for
Industrial Productivity (CNIPE), pointed to another factor:
"Only in recent years has sociology ceased to be a branch of
philosophy. Sociologists are usually either in the service of the

employers or rather abstract ideologists. So the unions are very suspicious—for them, a sociologist is either someone who doesn't meet their needs or an adversary."

Therefore, something new was added to the discussion with the appearance of a book called *Autogestion* (Self-Management) in late 1970, by Daniel Chauvey, which has stimulated considerable interest among managers, labor leaders, and impartial observers in France. Chauvey had the unusual notion of forming a philosophy of participation, based on modern findings of organization sociologists, with an ideological context. The basic idea is relatively simple: "To work in a more human manner and profiting from the intellectual potential of each participant. . . . The humanization of work must also pay its own way."[59] The objects of attack are "the robotization of work" and the resulting necessity for workers, on entering their place of work, to shed their intelligence in "the checkroom for ideas."[60] Chauvey is extremely familiar with modern management thinkers in the United States, Britain, and other countries.

Chauvey (a pseudonym—the author works in the personnel section of one of France's major industrial enterprises) explained to me that his fundamental idea was "to combine several scientific disciplines in an effort to adapt work activity to man—not the other way around." It is thus necessary to change, not only authority structures, but technology. "The present ideal," he said, "is to have machines which are extremely sophisticated but which can be operated by an ape. I say it would be more desirable to design the machines which demand the *maximum* of intelligence from the worker. Thus work would be much more than merely a conditioned reflex." He concedes, however, that "we are only at the beginning of this movement." Chauvey insists that his ideas would be most applicable in a system of "democratic socialism" (meaning neither centralized state socialism nor free-enterprise capitalism). That is arguable, but in any case the Chauvey ideas introduce some fresh thinking into the French "participation" discussion.

On the whole, one must conclude that the debate over "participation" in France has been extremely interesting and varied, intellectually stimulating, and productive of very little in the way of concrete results. However, the French experience has valuable lessons for other countries.

The most important is that the brutal alienation of workers under modern industrial capitalism is not a fantasy dreamed up by ivory-tower philosophers and social thinkers, nor is the deep need to exercise one's intelligence, to participate in decision-making, to carry responsibility, and to develop personally merely an abstract prescription turned out by intellectuals and irrelevant for ordinary workers. Astonishingly, the workers behaved in the completely spontaneous nature of their revolt and the nature of their demands exactly as they might be expected to, according to the theories of modern organizational science. This fact is of immense significance—not only for France, but for every other industrialized country.

Moreover, the events of May showed that a surface calm can conceal explosive hostility toward prevailing autocratic social structures, and that the built-up demands for democracy can explode at any time. Stagnation cannot be mistaken for stability.

Although the euphoric hopes of the rebels ("Tomorrow will be different,"[61] wrote one union leader) were not fulfilled, it is clear that if the desire for democratic rights is not satisfied, another explosion may take place. A 1971 poll among workers showed, even though there is nothing in the present picture to suggest that "self-management" might be a near-term realistic possibility, 44 percent of those asked rated it either "very important" or "rather important."[62] Some small changes have taken place, and there is a slowly spreading realization that more change must come. Whether rigidly bureaucratized France can accommodate large-scale change is an open question. But other societies, which face the same basic problems and have less restrictive social structures, have a great opportunity to learn from France and to make the needed changes—without any "events of May."

X. THE U.S.A.: SCIENTISTS

In general, the industrial democratic systems that we have been examining can be categorized under "representative democracy," in which the average member of the organization is rather remote from the real strings of power. In these cases, even where the desire to achieve real democracy is quite strong, there has been no appreciable effort to learn why some organizations work better than others, how the less successful might be made more successful, and how, if at all, the concept of democracy might fit in. All of the methods discussed so far give something to both employees and companies and are therefore better than nothing. But they also have defects, and most of the defects can be traced to the lack of attention to the real nature of organizations.

When we turn to the United States, we see an entirely different picture. There is a vast reservoir of knowledge of organizations. (Any group of human beings united to pursue common goals can be classed as an "organization"—a church, school, club, political party, labor union, and so on, though we are specifically concerned with work organizations.) During the past three or four decades the study of organizations by behavioral scientists has made enormous strides, and since the 1950s the knowledge has been seeping slowly into the management field. Previously, psychologists in industry were customarily restricted to technical chores such as testing, recruiting, and thinking up "human rela-

tions" gimmicks with which to create spurious feelings of belongingness among employees. And "organization specialists" were
people who concentrated on reshaping organization charts to
create clearer and more effective lines of authority, more or less
within the limits of traditional bureaucratic thinking. In recent
years, this has been changing, as the behavioral scientists have
increasingly persuaded managers to think of organizations in
terms of their human components. In 1957, a book called *Personality and Organization,* by Chris Argyris, a wide-ranging thinker
trained in both economics and psychology, gave many businessmen their first glimpse of the behavioral sciences and how they
might be useful in understanding work organizations.[1] Since then,
the teachings of Abraham Maslow, Douglas McGregor, Frederick
Herzberg, Rensis Likert, Warren Bennis, Louis Davis, and others
have become well known among managers interested in making
their organizations work better. There are departments of "organizational science" at a number of universities, and the literature on
the subject is enormous. There is a wealth of knowledge of organizations unmatched in any other country. And a great deal of it
suggests that democratic management methods are not only possible but are far superior to traditional authoritarian methods (although some of the aforementioned experts reject any connection with so shocking a concept as democracy). In a sense, then,
the potential for industrial democracy is thus far richer in America
than in any of the other countries we have examined.

However, there is only limited interest in industrial democracy
in America, and the implications of organizational studies for democracy are rarely discussed in business circles.

This anomalous situation cannot be expected to endure for
long, particularly in view of (1) the widespread and increasing
dissatisfaction with industrial capitalism and its damaging effects
on society and (2) the inescapably positive implications of the
organizational studies for industrial democracy. It is difficult to
see how a convergence of these two trends can be avoided—and
when the converging takes place, the impact could be enormous.

A central preoccupation of most of these organizational experts
is the accepted view of an organization. There is a certain classical picture of work organizations that most people involved, em-

ployees and employers alike, carry around with them, consciously or unconsciously. It is a highly formalized, static, and stable pattern. The function of every typist, welder, truck driver, salesman, supervisor, copy chief, draftsman, office boy, financial vice president, and everybody else is precisely spelled out, and his or her place in the hierarchy is located with great exactness. The requirements and limitations of each job—and often a single best way of doing the job—are rigorously defined. There is a precise order about who gives orders to whom, who has to obey, and who is responsible for what. The decision-making power is concentrated heavily at the top and is carefully filtered down through the lower levels according to formalized rules. The structure becomes pyramidal, because the higher we ascend the fewer people we find on each level giving orders to those below and accepting them from above. Close calculations can be made of how much of every needed commodity—raw materials, electric power, human man-hours—are needed to produce the desired output of goods or services. Things get done because there are rewards when orders are obeyed and punishments when they are not. The members of the organization are willing to work for the goals of the enterprise —producing the product or service and turning a profit—because of the lure of the rewards and the fear of the punishments. All these principles are necessary to insure stability, efficiency, and continuity.

The picture is similar to a machine. All the parts are designed to fit into the total apparatus and to produce a certain result. Moreover, it can be pictorially represented, on an organization chart.

This classical picture is heavily influenced by, among other things, two notable ingredients of industrial capitalism: bureaucracy, as described by Max Weber, and Frederick Taylor's scientific management. To some extent, the picture is not only accurate but essential. Large organizations could scarcely function without the division of tasks, allocation of responsibilities, and clarity of power lines it contains. As more than one theoretician has pointed out, the formalized bureaucracy is a marvelous discovery.

However, the picture also has some grave defects—and all the more grave for their not being generally recognized.

No organization is a static, mechanical, closed system, and no organization therefore runs according to a fixed, formal pattern. An organization is an open system and constantly changing, whether anyone wants change or not, and change is taking place with increasing rapidity. Today's organization chart is tomorrow's meaningless pattern of empty squares. Changes occur because of changes in the outside environment, the people involved, markets, technology, and over-all values of society. Moreover, power relationships develop in peculiar ways. A man nominally on a lower level somehow gains enormous influence in a manner unforeseen on the chart. Bosses who are supposed to possess unquestioned power lose control over their subordinates. Subsystems that are supposed to be separate come to grate against each other. The supposedly exact requirements of jobs get blurred, and unexpected phenomena arise—jealousies, internal politicking, and subtle sabotage. The goals of the organization get lost in bitter power conflicts and adherence to empty routines. The bureaucracy, which is supposed to be an instrument to promote efficiency through formalized rules, threatens to suffocate under the pressure of these very rules.

Obviously, it is a case of poor design. And the weakest part of the design is the assumption that the goals of the organization and of all the individual members harmonize exactly. The company's goals can be stated simply: the production of washing machines, insurance policies, or whatever, at a satisfactory profit. The individual's goals have been defined mostly in the form of money. The individual members thus fulfill their prescribed roles in the organization, and the organization pays them. The goals of both sides are thus fulfilled.

It is, of course, all wrong. As we have seen, a key ingredient in the alienation of workers is a deep desire to exercise control over one's own work and to use one's thinking powers. A clue to just why this simple fact should have been so long overlooked, but is becoming ever more obvious, is offered in the writings of Abraham Maslow, a psychologist whose thoughts have become familiar to many managers.

Maslow's special contribution was his view of the human being as constantly working toward fulfillment: "Apparently we function best when we are striving for something that we lack, when we wish for something that we do not have, and when we organize our powers in the service of striving toward the gratification of that wish."[2] The object of the strivings varies according to circumstances. Maslow felt there was a "hierarchy of needs," and that an individual did not move up the hierarchy from one set of needs to another until the lower-level needs had been satisfied. According to the theory, in fact, one does not even become aware of the higher needs until one gets past the lower levels. The lowest needs are physiological, and it is difficult to feel other, higher needs until these are satisfied: "For our chronically and extremely hungry man, Utopia can be defined as a place where there is plenty of food. He tends to think that, if only he is guaranteed food for the rest of his life, he will be perfectly happy and will never want anything more."[3] Other needs, in ascending order, are the need for safety, the need for belongingness and love, the need for esteem and, finally, the highest need of all, the need for "self-actualization," that is, for self-expression, creativity, and meeting challenges. The needs become progressively more complicated and more difficult to satisfy, but the need for self-actualization can be just as pressing, for the man who has arrived at that point, as hunger for someone still at the lowest level: "A musician must make music, an artist must paint, a poet must write, if he is to be ultimately at peace with himself. What a man *can* be, he *must* be."[4]

Maslow did not claim that the "need hierarchy" was an absolute dogma nor that the same needs exist for everyone in precisely the same way. He worked out the theory on the basis of his observations as a practicing psychologist. He had been particularly struck by the very solid nature of the higher needs and the personal damage that could result from being deprived at those levels: "I have seen a few cases in which it seemed to me that the pathology (boredom, loss of zest in life, self-dislike, general depression of the bodily functions, steady deterioration of the intellectual life, of tastes, etc.) was produced in intelligent people leading stupid lives in stupid jobs."[5] He was uncertain how common the potential for self-actualization might be, but suspected that it was "a widespread and perhaps universal human tendency."[6] It does not show up so often, however, because most people have not yet progressed to that level: "It is as if the average citizen is satisfied perhaps 85 percent in his physiological needs, 70 percent in his safety needs, 50 percent in his love needs, 40 percent in his self-esteem needs, and 10 percent in his self-actualization needs."[7]

The Maslow theory, while no doubt arguable in its details, goes a long way in explaining some common attitudes to work and some of the malfunctioning of organizations. In the early days of industrial capitalism, when physiological needs were paramount, workers were grateful to have only those needs satisfied—and their main interest was in the money needed to do that. As time has passed, workers have been able to climb the hierarchy of needs and are increasingly dissatisfied with a system adapted only to their low-level needs. Although the goals of the organization and those of the members meshed nicely before, they have begun to veer apart. To stick to Maslow's theoretical structure, we might say that modern industry is satisfying the physiological needs, the safety needs, and in some cases even the belongingness needs, but falls down badly when it comes to the needs for self-esteem and self-actualization. As the lower-level needs get even further satisfied, pressure to obtain fulfillment on the higher needs will surely increase steadily.

Maslow formulated his theory without any special knowledge of business organizations. He was primarily concerned with describing human nature as he saw it. Obviously, his view is an optimistic one. But coincidentally, this same kind of optimism is a central ingredient in the idea of democracy—the idea that judgment and ability to carry responsibility are not concentrated in an elite group but are well diffused throughout the population.

This view of the human being has not, however, had much of a chance in industry, because the notion of the worker as interested only in immediate, short-range satisfactions of his most pressing needs for food and other basics—and thus money—became so firmly implanted in the early days of industrial capitalism. Moreover, they were heavily reinforced by the scientific management of Taylor, whose gloomy view of human nature was quite the opposite of Maslow's. As we have seen, Taylor thought of man as incurably stupid and innately incapable of even understanding his work, much less of attacking it in a self-actualizing or creative fashion. Thus was set in motion a kind of self-fulfilling prophecy. Workers were treated as though they had no thinking ability whatever and would work only for the money—which was the only reward offered them. Eventually, however much thinking ability workers might have and however strong their desire to use it, the whole system became constructed to fit the original conception of human nature—it offers no interest or challenge whatever, and no thinking person would even dream of doing the work unless he were bribed, and even then only reluctantly. The circle is closed, the original concept is strengthened, and the money-instrumental view of work becomes ever stronger. The typical worker is lazy, unimaginative, and lacking in initiative and cannot be depended on. Daniel Katz and Robert Kahn, co-authors of a major work on organizations, point out that the fault lies not in the workers, but in the faulty construction of the organization: "The uniformity, the routinization, and the fragmentation of behavior run counter not only to the factor of individual differences but to the needs of people for self-determination, spontaneity, accomplishment, and the expression of individual skills and talents."[8]

The Maslow theories have had considerable impact on subsequent thinkers. Building partly on those thoughts, Douglas McGregor—who was a psychologist as well as a business consultant—described two quite opposite management philosophies representing two quite opposite views of human nature. Pointing out that all managers apply a "theory" of management whether they know it or not, he called the two extremes of philosophies "Theory X" and "Theory Y." Theory X assumes: "The average human being has an inherent dislike of work and will avoid it if he can. . . . Because of this . . . most people must be coerced, controlled, directed, threatened with punishment to get them to put forth adequate effort. . . . The average human being prefers to be directed, wishes to avoid responsibility, has relatively little ambition, wants security above all."[9] McGregor emphasized that this glum view of man was not imaginary, but was extremely popular among U.S. managers, and was hurting employees as well as the organizations. One obvious fault was that the bribes offered by managements had little or no connection with the worker's needs during his work life: "Most of these rewards can be used for satisfying his needs *only when he leaves the job.*" In many cases, "*work is perceived as a kind of punishment.*"[10] The refusal of managements to recognize the higher-level needs of workers must inevitably affect their behavior, both on and off the job.

Theory Y is at the opposite end of the spectrum. It assumes that work is not an abnormal activity, separate from the rest of life, but "as natural as play or rest." It is not true that a human being will work only because of a promise of reward or threat of punishment—he is prepared to accept responsibility, indeed, to seek responsibility, and exercise self-control "in the service of objectives to which he is committed." His most important goals are "the satisfaction of ego and self-actualization needs." The ability to "exercise a relatively high degree of imagination, ingenuity, and creativity" is far more widespread among the population than is generally supposed, but the capacities of the average employee are lamentably underutilized.[11]

These two theories were not supposed to represent the only two schools of thought in management, only rough outlines of two extremes. But McGregor's construction was the first to stimulate wide interest among U.S. businessmen that showed how traditional management methods, largely based on strict authority (Theory X), might be bad for both workers and companies. It had doubtless always been easy to see that heavy authoritarianism was unpleasant for workers. McGregor made the very important point that it was also bad for the companies, since they were wasting important potential assets—employees' intelligence and commitment—which they were in fact paying for, a mistake they would never make in the case of, say, a machine tool or a computer.

The central feature of Theory Y was its harmonization of the real goals of the individual and the company: "Its purpose is . . . to create a situation in which a subordinate can achieve his own goals *best* by directing his efforts toward the objectives of the enterprise."[12] Along the way, McGregor made some other important points. For one thing, the view of an organization as a predesigned machine to which people must adapt is a mistake. He wrote: "The conception of an organization plan as a series of predetermined 'slots' into which individuals are selectively placed denies the whole idea of integration."[13] The organization should be often adapted to the needs of the individual, not the other way around. Moreover, he bitterly attacked the idea, absurd though nonetheless widespread, that the manager is a unique, superior being. He described a typical manager's attitude: "He sees himself as a member of a small elite endowed with unusual capacities, and the bulk of the human race as rather limited. He believes also that most people are inherently lazy, prefer to be taken care of, desire strong leadership."[14]

McGregor's ideas were rather novel when his book, *The Human Side of Enterprise*, was first published in 1960, and that volume has been widely read by thoughtful—and successful—businessmen since. Robert Townsend, former president of Avis Rent-a-Car and author of the witty and irreverent *Up the Organization*, avowed that McGregor's book was one of the two best management books he had ever read, and his comments clearly reflect the deeply humanistic McGregor viewpoint and the distrust of confining, rigid, authoritarian management methods. In describing his success in switching Avis from a thirteen-year loss record into a career of fat profits, Townsend avowed: "If I had anything to do with this, I ascribe it all to my application of Theory Y."[15] One of his most radical moves was to depend on the employees. "The result of our outmoded organizations," he wrote, "is that we're still acting as if people were uneducated peasants. . . . All you have to do is look around you to see that modern organizations are only getting people to use about 20 per cent—the lower fifth—of their capacities."[16] He believes in avoiding bureaucratic entanglements and encouraging people to make their own decisions: "All decisions should be made as low as possible in the organization."[17]

One of Townsend's central points is his acceptance of McGregor's idea that his philosophy cannot be considered to be merely a set of tricks to be sprinkled around the company where needed, like so much "good management" fertilizer, but that, as McGregor said, "it is a strategy—a way of managing people."[18] The basic principles, once accepted, must inevitably permeate the entire organization and cannot be confined to small parts of it. Other experts on these modern approaches agree. Harold Rush, a brilliant young psychologist at the National Industrial Conference

Board, wrote in a survey of behavioral sciences in industry: "Because of the overlapping, reinforcing, and interrelated nature of the system's components, development or improvement of the organization is geared to improve all parts of the system."[19]

Numerous theoreticians have expanded and elaborated on such ideas in order to illuminate further the functioning—and malfunctioning—of organizations. One of the most rigorous in his approach is Chris Argyris, who has analyzed in depth the "illnesses" of organizations and how they can be cured. Like others, he traces the cause of the illnesses to the familiar authoritarian methods, the denial of the workers' needs to exercise their own initiative and intelligence, and the consequent split between the goals of the organization and those of the individual. He writes: "The strategy creates a complex of organizational demands that tend to require individuals to experience dependence and submissiveness and to utilize few of their relatively peripheral abilities."[20] The more management insists on strict obedience to orders and avoidance of thinking on the part of employees, the worse the situation can become. The employee reaction is quite understandable: "The employees perceive their apathy and noninvolvement as enhancing their individual effectiveness and, therefore, the effectiveness of the organization. Management tends to diagnose the same apathy as leading—if it has not already done so, to organizational decay."[21] Even while carefully removing any element of the work that might make it worth the attention of employees, managements still tend to expect the workers to become enthusiastic about it and, when this result is not reached, blame the workers for being lazy and unwilling to work at all without the customary threats, fears, sanctions, and rewards—a neat self-fulfilling prophecy. Under the circumstances, employees often agree wholeheartedly with this analysis. Having themselves insisted on employee apathy, management is stuck with the results: "A hostile employee will tend to resist any new responsibilities toward, as well as cooperating with, the organization."[22]

Argyris suggests that the ideal evolution will be toward what he calls a "mix model" organization, in which far greater flexibility and adaptability will be built in, so that the structure can change in line with changing external or internal demands. Such organizations can much more effectively operate in terms of their own goals as well as the goals of the employees for psychological growth, creativity, learning, and self-actualization.

Though all this detailed study of organizations has immensely increased knowledge of how they work, one of the results has been to reveal a vastly more complicated picture than one might have expected. Edgar H. Schein, a social psychologist specializing in organizations, points out: "The major impact of many decades of research has been to vastly complicate our models of man, of organizations, and of management strategies. Man is a more complex individual than rational-economic, social, or self-actualizing man. Not only is he more complex within himself . . . but he is also likely to differ from his neighbor in the patterns of his own complexity."[23] Therefore, no two organizations work in quite the same way—regardless of a similarity in organization charts—and all organizations are constantly changing character.

Organizations are more complex than is ordinarily believed, and the more complex an organization is, the more difficult it is to deal with. This picture of complexity, and the consequent complex network of employee needs, has met with much resistance among managers who believe that paying attention to such nice nuances is a luxury they can ill afford in the high-pressure frenzy of running their companies. Such attitudes are in great part responsible for the present ills of industrial capitalism; the organization is complex anyway, and hoping it is not only causes problems.

Advanced theoretical studies of organizations have been accompanied by studies of how they can be applied to reality.

As we saw in an earlier chapter, a first wave of organizational improvement was the "human relations" movement, based on the inadequate notion that conditions could be improved through a superficial manipulation of interpersonal relations in order to make employees "feel good."

The key difference between the "human relations" approach and more advanced techniques is the sharply different view of human abilities involved in the two methods. As management consultant Raymond Miles points out, when the "human relations" philosophy permits employees to participate in decision-making, it is only to "improve morale and satisfaction"—there is little faith that employees might actually have anything useful to contribute or that "participation may be useful for its own sake." In contrast to this "pseudoparticipation" technique, the more sophisticated manager strives to "continually expand subordinates' responsibility and self-direction up to the limits of their abilities," because putting these abilities to work benefits both the organization and the employees.[24] Naturally, only managers who are convinced that their subordinates' abilities are of value are likely to adopt such methods.

Thus more realistic approaches, based on the behavioral sciences and a more hard-headed view of human beings in organizations, have made steady progress, beginning in the late 1940s. Going far beyond a mere revision of an organization's social characteristics, practicing psychologists have been developing methods to attack the troubles at the source. If the monotony and boredom attached to limited, repetitive tasks was preventing workers from becoming involved in their work, and if they were not only able but also willing to carry more responsibility, a solution might be to overhaul the nature of the jobs themselves. Jobs were made, not more simple, but more complicated, through job enlargement, which gives the worker a broader range of tasks; job rotation, in which workers shift from job to job; and job enrichment, in which the job is not only varied, but requires more judgment from the worker. In a sense, this movement is retrogressive. Joan Doolittle, an organization research specialist at Corning Glass, described the approach to me: "The taylorites did everything they could to make work boring. We hope to go the other way."

The most prominent innovator in this area—indeed, the best-known living work psychologist in the United States—is Frederick Herzberg, who was one of the first to make a comprehensive effort to learn the real needs of workers and then to develop practical methods based on his studies.

In the 1950s Herzberg and his colleagues started with an exhaustive study of prior research into what "motivates" people to work. Concluding that the previous research gave no more than a few clues to the truth, Herzberg launched his own experimental study of the subject. Several hundred accountants and engineers were asked to tell "stories" about when they felt "exceptionally good or . . . exceptionally bad" about their jobs.

Analyzing the results, Herzberg, as he reports in the book *Motivation to Work*, divided job factors into "satisfiers" and "dissatisfiers." The former, also known as "motivation factors," include achievement, recognition, the nature of the work itself, responsibility, and advancement—the very same type of self-expression, creativity, and personal growth that other theorists and philosophers had pinpointed as key basic human needs. The latter group included such elements of, not the job, but the job environment—company policy and administration, technical supervision, salary, interpersonal relations with supervision, and physical working conditions. Although these features do not promote satisfaction, they can cause dissatisfaction if they are bad enough. Herzberg therefore called them "hygiene" factors (because hygiene cannot cure diseases, it can only prevent them from arising). A raise in salary may provide a temporary thrill; it will not transform a dissatisfied employee into a satisfied one.

Herzberg's theory thus provides empirical support for the notion, advanced by Maslow among others, that a need for self-actualization is basic and nearly universal, but Herzberg places other factors such as salary, working conditions, and interpersonal relations not only on a lower level but in a different category altogether. Moreover, those factors are weaker. Satisfied workers are satisfied about very different, and stronger, factors than the things that trouble dissatisfied workers.

If the theory is valid, it points to a definite course of action, according to Herzberg: "First, jobs must be restructured to increase to the maximum the ability of workers to achieve goals meaningfully related to the doing of the job."[25]

The principle has, in fact, been successfully put into operation in a number of companies. The best-known is American Telephone & Telegraph, which Herzberg invariably mentions in describing his technique. The first department selected for experimentation was one in which a number of girls were employed in answering letters from shareholders. Robert Ford, the Herzberg disciple at AT&T who has supervised the program, told me: "We were having excessive turnover, and we saw what was going wrong. These people were not really corresponding with the shareholders—they were only putting together standard paragraphs and signing the assistant treasurer's name." Therefore, the girls were told to write the letters the way they wanted, to use the standard paragraphs only if they thought them fully appropriate, and to check their own work. The results were astounding—turnover and absenteeism dropped, morale improved, and production increased markedly. The program was extended to other departments, even to some in which "enrichment" potentials would seem rather slim. One was a key-punch operation, where each of fourteen girls was customarily being given one-fourteenth of each job that came in. This was changed; each girl was given an entire assignment—a payroll for a single department, for example —and given the opportunity to check her own work. Again, the results were extremely good. In these programs, employees are left free to advance to the "whole job" concept at their own pace; if the new methods do not appeal to them, they are not required to adopt them.

The "job enrichment" thus added the "motivators" of achievement, responsibility, and interest in the job itself to the regular routine. Ford explained to me: "If you make a reasonable match between work and ability, everyone ought to be able to manage his own work."

The great significance of Herzberg's work was in demonstrating that the traditional bureaucratic and scientific management principles of work organization—which dictate that (1) each person's duties must be strictly defined and precisely separated from other layers in the hierarchy and (2) greatest efficiency is achieved when work is broken into the smallest possible pieces—are not necessarily universal truths but can be contravened to good effect. This revelation of the inadequacy of the orthodox view of organizations was of considerable value to subsequent researchers.

The Herzberg theories have some defects. The division of factors into two discrete categories is suspiciously neat, and Herzberg has been severely criticized for insisting on a complete separation between them. Victor Vroom points out that the methods used were questionable and that the findings are contradicted by other studies.[26] The Walker-Guest survey of auto workers, for instance, showed the boring, deadening, repetitive nature of the work to be a prime source of dissatisfaction, while the high pay and good

working conditions were virtually the only source of satisfaction—
which is not supposed to happen, according to Herzberg. It has
also been shown that Herzberg's downgrading of money is in
conflict with much other evidence.[27]

Moreover, even at best, the job enrichment brings about only
limited changes. The way in which the job is enriched is decided,
not by the employees concerned, but by the job enrichment experts. There is a fixed ceiling to the enrichment process, and
when the ceiling is reached, it is finished. There is no provision
for workers to discuss matters and propose improvements. Herzberg is against group action: Each individual is to be dealt with
individually. He is also against "participation." He told me:
"There is a danger you will participate beyond your level of competence." It is easy to suspect, in fact, that Herzberg's popularity
among U.S. businessmen depends to some extent on his method's
very limited objectives. It satisfies somewhat employee needs for
autonomy, but it is "safe"—it does not upset anybody, and it
does not rock the boat. And the classification of salary as a non-
motivator is clearly a welcome innovation for some businessmen.
Above all, it does not alter the traditional stiff hierarchical structure. Herzberg has written: ". . . the authoritarian pattern of
American industry will continue despite the propaganda for a
more democratic way of life."[28]

One reason for the restricted nature of the method is that
Herzberg himself, after having done his pioneering work in improving work, has not attempted to improve or develop his
methods. In recent years, he has concentrated primarily on his
appearances before management groups—a kind of globe-trotting
missionary preaching the motivation-hygiene gospel with great wit
and dynamism. In these appearances he tends to take a rather
dogmatic view, implying that research carried out since his own
has been on the whole quite unnecessary. After one of his lectures in Copenhagen, a Danish observer wrote: "Frederick Herzberg did not admit that there remain any unsolved problems worth
recognizing."[29]

Herzberg has written another book, *Work and the Nature of
Man* (1968). Essentially a restatement of his earlier work, it
cautiously intimates that something beyond a limited reform of
individual jobs might be in order. He writes: "The primary func-

tion of any organization, whether religious, political or industrial, should be to implement the needs for man to enjoy a meaningful existence."[30] He also mentions that jobs "must be open . . . to allow for possible growth." His follower, Robert Ford, has always maintained an open mind: "We do not yet adequately understand the great value of work to a human being. Surely it is not a constant; it changes as the society changes."[31]

In any case, Herzberg deserves a good deal of credit for having made solid progress in increasing worker satisfaction and organizational effectiveness, which has been of great use to subsequent researchers. His tireless vigor in promoting his ideas has also been of value, since to many managers they are still considered, as one British observer put it, "revolutionary."[32] It is only too bad that Herzberg stopped so soon; maybe he ought to work out a job enrichment program for himself.

Organizational thinkers, who have made further progress in essentially the same direction—that is, getting a smoother-working organization through integrating the goals of the organization and the individual members—have, for the most part, focused on groups. It is sometimes believed this is unhealthy, or perhaps unethical, because groups create pressure for conformity. But all organizations are composed of groups, and a group that works well would seem preferable to one that works badly. An individual unquestionably stands a greater chance of realizing his creative potential in an effective group than in one that is full of conflict.

A leading innovator along these lines is Rensis Likert, who was director of the Institute for Social Research at the University of Michigan for nearly twenty-five years before he stepped aside in 1970. Likert is, in a way, the Picasso of organizational research—he has been a prominent and respected figure for several decades, and he has never ceased making valuable contributions.

Likert agrees with most other work-reform experts that the central, and usually overlooked, elements for an individual in his work are the familar opportunities for self-actualization. He writes: "To be highly motivated, each member of the organization must feel that the organization's objectives are of significance and that his own particular task contributes in an indispensable manner to the organization's achievement of its objectives. He should see his role as difficult, important, and meaningful. . . . When jobs do not meet this specification they should be reorganized so that they do."[33] The problem is to integrate these needs with the goals of the organization: "The objectives of the entire organization and of its component parts must be in satisfactory harmony with the relevant needs and desires of the great majority, if not all, of the members of the organization and of the persons served by it."[34]

And Likert believes that all this can best be accomplished through building "well-knit, effectively functioning work groups"[35] that do not merely receive job instructions imposed from above, but are genuinely involved in the decision-making process: "Widespread use of participation is one of the more important approaches employed by the high-producing managers. . . . This use of participation applies to all aspects of the job and work, as, for example, in setting work goals and budgets, controlling costs, organizing the work, etc."[36]

The value of the participative approach has been demonstrated countless times. One classic description Likert cites concerns a clothing factory, in which cost-reduction changes were introduced in different ways in four roughly similar groups. In the first group, the production engineers designed the changes and instructed the group that they were to be introduced to. In the second group, management told the workers that costs had to be cut for competitive reasons, and asked that the group select from among themselves some machine operators who could be trained in new methods; these operators were then asked to contribute their own suggestions, many of which were adopted. The third and fourth groups went through much the same participative process, but all operators in the groups were included in the special discussions and the request for suggestions. Before-and-after figures showed that, in the first group, where the change was imposed autocratically, output dropped when the change was introduced and stabilized after thirty days at a level about 10 percent below normal. In the second group, which had partial participation, production rose after the change to about 10 percent above the prechange level; and in the total-participation groups, production rose by about 25 percent.[37]

Likert emphasizes that the participation must be authentic;

managements attempting to make employees "feel" they are participating, in order to gain acceptance of decisions already made, are playing a dangerous game. He warns against trying participation at all if the manager is not "genuinely interested in his subordinates' ideas and prepared to act upon them."[38] In addition to group decision-making, a main principle of good management is a "supportive attitude" toward subordinates—including confidence in their abilities, willingness to give them responsibility, and expectations of high performance from them.

The powerful potentials of cohesive, effective groups can be realized through what Likert calls the "linking-pin" structure. Instead of an organization chart consisting of a series of neat little isolated islands connected by lines, this flexible design is a jumble of overlapping circles and ovals, held together by "linking-pin" individuals who are members of various groups extending in all directions. If an organization is to work well, it must be possible for communication and influence to travel in all directions as constantly shifting conditions require. The "linking-pin" concept helps insure the necessary flexibility. In the ideal system, there would be no limits to this influence. Likert writes: "Every member of the organization would feel that the overlapping groups which link the organization together enable him satisfactorily to exert influence on all parts of the total organization."[39]

Likert admits that participative management methods are being used by relatively few managers, and that these methods are quite contrary to the customary hard-boiled management techniques in use. Yet he maintains that the few participative managements are the high-producing managers. This paradox exists because most managers start at the wrong point. In pursuing their goals—high productivity, low costs, low waste, low employee turnover—they are applying pressure on employees directly to achieve these goals, offering primarily economic rewards in return. But since this approach omits consideration of the real needs of employees, the result is the exertion of only minimal effort on the part of employees to reach the organization's goals.

Managements should therefore shift their attention to the "intervening variables"—that is, the most important factors by which management can affect the effectiveness of the organization. These intervening variables are the employee needs for self-expression and creativity. The key is to restructure management methods so that these needs and those of the organization are matched. A change in the causal variables (management behavior) will produce a change in the intervening variables (employee attitudes), and thence in the end-result variables (organizational success—e.g., profits, productivity, and so on). But it is no good attacking the intervening or the end-result variables directly; if management behavior doesn't change, nothing changes.

In the course of working out his management methods, Likert has developed a diagnostic tool that dramatically illustrates all this —it is a questionnaire which, when filled out by supervisory and management people, gives a "management style" profile of a company or department. It consists of about fifty items covering various aspects of the organization; each item offers four choices to describe the organization's customary practice, corresponding to four management styles: System 1 (exploitative-authoritative), System 2 (benevolent-authoritative), System 3 (consultative), and System 4 (participative-group). The questionnaire choices under System 1 describe management's feelings about subordinates as "Have no confidence and trust in subordinates"; motivations relied upon are "Physical security, economic needs, and some use of the desire for status"; upward communication is "Very little." The same items under System 4 are "Complete confidence and trust in all matters"; "Full use of economic, ego, and other major motives, as, for example, motivational forces arising from group goals"; and "A great deal" of upward communication. The System 1 to System 4 range of management styles is a continuum ranging from the highly authoritarian to the highly democratic, and the person filling out the form can pick out a rather accurate description of the organization in question, which will result in a number somewhere between 1.0 and 4.0.[40]

Likert says he has refined the form over a period of many years and has tried it out on several hundred managers. There is a very clear-cut correlation between management styles and effectiveness: "Those firms or plants where System 4 is used show high productivity, low scrap loss, low costs, favorable attitudes, and excellent labor relations. The converse tends to be the case for companies or departments whose management system is well toward System 1."[41] A company can be moved up or down the scale, but System 4, which includes group decision-making and interlocking linking-pin groups, is "appreciably more complex than the usual vertical structure . . . and requires greater learning and skills to operate it well."[42] Moreover, it requires considerable time before the changes in management behavior work through the intervening variables to show up in the end-result variables. On the other hand, a shift to System 1 cannot only be done quickly, but it can even yield some immediate, though misleading, results. This can be done by tightening up the organization, installing strict disciplinary measures, and de-emphasizing supportive management techniques—which can produce some quick profit gains but at the same time do irreparable long-term damage. It is small wonder that most managers, who after all have to answer to *their* superiors, prefer to stick to the "safe," orthodox management systems. Likert writes: "Orthodox ways of management, including *laissez-faire*, are readily recognized. The unorthodox styles of the most productive managers are . . . difficult to understand and to describe."[43]

All the work-reform theoreticians have much in common in that they aim at making much more use of employee abilities than is usually done and that this helps both the employee and the organization. But it may be said that Herzberg and Likert represent the two main approaches to work reform in America today. Herzberg's method depends on a precise study by management of individual jobs and a consequent repatterning of the jobs—also by management. Although the objective is to make the jobs more "complete" and thus more interesting, the employee himself is not involved in the change process, and nothing much is changed in the organization.

The Likert approach is much more "open-ended." The assumption is that there is no fixed limit to the abilities of individuals, that managers should encourage subordinates to use the full range of their abilities, and that managers should "establish a mechanism through which employees can help to set the high-level goals which the satisfaction of their own needs requires."[44] Job reform is not only a restructuring of individual jobs but drastically alters traditional methods by diffusing power throughout an organization. It is thus desirable and essential to work on the entire organization at once: "Every aspect of a managerial system is related to every other part and interacts with it."[45]

When we examine this approach more closely, we see that it is, in fact, democracy in the same sense as that word may be applied to political systems. Political scientist Dennis Thompson points out that an essential element in the concept of citizenship democracy is "a commitment to the presuppositions of autonomy and improvability." Thus it is assumed that each individual is capable of independent decision-making: "The presupposition of autonomy, treating each citizen as the best judge of his own interest, places few restrictions on what counts as being in a citizen's interest."[46] Moreover, "the presupposition of improvability . . . is an essential companion of the presupposition of autonomy." Put into business terms, this would mean that employees must be assumed to be capable of acting independently, and that if their decision-making talents are deficient, then they are susceptible to improvement—in this case by the application of proper management techniques.

The fact that democracy is completely compatible with the efficient functioning of an organization is of vast importance in any discussion of industrial democracy, since the road to democratization is completely in line with solid capitalistic principles. Though U.S. management thinkers do not commonly speak in these terms, the connection is clear and well recognized.

I pointed out to Rensis Likert that his "linking-pin" concept, in which influence can be exerted from any one part of the organization to any other, would bring about a continuum of power from the lowest levels of the organization to the highest, that this was what I called democracy, and wasn't this a revolutionary idea? He replied: "Oh sure, it's more than that. Getting everyone involved in the decisions is the whole idea. Every civilized nation will have to move towards that ideal, since it's the only effective system in today's world."

XI. BRITAIN: PROMISE

While we are examining advances in the study of group behavior, it is relevant to look briefly at Great Britain, since it is
there that some of the most advanced methods for restructuring
work groups have been developed.

The institution that has been most heavily, and over the longest
period of time, involved in this work is the Tavistock Institute
of Human Relations in London, which carries out various clinical
and research projects and which is especially noted for its work
with groups.

One of the earliest Tavistock projects in industry was its collaboration with Glacier Metal, a company headquartered in a
London suburb and making antifriction metals and industrial
bearings. *The Changing Culture of a Factory*, by Eliot Jaques
(Glacier's medical director at the time), which chronicles the project's beginnings in the early postwar period, has become something of a classic in the field of organizational studies.

Glacier was a bit atypical when Tavistock went to work. The
managing director, Wilfred Brown, held distinctly unusual ideas
about industrial management. He very much believed in democratizing his company; though he did not quite know how to go
about it, he assumed that more democracy would mean a less
profitable operation. Some of the more interesting developments
were signs that this assumption is not necessarily correct. At one

point, the company decided to set aside a sum of money to offset the expected costs of abolishing time clocks and instituting a paid sick-leave program, and was astonished to learn that neither absenteeism nor lateness increased. Though the company had made other steps toward a system based on justice and fairness for all employees, Brown sensed that there were some malfunctions, and this led to the Tavistock connection.

Thus when a team of eight psychologists from Tavistock moved in in 1948, for a stay of what was to extend over several years, they agreed that "a remarkably sound morale existed in the firm."[1] This atmosphere greatly facilitated the team's incessant probings, during which it uncovered an abundance of valuable information on the curious workings of power and authority in an industrial setting. The team attacked any problem workers and management agreed was worthwhile, and in almost every case it was discovered that the initial problem was not the prime difficulty at all, but that there were defects in the power machinery that badly needed attention. In a very real sense, the company thus underwent a deep and lengthy psychoanalysis.

One topic of investigation was a touchy pay dispute in a particular department. The workers wished to switch from incentive pay to a flat hourly wage. Management was agreeable, but no mutually satisfactory basis for change could be found. In the course of several months of abrasive worker-management discussions, in which each side sternly tested the motives of the other, it was discovered—with the help of the Tavistock people, who sat in on the discussions—that the true problems lay in the fact that the two sides simply did not trust each other, had no means for effective communication, and were seizing on irrelevant issues to start disputes. As a result, a shop council was set up in the department to remedy this fact. Almost in passing, the wage issue was settled to everyone's satisfaction. Jaques remarks: "What had begun as an issue to do with wages and methods of payment soon led into the complex ramifications of inter-group stresses so frequently tied up with wage questions."[2]

Perhaps the most significant project the team worked on was that involving the "Works' Council." In an effort to further democracy, the company had established this worker-management body to discuss questions of general company interest. It did not seem to be accomplishing much, and it was thought that some changes in its organization might help. But what resulted, after a lengthy and agonizing review of the body, was a thorough restructuring of the Council machinery. First, its "two-sided" nature, arising from the usual assumption that issues in companies have two sides—labor and management—was changed, to include office workers and to allow a more even representation from the entire company. More importantly, it was altered from a consultative body to one with real power to make final and binding decisions, which management would then carry out. Although this might seem a shockingly unconventional approach, it was in fact discovered that this actually strengthened management, since it began to receive authority from those below. As Jaques put it, the new arrangement "widened the scope of the sanctions given to those who occupy positions of authority, by providing them with the sanction of subordinates as well as superiors."[3]

Through years of painstaking work, the team helped the company sort out myriad hidden and half-recognized difficulties, to attempt to develop a truly democratic system, "a coherent executive system extending right through to the shop floor."[4] In the process, the inner workings of authority were clarified, making possible a more effective organization.

Glacier has since been taken over by a larger firm, but its unusual operating methods have been retained, apparently confirming management's faith that the bold efforts could work. Jacques wrote: "The new consultative system at Glacier may be regarded as an attempt to discover how far the extension of democratic rights inside an industrial organization can assist the ability of management to change."[5]

Many concepts that Tavistock took the lead in developing have, in later years, been widely and successfully applied in radically new types of industrial organizations. In a sense, the Tavistock work has been along the same lines as that done in the United States, described in the previous chapter and, like the U.S. research, much of it seeks ways to alter organizations so that the organizational goals and individual employees' goals can be efficiently integrated. However, the Tavistock work is in many ways more comprehensive and more advanced than work done in America.

A key Tavistock concept is the "socio-technical" view of organizations. Traditionally, industrial production is seen as a closed technical system, and human beings are forced to adapt to the requirements of the technology. A more advanced view is to look at, in Likert's expression, the "human organization" and to improve its functioning by altering management styles and personal interactions in the direction of more flexibility. This means that the organization must be seen as an "open system." But an even more flexible formulation is the "open socio-technical system," which considers neither the technical nor the human dimension as paramount, but instead focuses on the interaction between the two, in conjunction with considerations of effectiveness. It is conventionally accepted that there is one most effective way to construct any organization—based on scientific management principles and pyramidal bureaucracies. But when we see that the effectiveness of the organization can be damaged by poor coordination between the technical and the social elements, then it becomes apparent that the design of an organization—and of the technology—can be done in innumerable ways, and the most technically perfect may not be the best. As one Tavistock commentary puts it: "There exists an element of choice in work organizations."[6] This may seem an obvious idea, but it has been overlooked more often than not. In general, one can say that the Tavistock theories hold that organizations are most effective when they are based on small work groups that have a high degree of what might be called "democratic" status—i.e., independence and autonomy.

These ideas were extensively applied in a number of projects carried out in the British coal mines over some years, beginning in the early 1950s. The work was prompted by disappointments over two different kinds of change that had taken place: the nationalization of the coal mines in the early postwar period (expectations were that "management-worker relations would improve and that productivity would increase simply through change-over from private to public ownership"[7]—neither of which occurred) and rapid introduction of highly mechanized processes (which were not resulting in the expected productivity gains).

Traditionally, mining had been done through the "single-place method," whereby coal faces of six to eleven yards in length were worked by groups of six men working three shifts. All the men knew all the different tasks involved in working the coal, removing it, and advancing the roof supports, and each group of six men (members of each group selected their own coworkers) were paid according to productivity as a group. A technological advance was the "longwall method," in which straight walls eighty to one hundred yards long were worked with the help of complex equipment by a group of about forty men on the three shifts. Under the circumstances, some division of labor was inevitable, but the designers of the new arrangement neglected to consider the various choices available and broke the work up into the maximum number of jobs, in line with scientific management principles, on the orthodox assumption that the more highly specialized workers are and the more simple the tasks they are given, the more productive they become. Incentive pay rates were worked out for each individual job. In this case, as in so many other cases, the orthodox assumption was wrong; the work was made so simple-minded that the resulting boredom and noninvolvement of workers acted to damage productivity. And the full benefits of mechanization were therefore not being obtained.

In one experiment, the Tavistock team compared one unit using this conventionally organized longwall method with another in which the process was simply put in reverse—instead of each worker being assigned to a specific job, the group itself managed the entire job and assigned workers according to need and preference. Although not all workers knew all jobs, there was a sufficient mix of skills to allow workers to shift quite often. Specifically, the number of main tasks worked out climbed from 1.0 (in the conventional method) to 3.6 per person. Instead of being paid on individual piece rates, the workers were given productivity-linked wages, based on group performance.

The results were rather striking. The conventional unit registered only 78 percent of full potential productivity; the other unit registered 95 percent. Worker morale improved, partly because the workers could work together rather than separately, thus helping the formation of a cohesive team. Sickness absenteeism was 8.9 percent on the conventional unit, 4.6 percent on the other; absenteeism with no reason given was 4.3 percent on the conventional unit, more than ten times the 0.4 percent on the other. There were also other improvements, such as the virtual disappearance of the need for supervision in the improved unit, and more regular production.

The improvement in performance of the autonomous groups continued as long as it was possible to work a single coal face—up to two years. "At the end of this time," the authors write, "the groups were still growing in their capacity to adapt to changes in their task environments and to satisfy the needs of their members."[8] It is precisely this last point that is central to the success of the work rearrangement: The technical side of the system was reshuffled to suit the personal needs of the workers. The authors note: "It is the goodness of fit between the human work organization and the technological requirements that ultimately determines the efficiency of the whole system."[9]

The Tavistock researchers' startling findings, which went against all the preconceived ideas in industrial capitalism, were not enthusiastically received in British power circles. The coal mines (under state management) did not extend the methods, partly because they were too new and too difficult to understand and partly because, as one commentary put it, of "the threat to the larger social system of the implications of a thorough rational reform."[10]

The methods worked out by Tavistock have been applied in a few British companies (though they have been most widely used in Norway, as we shall see later). One wide-ranging series of projects took place in the refinery operations of Shell UK, after management became concerned about poor morale, poor labor relations, and similar problems. Tavistock helped the company give workers more decision-making power and more responsibility, and the results were generally gratifying. One account describes the changes made at the company's Teesport refinery: "Here the operators were trained to do four jobs, switching from one to the other, as the occasion demanded. In return they were given a pay structure that reflected these responsibilities."[11]

On the whole, however, considering the soundness of the techniques and the ample documentation of their effectiveness, the Tavistock methods have met with disappointingly poor acceptance in Britain. Michael Foster of Tavistock explained to me the reason why methods giving workers more freedom—which might, in conventional thinking patterns, be thought dangerous and inefficient—is basic and obvious: "The increased commitment is enough to offset any loss of efficiency." But it is difficult to get the point across in Britain, where traditional methods of designing production processes are considered the only workable ones. "Unfortunately," Foster observed, "jobs are now designed by engineers with no knowledge of social psychology." And perhaps the most important barrier, which scarcely fosters feelings of trust, is the strict British class system: "It's the structure in British industry—there is continuous fighting—a tremendous 'we and them' mentality."

It is perhaps ironic that the most popular work-rearrangement techniques among British managers are the "job enrichment" techniques developed in America, and it is these methods that progressively managed companies such as Imperial Chemical Industries use. The methods are far less comprehensive than those worked out by Tavistock—they do not involve workers in the alteration of jobs, they do not attempt to change the basic structure of the organization, and they customarily do not consider the role of technology at all.

Nevertheless, they can produce results, as is shown in a report on their use in ICI and other British companies.[12] In one controlled test, one group of salesmen was given enlarged responsibility and authority within certain limits, and a second group continued to operate in its normal fashion. After several months, the first group registered sales increases averaging 19 percent, while the second group experienced a decline of 5 percent.

The methods are intended to operate only within a limited scope; all the changes in the jobs are decided upon by management, and there is no attempt to build group cohesiveness or otherwise influence the over-all social system. As the report grimly explains the basic thinking behind the methods: "It seems that employees themselves are not in a good position to test out the validity of the boundaries of their jobs."

If there has not been much interest in Britain in democratizing industry through use of innovative management techniques, there exists a fairly constant discussion of the issue from a political point of view. This aspect of industrial democracy has a rich tradition in Britain, starting with the activities of G. D. H. Cole and others in the Guild Socialist movement of the 1920s. This movement took a dim view of *ownership* of industry, but favored worker *management* of industry. Cole wrote: "The proper sphere of the industrial organization is the control of production and of the producer's side of exchange."[13] Full-scale plans were drawn up for worker control of industry, particularly in the housing field, for the benefit not only of the workers but of society in general.

Not much came of the Guild Socialist philosophy, and for some decades the British trade union movement was deeply suspicious of anything that promised to suck them into a collaboration with the enemy, management. And this attitude has tended to be intensified by Britain's customarily stormy industrial relations climate.

It was thus something of a turning point when, in 1966, a report on industrial democracy by Jack Jones, assistant executive secretary of the Transport & General Workers' union, was published, in which a more positive view was taken. Jones declared: "I believe that spectacular increases in productivity could be achieved if the unions were given real powers and responsibilities in production, and if there were a strong determination to break through the barriers of outdated management and ownership." The main evil was seen to be "lazy and inept management," which was preventing the attainment of goals that both management and workers could agree on: "Good planning and efficient working methods plus realistic and high wage levels." Workers, through representation on boards and other types of involvement in decision-making, should be allowed to force backward managements to modernize their methods. Realistically, Jones considered that workers would need some training to be able to carry the additional responsibilities envisaged for them, but he emphasized that workers were basically able and willing to help improve conditions: "The most effective initiatives will come from the shop-floor." But Jones' plan was more than just a call for moves that would increase wages. It also aimed at promoting the psychological health of the individual: "There is a positive need to change the climate in industry to ensure that administration and manpower policies enable each person employed in industry to realize fully his individual potential."[14]

In 1967, the Labour Party adopted a resolution favoring industrial democracy, based on Jones' report. This served the purpose of getting the subject into the party's dialectical machinery, but the party, which was in power at the time, took no action before it was defeated in 1970. It was at one time considering a tough industrial relations bill (similar to the one subsequently passed by the Conservative government) to reduce industrial conflict, but gave only passing consideration to improving industrial relations through industrial democracy.

In the years since, there has been continuing debate, and a general sympathy for industrial democracy ideas may at times be perceived. In 1968, the first two volumes of a sociological study entitled *The Affluent Worker* appeared. This was a study of the attitudes of British workers toward politics and society as they were moving up from near the poverty line to something approaching middle-class prosperity. In the first volume, feelings about industrial democracy were studied, and most workers were decidedly cool to the idea: "In four out of five occupational groups, a majority felt that unions should limit themselves to their specifically economic functions: only among the craftsmen was the idea of greater worker control still largely upheld as a union objective." Some sample negative comments from workers: "The unions shouldn't run the factory—it would be a terrible thing." "Workers shouldn't manage the place they're working for. It's not right and they couldn't do it."[15]

Still, interest in workers' control existed among a sizable minority of the total sample, ranging from 22 percent to 61 percent (depending on occupation). And in the third volume, published in 1970, the authors came around to the view that industrial democracy could become a realistic possibility in the foreseeable future. This was partly because increasing prosperity was seen as having some unexpected and unwelcome consequences: "Affluence and its concomitants appear less as harmonizing influences than as likely sources of working-class discontent and unrest."[16]

This tendency seemed to fit in with political trends. Members of the working class appeared no longer especially drawn to the Labour Party, not because they were becoming *bourgeois*, but simply because the Labour Party, traditionally wedded to programs designed for the impoverished masses, had run out of steam. Predicting that Labour would likely lose the next election unless it found new issues, the authors theorized that Labour's best exit from its dilemma would be to find "political demands which may be as yet relatively weak and unformed but which are of a kind that the Conservative Party would find it difficult to accommodate." Here is where industrial democracy came in: "The most obvious examples here are demands for some substantial measure of employee participation in the control of industrial enterprises."[17]

The predictions turned out correctly. Labour did not find new issues, did lose the election and, since then, some Labour Party chiefs have been focusing their attention on industrial democracy. Wedgwood Benn, vice chairman of the party, has said he favors a wide-ranging series of changes in industry that would make work more human and industry more efficient by allowing workers more say over their jobs. Conceding that, in the past, Labour had overemphasized "economic management and budgetary policy," he said: "The man who actually has to do a job of work on the factory floor, or in a foundry, or in a shop or office is the best person to know how his or her work should be organized. There is nothing that creates more ill will in industry than when people are denied the elementary authority they need to plan and guide the work they are qualified to do." He mentioned that one of his most "horrifying experiences" while a minister had been to visit factories where the managers "obviously did not know what was going on." He thus pinpointed two of the most grievous ills in British labor relations: that workers are "consistently underestimated and their intelligence . . . insulted," and the class system, whereby "the grandson of the founder has inherited power he is quite unfitted to wield." Referring to the 1966 Jones report, he speculated that real democracy in industry could be

achieved within five years if the unions were to give it top
priority.[18]

It is not certain how soon the Labour Party will have a chance
to try out these ideas in Parliament, but it seems likely that political pressures, combined with pressures from increasingly well-
educated workers who tend to become easily alienated in industry, will eventually force greater political attention to be given
to the issue. To be sure, British experience with worker representation on boards of directors of state-owned companies has not
been particularly successful, and this has created some negative
feelings regarding other approaches to industrial democracy. In
1968, workers at the British Steel Corporation were given representation on the board on an experimental basis, but experience
has been so poor that it is likely the experiment will be aban-
doned. The worker representatives have little real power, and they
tend to be distrusted by their colleagues. Nevertheless, it seems
likely that efforts along different lines will have to be made to
meet increasing discontent with traditional management methods.

The evolution of industrial democracy took an unusual turn
in mid-1971, when the Upper Clyde Shipbuilders announced, after
being refused a state subsidy to offset heavy losses, that it was
shutting down, thus threatening six thousand workers with unemployment. Immediately, in a mood reminiscent of the workers' revolt in France in 1968, the workers spontaneously and
massively declared a "work-in" on the premises, took over control of all the functions, including the payroll, and continued to
operate as usual. The workers took great care to behave responsibly and to protect company property, and there was a heady, but
short-lived, call for "workers' control" of the yard. Wedgwood
Benn, after a visit to the yard, noted that the militancy of the
workers should be put to "positive purposes." He theorized that,
if the normal autocratic management pattern could be done
away with at Upper Clyde, the result would be better worker
behavior and more efficient operations, and he spoke of requiring the company to switch to a "workers' control" setup.[19]

As it turned out, nothing much happened at Upper Clyde, and
eventually, with government cooperation and fresh funds from

outside, the yard was saved. But while the revolt lasted, it did show again that there is a deep desire of workers to gain more control over their work.

Though there is some slow evolution in British thinking on industrial democracy, it must be said that present prospects for any appreciable movement are not especially bright. The tight class system continues to work against the spread of any great understanding of workers' needs and wants, and the assumption is general that workers have no interest in more freedom. Despite the evidence regarding workers' interest in obtaining more control, British journalist Anthony Sampson blandly writes: "The clamor for workers' control may often be cooked up or half-baked (for few workers really *want* control)."[20]

Though great promise for industrial democracy in Britain can be said to have been produced by the work of the Tavistock Institute, the subsequent developments have been a history of promise unfulfilled.

XII. THE U.S.A.: INFILTRATORS

Despite the unorthodox thinking involved in participative management methods, the benefits are sufficiently attractive that a number of U.S. companies have adopted them—most often with success, and sometimes with spectacular success. Relatively speaking, the number of firms is small, but it is growing rapidly as the result of the bold efforts of some highly imaginative behavioral scientists in industry. On the surface, the changes are not noticeably radical, and in many cases it has been possible to put them through without the full understanding of top management. Few executives in the companies concerned care to speak openly of "democracy." However, many of the scientists feel that they are dealing with something far beyond a new management technique—it is a question of a radical overhaul of the entire capitalist-industrialist tradition. And not a few of these people see themselves virtually as "infiltrators," quietly working to bring about far-reaching changes in "the system."

One of the best-documented case histories in this area is that of the Harwood-Weldon Corporation. The Harwood company, a pajama manufacturer founded in 1899, was taken over in the late 1930s by the founder's two sons. One of them was Alfred Marrow, who had a Ph.D. in psychology and a deep interest in applying his knowledge to promote intensive employee participation, which he did in his own company with rather gratifying results. He told me: "Machine operators know the factories where they can have some self-esteem, and they seek jobs there. We probably have the lowest turnover among employees in any similar plant in the United States."

The Harwood participative methods were put to a severe test in 1962, when the company acquired its major competitor, the Weldon Company. Weldon at the time was in financial trouble and was sliding rapidly downhill. It was being run along strict autocratic lines by two co-owners who made all the decisions—an unfortunately large number of which had been disastrous. Employee morale was low, turnover high, operations chaotic, and profits nonexistent. It was a classic old-line, autocratic company; shortly after the acquisition, the Likert organization made a survey among management and supervisory personnel, who gave it average ratings ranging from 1.87 to 2.67—that is, somewhere between "exploitative-authoritative" and "benevolent-authoritative."

A massive effort was launched to bring Weldon up to a reasonable standard, involving both Weldon and Harwood people as well as outside consultants. At one time, five consultant organizations were working in the Weldon plant. Weldon's rundown physical plant had to be improved, but a large part of the job was the gradual introduction of the Harwood participative philosophy which, in essence, is simply to get the workers' best efforts by encouraging them to contribute whatever they are able to contribute. Marrow wrote: "On matters which the workers know best—their own jobs, conditions in the shop, operation of machines—they have far more informed opinions than top managers who lack first-hand experience."[1] This idea was not easy to get across to the Weldon people, who had become accustomed to strict discipline and who felt disoriented when they were told they had to rely on themselves. At one point, the Weldon plant manager suggested to a Harwood executive that a group of Harwood top managers should come to the Weldon plant in Pennsylvania to meet the employees and tell them something about future plans. The Harwood man told him that was not the way they did things at Harwood: "The idea we want to get across to Weldon's em-

ployees is that when they think of the boss who's running the
show, they think not of New York, but of you."[2]

Through heavy reliance on group discussions, the Weldon
managers learned to trust each other, value the others' opinions,
and resolve conflicts in a more harmonious fashion than in the
past. Because they were more on their own, they developed more
self-confidence and more interest in their work. Moreover, they
were able to pass along these attitudes to their subordinates.
When thoroughgoing technical changes were made, employees
at all levels were fully informed of the changes, and their opinions were solicited. On the shop floor, supervisors and machine
operators participated in discussing, and finding solutions for,
problems. At first, many operators were skeptical; said one: "You
mean they are really going to let us talk about what is going on
even if we think they are doing things wrong?"[3] But when it became apparent that management would not only listen to complaints but would even put suggestions for improvement into
operation, even lower-level workers became convinced. Gradually, openness and mutual trust replaced the traditional atmosphere of noncommunication and no-confidence.

In 1964, only two years after the acquisition, the Weldon unit
had become a smoothly functioning, participative unit; its standing on the Likert scale was now seen as between 3.51 and 3.77—
that is, in the "consultative" area—not perfect, but a considerable
improvement. Employee turnover had dropped from 10 percent
monthly to 4 percent, daily absences from 6 percent to 3 percent. Employee earnings above standard (a method of figuring
incentive pay) rose from zero to 16 percent. Return on capital
invested shifted from minus 15 percent to plus 17 percent—
eloquent testimony that participation pays not only in human
terms but in money terms as well.

Nearly five years after termination of the formal change program, a team of observers returned to Weldon to study subsequent
developments. These observers expected that, once the battalion
of outside consultants had left the scene, there would be a re-
version to the previous unsatisfactory condition, and that they
could therefore "make some remarks about the 'Hawthorne effect'—about the superficiality and transient quality of organiza-

tional and behavioral changes induced under conditions of external attention and pressure."[4] To their surprise, they found that the process of change and development in the direction of increased employee participation had continued. Employee attitude surveys revealed that "the amount of supervisory supportiveness experienced by employees" had risen since the program ended. One aim of the original program was "increasing the total amount of control so that lower rank people—supervisors and operators— would have some added degree of control." Although there was scarcely any trace of this in the first stage, the subsequent changes were "in the direction intended and more substantial in degree." Perhaps most importantly, it had evolved toward a more democratic atmosphere; it had moved farther on the Likert scale toward "System 4," showing that the organization "progressed still further toward their ideal of a participative organizational system." At the same time, "substantial gains in efficiency and volume for the factory as a whole" were registered.

The observers concluded that there is something self-sustaining about the change process—that the transformation initiated from the outside creates new values in the organization, which themselves operate to generate further change in the desired direction. "The interdependence of elements tends to preserve, to enhance, and to 'lock in' the central characteristics of the system and thus to prevent retrogression."

A similar company that has adopted participation methods is R. G. Barry Corp., headquartered in Columbus, Ohio, maker of bedroom slippers, bathrobes, and other leisure-wear items. Management began looking into new management methods in 1966; a number of other companies had been acquired, the company was being decentralized, and there was a fear of losing control. The participation idea seemed interesting, but production was at that time organized, as is much work in this industry, on the so-called functionalized individual unit system, in which workers work for the most part alone, and it was difficult to see how group principles could be easily adopted.

A couple of years later, the company received an excited telephone call from a product licensee in Canada—he had developed a conveyor-belt production line involving about eight people for a single product group. The idea behind the system was of a rather highly mechanized, Taylorized system, but Robert Woodruff, Barry's personnel manager, immediately saw the potentials in a completely different light. "He showed us a way we could organize the operation around the people instead of the other way around," he told me. "He didn't even realize what he was showing us."

Beginning in early 1969, the company completely revised its main plant in Columbus along the lines of the new system, starting on a small scale with an initial experimental group of about a dozen people and gradually spreading to the entire plant. In every case, the operators themselves were involved in planning the production changeover, with the result that not all the lines are the same. Jacque Fisher, plant production manager, remarked to me: "We got the operators involved in setting goals because we wanted to have individual goals and company goals the same." At first, the operators thought they were being "conned" by management: "They had never been asked their opinions before."

While the participative system was being introduced, some other changes were also made. The incentive pay system was abolished, and everyone was put on straight salary. The time clocks were removed—a move that some said would lead to chaos. (Actually, absenteeism dropped.) Previously, all items produced were put through quality control, and that was also abolished. "We pulled the quality inspectors off the line," Fisher says, "and asked the workers if they would like to inspect their own work. The quality level improved tremendously." The basis of the system is full participation. Says Woodruff: "We give the groups all information on costs, markups, selling prices, competition, and so on, and we tell them they can do anything they want as long as they accept responsibility for keeping cost at or below the former standard." The number of maintenance men was reduced from seven to four—partly because the mechanics (who were also included in the participation) suggested some preventive maintenance and partly because the operators now did some of their own maintenance.

The change program was put through in nine months, and operations were disrupted for some time. Fisher explained: "Our biggest problem was that we didn't realize the cost of putting this thing into effect. People had to learn new jobs, and the training cost a lot of time and money." Some operators objected to the new system, and about 5 percent quit. Many supervisors resisted the change because, threatened by the strength of the groups, they saw their own importance reduced. Despite these initial problems, morale improved, the working teams developed remarkably cohesive feelings, and productivity rose. By mid-1970, production had risen to about 25 percent above the prechange level. Per-share earnings, affected by the production change and other factors, dropped by 16 percent in 1969, but in 1970 (a recession year) they climbed by 55 percent.

The company has also tried to extend participation into areas normally considered the exclusive property of the top-level decision-makers. In 1970, employees at the main factory were asked to help pick the site of a new facility, since some of them were going to be working in it. About 250 production people took part in a site selection survey, the results of which guided the work of a special site selection team. The team immediately eliminated some sites that were regarded as unsuitable by the workers and narrowed the choice down to two locations. All employees to be affected were taken on a tour to the two sites, and their opinion was accepted in making the final choice.

The Barry programs have upset some basic assumptions about managing a business. While Fisher was showing me through the factory, he pointed out that in some cases, identical machinery was positioned quite differently. He explained: "This girl wants to be closer to the line, and the other one doesn't. Personally, I think the first one is right, but if the other girl doesn't think so, that's her business." He suddenly stopped and looked around as though he had just discovered that someone had stolen his wallet. "This is completely unorthodox," he said, "my background is entirely in industrial engineering."

Nevertheless, the new methods work, and management is convinced it could work for others. Robert Woodruff told me: "It proves two things: First, people are basically honest; second, they really want to do as good a job as possible."

One of the earliest and best-known programs of job democratization has been at Texas Instruments, the electronics giant.

Having reached the six-million-dollar sales level in 1949, the company decided that, in order to retain its vitality, it would deliberately have to grow rapidly; otherwise, it could not satisfy the desire for personal growth for its best people, who would therefore leave the company in the hands of the less competent.[5] The result would not be good for anybody. In other words, the goals of the company were shaped in part to fit the personal goals of the individuals.

During the following decade, when the company was riding high on fast-expanding demand for semiconductors, in which it is the world leader, it enjoyed the benefits of the kind of euphoria that comes with continuing success, and a strong team spirit developed quite naturally. At the end of the 1950s, sales were well over two hundred million dollars, but the moment of truth (in the form of intensified competition) arrived. In the 1960–62 period, sales stagnated, and profits dropped by nearly half. It was then that management had to do something if the employees were to continue to contribute their best.

Under the aegis of Scott Myers, personnel director, the company began by testing the Herzberg motivation theories on several groups of workers. Though some minor differences emerged, the principal motivating factor for all groups, ranging from scientists to machine operators, was the same: achievement. Using these results as a guide, management started with job enlargement and job enrichment techniques, restructuring individual jobs. But Myers went much farther than this. He noticed that there was a wide and largely unnecessary gap between the functions of managers and those of workers. Customarily, managers are "planning, organizing, leading, controlling," while the workers are only "doing." This peculiar dichotomy, Myers says, creates a grotesque situation—"unintelligent, uninformed, uncreative, irresponsible, and immature workers who need the direction and control of intelligent, informed, creative, responsible, and mature managers."[6] Under such conditions, workers naturally regard work as having nothing to do with themselves, "a form of punishment," which they put up with only "to get the money needed to buy goods and services which *are* related to personal goals."

In combating this situation, Myers attempted to wipe out the gap and to involve workers in the entire process; as he puts it, the idea is to make "every person a manager." He argues that it is only in this way that work can become anything more than punishment: "People who work for themselves generally have meaningful work in terms of a complete cycle of plan, do and control."

Myers relates a story illustrating the philosophy. The company had won a contract for some radar equipment, but had mistakenly bid under actual manufacturing cost and was losing money heavily. A foreman took ten of his female assemblers off the assembly line, met with them in a conference room, explained the situation fully, and asked for their suggestions. The girls broke down the operations required in assembly, studied every operation, and after several hours had made some forty suggestions. At the time, manufacturing the equipment required 138 man-hours, and it would not be profitable unless that figure were brought down to under 100 hours. The girls' suggestions would, they assured him, result in a figure of 86 hours. The foreman did not believe it could be done, and he was disturbed because he feared the girls' failure would lead to a loss of self-confidence. But, having asked their opinion, he felt trapped, and he reluctantly gave them the go-ahead. As it turned out, both the foreman and the girls were wrong—they actually reduced assembly time to 75 hours; then they asked for another meeting, which cut the time further, to 57 hours, and, finally, to 32 hours.[7]

Word about such events tends to spread, Myers points out, and soon other foremen are involving their workers in similar projects, and most of them are soon experiencing not only increasing productivity but lower employee turnover and absenteeism. Moreover, the girls on the assembly line suggest changes that affect process engineers and manufacturing engineers, so that bureaucratic tendencies break down and employees become increasingly committed. So involved do they become, says Myers, that management has had to construct "safeguards against overcommitment," reminding employees that they also have responsibilities to their families.[8]

The direct, concrete involvement of workers in their work is accompanied by some more subtle forms of democracy. As one way of disabusing supervisors of the idea that they are members of an infallible elite, to help them "gain early acceptance of their limitations," Texas Instruments lets the operators help train the supervisors. Myers says it has a big impact on the supervisors' values.[9] There are no status symbols in the company, no hierarchy of office furnishings, no executive parking places, and no executive dining rooms. Charles Hughes, a personnel executive, remarked to me: "We have one class of people—employees. Everybody is on a first-name basis, and everybody has the same benefits as far as possible under the laws. We post all jobs available in the company newspaper, and anybody is free to apply for any job."

The Texas Instruments approach demonstrates, says Myers, "the wastefulness of bureaucracy and the advantages of democracy."[10] But he emphasizes that it is not just a matter of "liking" people, which he says is irrelevant. The real point is both more human and more hard-boiled: "It is necessary that we recognize people as individuals and realize that if they do not achieve their personal goals, they won't achieve company goals."[11]

The striking participative program at a New England electronics plant of Corning Glass began with the rather vague feeling that, since the plant was relatively new and therefore had no traditions, it was in a position to try new management techniques—though it was not certain what might be possible.

The challenge was enthusiastically taken up by Michael Beer, the company's manager of personnel research. The first step was an attempt to create a favorable atmosphere among employees (eighty production workers, mostly women with less than a high school education, thirty technical and clerical employees, and fifteen professional and managerial personnel) to let them know that their ideas, opinions, and questions were genuinely desired by management. The campaign, which involved weekly and monthly meetings, bulletin boards, and a plant newspaper, took about a year to get this novel idea across. Gradually, however, the initial suspicions faded, and employees who at the beginning would confine their comments to a cautious questioning of the functioning of the coffee machine started asking searching questions about the company's long-range planning and other policies.[12]

Two central techniques were job enrichment and autonomous work groups. All employees were given maximum responsibility, and decision-making was pushed down as far as possible. The first concrete project was in a department producing hot plates for laboratories and hospitals, using an orthodox assembly line with each girl doing a tiny part of the job. The assembly line was abolished, and everyone was given the job of assembling entire products. This change had a powerful impact. One girl remarked proudly: "Now it's *my* hot plate." Absenteeism dropped from 8 percent to 1 percent in six months. Rejects dropped from 23 percent to 1 percent, and productivity rose by 47 percent. In another department, a change was carried out when the supervisor suddenly announced that the girls were to be split into two groups, that each group would be responsible for planning and scheduling the work and assigning tasks among the workers. After some grumbling about the supervisor's abdication of responsibility, they accepted the new setup and became so involved that they soon found themselves voluntarily staying late at work to work out planning details. Perhaps the most astounding project was in a department producing complex electronic instruments, some consisting of up to 250 parts and selling for four thousand dollars. Again, the line was abolished and the operators were given the entire products to assemble. Again, absenteeism dropped, from 8.5 percent to 3.4 percent. Productivity rose about fifteen hundred dollars per year per worker. Rejects dropped from 25 percent to 13 percent. This was all the more astonishing because, during the period in question, four new instrument models were introduced, one of which had been rushed through design so rapidly that no drawings were available and the girls had to learn assembly on the basis of a prototype model.

After three years of such projects, the most obvious result of the program is a unique spirit in the plant. Michael Beer explains: "New production employees . . . report more openness, greater involvement by employees, more communication, more interesting jobs, and better supervision." Visitors "are struck immediately by the culture of the plant," and managers who have been transferred to other locations "showed cultural shock at the change." Employee turnover is less than 1 percent (which compares with 3.5 percent in that region). And economic performance, even though it cannot be directly compared with that of other plants, is good.

The workers' own comments reflect the change: "I love it. . . . Everyone is so tremendous. They seem friendly, interested, and concerned about us. I also feel that I know everything that's going on in the plant and feel that this is very important." "You get very involved in your job here and won't stay home because you have a goal to meet." "I am now interested in the team and what we can do as a team in terms of our goal. Sometimes I sit at home and think of how we can better the goal, whether we'll make the goal, and how we can improve the goals."

Perhaps most importantly, the plant's unusual atmosphere does not depend on the personality characteristics or opinions of any one person or any set of persons, because management people are constantly being transferred in and out. The plant has developed a "culture" of its own that is self-propelling and self-reinforcing.

Like many others, Beer emphasizes that the idea is not to create a "country club" atmosphere or a "soft" management philosophy to replace a "hard" one: "It is a third alternative . . . which is tougher than directive leadership because the direction and control come from within the individual through commitment."

Among the more significant work-reform programs being carried out in America are those in the auto industry—long famous for its alienating and mind-deadening jobs. As summed up by one worker, whose function it is to remove tires from a rack and place them on a moving line, "I don't know what it is they can do, but they got to change these jobs. If you don't get a break off that line, you can go crazy."[18]

The auto companies don't know what to do either, but they have all become painfully aware of an approaching crisis. The situation was dramatically illustrated by the disaster at Lordstown, Ohio, where one of General Motors' newest and (supposedly) most efficiently engineered plants foundered in early 1972 under the sullen resentment of a young workforce that had no sympathy with the militaristic precision and dehumanizing character of the high-speed assembly line. The resulting twenty-two day strike was not about wages, but was a protest against the unbearable working conditions.

Though no U.S. auto company has taken so drastic a step as to abolish the assembly line (as is being tried in Sweden, as we will see later), they are all worried about high turnover and absenteeism, sabotage, and other impolite practices on the part of their employees.

This is clearly shown at General Motors, which was keenly aware of the problems and was striving to attack them well before the Lordstown affair. In 1970, Delmar Landen, director of employee research, told me, somewhat prophetically: "We are on a collision course. We have built institutions which were very effective in their time, but now there are increasing levels of aspirations and different value systems are pressing against these institutions." At that time, Landen's entire headquarters staff of researchers consisted of half a dozen behavioral scientists. In 1972, this staff had more than doubled, and in addition there were some fifty collaborators doing similar work in the various divisions. Landen told me: "We know that we have to take action to avoid situations like Lordstown. We've got to learn how to prevent those problems."

To be sure, the difficulties are awesome. For one thing, nobody is quite sure how objectionable the assembly line really is (although sociological studies indicate that it is by no means well liked). In one GM facility manufacturing electric switches, employing women, in which each woman constructed an entire switch, part of the plant was changed to an assembly-line operation, where each woman did only a single repetitive operation. Upon interviewing the women, the company found that many of them considered both jobs equally boring, but that the assembly line at least gave them a chance to socialize. Landen explained to me: "If we assume that the work itself is too boring, then the only way to increase feelings of personal worth is to enrich the job vertically—and that means that the assembly line has to be redesigned. But if we look at the organization as a whole and how we might involve people in the total organization, then the 'job' takes on a much broader meaning. I'm not sure we have even begun to explore all the possibilities." In order to get more precise knowledge about the "assembly line blues" and why different employees react differently, the company has begun a massive study of worker attitudes. "We're going to find out for ourselves," says Landen, "how much disaffection there is among people do ing assembly line work, what accounts for it, and what kinds of changes they might want."

Meanwhile, the company has initiated a wide-ranging series of projects designed to involve workers more deeply in their work. Much of this is classified under "job matching"—that is, an effort to obtain a more precise fit between the worker and his job—principally by changing the job. One important technique is "team building"—a process that aims at increasing a "work group's ability and motivation to do its work well." Where it is possible to build cohesive groups, it is possible to bring about a healthier and less autocratic atmosphere: "Gradually, the group acquires a capability for self-diagnosis, self-evaluation, and self-correction; and it will hopefully reach the ultimate objective of requiring no outside direction to accomplish its work effectively." But the active participation of employees must be obtained: "To be successful, the effort requires that all employees be given the opportunity to set goals, contribute ideas, and obtain feedback on their performance and progress."[14]

At this writing, GM's reform efforts are admittedly "somewhat isolated and of recent origin," but in some cases it has registered tentatively encouraging results in bringing down absenteeism and turnover and improving morale—without damaging productivity. The most ambitious program is an "organizational development" project begun in 1969 in cooperation with the Institute for Social Research at the University of Michigan. On the basis of attitude surveys, it was decided that management should "be more receptive to employee ideas, give them more opportunity to participate in establishing goals and solutions in their areas of work, stimulate more team effort among employees, and more effectively coordinate total resources toward common efforts." To try out these ideas, four plants were selected for experimental efforts. Through more active communication with employees, aggressive attempts to elicit their ideas and involvement, and management readiness to listen to their complaints, some positive results were achieved. In one case, employee grievances were reduced by more than 90 percent, absenteeism was cut, and over-all labor costs were trimmed.[15]

Chrysler has also been attacking the problems of worker discontent, through more effective communication with workers, requests for their advice, and the introduction of some flexibility in assembly lines. However, there have not been any far-reaching changes in the basic production methods, nor has any attempt been made to alter the technology of the assembly line. One account of Chrysler's moves noted that there has resulted "a new atmosphere, a new team spirit," but that there "is little possibility in the near future that assembly lines will change significantly."[16]

All these efforts are admirable, though they have not brought about radical changes in the nature of the work; neither have they changed the deadly mechanical autocracy of the assembly line. And they constitute only a small step in the direction of true democracy. The large barrier, as Landen reminded me, is painfully obvious: "The point is, how do you get the same volume production with a modified assembly line?" Nevertheless, GM began, in 1972, construction of a facility in Canada to produce radios based on teams rather than assembly lines. It was also readying a plan to introduce, in one plant and on an experimental basis, a team concept involving six to eight persons for the final trim on passenger autos.

The auto industry may be, in some respects, behind the times, but it is struggling hard to catch up.

Like General Motors, a steadily increasing number of companies are establishing headquarters service functions in which behavioral scientists work out methods of overhauling organizations and reforming jobs to alleviate worker discontent. Typical is PPG Industries in Pittsburgh, maker of glass, paint, chemicals, and a variety of other industrial products, which in 1971 engaged William H. Mobley as its manager of employee relations research and planning—a new position. Though when I spoke to Mobley (in mid-1972), he was just getting started, he had some firm and rather original ideas about his company's problems and the opportunities they represented.

One project he had launched was at a PPG plant in the Midwest making architectural metals. The workforce was young, and discontented, as shown by a high rate of absenteeism and employee turnover. Two auto plants in the area had the same problems, despite higher pay scales. Mobley told me: "We feel if we

can make our jobs more desirable we can compete more effectively for people."

Two departments in the plant were selected for reform. In a
drafting department, some draftsmen were making original drawings for jobs, others made shop drawings, and still others, correc-
tions. "Nobody was identified with any project," Mobley told
me. Therefore, the aim was to increase identification by tying
draftsmen to "whole" projects and giving them feedback, where
necessary, directly from the field. Another department selected
was in the factory, where efforts were being made to redesign
small, separate jobs into larger, more meaningful units.

One unusual aspect of Mobley's approach is an insistence on
combining research with actual projects. "We want to answer
two questions," he said. "First: What specific outcomes do people
find desirable in their jobs? And second: To what extent does the
performance of their jobs lead to these outcomes? We are asking
these questions on a before-and-after basis. If job enrichment has
the effect it's supposed to have, then a change should show up.
If so, I think we will have learned something." Mobley was just
winding up taking his "before" measurements when I spoke to
him; though full results would take some time, he expected that
when they came they would show "not only what happened but
why."

Another special feature of this project was that it was taking
place in a union plant. Mobley was bravely preparing to face that
problem: "We anticipate complaints on job classification. Why
can't we go to the union, say we're concerned about what we're
doing, and propose setting up a cooperative six-month study?
We might run for six months with wage rates frozen, after which
we would re-evaluate jobs."

Another PPG project was in a department of a glass plant in
Ohio. It was thought that if goal-setting, management by objectives, and other sophisticated suggestion-seeking techniques
worked so well on the management level, perhaps they should be
tried among production workers, and this project was set up to
test the notion. A first step was to supply the approximately
forty workers at this location with full information on costs, production, competition, and so on—far more data than is normally
released either to employees or to shareholders. They were then

asked to help establish production goals, quality standards, speeds, and so on. Feedback was arranged to let employees know how they were doing at all times. Management emphasized that employees could ask for any information they wanted, and that the goals were to be the employees' goals. The workers enjoyed greatly increased freedom; for example, they could decide when the line was to be turned off—previously a management decision.

There are no precise data on results, but productivity rose far beyond expectations, and management was convinced that it was due to the changed treatment of employees. A good part of the increase was in the form of higher quality. Since a small scratch or a flaw caused by faulty temperature control could be extremely costly, even a small increase in careful handling can be significant. Mobley explained the incentives working among the employees: "The norms are not being imposed on them—it's their own goals they're working toward. Also, there is the willingness of management to disclose information normally held confidential. It shows management believes workers can be trusted. That tends to wipe out the artificial gap between management and workers."

The system worked so well that it is being extended to other areas in the same plant. Because the plant is highly capital-intensive and it is difficult to change the technology, the extent of change is limited. However, Mobley notes: "It's an evolutionary process. We might next see if we could restructure the process itself; even if we can't change the basic technology we might split up the tasks differently." Moreover, there is the possibility of involving operators in the design of new production facilities: "I think plants are too often designed by engineers, without any thought of the workers. One thing I would like to do is to get a chance to look at the jobs before we get locked in."

Mobley does not take a doctrinaire approach, but believes in adapting the approach to the problem. "Goal-setting doesn't preclude job enrichment," he notes. "And job enrichment might lead to goal-setting. It doesn't matter so much where you start. What we need is to know how to integrate the needs of the individual with the needs of the organization. I don't think any one technique can do it all."

Like many others in similar positions, Mobley is greatly concerned with collecting hard results with which to persuade managers to accept new techniques. "When we get some data," he says, "then we can talk to managers in their own language." He is convinced that the youthful workforce with radically new values is creating irresistible pressures of change, as shown in the Lordstown affair. "Lordstown had a big shock effect," he points out. "Managers are seeing a brand-new challenge. Maybe they only thought of it a few months ago, but now they're really aware."

One company whose headquarters problem-solvers have been quietly building up a considerable body of experience in restructuring jobs over a period of years is the Monsanto Company, a St. Louis-based maker of chemicals, synthetic fabrics, and other products.

J. I. Johnston, director of personnel planning and development, told me that, though he does his best to stir up interest among managers in his advice, he does not believe it possible to impose new methods on unsympathetic managers: "The corporate group provides resources and encouragement, but we don't give orders. We only try to show managers how production can be increased by giving workers more decision-making power." Johnston is very pragmatic. "We are extremely eclectic in our philosophy," he told me. "We will try anything that works."

One method that has been found particularly valuable is "shared goal-setting," which can be used on virtually any level (it has been used mostly in working with managers). Employees discuss with their superiors the levels of results they wish to attain and the methods by which to attain them, the employees participating fully in making the decisions. After a time, the situation is reviewed and new goals set on the basis of new discussions. Johnston says: "We find that very effective. The worker develops an understanding of what the whole business is about, and the foreman understands how he can help the operators. But it only works if you mean it—and make sure the operator has enough information. What we're driving at is self-determination and self-control."

Another technique is "joint training," in which a group cutting across supervisory lines but with a common interest in a particular process takes part in either training projects or actual problem-solving. Johnston notes that it is very helpful in "changing attitudes, building more understanding and more respect among people."

A plant where both methods were put into practice was at Long Beach, California, producing chemicals and plastics and employing about two hundred persons. The plant is nonunion, and management began to suspect that employee discontent was rather high when the pro-union faction in plant elections (which had been held regularly for nearly a decade) began to near the 50 percent level. Johnston told me: "We figured that whatever we were doing, it wasn't working." An attitude survey harvested a large number of bitter, anticompany complaints (poor supervision, the company has no respect for employees, and so on). "It gave us a bit of a shock," Johnston said, "but if people were bored with us, it showed we had to do something. If you have trouble with production workers, it is usually the result of management practices higher up."

At the request of the plant management, the central corporate people drew up a program for a reform, including goal-setting and joint training, especially the latter. "We trained most of the foremen and operators," Johnston says, and the result was a new basis for cooperation and understanding: "It gave them a very effective vehicle in getting more participation from the workers."

The following year, the pro-union bloc in the election dropped significantly, and the atmosphere improved sufficiently later so that no further elections have been held. The plant's "hard performance data" also improved, and three years after the program was launched it was performing better than at any time in its fifteen-year history. Johnston concludes: "The plant management attributes this to opening up the organization across supervisory lines and improving management practices. The employees were in effect saying: 'The company finally asked for our help, and that's what we're giving.'"

A more radical approach was taken at an organic chemicals and plasticizers plant in Bridgeport, New Jersey. The plant manager, having become intrigued with modern participative theories, decided to cut away the entire power structure; as one account put it, the aim was to "change the workforce from a pyramidal structure to a team-based operation . . . and eventually eliminate

departments as such."[17] The organization was broken up into
product teams, each of which sets its own goals in line with
those of the plant as a whole and measures its own results. Instead
of being closely supervised, operators now do almost all their own
process control (foremen have been eliminated entirely on two
shifts).

Though both these plants were nonunion, Johnston told me
that similar programs have been started in unionized plants, with
little difficulty. "A union in a plant can block change if it wants
to, and if we don't take time to explain and justify the change,
they will block it. In general, the unions we deal with *like* the
idea of increased responsibility, because that usually increases the
rate of pay."

The key, he pointed out, is to put more challenge in the work
by giving people the opportunity to widen their scope: "That's
what I mean by opening up the organization. Invariably, people
want to do more." As a result, challenge and responsibility are
built into jobs wherever possible: "We design a very high-level
job for a control-room operator with a thirty-million-dollar plant
under his control. We could easily break it down smaller, but
we're constantly opting in favor of a more challenging job."

Monsanto is totally practical about this program. Johnston
explained: "More effective work is performed at any level if the
individual is enriched by it. He should derive strength from his
experience—not from a social point of view, but because it promotes productivity." He added: "The objective is to improve
management—*in our terms.*"

So far, projects of one sort or another have touched some 30
percent to 40 percent of Monsanto's workforce—a rather high
figure considering the relatively brief history of the program
(Johnston's function was established only in the late 1960s).
Johnston avers that "Our intention is to make possible change
that is self-sustaining." It is not known to what extent that is being achieved, since—in line with company principles of decentralized control—managers of individual operations are not compelled to maintain contact with Johnston, and there thus is no
mechanism for following up projects. Moreover, Johnston candidly
says he does not have any picture of where this momentum for
change might eventually carry the company, when larger numbers

of employees are involved in ever-widening spheres of decision-making. Might that one day result in some basic changes in company organization? Johnston confessed he doesn't know. "We have developed a description of an ideal situation," he told me, "but we keep changing it." For someone whose business it is to promote change, perhaps that is a wise attitude.

That democratic management is not synonymous with "soft" management is well illustrated in the case of Syntex Corp., maker of pharmaceuticals, especially oral contraceptives. Syntex has been steadily striving to give employees greater freedom from autocratic controls, greater autonomy, and greater pratication in decision-making—but at the same time increased personal responsibility.

Syntex management decided in the mid-1960s that the ideal form of organization would be Rensis Likert's "System 4," with emphasis on a high degree of confidence shown in subordinates, motivation based on challenging assignments, decisions pushed down as far as possible in the organization, and a free flow of communication. In implementing these principles, management has attempted to reshape the entire organization. One executive has said: "The real pay-off comes not from developing individual managers, but by developing the organization's climate."[18]

Many of the company's programs are arranged in such a way that employees are rewarded if they wish to take on additional responsibilities, but are not penalized if they do not wish to do so. One plan is a "career development laboratory," designed to assist ambitious employees in planning their future in a knowledgeable fashion and to assure the company a continuing supply of promising management material. Though a principal value of the program is to prepare future managers, it was in fact originally developed to select supervisory personnel from the ranks of low-level workers, and it is therefore not confined to any particular level.

John Zenger, director of employee development, explained to me: "Our thinking is that organizations need authority but not autocracy. We need leadership—the best leadership is one that sets high standards, builds teamwork, supports individuals, and provides people with the tools to get the job done." The company therefore believes in firm controls, but not of the orthodox variety: "The information you are gathering has to be fed back to the people who are doing the work. That's the best kind of control. We don't see information as being given to a few selected people who are then clubbing the people below."

Dale Miller, director of career development, told me that the heart of the program was focusing employees' attention on their future: "Typically, people have not planned their careers—they are waiting for the opportunities to fall on them. But we think the individual must take the responsibility for his own career." Everyone is encouraged to discuss the position he desires. "This way," says Miller, "we find out who is interested in management careers and who is not. The people are given the opportunity to demonstrate their strengths and deficiencies." Once that happens, the individual is informed of where he stands, what deficiencies might need correcting if he is to reach his goal, and what training facilities the company will provide if he chooses to persevere. In any case, there is no attempt either to dissuade him from his goal or to push him if he himself does not wish to make the necessary effort, since the company has found that it benefits as much from leaving contented lower-level people in peace as from spotting promising high-level talent. "The employee makes the choice," Miller told me. "The program does not make judgments of what should happen to any particular man. In most cases there is a gap between what a man is capable of doing and what he is doing. But he may not want to pay the price to close that gap. We tell him that's O.K.—but now he knows the ball is in his court."

Miller emphasizes that the program goes beyond the rather mechanical-sounding function of fitting the right man to the right job; it is also a question of enriching the lives of employees. "Some executives," he says, "make the assumption that employees want the extrinsic rewards. But we find they are much more interested in the intrinsic, they want a more meaningful involvement with the organization. The whole idea of the quality of life in this country has to do with careers. There is quite a lot of career changing, because people are just dissatisfied with doing meaningless work."

Another attack on the organization's over-all climate was the creation of "natural work groups." Better understanding in such small groups is promoted through use of small "laboratory" sessions in which individuals—collected either from different departments or from the same work area—meet for several consecutive days of frank, open discussion of the members' personalities and behavior patterns—with reference to group functioning and company goals. These meetings, similar to what are sometimes called "T-groups," are often believed to be potentially dangerous, since they may uncover serious emotional sore points but offer no cure for them. But Syntex doesn't agree. One of its experts says: "It's not necessary to be cautious. . . . We have moved fast and effectively in a short time. It takes guts, but we are committed to candor and openness in this organization."[19]

One experiment suggests that the company is on the right track. Salesmen from four different regions were selected for an experiment: Only those in the second-ranking and fourth-ranking groups (ranked in terms of success in selling) were put through the laboratory sessions. After six months, the two groups had moved up to first and third rank, respectively, and had scored increases of 116 percent and 207 percent in sales, while the groups not receiving training registered gains of 53 percent and 56 percent.[20]

A rather thorough implementation of the company's philosophy is at the plant of its Arapahoe Chemicals Division in Colorado. Described as "pretty radical" by Miller, this program aims at including all of the roughly 130 employees in company decision-making.

The program has been of special value with regard to the division's scientists, who formerly were being severely frustrated in their work. One spokesman described the situation: "We used to seek men with doctorates in chemistry and men with innovative minds, then give them jobs that required nothing more than 'cookbook chemistry' that a technician could do."[21] As a result, scientists were apathetic, indifferent, and alienated. To remedy this appalling situation, the company reordered its entire system so that chemists were given whole projects, not sliced-up sections of jobs, to work on, and were held responsible for working out solutions to a customer problem (including ordering of raw materials, planning a pilot process, costing the production proc-

ess, and setting up a production schedule). Any difficulties are reported directly back to the chemist for correction. As a consequence, morale among scientists has improved vastly.[22]

More control over decision-making has also been extended to
the lower-level workers. Miller told me: "There is much greater
participation among employees in building jobs from the ground
up instead of the top down." Monthly meetings are held at which
employees are invited to air their complaints and suggestions for
improvement. The top executives discuss these employee comments, but they then leave the meeting, and the employees discuss "more touchy subjects" with only an employee relations
supervisor present. The supply of valuable suggestions to management has improved markedly.

As a matter of routine, employees are involved in any change
in production methods. In one notable case, a sizable customer
notified the company that he would no longer pay the current
price for a certain product. Since Arapahoe had constructed a
plant specifically designed to produce that product for that customer, management was concerned, and called together the workers
to discuss the problem. The workers did indeed point to some
production bottlenecks and suggested adding an additional pump
in a refrigeration stage, a larger pipeline for transmission of the
product between two stages, and the use of an additional cen-
trifuge. The suggestions were adopted, and the intended savings
were achieved.[23]

Though Syntex has long been renowned as a spectacularly
successful company, it must be said that its success has been
primarily due to its products, not to innovative management
methods, which are of recent vintage. Says Zenger: "The product of our management methods will only be seen five years
from now." Nevertheless, the feeling is that the new methods
have been of value in applying a rather simple philosophy. Dale
Miller puts it this way: "It tends to mean that employee needs
and company needs go hand in hand."

Some companies have "backed into" more democratic management methods and discovered, somewhat to their surprise, that
such methods can generate excellent results, thus stimulating a
wider application of these techniques.

One such company is the Cleveland-based Eaton Corp., maker of auto parts, fork-lift trucks, and a variety of other industrial products. The company has about seventy plants in the United States employing more than twenty-five thousand persons. Since almost all the plants are unionized, the company's personnel policies are heavily dominated by its relations with the unions, which, as D. N. Scobel, manager of industrial relations, told me, are "good at some plants, and at others, not." Naturally, it is the latter group that causes worries: "I don't know if we have any 'Lordstowns,' but in some cases we're probably pretty close. We're therefore asking what we can do in our new plants to prevent what has been happening in some of our old plants."

The company had occasion to take a hard look at its employee relations practices when it was planning a new engine-valve plant at Kearney, Nebraska, in 1970. During the site-selection stage, some headquarters employee-relations people visited Kearney and talked to city officials, other local companies, and a number of prospective employees. They discovered a rather special Kearney atmosphere—a high degree of stability, closely knit relationships among the populace, and a rather strong anti-union feeling —but also a measure of hostility to large industrial employers. One deduction from all this was that any new employer's treatment of people would become quickly known in the town—creating dangers, but also opportunities.

"We asked ourselves," Scobel told me, "if there was anything different we could do in Kearney to take advantage of the factors we thought we sensed. One thing we thought about was a rather common practice in industry—we use one set of standards for factory workers and another for salaried employees." Such differences are reflected in probationary periods for factory workers, less liberal paid-days-off rules and pension plans, ubiquitous posting of rules in factories, time clocks, and other practices. Scobel explains: "What we're basically saying is, 'Mr. Stupid Factory Worker, we don't trust you—if someone doesn't tell you not to steal, you'll steal.' And we can't blame the unions for it because we're doing the same thing in nonunion plants."

At Kearney, therefore, factory workers and salaried employees are treated alike—the same pension and paid-days-off policies, no probationary periods for anybody, no posted disciplinary rules anywhere, no time clocks, and no disciplinary reprimands for anybody. In addition, factory workers are given responsibilities normally reserved for others—they show visitors through the plant, they sit on such bodies as safety committees, and they help plan new work processes. Rather surprisingly, Eaton also places great emphasis on "human relations"—foremen are encouraged to spend much time advising and counseling subordinates—though most experts believe such techniques are rather unproductive.

All this is combined with a broad attempt to make jobs more interesting, wherever they can be shifted around, through job enrichment techniques. "We take Herzberg rather seriously," says Scobel. "Good human relations is important, but that real extra effort will come from an enriched job." There are, for example, no "setup men" who set up a machine for a particular job. Scobel explains: "Even when the job itself is rather boring, setting it up is quite interesting." So each worker does his own setups. Workers are also encouraged to do their own maintenance. "We get the maintenance men to show the operators what they're doing, so the next time perhaps he can do it himself. If a man can fix his own equipment he will be much more involved in his job."

In the process of reworking jobs, Eaton's management people have learned a great deal. Scobel told me: "We found there are some fantastically simple things that can be done. For example, our sweepers keep their own inventories of supplies. Now for some reason we seem to be getting janitors who are really interested in keeping the plant clean." Some of the new techniques discovered only by chance have been installed as permanent features of the plant's operations. At one point, because of production growth, management saw it had to hire another man in what was previously a one-man operation, covering the reception of steel rods, the accompanying paperwork, taking the rods to a cut-off machine, doing the cut-off work, and distributing the slugs to extruding machine operators. The conventional approach would be to slice the job in half, with one person doing nothing but running the cut-off machine all day. "You couldn't think of a duller job," Scobel points out. But as it happened, the job was divided vertically, with two men responsible for two different product groups, but each doing all the chores associated with his material. The rearrangement was made by management, and when the reshuffling was announced to the man in the job, he profusely thanked management for handling it that way, as he had been scared stiff the job would be broken up in the conventional manner—which gave management a fresh view of worker thought processes. Scobel told me: "That changed our thinking about the idea of consulting employees on job changes. So now we consult employees before changing any jobs, and in fact workers are now represented on the work process committees." This has worked so well that the chief product design engineer has urged management to consult employees before finalizing designs. "Normally," says Scobel, "the distance between the product engineer and the employee in the shop is like from here to China."

The process has thus to some extent become a continuing one —though it was not actually planned that way from the start. "One of our concerns is that the system might get stale," Scobel says— but the company has not made any detailed evaluation of the Kearney plant, and nobody knows exactly where it might end. Nevertheless, the results have been heartening. Casual absenteeism is under 1 percent, and all absenteeism (including sick leave) is under 2 percent (the company average is 6 percent). There is virtually no turnover, and the plant has a backlog of about 3000 applications for jobs (there are 350 factory workers and 100 salaried employees in the plant). Productivity (including considerations of quality) is 100 percent above that of a similar Eaton plant managed in the orthodox manner. The company has been astonished at some of the developments. "Some really surprising things happen at Kearney," Scobel says. "A man comes to work when he's sick, so the foreman sends him home. He goes home, but a few hours later he's back on the job—he says he got bored sitting at home."

The "Kearney thing," as the new approach is known within Eaton, has been extended to half a dozen other Eaton plants, but most often in a watered-down version. "We have great difficulty selling managements on these ideas," Scobel says. "At one place we couldn't sell them on pay for days not worked, for example. So we've had to make compromises. I'm a little worried about these hybrids; it's like we're saying, 'We trust you—but only so far.' The deepest level of involvement is at Kearney."

So far, the company has not dared to try the method in a unionized plant, for fear of stirring up disputes over job descriptions and other inflexible practices common in organized locations. But that is Scobel's next ambition. "We'd like to introduce these methods in an established plant with a union—we'd make a completely new type of agreement." Through careful planning and selection of the right place to start, Scobel hopes to attack a unionized plant eventually, though he is fully aware of the difficulties: "We have trouble with both managers and unions—but more with unions."

In a way somewhat similar to Eaton's Kearney experience, the Spalding Division of the Questor Corp. launched an entirely new philosophy when it built a new golf club factory in Fort Smith, Arkansas, in 1969.[24] Spalding's management started with the idea that employees should have "more participation" and "more to say about how the plant should be run," and the further notion that conventional industrial friction should be avoided if possible. James Long, Spalding vice president, said: "We didn't know exactly where we ought to go, but we knew that we didn't want to do what had been done. Most production operations are interrupted from time to time by misunderstandings . . . which affect either the output or the quality of the product or both, and even the most efficient, best-known engineering approaches have not solved that problem."

Therefore the company based its new approach, just as Eaton was doing at about the same time, on the idea that "people can be trusted" and that they very much seek "achievement" and "recognition for achievement." These principles led to some innovations at Fort Smith. Everyone is on straight salary. There are no time clocks. Supervision is at a minimum (there are no foremen). There are no inspectors in the strict sense of the word (if any working group receives materials that are faulty they pass the word directly back to the group from which they received the materials, not through an intermediary). Workers are given wide latitude in changing their work assignments.

In addition, efforts were made to create an open atmosphere to persuade the workers that their suggestions and recommendations were very much welcomed by management. Some extraordinary suggestions have been received. One worker detected a flaw in a stamping machine, which was leaving a costly defect in the golf club heads. The flaw was quickly corrected when pointed out by a worker in another department. A girl, noticing a safety device on a machine in a department other than her own, which required clumsy and uncomfortable hand movements by the operators, called it to the attention of the engineers, and told them how it could be fixed—which it was.

When word got around—in the community and the company— of the plant's unusual operating philosophy, where "everybody is having a wonderful time" but nobody does any work, management hastened to set the record straight. In fact, Spalding says the plant's costs are 15 percent lower than those of comparable plants, efficiency is higher, safety is "outstanding," absenteeism is "minor," and turnover is almost zero.

The workers, needless to say, find the system much to their liking. Darnella Newman, employed in blending the finish on the golf clubs, said: "When I was working at other places I didn't like to be told what to do, just like being a robot, you just carry out orders and they give orders. I don't think I like that too much." The Spalding plant is different, she says: "When we come in in the morning we know what we have to do, what we're supposed to do, so we do it." Larry Montgomery, a twenty-one-year-old worker, has his eye on a management job: "I'd like to make it in Spalding, though, and nowhere else. 'Cause I like the philosophy we got here. There's nobody to stand over the top of you. They feel that this way you get your work done and nobody's pushing you and there's no time clocks you have to worry about. It's really you're your own boss." Some managers are disturbed by the new methods, since it leaves them little to do, but on the whole Spalding is well satisfied. Jim Long, who has been with the company for more than forty years, said: "It's the most wonderful experience I've had in my forty years; I think it's wonderful."

In general, we might say that the central problem in a democratization process is the development of responsible behavior among workers, to accompany the increased freedom that democracy implies. If democracy is to be economically viable, employees who are freed from bureaucratic and mechanical restraints must also be free to utilize their latent abilities, which are crushed or severely repressed under orthodox management methods.

It is therefore altogether natural that psychologists and sociologists, armed with sophisticated knowledge of the behavior of organizations, would be especially skillful in actuating this process, and most of the progress toward democratization in the United States has stemmed from the efforts of behavioral scientists.

But it is obvious that it does not really matter by what mechanism an organization develops, as long as it is in the desired direction, and it is therefore worthwhile to look at some "homegrown" management systems incorporating some degree of democracy but put into effect without any specialized scientific knowledge. (In fairness to behavioral scientists, we can note that the great majority of such home-grown systems—such as most of the profit-sharing and employee stock-ownership plans—have failed; we will look only at some that have succeeded.)

Whatever the differences between these systems and those planned along more scientific lines, they have one element in common: a "Theory Y" orientation of the part of management, a basic belief that the average person is eager to perform at the top of his capacity, if management will only provide credible evidence that that is what is wanted and that an extra effort will be appreciated. This point is clearly illustrated at Lincoln Electric Company, a Cleveland maker of arc welding equipment, which has been following its own unique "incentive management" system since 1933. Although James F. Lincoln (the long-time head of the company) devised the plan more or less by instinct, his basic statement of principles is one that few behavioral scientists would quarrel with: "The personnel of any organization has inherent in it the making of a company of unique and outstanding ability if only their environment will stimulate in its members a strong desire to develop their latent abilities. Man has endless possibilities."[25] The trouble with most companies, Lincoln said, is that they do not place any demands on the workers: "The usual individual in the usual industrial environment has no challenge presented to him."[26] He urges that this be corrected: "Occasionally give the person whom you wish to develop a job that is over his head. Show him that you expect him to do it." The challenges must be constantly increased: "Keep the pressure on. After the first step in development has been accomplished, have the next follow quickly." Moreover, everyone must be made to realize that they are carrying responsibility: "That must be a reality, not an act. . . . When any man makes the team, accept him as a teammate. You are not a boss, you are a leader." Finally, a high level of effort must be recognized: "The worker must feel that he is recognized in accordance with his contribution to success."[27]

At Lincoln, this recognition is primarily in the form of money. While money alone, as we have seen, does not guarantee that workers will be involved in their work—very often quite the contrary, in fact—at Lincoln the amounts of money are so large, and are so closely linked to individual achievement, that no employee can doubt the sincerity of management's insistence that it genuinely wants the worker to do his best and that he will be rewarded accordingly. In 1933, the company was running at a heavy loss, and Lincoln therefore told employees that, if the loss could be eliminated, fat bonuses would be paid in proportion to each person's contribution. In 1934, the company ran at a profit, and bonuses totaling 38 percent of the total wage bill were paid. Since then, the bonuses have ranged between 50 percent and 150 percent of the wage bill, and the company has continued to be successful. Despite the largesse to employees, growth has been steady (sales grew by nearly 100 percent in the 1962–71 decade), and the company is now the world's largest in its field, with well over half the market in the United States and considerable operations abroad. According to figures compiled by the company, despite total payouts to workers roughly double those of competitive companies, the productivity of Lincoln workers has been sufficient to outrun all competition. During the 1934–50 period, productivity per worker rose at an average rate of 15.35 percent at Lincoln, compared with 3.11 percent in all U.S. manufacturing industry. This astonishing record is, Lincoln wrote, based on a rather simple equation: "Their productivity is more than four times that of competition. They are paid only slightly more than twice the wages of competitors."[28]

Unorthodox though the system is, it has nevertheless succeeded in bringing out the full "participation"—in the full meaning of that word—of all employees. Because everyone knows he is responsible, a great deal of overhead—for foremen and inspectors—can be eliminated. Some workers operate virtually as independent businessmen within the factory; one man might make, for example, gas tanks, receiving the formed plates from a previous production stage, mounting a copper spout, welding the plates together, testing the product, and then passing it on to the production line. He is not supervised, and he is solely responsible for the quality and quantity of his production. Every worker is rated for his contribution by his superiors, and his share in the bonus payments is figured accordingly.

There is no doubt that the atmosphere at Lincoln is affected by this unusual system. Mitchell Fein, a consulting engineer, gives this account of a plant visit: "Most unusual is Lincoln's employees' identification with their work. At one work station, I saw a worker operate five different machine tools to produce a rotor shaft from a blank. He operated a tape controlled engine lathe, a tracer lathe, two small milling machines, a hydraulic press, and he performed all his own inspection. . . . These employees participate in their work to a far greater extent than visualized by psychologists in their writings. The key to this participation is that the employees *want* to do it; there is no holding back."[29]

Lincoln does not practice "democracy" in any very advanced sense, and worker participation in over-all decision-making is not encouraged. (Many do make their opinions known at stockholders' meetings, however, since many have been given the opportunity to purchase stock.) However, the Lincoln system does go far in meeting the true human needs of its workers and rewarding them for their contributions. No detailed studies have been made of the company's performance in recent years, but in 1971, despite bonuses to employees amounting to some 90 percent of wages, the company still earned 10.7 percent on net worth, which compares favorably with the 9.1 percent for the five hundred largest U.S. companies.[30] Not much is known about the inner workings of the system, and the company refuses to allow outside researchers to study it in the plant. Moreover, Lincoln is not much interested in improving its basic plan. A spokesman tersely informed me: "Once we find a good way to do something, we don't change it. Our results lead us to believe we have a good system. When we no longer have the results, we'll change it."

Apparently, the Lincoln formula still works, and it seems to confirm James Lincoln's original feeling that work can be transformed from the "degrading thing" it usually is into the challenging activity it should be, through mobilizing each person's natural desire to excel. He saw with great clarity the obvious but often overlooked fact that everyone is quite ready to perform far above the usual standard, if only he sees that it is of interest to him to do so. As Lincoln wrote: "If the enthusiasm of the amateur athlete could be put into industry, results ten times greater than anything yet accomplished would become automatic."[31]

Another system born during the Depression of the 1930s was that of McCormick & Co., Baltimore maker of spices, tea, convenience foods, and other products. In 1932, Willoughby McCormick, who had founded the company in 1889 and had ruled it with an iron hand since, died, leaving the presidency in the hands of his nephew and heir apparent, Charles. Having worked for the company in various capacities for some years, Charles was convinced that his uncle's tyrannical management methods, which arose from a basic distrust of human beings, were all wrong. Further, he felt that a change in the management philosophy could be of considerable help to the company, which at that time was deeply in the red. He therefore called all the workers together, told them that a new era of mutual trust was opening, and called for their cooperation in revising the firm's fortunes. As evidence of his own faith in them, he announced that all wages were being raised and working hours were being reduced. Within a year, the company was in the black, where it has been ever since.

McCormick's philosophy was based on the idea that people work better and more productively—for themselves and the company—if they have an involvement in their work. He wrote: "People cannot be coerced—they can only be led through the contentment they find in their work."[32] He therefore sought to find mechanisms to improve two-way communications, "to extend management so close to the worker that the two understand one another and work together as a team."[33]

McCormick's special invention was what he called "multiple management," a system of employee boards, operating in much the same way, though on a lower level, as the board of directors. These boards examine various aspects of company operations and make recommendations for improvement. One board is a "junior" version of the board of directors, and the others operate in special areas (e.g., sales, real estate, manufacturing, administration). Membership is changed every six months, and the boards elect their own new members. Each board has about fifteen members, usually drawn from middle management, and they are free to take up any issues they like in their areas, except wages and questions regarding individuals. Their decisions are not binding, but the overwhelming majority of their recommendations are accepted. During one five-year period, one board logged more than two thousand recommendations, and all but six were adopted as policy. The areas probed by the boards range from the design and labeling of containers to new-product development, financial policies, office procedures, and manufacturing methods. At a meeting of a junior board I attended, the members discussed at great length the advisability of allowing stockholders to receive dividends in stock instead of cash (it was tentatively decided to propose the idea to the board of directors).

Aside from the very solid value of the suggestions received, the boards give middle managers a larger view of corporate operations than is customary. Fred Ogburn, director of human relations at the company's McCormick Division, told me: "The members get into discussions on subjects they would otherwise never be exposed to—engineering, marketing, financial problems, for example. There is no agreement on the principal value of the board system, but I think its greatest value is the contribution it makes to the development of its members."

Employees also participate financially in the company's operations. There is a profit-sharing plan into which is paid 7.5 percent of pretax earnings, and employees are given the opportunity to buy stock (about 70 percent to 80 percent do, and more than half the company's stock is owned by employees and the profit-sharing fund).

Though Charles McCormick (who died in 1970) was proud of having found "a way for people to participate,"[34] he did not feel that participation should extend to the very lowest levels. One top executive told me: "Charlie McCormick used to say that one man out of ten knows how to think"—and membership on the boards is still largely barred to the lower nine-tenths or so of the employees. A great many efforts are made to keep track of employee attitudes (through frequent meetings and attitude surveys made by outside organizations), and a very democratic spirit is maintained (there are, for example, no executive dining rooms or other irrational status indicators). But genuine participation at McCormick is still largely an upper-crust affair.

Some managers feel this must be changed. Ogburn told me: "We have not got to the point of each department setting its own objectives, but I see this as a definite possibility. The future of participative management is in carrying participation to all levels of the organization." Robert McFadden, a young, sophisticated personnel specialist who is corporate director of human relations, explained to me that the system may have to be changed to keep up with changing times: "Up to now we have been a very security-oriented company—we thought as long as we shared profits with people, that was enough. Now we are beginning to see—as other companies have seen—that that is no longer sufficient for today's employees." Thus McCormick's ideas may eventually be revised.

By most measures, the ideas still seem to be working well. In the 1962–71 decade, sales rose more than 150 percent to 140.6 million dollars, and per-share earnings by more than 200 percent. In 1971, after a 750,000-dollar payment to the profit-sharing fund, the company earned five million dollars, for a well-above-average 15 percent return on net worth. Moreover, employee morale is high, absenteeism is low, turnover is negligible, and the company receives from four thousand to five thousand applications to fill the seventy-five to eighty jobs it has to fill each year. As limited as it is, McCormick's idea of participation would still seem to be functioning. As expressed to me by Harry Wells, the company's president, the idea is admirably uncomplicated:

"We try to get everybody to take an active role in the business rather than just show up for work every morning."

No doubt the best-known of the Depression-generated management systems is the Scanlon Plan.

This plan is named after Joseph Scanlon, who originated it in the late 1930s. It is based on some rather strange principles, mainly arising from Scanlon's peculiar background: He had been a cost accountant, an ordinary worker, and a union official, and all of this experience is reflected in his plan. The plan arose, as so many others have arisen, largely by accident. Discussions in a company that was experiencing heavy losses and fighting for survival in the Depression had reached an impasse, and it was decided to make one last, desperate effort to correct the troubles: Management would simply inform the workers of the situation, plead with them to make every effort to cut costs and increase productivity, and promise them that they would be generously rewarded if the company did survive. To everyone's surprise, the technique worked marvelously well. The principles were then formalized so that other companies could use them, and the Scanlon Plan was thus born.

The plan is based on some extremely simple principles. First, some realistic, practical measure of a company's efficiency must be found. It might be production volume, operating profits, or whatever, though in later years it is usually total payroll divided by production value. Second, management and the union pick a "normal" past period and agree that, when results are above the ratio for that period, a portion of the increased profit (usually 75 percent) will be handed over to the workers, the total pot to be split among all employees (including white-collar and executive employees) in proportion to salary. (In case of unusually heavy capital investments or other changes, the formula might have to be refigured, but this is not often necessary.) A network of committees is set up to consider suggestions made by employees—which may affect any aspect of company operations—and those deemed of value are put into effect. The benefits are divided equitably among all, regardless of who makes the original suggestion.

The plan has been applied in dozens of companies in the

United States, generally with gratifying results. One study found that, among ten companies that had adopted the plan, productivity improved an average of 22.5 percent in the first year after the plan was adopted, and another 23.7 percent in the second year. The worst result was in a company that improved only 6.8 percent in the first year and 13.7 percent in the second year.

The secret of the plan's success, according to Fred Lesieur (who took over promotion of the plan after Scanlon's death) is its fulfillment of a basic need: "This plan doesn't mean giving people a 'sense of participation'; workers don't want that. This plan means giving them real participation."[35] Douglas McGregor, who greatly admired the plan, pointed out that the formal elements—the union-management agreement, the committees, the formula, and the solid system of rewards—meshed together to impel employees and managers to "literally discover a new way of life."[36] The real key is the spirit of participation created, though that was not itself part of the original design. In the more scientific methods of work reform we have looked at previously, great skill, ingenuity, and delicacy are used to create conditions under which workers can become more involved in their jobs and thus interested in giving their best efforts. The Scanlon Plan, in its own crude way, does the same thing more directly—by making it immediately apparent to employees that they themselves should take the initiative in becoming more involved. Thus it is in one way more honest but in another more devious—since it exploits the widely held belief that people work primarily to earn money and that, if bribed to work harder, they will work harder. The assurance that efforts will be rewarded in an equitable way undoubtedly provides the necessary initial impetus. Workers can produce at top capacity and can help each other instead of competing. The subtle sabotage and deliberate underproduction that is so common in industry is no longer needed. There are numerous examples of individual workers' output doubling or more the first day the plan is in effect. But the longer-range impact of the plan goes far beyond mere money. Gradually, the value of group effort becomes apparent, and group feeling becomes increasingly strong. These factors eventually outweigh the bonus payment in importance (when the bonus drops or evaporates temporarily, the cooperative atmosphere nevertheless re-

mains). A bonus payment alone is not enough—as is shown by
the widespread failures of profit-sharing plans and incentive payment techniques.

A brief review of the Scanlon Plan written by Fred Lesieur
and Elbridge S. Puckett (both of whom have been helping companies, as consultants, to put the plan into action) in 1969
notes that the plan is alive and well and continues to be adopted
by new companies—though the total number of companies using
it continues to be relatively small.[37] The plan works just as well
with the "normal, healthy cases" as with the "Depression cases"
originally touched by it; nevertheless, the fundamental principles
are the same. The authors note: "Probably most important to
the success of a Scanlon Plan is that everyone in the organization knows management wants to work with employees to improve
operations. . . . Collaboration is part of the job."

The above-mentioned "home-grown" management systems arose
in the crisis atmosphere of the Depression, but unusual results
can still be obtained through the introduction of drastic, though
common-sense, reforms.

One example is Overnite Transportation Co., a trucking company headquartered in Richmond, Virginia.[38] Faced with a
sharp decline in earnings and a sharp rise in lost and damaged
cargo claims, Harwood Cochrane, Overnite president, put into
effect a bonus system for terminal managers to cut expenses and
a stock-purchase plan for all employees to stimulate initiative,
both in 1970. The results surpassed all expectations, because the
plan was sufficiently closely tied to performance that employees
contributed their maximum effort to improving matters. Terminal
managers were so zealous in improving operations that claims
dropped by 80 percent in one year. Drivers also bore down
harder. Charlie Newsome had worked for the company for more
than thirty years, but the stock-ownership plan gave him a whole
new perspective: "After I became a stockholder, I felt I had to do
a better job. I really love my company."

Other people who love the company are the stockholders. In
1969–71, the company opened new territory, and its sales rose 44
percent—but net income rose 240 percent. The stock climbed
125 percent in calendar 1970 and another 145 percent in 1971,

thus generating considerable affection for the company among security analysts. One analyst at a Richmond brokerage firm remarked: "They've done what they should by their employees, and it's really paid off."

All the U.S. approaches to industrial organization that we have been discussing contain elements that may be characterized as "democratic"—that is, they alter conventional power structures, they give increased power and freedom to lower-level employees, and they help diffuse decision-making throughout the organization. But they all tend to be limited in that they do not contain a total management commitment to a continuously developing system of autonomy. All the above-discussed companies may, and probably will, develop further in the direction of democracy, but most of them have launched their programs with rather restricted aims in mind.

The companies that have gone farthest are those that have adopted a more far-reaching philosophy, variously described as an "open systems" or "total systems" or "socio-technical" approach. One key feature of this attack is that the limits to employee influence are placed as distant as possible (ideally, no limits at all should be placed). Another is the integration of technological systems with social systems, in a way that promotes the positive interaction between the two. In general, it may be said that this is the philosophy pioneered by, and largely identified with, the Tavistock Institute in London, as we have seen earlier.

The two companies that have made the most concrete progress along these lines are General Foods and Procter & Gamble.

The General Foods philosophy has been put into practice at a pet food factory in Topeka, Kansas. Lyman Ketchum, an organizational specialist at General Foods headquarters in White Plains, New York, explained to me that the new approach grew to a great extent out of experience at a pet food plant in Kankakee, Illinois, of which he had been manager. In the late 1960s, with the advent of an ever-younger workforce, an unfamiliar atmosphere was developing. "We discovered there was something different happening," Ketchum told me. "People were not aware of why they were behaving differently, they were just reacting in different ways." Ketchum mentioned poor quality production, horseplay, vandalism, and graffiti on the walls as symptoms of the discontent. He told me: "Bad quality is inevitably a product of alienation."

To attack these problems, management took an entirely new stance at the Topeka plant. "We used a total systems approach," Ketchum observed, "to match the business conditions with our beliefs about human beings. We intended to design certain principles into the system, and out of this would come high productivity as well as satisfaction." A planning group (which included an outside consultant, Richard Walton from Harvard) pointed to changes in society as a principal influence on the new approach: "Present business, educational and social trends indicate that organizations must consider ways to more fully utilize individuals' potential and meet their needs. Yesterday's employees that were depersonalized by organizations merely became apathetic but generally compliant. . . . But today's employees who become alienated by the organization are more likely to actively challenge or even attack the organization."[39]

The planning group analyzed the nature of the plant's operation in connection with the needs of people—e.g., self-esteem, sense of accomplishment, autonomy, increasing knowledge of and data on their performance.[40] This early consideration of employee needs had an impact on planning the plant (although the group started too late to be able to make basic alterations in the technology). Ketchum explained to me that each point on the list had a tangible meaning: "If people are to have self-esteem, you have to do things to satisfy this need. If they are to have a sense of accomplishment, they have to be able to finish their tasks. Autonomy—they have to be able to plan the work, check the quality, change the design of jobs. They have to have real control, and not just over simple stuff like when they can take a coffee break—it's the real guts of the job." One consequence was minimization of the workforce to make the job more challenging. "Usually, there's an awful lot of overcrewing and overmanagement. This time we didn't do that. We started with the bare bones and want to keep it that way." Along the same lines, the planners omitted as many specialized functions as possible. "We tried to put all the responsibilities and all the skills in the teams," Ketchum said. "It's totally different—a whole new approach." Other features of the new plant were elimination of time clocks, a management style encouraging people to participate, a minimum of supervision (there are no foremen—there are "team leaders"), information systems that promote decentralized decision-making, provision of broad educational and personal improvement opportunities, and a minimum of status symbols.

After about eighteen months of operation, the Topeka plant appeared to be working out very much as planned. Ed Dulworth, plant manager, told me that all the unusual features had been retained; indeed, employees were being given more freedom than planned: "People have much more responsibilities here, broader jobs, more authority, a lot of freedom. There are very few written statements as to what is expected in terms of behavior. There are no time clocks, and people are free to come and go when they wish. In the plant, operators are free to arrange the tasks among themselves. The scheduling—who does what and when—is all handled by the people in the plant. Everybody is very involved in all aspects of the business. We have committees for safety, fire-and-disaster, spare parts, welfare and benefits, recreation, and so on. Almost everyone has some part in the committee work."

There are two teams—an eight-man processing team and a sixteen-man packaging-warehousing team—operating on each of three shifts. There are about ninety employees, including office staff. Normally, there would be cleaners, helpers, process operators, mechanics, boiler operators, quality control technicians, fork truck drivers, grain unloaders, and others on each team. But here there are no job categories for operators—everybody learns every job. When I visited the plant, employees were just finishing the process of learning all the jobs on their team, and the movement from one team to the other, to learn additional jobs, was just beginning. Everyone learns at his own pace—his progress being judged by his fellow team members—and moves up the pay scale according to his own progress (regardless of seniority or how many others are moving up at the same time). Starting pay in mid-1972 was 136 dollars a week; by learning a full team's jobs, employees move up to 142 dollars; by learning more jobs "across the plant," they move gradually up to 170 dollars; and by acquiring an unusual skill or expertise, they can move up to 192 dollars (a step nobody had reached at the time of my visit). Dulworth says: "We feel that the more jobs a person knows the better he can do any job, since lots of things that happen affect several jobs. We're paying for knowledge beyond what is required. For example, you can get people to do jobs like loading materials eight hours a day rather cheaply. But that's an undesirable job, and the people here share the undesirable jobs." Among the unplanned responsibilities taken over by the employees is the job of hiring and firing. Potential new employees are screened by the teams and, occasionally, they are expelled on the decision of their teammates. The system has undergone changes in other ways. Dulworth notes that there were complaints about holiday pay, so that was changed. "The operating group analyzed the packaging operation," he explained, "and decided more people were needed there—so we hired more people." One unexpected development carries some legal risks. "Our guys are supposed to be paid for time worked," Dulworth told me, "but it's not always so. People come in outside working hours—there's quite a lot of that. For example, we were working on installing a recreation room, but the cost was taken out of our budget—so the employees are working on it on their own time."

Dulworth emphasizes that more change in the system is expected. He said: "The willingness not to be static is critical. What we have may not be right. Everybody's learning. We have to be ready and willing to change."

Over-all costs of the product are considerably lower than would customarily be expected in a conventional plant, and quality is higher because of greater worker involvement.

But perhaps the most significant measure of the plant's merits is in the attitudes of workers, which are overwhelmingly positive. Jim Weaver, a thirty-four-year-old operator, gave me his reaction: "I started in bulk unloading, then went to the utility building, where I learned to operate the boiler, heating and ventilation system, and the cooling tower. Then I went to the central control room in the process tower, and now I'm an expander operator. There are seven people in the process tower, and all seven know all the jobs. If we get some time ahead, we go down to the packaging department so we get ahead in learning those jobs.

Next I'll be switching to the packaging department. It's much better to move around. I get bored staying on one job. When I came here I didn't know what an expander was, they just said this is your baby, you do it. We had to learn everything from the ground up. When you learn one job, you teach it to the next guy, and every guy finds a new and better way of doing things. Some guys have designed their own tools to make the work easier. We do our own maintenance work and lubrication. Everything that goes on here, we do it. Moving from job to job makes it more challenging. A man comes to the point where he knows all about one job—it's possible to be *too* familiar with a machine, and then you take risks. Moving from job to job, it makes you more alert. I get a kind of joy out of it because it's challenging. If they ask me to go over to the utility building to help out, I go because I know the job. I think we save the company money that way because otherwise they'd have to have more overtime. Ninety-five percent of the employees are sold on the system. We're the foundation of what it's going to be in the future—the Topeka System. We've had our problems, but we can sit down and work them out. I like General Foods. It's the only job I ever had where I felt I was part of the company. General Foods put responsibility on me, and I can accept it. I feel, being chairman of the safety committee, I should be paid extra, but I like it. I feel wanted. I've been ill and come to work anyway because I know I'm needed. General Foods affords me happiness. If a man is happy in his work he'll be happy at home. Before, I'd never been anywhere in the United States. But now I've been to all the safety meetings in New York, Michigan—they don't send management, they send me. When a salesman comes around to sell safety equipment, Ed Dulworth sends him to see me. I suggested that our committee go to the National Safety Council meeting in Chicago—it was going to cost three thousand dollars—so Ed said O.K., you set it up—I thought he was kidding, but the whole committee went. Being black, I always wanted to be a part of something, but it seemed every time I tried something I got pushed back. I feel many people could do things but they're not given the opportunity. These people make me feel important. Two years ago I wouldn't have thought it possible to find this many people who took such pride in their job. I feel in the future that the Topeka

System will be such a success that other people will be asking us to help them out."

In fact, the system is already sufficiently successful that the employees have been asked for help—in designing an addition to the plant. Operators in the existing plant were asked to contribute ideas for the new addition; one suggestion was that the core group being sent to the new plant to help train new workers should not be paid extra for taking on extra responsibilities, since that would be unfair to the other workers.

Bill Easter, manufacturing manager of the new plant, explained to me that the special management system is to some extent built into the technology of the new plant: "Some aspects of the plant are different from what they otherwise would have been—to suit the open style of management." The technology has been revamped to change the character of the jobs. "Often," says Easter, "there is no opportunity for operators to see what goes on before or after their stage, so we've grouped operations together so operators can relate to each other and to the process better. They have more of an opportunity to sense their responsibility. We're trying to get all operations under one team grouped together so they all have visibility." Easter explained that "maximum automation" is not always the best answer: "If your aim is to make an idiot-proof factory so nobody can fuck it up, that's right. But not if you want to have systems arranged so people have control over more things and are able to see their part in the process. For our products you can't take the man out of it completely. His judgment is absolutely necessary. We find that when we've taken automation as far as we can, then the man becomes uninvolved—and that affects quality. We have to have people on the alert so they can make changes minute by minute."

The plant designers have seized every opportunity to design more interest in the jobs. Easter says: "Traditionally, one job is picking up packages of frozen meat and stripping the paper off—that is all the man does. We are now providing a hydraulic lift table the man can adjust to the height he wants, and he also has a window where he can see the process, and he works a control board—he will be really involved in the process. Ordinarily, all this would be split up into several jobs. We will have three guys in all, but all of them are involved in the job." The "lean" crewing principle is being followed in the new plant, which will have 85 to 100 people, instead of 150 to 175 under orthodox methods.

Could a new manager with more conventional ideas destroy the "Topeka System"? Actually, clever as the technological designs are, there is nothing to preclude the use of orthodox autocratic techniques. But Dulworth doubts it could happen: "We have some outstanding performance—it's as good as they've ever seen in the company. Also, we have an established culture. It would be very difficult to change that. If anybody came in here and wanted to change it he would have a fight on his hands. It wouldn't be impossible, but the reaction would be extremely quick. Things would start coming apart almost immediately."

Considering the employees' almost incredible attachment to their plant, this seems believable. When asked how he might like to work at another company, Jim Weaver answered: "You'd have a hell of a time getting me to leave this place."

Without doubt the most radical organizational changes made on a practical, operating, day-to-day basis in the United States have taken place at Procter & Gamble, America's twenty-first largest company and well known for its hard-boiled, aggressive management practices. The P&G experience is of great significance for our discussions because of the size of the company, the radical nature of the changes that have taken place, and the scope of those changes. Primarily devoted to making good soap and fat profits, P&G has minimal interest in "in" management methods or modish nomenclature; but Charles Krone, the dynamic head of organizational development at P&G's "Ivorydale" Cincinnati headquarters, in discussing his approach, says: "I call it industrial democracy."

The new P&G program was first put into operation in the late 1960s at a plant in Lima, Ohio, employing about 125 people in three shifts, producing two consumer products, one in a batch process and the other in a continuous process. Krone explained to me that the new ideas were designed into the plant—which uses rather advanced technology and is highly automated: "The plant was designed from the ground up to be democratic. The technology—the location of instruments, for example—was designed to stimulate relationships between people, to bring about autonomous group behavior, and to allow people to affect their own environment." Conference rooms, laboratories, and other service functions are located immediately adjacent to the production area, so that any needed action can be taken without delay. The basic principle, as enunciated by Krone, is that the human being has "growthful potential." And a key to the design and operation of the plant is that no barriers should be placed to hinder that growth. Just as there are no physical barriers, so there are no barriers between jobs. Indeed, there are no jobs at all in the ordinary sense. In an orthodox plant of this type, there might be sixteen to twenty job classifications—at Lima there are none. Not everybody can do every job, but every member of "the community" (as Krone refers to the employees) is constantly adding to his own skills in some specialized field. Krone says: "Each individual defines the direction in which he wants to grow." The community decided, however, that every member must continue to share responsibility for day-to-day operations. "You might be a laboratory technician," Krone says, "but you also handle operating jobs. Everybody carries the same minimum responsibility. No matter where you go, you always have to go back to the operation—you cannot become exclusively a specialist. Everybody is responsible for the throughput." Since the members of the community have taken over responsibility for hiring and firing, the nonspecialization characteristic has become an accepted feature of the plant. Krone says: "One guy became a very skilled machinist and wanted to concentrate on his skill—so the community fired him. They told him there was plenty of opportunity for that on the outside. This system grew up naturally at the wish of the members—it was not imposed." (In passing, we can note the remarkable similarity of this P&G plant with the kibbutzim in Israel, where cabinet ministers and engineers routinely share in the jobs of serving breakfast and washing dishes.)

In reaching out beyond the operating jobs to handle special problems, the members of the community are constantly acting upon and enlarging their environment; the environment does not stop at the walls of the plant. Krone says: "A person is part of a total social system, a product system, a total environment made up of all the environments he relates to. Rather than looking intensively inward at the technology, employees are constantly mediating their environment." They might, for example, need to confer with suppliers, with corporate headquarters line specialists, or with outside consultants—all of which they are encouraged to do. They might meet with the marketing manager to help plan, say, a special promotional campaign to fill up excess capacity they know is coming up. Krone says that this can on occasion be a great help to a marketing brand manager: "If he knows what they are thinking about and what they are able to do, he can fit his problems and their capacities together."

The members of this unusual community were judged to have, when they were hired, "high innate capacity," but they did not have any special training or skills. "However," Krone points out, "after the plant has been in operation for three years, they are by now probably among the most highly skilled people in the company. One man who was a farmer would now be called a very highly skilled instrument specialist. He designed the plant's whole instrument control system, and did it entirely on his own initiative, working with manufacturers."

The members of the community have virtually complete control of the plant. There are no time clocks or other symbols of petty "class" distinctions, and everybody is on straight salary. "The manager," says Krone, "has very little decision-making power. Usually, instead of being seen as a resource, he is seen as an invader, fulfilling a directive and controlling role—there is much less of that here." Among other things, the members of the community work out the pay scales themselves, and all the salaries are known to everyone. In order to do this, workers are given information or community averages, costs, and the like. I asked Krone if the company gave them complete financial figures on their operation. "Well, no," he answered, "they give them to us. One guy is interested in accounting, and he develops all that information. They draw up their own budgets and so on." Isn't this a dangerous method of setting wage scales? "Sure," Krone says, "they could hold us up and say you're not paying us enough. But by now you could almost say those employees have less interest in their pay than management people do, who think the Lima people are not being paid enough."

The unorthodox methods at Lima have proved somewhat perplexing to the rest of the company. A technical services group from

corporate headquarters was constantly asking for the plant chemical engineer—it took a year for the fact to sink in that there was
no chemical engineer.

However, the plant's hard data are easily understandable. Even
though the pay scale is considerably higher than is customary,
over-all costs are approximately 50 percent of a conventional plant.
Though much of that is because of the advanced technology, the
advanced technology could not function properly if there were
not an advanced social system. Quality is also affected. Krone told
me: "It has the most outstanding quality record of any plant we
have—it is virtually perfect quality."

The results have, in fact, been so good that the open-system
principles have been applied to a number of other new P&G
plants constructed over the past few years, and as this is written
the employees in such plants total close to 10 percent of the
company's twenty-eight thousand U.S. employees. Considering
the very different nature of the new approach and the short time
it has been in operation, this is an astonishingly high figure. Since
the open-system methods have proved spectacularly profitable, it
is highly likely that this figure will rise farther in the future.
Though the introduction of bold new management methods at
P&G took the form of a kind of "guerrilla warfare" in the beginning, when top management had only a dim understanding of
what was going on, the new principles seem now to be firmly
and inextricably established.

Indeed, perhaps the best test of the new methods is that they
are being introduced successfully in long-established operations.
Obviously, creating a special atmosphere in a brand-new environment is quite a different matter from working in a location that
already has its own climate. But now, increasing efforts are being
made at "Ivorydale," the sprawling collection of aging structures
housing half a dozen production operations as well as corporate
headquarters. "A few years ago," says Krone, "the attitude was
that if you wanted something to work, don't put it in Ivorydale."

The initial attack at Ivorydale was on a modest level. In rearranging a warehouse conveyor-belt system, which resulted in
job changes for some two hundred employees, management discovered that the change, made without the involvement of employees, had generated a tremendous amount of friction and dis-

content. Therefore, when plans were being drawn up to make a similar change in a nearby location, an effort was launched a year in advance to inform every person affected. This might seem pointless, since the essential nature of the change had been decided. Nevertheless, it was learned that the employees had strong opinions about the allocation of the new jobs. Marlyn Rabenold, a P&G internal consultant, told me the solution was rather a simple one. "The people themselves made the decisions about who got what jobs," he told me. "It was tremendously important to them, and of no importance whatever to management. The change went extraordinarily smoothly, in contrast to the great friction in the first change."

After some other promising experiments in getting employee participation, management is, at this writing, in fact planning construction of a new manufacturing facility at Ivorydale, and is discussing the plans with more than a hundred persons who are involved—management people and engineers as well as production, clerical, maintenance, and crafts people. Rabenold explained to me: "We're giving people increasingly more choice. This will be a much better design because we're getting the opinions of the people who will be running it." Aren't all these meetings and discussions rather costly and time-consuming? Probably—but the benefits appear to outweigh the extra costs. In the new facility being planned, for example, the project has so far been underspending its budget.

The outstanding characteristic of the P&G approach is its insistence on a truly "open" attitude. In line with the notion that the employee is a "growthful potential human being," no borders are erected to limit employee influence on company affairs. That these principles have been applied in a major U.S. company over a period of some years and in widely scattered locations— with excellent results—is strong evidence of the benefits of giving power and freedom to employees. So far, the company appears to be succeeding in the objective, as described by Charles Krone: "What we're trying to get to is something dynamic, creative, and democratic."

Even the most casual—and most skeptical—glance at the experience of companies such as those discussed above should convince most observers that democratization of organizations not only enriches employees' lives on and off the job, but also tends to generate fat returns in the form of higher productivity, as it logically should, since it permits each individual to contribute his maximum effort. As Katz and Kahn state in their authoritative study of organizations: "It is paradoxical that the standard justification for autocratic practice in industry is its alleged efficiency, since the empirical research results do not support that conclusion."[41] But this is the aspect of industrial democracy that is most often questioned, and disbelief in the profitability of democracy is a formidable barrier (though by no means the only one) to the acceptance of industrial democracy.

Therefore, it is quite significant that the collection of precise details on the relation between profits and management styles is now under way. A massive research effort, launched in 1970 and scheduled to run at least through 1975, involving eleven thousand persons at twenty organizational sites in eight different companies and costing several million dollars, is designed to provide detailed information on just this question. The project is known as "Inter-Company Longitudinal Studies" and is being carried out by a team headed by William C. Pyle at the Institute for Social Research at the University of Michigan.

This high-powered project is the brainchild of the imaginative Rensis Likert. As noted earlier, Likert has long believed that "the highest producing managers in American companies are using, on the average, the same basic principles of managing the human organization"—that is, the participative methods embodied in System 4. Moreover: "These principles differ in fundamental respects from the principles being used by managers who are achieving only average results." And both these points, Likert notes, have been documented in hundreds of companies through use of his rating forms.[42]

Gradually, Likert realized that there was one formidable factor that not only tended to deter managers from introducing democratic methods but actually encouraged them to use the old-fashioned autocratic techniques. This factor is time. A first inkling of this fact emerged from an experiment with clerical workers, in which two substantially identical groups of workers were treated in two different ways—one by authoritarian methods, the other by participative methods. Unexpectedly, the experiment had to be broken off after a year. At the end of that time, some of the hoped-for results had been obtained: In the participative group, "the perceptions, motivations, performance goals, and turnover" had improved, while all these had worsened in the authoritarian group. Productivity rose in both groups, but, surprisingly, by 25 percent in the authoritarian group against only 20 percent in the participative group. This was puzzling, because it was apparent that the conflicts and poor morale in the authoritarian group would inevitably damage results.[43]

Thus attention was focused on the time factor, which appears to be a critical one because of the customs of American business. Impressive short-term results can frequently be produced by hard-hitting managers who are generating a long-term catastrophe. Such conduct, says Likert, is encouraged by corporate reward systems that "enable a manager who is a 'pressure artist' to achieve high earnings over a few years, while destroying the loyalties, favorable attitudes, cooperative motivations, etc., among the supervisory and non-supervisory members of the organization."[44] Such steamroller managers are frequently even promoted in recognition of their talents after, say, two or three years, which is just about the period that elapses before the damage begins to show up in the figures, leaving someone else to clean up (and no doubt take the blame for) the wreckage. (Conversely, a manager interested in building up a smoothly running organization based on participative methods must realize that his efforts will most likely not show up for two years or probably more, during which time he will be expected to answer for his unorthodox strategy to his superiors.)

What is happening, in effect, is that valuable resources are being disposed of and earnings being given a short-term, artificial boost. No management would stand for such cavalier treatment of physical assets, and even if management were willing, the auditors would not be. Since human resources do not appear on the balance sheet, they can be liquidated at will by managers oriented to "the bottom line" (where net profit appears), in order to give a spurious injection to earnings.

In recent years in the United States, bottom-line-oriented managers have no doubt been in the ascendancy, in great part due to the vogue for "conglomerates," which are concerned much with money, little with people. Nancy Belliveau, in a survey of financial-minded managers, cites one conglomerate that acquired a company consisting primarily of scientists who did not care for the hard-driving philosophy of the acquiring company and all of whom left within a year.[45] One insider was quoted as saying: "They paid $5 million for nothing." Outstanding examples of financial-minded conglomerates are Litton Industries, some of whose recent problems, it is felt, "can be traced directly to the financial man's insensitivity to human factors," and ITT, about which one observer says: "The name of the game is perform or get out. It's much less important to be people sensitive." It is quite possible that this heavy bottom-line orientation explains the troubles of many conglomerates recently and, consequently, the decline in the popularity of that particular fad in Wall Street.

The Michigan research project is aimed at clarifying such matters through "human resource accounting," which will, ideally, reflect immediately any deterioration or improvement in a company's human resources where it can be easily spotted—in the financial statements. To be sure, that the efforts of human beings have considerable monetary value is hardly news. Indeed, it is one of the fundamentals of capitalism and one that, in his commentary on the theory of surplus value, Marx found quite irritating. "The value of labor-power," he wrote, "and the value which that labor-power creates in the labor process, are two entirely different magnitudes."[46] The point is of great continuing importance in capitalism. Benjamin Graham and David Dodd, in their classic work on security analysis, wrote: "The appraisal of management is considered an essential—perhaps *the* essential —factor in determining whether an investment should be made in a given business."[47] Bernard Baruch flatly stated that the "most important" factor in evaluating a company was "the character and brains of management."[48] Surprisingly little effort has been devoted to gaining a more precise picture of that factor, partly, no doubt, because it seems a trifle immoral. The Michigan team notes: "We also have difficulty thinking of people individually as assets since they are not legally owned by the firm and because of cultural constraints or taboos on the notion of valuing an individual in monetary terms."[49] Still, a standard bromide in every company annual report is a tribute to "our most valuable asset," the employees, and if such statements have any sense at all, there should be no objection to making them a bit more precise.

The Michigan team has laid out three basic approaches to the problem, by computing figures for (1) the value of investments in human resources (approximately corresponding to book value for physical assets); (2) replacement values; and (3) economic values, that is, the capitalized value of earnings directly attributable to these resources.

A good start has been made on the first two, which include "expenditures in recruiting, hiring, training, developing, and organizing employees into effective work groups" (except for changes in general price levels and training or other procedures, these first two values should be roughly the same). Since 1966, the R. G. Barry Corp., discussed earlier in connection with its participative management program, has been developing, with the help of the Michigan team, methods of calculating these figures. By 1970, "book value" figures had been computed for all 147 managers in the company and 425 factory and clerical personnel. It was discovered that a first-line supervisor called for an investment of about three thousand dollars, a middle manager, fifteen thousand, and thirty thousand or more for a top executive. The figures are modified occasionally, and the investments are amortized over a period of time corresponding to an employee's estimated tenure with the company.

In 1969, Barry drew up, for internal use, a "capital budget for human resources," believed to be the first of its kind, which can answer questions in such areas as new expenditures for training programs, the real costs of employee turnover, and whether the human resources in any particular department are rising or falling. In this way, if any manager attempts to juice up short-term profits at the expense of human resources, top management will be alerted immediately. In its 1969 annual report, Barry gave some actual dollar figures relating to the value of its employees. Thus it was shown that, because of heavy employee-development costs (which, logically, might be better capitalized than expensed), reported earnings were understated by about 10 percent, and that when "net investments in human resources" were added to the asset side of the balance sheet, total assets rose by some 15 percent. (When word leaked out about the unconventional report, the Securities & Exchange Commission nervously asked Barry to delay releasing it pending a closer look, but relaxed when it saw that the figures were illustrative, experimental, and unaudited, and clearly labeled as such.)

The Michigan team hopes that, within a very few years, the value of this approach can be more concretely demonstrated. Eventually, the "economic value"—that is, the real earning power —of human resources can be measured. William C. Pyle writes that such measurements would take into account "group" values: "It is well known that human resources value exists not only in capabilities of individuals, but it is also dependent upon the effective interaction of employees."[50]

The practical value of the idea is already quite clear. Edward Stan, treasurer of the Barry Corp., says: "Representatives of the banks with which we deal and representatives of other of our long-term creditors have been to our plant, talked to our people, and then made their evaluations. With our Human Resources Accounting system, we can assist them in their evaluation and hopefully improve the accuracy of their assessment of us."[51]

As understanding of human resource accounting becomes more widespread, it will unquestionably spur managements to adopt more democratic management methods, if only to more effectively pursue that primary capitalistic goal: profit.

The advanced management methods we have been discussing have been introduced in U.S. companies primarily because they "work" in conventional terms, but we have seen that they are of excellent help in bringing about a true democratization of companies—breaking up orthodox power patterns and diffusing influence throughout the organization. If knowledge of these techniques had been available to the creators of the self-management system in Yugoslavia, the *Mitbestimmung* system in West Germany, the Histadrut democratic experiments in Israel, or the Guild Socialist movement in Britain in the 1920s, the subsequent histories of these phenomena might have been very different.

Yet there is little or no recognition of, or interest in, this fact in America. Most of the people who have been developing these methods dislike the use of the word "democracy" to describe their work. Frederick Herzberg, truly a pioneer in recognizing employee needs for carrying greater responsibility, flatly rejects the "democracy" label for his work. So do many others, with varying degrees of insistence. J. I. Johnston of Monsanto frowns on the use of the word, preferring "collaborative environment." George Raymond, president of Raymond Corp., which has made some far-reaching organizational changes—time clocks have been abolished, all employees have been put on straight salary, and the opinions of workers are elicited when production changes are made—told me he would definitely not characterize his company as democratic: "No, definitely not. This is not a democracy. To me, democracy means majority rule, and I'm not going to take a vote on running the company."

The issue extends far beyond mere terminology. In much of the recent discussion of work-related problems in America, there is the assumption that, since a main culprit is an abundance of tedious jobs created by short-sighted managements, the answer is the creation of fascinating jobs by far-sighted managements. A great deal of attention is given to the rearrangement of tasks in "job enlargement" or "job enrichment" or "job design" projects by managements which, having noted worker discontent and desire for more control, are sagely expanding the worker-control area by a fixed amount and therefore assuming they have liquidated the root problem.

But the root problem is not a faulty arrangement of jobs, it is a question of faulty power patterns; the arrangements of jobs are only surface symptoms, and projects that do nothing but rearrange jobs without altering the power structure are only surface solutions.

To be sure, any job reshuffling that gives workers increased control is a step on the road to democracy, and the assembly-line worker who sees the time span of his job increased from, say, forty to seventy seconds, and his task widened from tightening one bolt to tightening two bolts, will doubtless warmly appreciate the change. But we might logically describe as *fully* democratic those organizational systems that regard employee influence as a healthy and desirable phenomenon, are planned from the ground up to nurture and encourage such influence, and therefore do not set narrow, management-fixed limits to the scope of that influence. We have referred to such arrangements as the "open systems" or "total systems" approach and have seen them used with spectacular effect at some plants of General Foods and Procter & Gamble. A central key in these systems is the extent to which employees are allowed to deal directly with their own environments, and thus achieve the freedom, autonomy, and opportunity for personal development that must be contained in a truly democratic system. Any person confined within the strict limits of a management-created fixed "job" and therefore barred from dealing with his environment is still functioning only at half speed. And if we allow that a person must be allowed to deal directly and freely with his environment, then we must also allow that, in a dynamic and changing organization, the environment is also dynamic and changing. Charles Krone of P&G pointed out to me: "Most scientists in this field have failed to grasp the over-all concept. They aren't thinking in large enough terms. If you don't have a workforce that is transacting with its environment, then it's a static system and out of phase."

This point is being increasingly recognized by companies, though in a somewhat dim way. In a great many cases, an evolutionary transformation of a system occurs quite accidentally—as when, at Eaton's Kearney plant, a chance remark by a worker following a job change showed management that workers should be included in planning production changes—dramatizing the fact that systems do tend to grow whether they are planned that way or not. Job-enrichment experts in America are increasingly recommending that the employees themselves must participate in reforming their own jobs and that the change process, in order to work, has to be continuous. Moreover, it is recognized that job design projects cannot be confined to one part of a company. If they are to have any life or usefulness at all, plans must be made for gradual extension beyond one or two departments. In other words, a vital part of a truly dynamic and useful system is one where growth is not only tolerated but expected and prepared for.

We can remark in passing that the difference between these two approaches—the limited job-rearrangement and the unlimited "open systems" concept—might also be said to mark the difference between "manipulative" and truly employee-oriented practices. The suspicion of "manipulation" for management's narrow purposes is of course common, and employees are justifiably hostile if they see spurious benefits to themselves being offered in return for changes of great benefit to management. On the whole, the case histories we have been reviewing have given benefits both to management and to workers. As a rule of thumb, we might say that the deciding factor is one of "choice." If the reorganization process results in increased choice for the employee, we can fairly say it is operating in his best interests. If not, if management-decided changes merely substitute a modern straitjacket for an old-fashioned straitjacket, then we may fairly conclude that the system is dishonest and manipulative and has little regard for the employee. A completely open system provides, of course, maximum choice.

However, some of the methods have sometimes been used primarily to suppress employee grievances. One major insurance company that instituted a broad job-enrichment program happily concluded that the principal benefit was a decline in the number of requests for wage increases on the part of the workers. Yet the employees were not being given any appreciable benefits to offset this development. It may be presumed—indeed, it may be hoped—that this type of practice will backfire.

Just as we see that, in scientifically planned open-systems organizations, there are no artificial barriers to employee influence within a company, we can also see that the natural "environment" does not stop at the walls of the company. It is obvious that the experiences of employees on the job affect their total existence. As Jim Weaver of General Foods puts it: "If a man's happy at his work he'll be happy at home." The beneficial effects of satisfying work on workers' private lives have been often noticed. Richard Walton, consultant at the General Foods plant, notes: "Team leaders and other plant managers have been unusually active in civic affairs—apparently significantly more active than is typical of other plants of the same corporation or other plants in the same community. It's possible that participatory democracy introduced in the plant will spread to other institutional settings."[52] Will McWhinney, a UCLA psychologist who has worked as a consultant with P&G, reports: "One of the striking features in our pure 'open' systems plant is that workers take on more activities outside the workplace. The most visible involvements had to do with community racial troubles. Following major disturbances in the small city where they lived, a number of workers organized the black community to deal directly with the leaders of the city and of industry. . . . Blue-collar workers won elections to the school board majority office and other local positions. Nearly 10 percent of the work force of one plant holds elective offices currently. . . . We have noted that 'open' systems workers join more social clubs and political organizations."[53] Similarly, experts are recognizing the massive impact of social developments on job attitudes. Louis Davis, a UCLA work psychologist who began arguing for a total-systems approach to work organizations long before most experts realized there was anything wrong with their orthodox organizations, has said: "The social and the technological forces can be seen working toward the same end, for 'job characteristics that develop commitment' and thus promote the economic goals of the highly automated enterprise are exactly those that are beginning to emerge as demands for 'meaningfulness' from the social environment—participation and control, personal freedom and initiative."[54]

Surprisingly few of the companies I have visited have given much thought to where the changes they are promoting in their organizations might ultimately lead them, even though they often see a process developing that tends to have a life of its own. But it is apparent that the ultimate scope of the changes may be rather large. Many behavioral scientists, a group not generally noted for revolutionary fervor, thus find themselves engaged in a potentially explosive social movement. Stanley Seashore, at the Michigan Institute for Social Research, told me: "If you want to think large thoughts, you could say that it is a whole new phase of human existence." This is a rather new thing for these scientists, who have in the past tried to copy the physical sciences and confine themselves to measuring, weighing, testing, and other such chores. This is changing. In 1969, George Miller, president of the American Psychological Association, said: "Our obligations as citizens . . . are considerably broader than our obligations as scientists. . . . We are in serious need of many more psychological technologists who can apply our science to the personal and social problems of the general public."[55]

In general, company top managements have not been terribly aware of the radically new techniques introduced in their companies, and they are especially not aware of the potential social implications they may be promoting. Nor are those who are most instrumental in bringing about the changes all that eager to provide careful explanations of their activities. Some of the most impressive projects have thus been quietly engineered by executives working as "infiltrators" who have kept their projects quiet for years. The unorthodox management methods used in one plant of a major American company were kept hidden from top management for more than ten years. (When asked why, the plant manager replied: "I don't trust this company.") Though increasing attention is now being paid to these advanced management methods, many scientists still feel that keeping quiet is the best policy. One young psychologist told me: "I don't try to mislead people, but if I know we're going quite far along this road I don't necessarily say that to every manager. I deal with them on the level they can understand." Another scientist who has been responsible for some extremely successful projects in his company remarked: "My predecessor created this job more or less by accident and in my five years here I have had to struggle to have my ideas accepted. I think that management can accept participation on a pragmatic level but not otherwise. If they thought there were any further ideas involved, they would reject it."

But regardless of some reluctance, most of the scientists are optimistic. Charles Hughes of Texas Instruments observed to me: "I am convinced that there is going to be a massive attack on this within this decade." More strongly, one plant manager, whose top management has been deeply suspicious of the peculiar participative methods he is using, when asked if his methods were supposed to be revolutionary, replied: "You damned right —and it's about time!"

XIII. SCANDINAVIA: MODEL (AS USUAL) FOR THE WORLD?

Most of the thinking about industrial democracy and most of the systems that have been put into effect have revolved around intuitive, trial-and-error theorizing about formal power relations, incorporating only hazy or nonexistent understanding of how power actually functions in organizations. In America, a vast quantity of knowledge of organizations has been developed, but its relevance to democracy is generally unrecognized (or at least not openly admitted), and there has been approximately zero interest in applying this knowledge to industrial democracy.

The blending of the ideology of industrial democracy with sophisticated scientific knowledge of organizations is thus a matter of critical importance. Ideas of democracy and justice are no doubt admirable in themselves, but if they are to have any practical utility, it should be possible to present some solid evidence of the fact. As it happens, a rather impressive body of such evidence has been accumulating over the past decade or so in Scandinavia. It constitutes the best demonstration to date that industrial democracy is a sound and workable idea. It seems inevitable that large changes will take place in industrial organization forms in Scandinavia, very possibly forming a pattern that the rest of the world will find it difficult to ignore.

The first marriage of industrial democracy ideology and scientific methods took place in Norway, beginning in the early 1960s. Around that time, there was a widespread feeling among the general population that, in a democratic society, the application of democratic principles in business organizations was not only logical and necessary but a matter of urgency. Norway had a strong and unified labor movement and a system of workers' councils, but they were considered inadequate to give workers real power in company decision-making. Alf Andersen, a union leader, said in 1960: "We must go further. In the life of workers and companies there must be created an internal democracy where consultation and cooperation give employees a stronger position than before. Employees must be granted a real role in decision-making in the individual company."[1] This view was fully shared by the public. A survey at about that time showed that 56 percent of blue-collar workers and 67 percent of white-collar workers wanted more control over their own work and working conditions, and 16 percent and 11 percent, respectively, wanted to participate in over-all company decisions. Only about a fifth of both groups professed to have no interest in such matters.[2]

It was one thing to recognize the problem, quite another to solve it. In 1961, a committee was established jointly by LO (the central labor confederation) and the ruling Social Democratic Labor Party, with labor leader Tor Aspengren as chairman. In 1962 the Aspengren Committee made its report, in which it recommended that a new company body should be created, known as the *bedriftsforsamling*—literally, "company assembly"—to be interposed between the board of directors and the shareholders and to consist of one-third worker representatives. The idea was thus similar to the West German *Mitbestimmung* system, with that arrangement's overformalist weaknesses.

At the same time, a thirty-seven-year-old psychologist named Einar Thorsrud, at the Institute for Research in Industrial Environments in Trondheim, was becoming interested in the same questions. He thought that the longings for industrial democracy had a readily recognizable basis. "Many of us felt," he told me, "that the feelings of alienation, the problems of tediousness, were connected with lack of control over work and personal participation." While the Aspengren Committee was working on the question from one angle, Thorsrud began a series of discussions with labor leaders, with a completely different orientation.

Thorsrud had been much impressed with the work of the Tavistock Institute in London on work organizations, and particularly with the concept of the socio-technical system and the methods developed in that work to grant increased power and responsibility to lower-level workers for the management of their own work, with a minimum of supervision. This, he felt, was the real key to industrial democracy: Worker control over matters that were of intimate interest to workers on a day-to-day basis and about which they had great knowledge. If the scientific methods worked out at Tavistock could be somehow coupled with the ideological demands just then being raised in Norway, Thorsrud felt that this could be a momentous breakthrough—and he was right.

Fortunately for the Norwegians, Tavistock's startling findings, which went against all the most cherished principles of industrial capitalism, did not—as we have seen—strike a responsive note in British power circles, and Thorsrud was therefore able to interest some of the leading minds at Tavistock in working in Norway.

Therefore, in early 1962, Thorsrud, who by this time had managed to persuade both labor and management leaders in Norway to underwrite a more scientific survey of industrial democracy (the labor unions agreed to abandon their support of the legislative proposal for the time being), began to develop plans for actual on-the-spot experiments in Norwegian companies with the collaboration of people from Tavistock. Thorsrud recently recalled: "One reason we were able to accomplish something was that we got the best people from Tavistock to work with us—they had no chance to work in England. Now the English are coming to Norway to learn about what we got from England."

The first phase of the project was a study of the more customary approach to industrial democracy: the appointment of worker representatives to boards of directors. Thorsrud and his colleagues studied West Germany and Yugoslavia as well as certain state-owned companies in Great Britain and Norway, where worker representatives had been granted places on the boards, and published a report of their conclusions in 1964. The disadvantages of board representation were found to far outweigh the merits. The subjects normally discussed at board meetings were judged to be neither of much interest to workers nor of direct value in promoting industrial democracy, and most workers were seen to lack the proper training to actively participate in these high-level discussions anyway. They thus can be easily manipulated by the other board members. Moreover, the status of the worker representatives as "hostages" of management, where they must share responsibility for decisions that they do not really take part in formulating, tends to weaken the workers when it comes time to enter into normal bargaining.

The problem is the distinction between *formal* power, completely and legally vested in the board of directors, and *real* power, which, as everybody in any company should be able to recognize, belongs to day-to-day management. The report concludes: "If democratic participation is to have any reality, it seems absolutely necessary that it begin on a level where the majority of the workers have both the ability and the willingness to participate. In our opinion, that means that we must begin at the individual's work situation and improve conditions for personal participation there."[3] The report was a little unfair in that it concentrated almost exclusively on the negative aspects of the systems studied, skipping lightly over their positive sides, but it cleared the way for the very original work done by the Thorsrud team later.

In the next phase, the team undertook to introduce work methods, similar to those developed in the coal-mining industry in Britain, in Norwegian industry. All the work was placed under a coordinating committee appointed jointly by the central labor confederation (LO), the employers' confederation (NAF), and the researchers. Four companies volunteered to take part in the experiments, which were to be independent of the regular union-management relations, free to try various work-reform arrangements, and separate from conflict dangers. The labor-management agreement to shield the experiments from outside interference was of vital importance.

The great significance was that, for the first time in history, a scientifically guided work-reform program was to be launched, clearly and unambiguously labeled as "industrial democracy"—an expression that both labor and management agreed not to be frightened of.

Thorsrud's approach is very much influenced by his view of man as a thinking being capable of learning and developing, but also capable of being crushed and mentally crippled, in his work. He postulates six basic needs that an individual seeks to satisfy in his work: a real content, including possibilities for variation; continuous learning opportunities; the chance to make decisions; recognition and respect; an understanding of the connection between the job and the rest of the world; and a view of the job as a step toward a desirable future. Thorsrud explained to me that he had been attempting to apply these principles to the unfortunate circular development in most industrial production: "We must be aware of the consequences in a process where (1) jobs are simplified, which leads to (2) reduced learning possibilities, then to (3) centralized control, meaning we have to rely on (4) pay as motivation, which in turns produces (5) high turnover and (6) reduced trust, and alienation of workers. With all these unanticipated consequences, you are then back to the beginning, and it becomes a *necessity* to simplify jobs. So we wondered if it would be possible to go in the opposite direction, (1) to enrich the job, complicate things, which would lead to (2) increased responsibility, (3) increased learning possibilities, which intensify the complexity further through feedback, (4) increased mutual respect, and (5) increased understanding of the total job and its relation to the world inside and outside the organization."

The first company to volunteer for an experiment (though not the first actually to get started) was Nobø Fabrikker in Trondheim, maker of heating equipment, steel office furniture, and other fabricated products. In 1965, the company invited the researchers to begin work in one department, employing about thirty people, in a plant making metal furnace panels. Though management was willing to cooperate, the thought was that the experiment would run for a certain period of time and then would be finished. The workers were skeptical. They were not much interested in industrial democracy and were not overly impressed by the researchers' attempts to describe something the workers had never seen. "It wasn't so easy to give a concrete explanation of the new principles of job reform and organization development since we lacked local examples to refer to."[4] The employees agreed to cooperate, but only on condition that they could break off at any time and that they could return to the former setup at the end. They were persuaded partly because one of the basic principles of the researchers—entirely logical in a democratic process—was that the workers would themselves participate in any decisions to change work methods.

At the time, the operation was organized on traditional scientific management principles, with production broken up into discrete functions. Each worker had a fixed job covering a small part of the process and was concerned with a time span of only a few hours. Payment was on individual piece rates. The functions broke down into three natural divisions: simple working of the steel sheets (pressing, welding, and polishing), surface treating (washing, painting, and drying), and assembly along a moving line. The workers were therefore reorganized into three groups corresponding to these categories. Within each group, the workers learned four jobs instead of one, so that they could shift from job to job according to circumstances. For the workers, this was a valuable antidote to the previous monotony and gave them a better over-all picture of the production process; it improved efficiency in reducing bottlenecks and gluts of work-in-process at the different work stations. The groups were autonomous—that is, there were no foremen or other supervisory personnel, and the workers met briefly each morning to discuss problems, plan production, and assign the jobs. Management's role was limited to supplying new materials and keeping track of production schedules. Individual piece rates were abolished; a new pay system split a group incentive equally among all the workers. In addition, a small hourly bonus was paid to workers who learned more than four jobs, in partial recognition of the principle that blue-collar workers, like white-collar workers, should be compensated not only for what they do, but for what they know. Some technical changes were made in equipment to suit a system based on groups and where no worker had any fixed job.

All the changes were aimed directly at improving the *technical* system, but, through the establishment of groups with common aims, the changes also indirectly worked for building a more cohesive and more smoothly working *social* system as well.

The experiment ran for about seven months, at the end of which production of furnaces per man-hour had risen more than 20 percent. According to the original agreement, the experiment

was finished. But as one worker said: "There was never any discussion about going back to the old system. Everybody agreed
that the new system was better, and both management and
workers wanted to continue." The new methods spread to the
entire plant, employing about seventy-five workers. After a year,
the researchers took an opinion survey, which showed an overwhelming acceptance of the new system. Here are figures showing those who favored the new system over the old (leaving out
the neutrals and "don't knows"): with respect to variation of the
work, 55 percent to 3 percent; participation in decision-making,
64 percent to 0 percent; degree of responsibility, 77 percent to
0 percent; education on the job, 47 percent to 6 percent; relations
with fellow workers, 67 percent to 4 percent; and contact with
management, 60 percent to 4 percent.[5]

After the systems had been in operation for three years, workers
still were quoted as expressing high enthusiasm. Gerhard Lindberg,
a welder, said: "I stood here for eight years welding together metal
plates, always on the same spot and with never any change. I
hardly knew what the plates were being used for. I never thought
about the job and never asked anybody—I just did what I was
told. The work was a vacuum. . . . Now it's much better. There
is variation in the work. We discuss production and plan the whole
thing ourselves—everybody is interested in seeing that it runs
smoothly. You jump in where you're needed and then you get
help from the others another time. But the most important thing
is that you feel freer." Ole Pettersen, chief engineer (whose job
is limited to giving advice when asked and handling raw material flow), said: "We've never had such a satisfactory year at
Nobø as we had last year. The mood is much better. We want to
reorganize the whole company this way."[6]

As this is written, the methods have been extended. Productivity has continued to increase, and management has withdrawn
almost completely from day-to-day operations. Employees are organized into groups with from fifteen to forty members each, all
of which groups work almost completely autonomously and in
which all workers are equal. Each group elects, annually, a "contact" person who coordinates with other groups and with management. Gradually, the workers' task time span has grown from

less than a day to three months (corresponding to marketing cycles). As the workforce in the plant grew, new employees were included in the revised methods. When production outgrew the old premises, a new and larger plant was constructed, and the workers were actively involved in the planning. For example, in order to better coordinate production with marketing, they suggested that computers be located directly on the factory floor. By mid-1972, the radically different methods were still generating excellent results, and the workforce (an expansion to nearly five hundred persons was under way)—remained enthusiastic.

One very significant result was that, once the workers had a taste of participation in management, they clearly wanted more. Ulrik Qvale, one of the research team, noted in 1970: "From an industrial democracy point of view perhaps the most interesting fact is that the workers are continuously active in pushing the project further. Their principal demand today (which is shared by management) is for more education . . . so that they can take part to a higher degree in the development of the department." Also: "Returning to the old pattern has always been out of the question."[7]

A complete contrast to Nobø was shown by another of the experimental companies, Norsk Hydro, one of Norway's major companies, with eight thousand employees and interests in power, chemicals, oil, metals, and other fields. Moreover, management did not look upon work reform as merely a temporary experiment, but as the first step in finding a new organization form that could be applied in the entire company. This was in great part because of some critical problems—labor-management relations were poor, the structure was suffering from a paralyzing bureaucracy, and channels of communication had almost completely broken down—and these problems were intensified because the company was facing severe competitive conditions on the world market for fertilizer, a major product. Management felt that the only practical solution was greater democratization, that is, the maximum participation of every employee in shaping decisions. An official pronouncement from the mid-1960s stated: "In industry, demands on the individual are increasing. . . . Now, as never before, the key to a successful society, for every company and every individual, is in making real use of the human being's abilities and willingness to contribute."[8]

Initial efforts were made where the need was greatest—at the fertilizer works in Herøya, consisting of one old production facility (with about seventy-five employees) and a new one under construction. The development plan was handled directly by the company, with the researchers acting as outside consultants. The first step, in 1967, was to form a "Future Group," consisting of a foreman, a representative, a personnel officer, a man from the Oslo head office, and a researcher from the Work Research Institute in Oslo (to which Thorsrud had by this time transferred). The Future Group acted as liaison between workers, management, the union, and the researchers. "Morning meetings," similar to those at Nobø, were started, where all the plans were discussed and suggestions received. Gradually, a "model" of the ideal organization took shape. It was decided that the workers should be organized into small autonomous groups, that considerably greater flexibility was necessary, that every worker should master several jobs, and that, therefore, increased training was necessary.

Fertilizer manufacture is a highly technical process, and modern fertilizer plants are automated to a great degree. Considerable scientific and technical knowledge is necessary, particularly if workers are to be able to shift jobs quickly according to need. Production is continuous, and the avoidance of costly breakdowns depends both on knowledge and acceptance of responsibility to act in emergencies. In line with these conditions, one of the first concrete steps was to give solid additional training, both theoretical and practical, to workers who were to be employed in the new plant. A new pay system was introduced, based on the principle of pay for knowledge, not for production; higher pay grades could be achieved by acquisition of additional knowledge, regardless of the particular job handled. New workers needed for the new plant were recruited, with advertisements clearly spelling out the company's new organization form.

Progress toward the ideal organization came slowly, since nobody could really explain how it would function in practice. The first stage was the dissemination of full information. The second stage was to be commitment on the part of the employees, but that was more difficult. Some unexpected critical incidents helped. At one point, an outside commercial consultant firm, which had been engaged by management, was trying to refine piece-rate payment systems and was recommending some staff reductions. The workers insisted that the new organization could not function if the consultant firm had its way, and management accepted the workers' views. The workers refused the compensation plan suggestions, and came up with their own plan for staff reductions, all of which management accepted. It was the first tangible sign that the employees were indeed going to be listened to. Another dispute over wages, which at first management declined to discuss on the grounds that agreed rules were being adhered to, was forwarded to the Future Group, which obtained immediate action in favor of the workers, showing that this group did carry real weight and was not merely a management trick. A different kind of emergency arose when an accident occurred in one part of the plant the day before some foreign customers were to arrive. Without hesitation, the workers on that shift repaired the damage on their own initiative, through a massive crash effort, so the plant would be in perfect order for the visitors. Thus the employees were given a real chance to exercise responsibility. Perhaps the clearest indication that the new organization form was taking shape came when the old fertilizer plant was being shut down for a complete reconstruction. Normally, all the workers would be transferred to other jobs during the reconstruction, but they suggested that as many of them as possible might be profitably employed in the renovation, and management accepted. This required some additional training, but these extra costs were more than offset by the valuable contributions the workers could make.

Gradually, progress toward a new organization form, based on autonomy instead of autocracy, accelerated, and became a self-propelling, continuous process. In the new plant, the workers participated from almost the beginning in planning and, eventually, management. All jobs were being rotated except maintenance and janitorial duties. The workers decided they should take care of their own maintenance as far as possible, for reasons of efficiency, as well as their own cleaning up, because it was deemed unfair to unload these undesirable jobs onto other employees. This turned out to be an excellent idea: "Visitors to the fertilizer factory are struck by the unusual cleanliness and neatness. This is the workers' 'own factory' which they take pride in keeping in order."[9]

All parties were well pleased with the results. Management found that, largely due to the fewer employees needed to run the plant, cost per ton of fertilizer produced dropped by 30 percent. A management comment: "It's not only a question of production, it puts human values in the center."[10] Employees were also very content. Said one: "It would be unthinkable now to go back to the old organization. . . . It was real forced labor in the old plant, no contact, no cooperation, no fun in the work."[11]

Steps have been taken to extend the new spirit, in line with the original intention, throughout the company. After only a few months of work in the fertilizer operation, reform projects were launched in a carbide plant and a magnesium plant. The introduction of these radical methods required careful nursing and considerable time, but by 1971 department reorganizations had covered more than 10 percent of the company's employees. More importantly, a new atmosphere was gradually gaining ground in other departments. Reidar Tank-Nielsen, personnel director, told me: "We have just started. But if you really want to adopt a policy like this you can apply it to some extent without any formal projects." He noted that the main obstacle to rapid change came not from workers but from the upper levels: "It takes time to change the mentality of people. There are people working here twenty-five years who are accustomed to a certain type of leadership. It can be quite difficult to learn new things, and this is our most important problem. It occurs at all levels—with foremen, middle management, and even top management. It's a mentality problem." Nevertheless, the company has made rapid strides and is setting no limits on the type of decisions employees may influence. When asked if employees might be permitted to have a say in over-all management matters, if they should demand it, Tank-Nielsen added: "Definitely; that is our goal, and we hope it will come. But it takes time."

The Norwegian experiments were not all as successful as the two summarized above. In fact, one had to be put down as a failure because of poor communications, inadequate experience on the part of the researchers, too great haste, and other problems.

Too, the movement is still in its early stages, and Thorsrud and his colleagues have deliberately slowed the pace of development, in order not to jeopardize its future. Because the full research results have been available only in Norwegian and because the reality seems—against a background of hundreds of years of authoritarian thinking in industry—incredible, some skeptics have been inclined to doubt the significance of the Norwegian work. Thorsrud says: "Many people have come to Norway just in order to convince themselves it can't be done."

Nevertheless, objective observers who have followed the experiments carefully have become convinced that they are a great event in the development of industrial democracy. They offer overpowering evidence that many of the common objections to giving workers authority simply have no foundation in reality. The original premise of the labor leaders in the early 1960s that workers want and need, and can very well handle, more decision-making power in their work place has been abundantly confirmed. Inasmuch as the work was conducted under rigorously objective conditions, but within an ideological framework related to industrial democracy, it constitutes an obvious threat to established ideas of power and authority in industry. In Norway, the implications are clearly recognized and accepted. One highly placed figure in Norwegian industry told me, quite without alarm: "In the long run I suppose it will influence the whole system. One main idea is to remedy one of the dark sides of the present state of affairs—it's a fact that many people in industry today are very discontented."

The principal concept applied by the Thorsrud group was the notion of "autonomous groups," which, when properly established in manufacturing plants, develop a powerful dynamism and momentum of their own in harnessing the latent abilities and ideas of workers. The intelligence of the employees, so long suppressed in the normal authoritarian environment, is released and allowed to develop. The notion has been, in fact, so much emphasized in writings in Scandinavia about the research that some employers have come to believe that they can get some of those magical autonomous groups installed in their plants in the same way they can order a new turret lathe. It's not quite that easy, particularly since it calls for a management acceptance of a change in organizational form that carries with it drastic alterations of power relationships. Moreover, Thorsrud stresses that autonomous groups, which have worked well in some cases, might not work in all, and other approaches might prove more fruitful in other circumstances.

Recently the Thorsrud group has been developing its methods further. A major effort has begun in the shipping industry. On board ships there are rather special problems, but experiments with forming workers into groups, letting them alternate within various jobs, giving them responsibility for assigning work, and breaking down to some extent barriers between officers and men have, after a couple of years' duration, shown encouraging results. In addition, at the beginning of 1971, formal projects were begun in a dozen or so companies, including service industries and white-collar operations. Attention is also being paid to methods that might result in more rapid change in companies. Says Thorsrud: "When we go into a company, now, we will not be starting on the shop floor. We don't need to spend another five years proving it can be done. So we start on a higher level where there is greater leverage."

Superficially, the work-reform methods used in Norway may seem quite similar to those used in America. But by comparison, the innovations introduced even in the most advanced U.S. companies are far less comprehensive. Most importantly, the revolutionary point in Norway is that there is a clearly stated intention to promote industrial democracy in the widest possible meaning. Ultimately, no limits are to be set on worker influence. The wide gap between American thinking and Norwegian thinking was illuminated during a seminar at which Einar Thorsrud, the best-known Norwegian work psychologist, and Frederick Herzberg, the the best-known American work psychologist, were present. Herzberg was expressing his gloomy views on the dangers of worker participation, and Thorsrud commented: "You are against participation for the very reasons we are in favor of it—one doesn't know where it will stop. We think that's good."

Sweden, Norway's neighbor, has been somewhat slower in getting started in industrial democracy, but by now is, in some ways, even more advanced. The idea of industrial democracy has a long

and honorable history in Sweden. In 1920, a parliamentary committee was assigned the task of studying the question, and it made
its report in 1923. One of the members, Ernst Wigforss, a well-
known politician in the Social Democratic Party (and later, for
many years, a creative and resourceful finance minister), submit-
ted, as part of the report, a thoughtful, lengthy memorandum. Astonishingly perceptive for the time, this memorandum pointed
out that modern industrial organization was bringing with it
"dissatisfaction because of the nature of the work, monotony, and
lack of room for initiative and freedom of movement." Wigforss
asked if labor unions should not turn their attention to negotiating on "the psychological atmosphere in the factory . . . is it not
of significance for the worker just as well as the physical aspect?"[12]
With great clarity, Wigforss saw the fatal flaw in the argument
that, if workers could only be adequately paid, they could acquire
real satisfaction from life outside of work: "The more monotonous
and mechanical, the more tiring and soul-deadening daily work
becomes, the more difficult it is to engage in more creative occupations with cohesive relationships and meaningful goals, and the
easier it is to seek substitutes for the daily burdens in titillating
amusements, in idle dreams and fantasies, lacking connection with
reality."[13] The problem lay in the alienating conditions typical of
modern industry, and an effort should be to create conditions favorable for real life in—not outside of—work. Moreover, Wigforss saw that, in granting demands for workers' "freedom and
independence," the production process "had nothing to lose . . .
but quite the contrary."[14] He painted a picture of the ideal industrial operation, involving "voluntary cooperation under elected
leaders, with equal opportunities for all workers to exercise their
abilities, to carry their share of responsibility and decision-making
. . . to realize the principles of *freedom* and *equality*. . . ."[15]
There was no thought, however, of proposing really radical solutions. There was a vague feeling that the goals might be reached
through the creation of consultative workers' councils, but nothing happened even on this modest front until after World War II.
In his memoirs many years later, Wigforss conceded that the ideas
were too shocking for the period: "There are some questions that
don't get answered, simply because the time is not ripe."[16]

In the ensuing decades, these ideas were largely forgotten, and

Sweden became justly famous for its harmonious and peaceful labor-management relations, reflecting the "spirit of Saltsjöbaden."
This refers to the seaside resort where, in the mid-1930s, representatives of management and labor worked for many months ham-
mering out an agreement whereby conflicts could, it was hoped,
be minimized. The intention was achieved, and for some decades
Sweden had one of the world's lowest rates of days per worker
lost through strikes.

From the unions' standpoint, the key principle is that managements should be left completely free to automate, mechanize,
introduce Taylorized work routines, or anything else—on the sole
condition that workers could be compensated (materially speaking) for their contributions to general economic progress through
fat wage increases, which the companies thereby became ever
more able to pay. If this meant that the Swedish unions could be
accused, most of the time, of excessive docility (as they in fact
often have been by foreign observers), they were able to show
their awesome, and rewarding, toughness when contract-negotiat-
ing time rolled around.

An essential element in all this was a statement of policy called
"Paragraph 32," which ordains that management has the right "to
freely hire and fire workers, to manage and assign the work, and
to use workers from any union whatever or workers outside unions." This principle has actually been embodied in virtually every
contract signed since 1905, but it was the unions' post-Saltsjöba-
den acquiescence in its strict observation that led to some of the
more famous features of the Swedish labor scene: no featherbed-
ding, no make-work, no union shops, no closed shops, no protests
over automation, and no complaints about time-and-motion studies. Indeed, so fully did LO (the central labor confederation), em-
brace management's rights to reorganize work procedures that for
some years it conducted training courses in time-and-motion studies to create receptivity to Taylorized work methods among union
members and thus facilitate the introduction of such methods by
management.

The positions remained largely unchanged for some decades.
At the quinquennial congress of LO held in 1961, a special report
examined the question of industrial democracy anew, and concluded that workers already had sufficient leverage through tradi-

tional bargaining procedures to get anything they wanted; besides, if workers were to get too involved in management decisions, they might get involved in decisions that were against their own best interests.[17] Regarding the tenacity with which the union leaders held to their fixed positions, British labor expert T. L. Johnston wrote: "In discussion of this theme (industrial democracy), there has never been any great preoccupation with fundamental philosophical or moral concepts based on the Dignity of Man. . . ."[18]

Attitudes slowly began to change in the 1960s, and interest in industrial democracy again began to manifest itself in numerous discussions in the press and elsewhere. A good deal of the discussion was hopelessly obscure, meandering around the general (and very defensible) view that working conditions would be improved if everybody treated everybody else in a nice way. In 1964, Eric Rhenman, a young professor of corporate finance, published a detailed study of the subject, which subjected the various ideas to critical examination and, most importantly, pointed to the links between democratic ideas and the scientific study of organizations carried out in Britain and the United States. Rhenman expressed skepticism that it would be possible to "find general recipes for treating the problems in question here."[19] However, his book served the useful purpose of adding some clarity to the discussion.

In 1966, candidly borrowing ideas from the Norwegians, the Swedish employers' confederation (SAF), the white-collar central union organization (TCO), and LO jointly established a "Development Council for Cooperation Questions" and agreed to carry out experiments of various kinds (even though the word "democracy" was studiously avoided, that was the central idea) and that they would not be considered to conflict with normal labor-management relationships.

The Development Council did not do much developing until 1969, when the first comprehensive report on Thorsrud's Norwegian work was published; it had a rather electrifying effect throughout Scandinavia. Suddenly, "industrial democracy" became the fashionable expression and the simple key to everlasting peace and prosperity. Enthusiasm was probably running higher among managers than among workers. The first conference in Sweden on the subject was, in fact, organized by SAF, the employers' group, with arrangements made for thirty-five participants. All tickets were quickly sold out, and the waiting list bore more than a hundred names.

Olle Gunnarson, a top labor official, said in 1969: "People who are growing up today will no longer be willing to accept authoritarian managements. In five or ten years these people will be beginning their working lives. We have that long to find new forms of organization."[20] As a matter of fact, that prophecy fell short of the mark, and Swedes began clamoring for new forms within only a couple of years.

It is difficult to convey the mood of the Swedish public regarding industrial democracy, so different is it from that in other countries. A distinctive peculiarity of Swedish society is the thoroughness with which any popular question is thrashed out, discussed, and painstakingly argued in public. Once industrial democracy, and its potentials, began to seep into the public consciousness, the subject was endlessly debated. The discussion has not always been terribly knowledgeable, but it has kept the topic vividly alive in the mind of the public and has created immense pressures on companies to take action.

The Swedes' intense interest in the subject is understandable. It has gradually become clear that the workers' councils have failed, having been primarily used for the announcement of management decisions after the fact. More importantly, as people have obtained better educations (one of the central elements in Sweden's welfare state has been a massive expansion of educational opportunities), better job security (a full employment policy aims at unemployment of "o percent"), and more prosperity (Swedish GNP per capita is the highest in Europe), they are no longer so ignorant or so needy that they wish to tolerate the "robotization" characteristic of much modern industry.

A public-opinion poll in 1969 showed that 72 percent of all Swedes believed there was a "very great need" or a "rather great need" for "increased influence from employees' side in industrial companies."[21] Industrial democracy is so widely discussed that one is scarcely surprised to find even children displaying a measure of sophistication on the subject. One newspaper asking teen-agers for their view on various subjects found that twelve-year-old Malin

Löfgren defined an undesirable job with ease: "A bad job is one where others make all decisions, and where you have to do what others say." And fifteen-year-old Miklas Hellberg agrees: "It wouldn't be so bad to be a dishwasher, as long as you could take part in making the decisions on hours and pay and working conditions."[22]

By the time the 1971 LO congress rolled around, the labor movement had drawn up a completely new program. In essence, it reversed its entire philosophy. While previously its efforts had been aimed at getting maximum means for workers to enjoy life outside their work, it now focused on improving the work experience itself, candidly conceding its earlier mistakes. Inge Janérus, an LO official concerned with industrial democracy, wrote: "It should be clear that those who have the most monotonous, least intellectually stimulating and least developed jobs cannot compensate for that in their leisure time."[23] The dangers to mental health in modern industry have become increasingly clear. A study commissioned by LO found that less than a quarter of LO members felt they were free of undue stress on the job.[24]

The program revealed at the congress demanded worker representation on boards of directors, abolition of Paragraph 32, worker participation in shop-floor operations, authority to appoint auditors to examine company books, and a share in decisions on hiring and firing, selection of management personnel, and long-term budgeting and planning.[25] In other words, it wants power at all levels, and it wants it guaranteed through legislation. At the Congress, it was obvious that a new day was dawning. One official succinctly summed up the new spirit: "We are going to be saying 'No' to any more of this 'cooperation waltz.'"

Office employees are also involved in the industrial-democracy movement. Karl-Erik Modig, an official of TCO (the central organization for white-collar employees), points out that his normally rather placid organization is also radically altering its views. "There are going to be some large changes," he says, "regardless of what we do. So it is much better that we participate in bringing them about." TCO has accordingly taken a formal position that employee influence in companies must be increased, and it is working to achieve that goal.[26]

Inasmuch as it has become obvious that democratization will be achieved one way or another, many companies have been taking steps to keep up with, or ahead of, the trends.

Much of the action being taken is under the guidance of the Development Council, which during the first couple of years of its active phase launched about fifteen projects in various volunteer companies. In line with the Swedish preference for careful, well-thought-out progress, the movement has been glacially slow, but the direction is clear.

The direction—and the slowness—is well illustrated in one Development Council project begun at a plant of Atlas Copco just outside Stockholm, producing rock-drilling machinery and related equipment. Management had long been interested in encouraging worker participation, had built up an elaborate system of workers' councils, and had offered workers courses in corporate management to stimulate their interest in the company (efforts that were admittedly only partially successful). The company was thus keenly interested in cooperating with the Development Council.

One department was selected as a testing ground—a workshop responsible for assembly of rock-drilling machines. Consisting of twelve workers and a foreman, the department was producing about twelve thousand units per year, of about fifty different products. There are seven functions, including machine adjustment, assembly, honing, cleaning, testing, and painting; before the project began, each function was handled by one or more workers, in line with traditional assembly-line methods, and each worker stuck to his specified task. Payment was on individual piece rates.

The department was reorganized for the project, and the workers were divided into four three-man teams. The assembly line was broken, and each team followed an entire batch of machines through the line from start to finish. All workers were given additional training to allow them to shift from job to job as the need arose, and they distributed the job assignments themselves. After considerable discussion of various alternative payment methods, the workers agreed to a single rate for the entire group, consisting of a fixed sum plus a variable based on production volume.

This may seem a trivial, and perhaps almost insignificant change, in a rather tiny department. But in fact it amounted almost to a revolution. Most of the workers had been at their jobs for more than ten years and, though all changes were decided by the workers themselves, the abandonment of accepted methods did not come easily. Björn Askert, production chief, told me: "We thought we would be finished with the project in about six months. But in fact it took more than eighteen months just to move from an initial proposal to actually beginning the experiment."

After a year, the "experiment" was ended and a massive amount of data collected which, as this is written, is being analyzed. In some senses, however, the success is apparent. For one thing, the workers, given a choice of continuing in the reorganized line or reverting to the old methods, unhesitatingly chose to continue with the new program—even though, for a few of them, it meant slightly lower wages. Göta Ström, assistant shop steward, who was mildly skeptical of the whole business, nevertheless told me: "There has been a completely different atmosphere in the department. They are now able to discuss problems together, because all the problems are now common problems—before, it was every man for himself." Moreover, a small gain in productivity was registered, from 21 percent above standard at the beginning of the project to 24 percent to 26 percent at the end of a year. No technological changes were made during that time, and the total wage bill rose less than productivity.

Although one company spokesman described the new method as a kind of "grass roots democracy," Göta Ström is not convinced. "This is a very little part of company democracy," he says. "It's an effort to create a more satisfying work-place, but there is not much difference in decision-making power. It will have to be much larger to be real democracy." On the significance of the experiment, however, both sides agree. Ström says: "If there is any meaning to this, it must be expanded to the whole company—otherwise it's just a waste of time."

However, as the experiment has proceeded, the mood in the company has also been changing. For one thing, management has increasingly focused its attention on encouraging workers to contribute ideas for changing things. One engineer told me: "It's not new for the systems planners to get ideas from workers. What is new is that now there is an insistence on seeing that it happens."

One of the more thoroughgoing Swedish programs is that of The Grängesberg Company, a vast enterprise with interests in steel, mining, and shipping. For many years, it has been developing a large assortment of techniques to reshape the organization away from the traditional autocratic pyramid, where everybody on lower levels is told what to do and how to think by those higher up—sardonically described as the "papa knows best" system by Karl-Johan Edström, personnel director. The company no longer has a single president in practice (though, technically, it must have, according to Swedish company law), but a three-man governing board, the members of which have equal rank and equally distributed authority.

The ultimate goal is to change the basic company structure, and the entire organization is thus being overhauled. Edström told me: "We want to give every individual influence in every job, and the old organization just won't do." The goal is to help the worker as well as the company. Edström says: "With the abolition of the 'papa knows best' system, power and decision-making will be distributed more evenly. We will therefore have the opportunity to coax out the unutilized resources we know are in the group."

There is, however, an overriding moral element in the program. Edström says: "There is no more authoritarian situation in our society than the traditional work organization, where the boss can kick people out when he wants and where there is no appeal to such decisions." One of the company's more startling innovations is a "no-firing" policy. Inge Selinder, a recruiting specialist, told me: "The employer's absolute right to fire people must be taken away. If someone doesn't fit the organization it means we recruited badly. And if we make a mistake we must take the consequences."

The company's new philosophy shows up often. One example was a dispute in a department over how that department, which was being reorganized, should be set up. The employees had one plan, and the management, another. After lengthy discussions, the employees' plan carried (its main feature was the abolition of the position of head of the department).

One section of the company that has been reorganized is Essem Sintermetall, a sintering works. Its sixty employees were given the choice of continuing on individual piece rates based on MTM (a system worked out with time-and-motion study) or monthly salaries. One worker was quoted as saying: "With MTM you just stop being a human being."[27] The monthly pay is 80 percent a fixed sum, with the rest figured on finished production, split evenly for all. The workers are divided into six groups—powder pressing, sintering, inspection, and so on—and each group selects its own leader. Whereas formerly there was one foreman for each fifteen workers, there is now one and a half for all sixty. Since all workers are bunched in the same pay program, they feel they can work more closely together than formerly. All workers participated in deciding on the reorganization, and all take part in the day-to-day decisions. Morale is high, and turnover is the lowest in the entire company. One worker, who had been one of the most highly paid under the old system, said: "We who were highest up got the least when the change was made, but that's O.K. . . . The job is no different but now we have a goal to work for—we can plan one or two weeks ahead, not just stand here like a robot."

It was at this plant that Sweden's first "full-time industrial democrat" appeared in 1972. Bengt Gustafsson, who had been a milling machine operator for some twelve years, was given the experimental job of looking after industrial democracy matters. It is a rather vague position, but he sees some value in acting as a kind of channel for opinions, to make sure worker views are heard. "The most important thing," he says, "is to be able to influence your own situation in the daily job, right at the work place." He notes the rapid shifts in thinking that have occurred: "Ten years ago it was only pay people demanded. Now it's more—the work environment, the forms of pay, democracy. . . . The fact that my job exists is due to a change in attitudes. There have been increasing pressures from below."[28]

The company has become accustomed to seizing every opportunity to give decision-making power to workers. When a two-hundred-dred-thousand-dollar program of improvement of the immediate work environment was being planned at a mill, employees were given the right to decide how most of the money would be spent.[29]

The democratization of the company is being actively promoted by management. One top executive, Bertil Liljeqvist, says: "We are pushing down decision-making as far as possible within the company. In this way, decision-making will be shared by more people. Decentralization is the key word." That the program is taken with intense seriousness by the company is shown by this statement in the 1971 annual report to shareholders: "The quest for suitable forms of company democracy resulted during the year in an expanded experimental scheme, chiefly concerned with means by which the employees can exert a direct influence on conditions at their own workplaces."

Since there are more than twenty-five thousand employees, providing machinery for all to have their influence felt presents some problems. To solve them, a complex network of boards and groups has been set up, topped by a company-wide "Gränges Council," with twenty-eight members representing employees and thirteen representing management. It is estimated that 10 percent of employees are directly engaged in some phase of this activity.[30] In addition, the company has given nonvoting places on the board of directors to two workers and one municipal official in a town where its plant is a major employer.

Though it is estimated that some 60 percent of the company's employees have so far been affected by one or another of the experiments, reorganizations, or reshufflings, no large claims are being made. Edström emphasizes that the transformation of the company will not be quick. He speaks in terms of ten to fifteen years to find the new forms that are needed, but in a sense the process never ends: "We must be prepared to change the organization constantly in order to adapt to new needs."

Another work reform program is at the famous Orrefors Glass Works. When it built a sleek new factory in 1968, the organization had to be shaken up. An American consulting firm advised instituting a system of closer control, and more work supervisors. Johan Beyer, president, was not a production expert, but he strongly felt that to *increase* control—when everybody in Sweden was discussing ways to *decrease* management control—was somehow wrong. So he went in the opposite direction and worked to reduce control and to increase responsibility for workers. The new system was begun in a department with twenty-two workers where products go through eight operations—e.g., polishing, washing, inspecting, labeling, and packing. Previously, each worker had to stick to one post because pay was by piece rate and any change had to be accompanied by complicated discussions on adjusting the rate. An hourly scale with a small premium for production was introduced, workers were allowed to learn additional jobs, and they were permitted to move up and down the line as needed. As a result, quality has improved, production is smoother, money is saved by reducing buffers between stations, and workers are far more satisfied. Allen Liedberg, a worker on the line, told me: "This is the 100 percent right system. Now we decide how everything is to be done on the line. The workers all like the new system—much better not to have to stay at the same spot." How about industrial democracy? "It's the key to the whole thing. We must be included in more decision-making, but we have already come quite far." As a matter of fact, employees, after about a year of the new system, not only did not want to go back to the old, but were asking for more decision-making power. The Swedish glass industry has been experiencing bad times, and the workers have been free with their suggestions for improvement. Birger Frööjd, a shop steward, complains that design is being handled badly. The workers did win a place on the design committee, but he feels further improvement is necessary. Moreover, he asserts that the Orrefors "exclusive" selling policy, under which only a few stores in any area are supplied, designed to maintain an aura of rare elegance, is outmoded. "They say we profit from making the glass hard to get—but times have changed." He insists that workers' views on this and other problems must be listened to: "The democratic principles we have begun with must be expanded."[81]

Numbers of other Swedish companies have been moving toward democratization. One of the most dramatic is at Saab-Scania, which, in 1972, put into operation, at Södertälje, the first production facility in the history of the automobile industry based on the abolition of the assembly line.[82] Instead of a single massive line moving at a fixed rate past the workers, the plant consists of six separate assembly areas, in each of which three workers receive the formed engine case and assemble parts in it. The workers can vary the pace and divide the work among themselves as they wish. Miss Marja-Liisa Karpinen describes her job thus: "I work on assembly of the Saab 99. There are three of us in the group. . . . We can decide for ourselves how we want to do the work. In our group we usually do ten minutes' work each on an engine. But today there are only two of us here, and we decided we would each do complete engines. I'm supposed to do one engine in half an hour. That is fixed. But I can also work faster if I want—then I can take it easy later on. We can look after ourselves, and the job is certainly more pleasant than working in a trousers factory."

Production manager Tore Nilson, who designed the system, says: "The main advantage we hope for is increased work satisfaction. But the system also has other advantages over a moving line." One of these is greater flexibility. When the workforce is below normal, or when production targets vary, management can simply shut down some of the assembly areas. Moreover, one area can be used for training, allowing new workers to learn at a calm pace. "Finally," says Nilson, "we believe we will gain in quality. The groups themselves are responsible for the engines they produce."

Boliden, a mining and metals company, in planning a new workshop, decided to let the employees—seventy-five workers and twenty supervisors—participate in the planning of their future work place. As a result, the planning took a month less than expected, the planning was "more down-to-earth" than is usually the case, and a number of excellent suggestions were made and accepted. One of them called for a capital investment of some forty thousand dollars, but it would mean total savings of some eight thousand dollars per year. Planning of this new facility was one of the ways the company had found to push its own democratization program, which is intended to eventually affect the entire company.[33]

Much of the progress in Sweden is directly linked to social tendencies, and the general unwillingness of people to accept boring and monotonous jobs. Nowhere is this fact more striking than at Volvo, Sweden's largest company, where absenteeism has been running around 14 percent, and annual worker turnover, 30 percent to 40 percent.[34] The company has taken a number of steps to ease the situation. For one thing, reasoning that, if employees disliked their jobs they might in some cases be persuaded to remain with the company, it set up an "internal employee agency" in 1971.[35] It also gave places on the board of directors to two workers, one blue-collar and one white-collar.

For some years, the company resisted the idea of modifying the assembly line, maintaining that automobile production would be impossible without it. However, rising turnover and absenteeism as well as increasing difficulties in recruiting forced the company's hand, and in mid-1972 it announced it was investing fifty million dollars in two new "experimental" plants lacking assembly lines. The most radical departure was an auto assembly facility, budgeted at twenty million dollars and scheduled to begin production of some thirty thousand autos a year in 1974. The move goes a step beyond Saab's team-based engine production facility in that it attacks directly what is no doubt the world's most hated production place and the favorite object of study among sociologists seeking material on extreme worker alienation: the line on which the automobile itself is assembled. The moving, fixed-speed line is being completely done away with and the work organized in small groups. The six hundred workers are to be divided into autonomous teams of fifteen to twenty persons, and each team will be responsible for a particular section of a car—e.g., electrical system, gear box, brakes. Each group will set its own pace, and goods in process will be transported between team stations by hand trucks. The other plant is an engine factory, scheduled to cost thirty million dollars and to employ six hundred workers beginning in 1973. It is also to be based on teams.

Although the company emphasized that the effort was an experiment and warned that the plants might not prove out economically, it was noted that action had to be taken if the company was to retain enough workers to operate at all. Pehr Gyllenhammar, president, said: "We are making a real effort, on the basis of all our experience and trials, to create a workplace that meets the modern human being's needs."[36]

At SAPA, an aluminum-fabricating company, employees are assigned to different wage categories by a special board—on which

the employees themselves are in the majority.[37] At Götaverken, a
major shipyard, Bengt Tengroth, a former local union official, was
named vice president in charge of personnel in 1971 when the
company, after nudging by the state, was taken over by another
firm; in addition, a board was set up to make decisions on a
number of employment issues, and the employees are in the
majority. Tengroth describes a main goal of the new management
to be "democratization of the decision-making process regarding
planning."[38] The Matfors paper mill of Svenska Cellulosa introduced a system to improve communications in 1969 by inviting
worker representatives to take part in the regular daily meetings of
the mill's management. One result has been an improved flow of
valuable suggestions from workers and improved job satisfaction;
on the latter point, plant manager Karl-Erik Lockmark defines it
as "work which has some content demanding something more
than just endurance . . . when it can give the individual the opportunity to make decisions, at least within an area he can call his
own, when he can see his work as compatible with some desirable
future. . . ."[39] And one company, a brewery named Top, which
was to be sold because it had declared bankruptcy, asked the employees to vote on which offer should be accepted, and their recommendation was the deciding one.[40]

One factor in the strength of the Swedish democratization movement is undoubtedly a basic philosophical point accepted by most
Swedes. Edmund Dahlström, Professor of Sociology at the University of Gothenburg, writes: "Regarding the division of power
and influence there is a broad philosophy of equality . . . in our
society, which on the whole means that an even division of power
is to be preferred."[41]

Swedish businessmen are obviously more favorably inclined to
democracy than their counterparts in other countries. In 1970, a
poll showed that 75 percent of managers questioned favored sharing decision-making in all departments. Even so radical a suggestion as "replacing supervisors' decisions with collective decisions"
drew favorable responses from 11 percent of the managers.[42] A
similar poll in 1971 showed that 20 percent of managers saw giving workers full membership on the boards of directors as an advantage, and 25 percent thought nonvoting membership would be

advantageous.[43] In commenting editorially on businessmen's opinions in this area, *Veckans Affärer*, the leading business magazine—which, like business magazines in most countries, generally reflects businessmen's thinking—termed "intensified democracy within companies" as "inevitable."[44]

Among the institutions working to influence businessmen's opinion in this area is one that is the creation of SAF, the employers' confederation. This is called the Personaladministrativa Rådet, in English generally referred to as the PA Council. It was formed in 1953, to carry out research and handle company assignments in personnel policy. Originally, it was much concerned with testing, recruiting, conducting management courses, and the like, but it has moved increasingly into active promotion of industrial democracy, using methods borrowed from Norway, Britain, and the United States. Very much in the Swedish habit of tolerance and broad-mindedness, SAF has voluntarily relinquished control of the council by inviting representatives from unions, the cooperative movement, and other organizations to take places on the governing board, yet it continues to subsidize part of the council's budget. The council is independent both in its operations and its attitudes. Lennart Lennerlöf, head of the council, sternly lectured a group of businessmen that their methods of mechanizing and Taylorizing operations were all wrong: "The direction of development has thus been diametrically opposed to the increasing needs of individuals to participate in decision-making." He pointed out that a "personnel gap" was developing—"the difference between companies with respect to work, knowledge, work habits, motivation, and cooperation"—which could become increasingly critical as individuals become increasingly choosy about the types of work they will accept. The answer, he went on, is obvious: "A company's personnel administration must aim at increasing both productivity and work satisfaction, and it should be formulated in such a way that progress in the direction of industrial democracy is facilitated."[45]

Denmark is somewhat behind its neighbors Norway and Sweden in the development of industrial democracy, but interest in industrial democracy is nevertheless widespread. A public-opinion poll in 1971 showed that, when asked to name the single most important desire in their working lives, 48 percent of the population put "more influence on decisions" first, as against 14 percent for "higher wages" and 12 percent for "shorter working hours."[46] Moreover, the same alarming signs of discontent with work are evident in Denmark as in other countries. One study showed that absenteeism in Danish companies rose by 50 percent in the 1967–70 period.[47] Hilmar Baunsgaard, the former conservative Prime Minister (his government left office in 1972), at one time said: "A sharing of influence and responsibility in day-to-day production will probably be the most pressing task of the 1970s. We will not be able to get through the decade without solving this problem."[48]

In line with this sentiment, a great many reports, studies, experiments, and so on have been made, though none of them has yet led to official action. One committee appointed by the government, under the leadership of Professor Torben Agersnap, spent some five years studying the question, producing in the end a rather thin volume with even thinner suggestions for action.[49] The report's recommendation was that the question should be studied and that cooperation between labor and management continue in an effort to find workable forms that might satisfy both parties. Professor Agersnap explained to me that the level of interest in the subject was still low compared to Sweden, in great part because Denmark has only recently emerged from being predominantly agricultural and has thus not yet had the opportunity to develop the problems of highly industrialized countries. "This is still a country of small firms," he pointed out.

Nevertheless, the pressures have impelled a number of companies to launch democratization projects, many of them experimental and research-oriented, but others designed to transfer decision-making power to employees with a minimum of delay. The approach taken has been roughly the same as in Norway, though ideas have also been freely borrowed from Britain, Sweden, and the United States.

One of the most comprehensive projects included seven manufacturing and service enterprises, aimed at increasing job satisfaction and improving coordination by making jobs more challenging and demanding, including the Norwegian conception of autonomous groups. The groups were given greatly increased collective responsibility for quality, meeting delivery schedules, and distributing jobs among group members. In some cases, the groups were also given authority over hiring and firing (not all cared to take on that task). After more than a year of experience, a preliminary report showed that both workers and managements were pleased with the results. Nobody cared to return to the orthodox systems. There were problems with expanding the novel methods rapidly enough. One report stated: "Experience is already so good that some envy has arisen among others in the companies who cannot yet be given comparable working conditions." Though higher productivity was not an objective, none of the companies experienced lower productivity, and some had a slight increase.[50]

Other companies have begun projects independently. A textile company in Odense, Nordisk Tekstil Væveri, has divided its two hundred employees into autonomous groups, in great part because of the severe competitive pressures in this industry from foreign producers. One executive notes: "More than most other companies, we must have all of our employees actively interested."[51] Schades Papir, a small paper-converting firm, has developed a peculiar system of fixed salary plus incentive payments based on production, plus an opportunity for workers to purchase shares in the company. The basis of the pay system is that, to a great extent, each worker can decide his own work pace and thus his own pay. An executive remarked to me that, in the first five years of the system, volume output had increased by some 200 percent, while the workforce and the technical equipment had remained the same. The central key: "Every worker is responsible himself for what he does."[52] Lennart Larsson, who owns a clothing company named Elson, has developed a system whereby the places on the board of directors are divided among blue-collar workers, white-collar workers, management, and capital.[53] After the employees of *Information* took over ownership of their ailing daily newspaper in 1970, both finances and morale improved markedly. At the first annual meeting under the new regime, board chairman and journalist Knud Vilby reported that a switch to profit from loss could be attributed to the new ownership situation. "Everybody knows where things stand at all times," he said. "One of the sad facts in some places is that it is difficult to convince employees of the seriousness of a situation because management does not wish to talk to the employees."[54] A number of firms have given employees places on boards of directors. A/S Marius Pedersen, producer of construction materials, gave three of seven places to employees in 1972. Management explained: "The employees, like shareholders, have a risk in the company. The shareholders risk money, the workers the basis of their existence. They should therefore share in the decisions."[55] At J. H. Schultz, a printing company, a third of board seats were given to employees in 1970, and president Ole Trock-Jensen said: "It has been a great advantage for the firm. It has improved cooperation and prevented misunderstanding and mistrust. I must frankly admit that I have been surprised at the maturity of the employees."[56] At F. L. Smidth & Co., one of Denmark's largest companies, democratization of particular parts of the company is seen as preparation for giving employees board seats. At a 950-man machine factory, a management-worker board is kept constantly informed of company affairs and makes recommendations for action. Also, there are temporary project groups to look into special problems. Says factory manager Aage Uht: "In 99 percent of cases, management follows the groups' opinions. The man on the shop floor often knows more than the guy sitting at a desk."[57]

One of the difficulties in Denmark is that industrial democracy has gotten entangled in what LO, the central union confederation, calls "economic democracy," a complex plain calling for employee shareownership in industry. Though the plan undoubtedly in some legal sense increases workers' "influence," it does nothing to improve jobs or attack the basic problems of worker alienation. Neverthleless, the proposal was adopted as official policy by LO at its 1971 congress.

A somewhat more logical proposal is that of DASF, a union of semiskilled workers, and Denmark's largest. This one aims at putting workers on boards of directors. Anker Jørgensen, DASF chairman, noted at the union's 1971 congress: "The demand for worker influence is accelerating, and I believe that, very soon, one goal for the labor movement will be that workers and capital be given equality on corporate boards."[58] The general principle was adopted at the congress.

Jørgensen told me that, so far, probably not more than 10 to

20 percent of his membership was yet interested in such matters, but that "they are the most intelligent" and that the numbers would grow rapidly. One reason was that the problems of work were growing increasingly serious, but the union had no power to nudge management methods into more human channels. One of his union's unusual practices has been its close study of various management attempts to improve motivation through use of participative methods, autonomous groups, and the like. In 1971, it published a well-informed booklet on the subject, in which it noted the union's support for new management methods but also its desire to follow such moves closely, "especially to assure that employees are not being manipulated, but also to assure that the union is not being maneuvered out of the picture."[59]

Jørgensen explained to me that the union was interested not only in a democratic division of power at the top—that is, on the boards—but also at the work place. However, the one complements the other: "If we go in at the top, I think we'll have better possibilities to give people on the shop floor more democracy." Jørgensen is promanagement in that he favors use of advanced management methods, and it is just for this reason that he wants power at the top—to make sure they are used, and that they are used in the best interests of the workers. It is an unusually enlightened and progressive view, particularly when compared with the backward opinions of union leaders in some other countries (particularly the United States).

Scandinavian democratization is at present being concretized in legislation in all three countries. This occurred first in Norway. In 1968, a parliamentary committee headed by E. F. Eckhoff, a member of the Norwegian Supreme Court, was set up by the center-conservative coalition government in power at the time, to study possible needs for legislation in industrial democracy. In early 1971, the committee published its findings. The majority on the committee suggested that a few companies should be selected for experimental projects involving placing workers on the boards of directors. The minority, representing more leftish tendencies, revived the ten-year-old suggestion of the Aspengren Committee —not altogether surprising, since Aspengren, by this time head of LO, was on this committee. As before, the proposal was for

creation of a *bedriftsforsamling* in companies with more than two
hundred employees, situated between the shareholders and the
board of directors.[60] The minority vowed that it would push the
proposal through parliament at the earliest opportunity, and, in
mid-1972 (after a shift in government in 1971), did so. At the
same time a provision was added requiring all companies with
more than fifty employees to appoint worker representatives to
boards of directors as well—a minimum of two on each board.
The legislation was made effective at the beginning of 1973.

The change in composition of the boards of directors did not
generate much opposition. Creation of the *bedriftsforsamling*
was more controversial. Though workers would have only a third
of the places, labor leaders were satisfied that they would get a
fair hearing for their views. The main function of the new body is
to appoint the boards of directors. It also must be consulted on
major company moves, such as large capital investment programs
or rationalization moves that can affect employment.

The NAF, representing the employers, strongly opposed the
new legislation. In a joint statement issued with the Federation
of Industries, it attacked the proposal because it would make the
"decision-making process in companies less effective and could be
inhibiting on management and on day-to-day operations." Fur-
thermore, it would create "uncertainty and confusion in responsibility and competence relationships within the company."[61]

That was the official reaction. However, insiders say the position
was largely artificial. One observer told me: "If the officers of the
NAF had been able to express their own opinions, they would
have been much more liberal. But they had to represent the
majority view of the members of the group. In this case, the
members are lagging a bit behind." Indeed, management people
in general do not seem overly upset by the new ideas. Edvard
Brøvig, an expert on management education at NAF, remarked
to me: "Many workers are more competent to sit on boards
than shareholders are. Many of them know the factory from top
to bottom and are certainly more qualified than shareholders who
visit the factory once a year—or perhaps never."

Following the democracy program presented by the Swedish
LO at its 1971 congress, the Swedish government drew up legislative proposals, to be presented to parliament in 1972. The main

point was statutory memberships on boards of directors for worker representatives—a minimum of two on each board—for all companies with more than one hundred employees. In addition, a parliamentary commission was appointed to investigate LO's wish to abolish the detested Paragraph 32, replacing the employer's unquestioned right to make unilaterial decisions with some sort of joint labor/capital jurisdiction over working conditions.

One large step on the road to giving workers more say over their immediate work environment was recorded in mid-1972, when LO and SAF drew up a new agreement covering management moves to increase efficiency through automation, work studies, and similar action. Replacing a 1949 agreement on the same subject—in which both parties had agreed to strive for "higher productivity" as being everybody's principal goal—the new document sets up four objectives to be kept in mind in any such activity: increased productivity, increased work satisfaction, improved work environment, and security of employment. Moreover, the agreement gives workers access to all management records used in planning work changes, requires them to be included in the planning during the initial stages of discussions, and gives unions the opportunity to discuss changes before they are made. The agreement states that changes in jobs should, "as far as possible, not only consider technical and economic viewpoints, but also strive consciously to create work which, from an individual's point of view, can be experienced as meaningful and involving."[62]

In late 1972, labor leader Anker Jørgensen was named Prime Minister of Denmark, and shortly thereafter the government unveiled a legislative proposal covering the "economic democracy" shareownership idea as well as a requirement that all companies with more than fifty employees give at least two places on their boards of directors to employees.

In view of the excellent results achieved in the experimental shop-floor democratization, it might be assumed that there is no need for legislation. But that is not the way the labor leaders see it. Even though Scandinavian managers are doubtless more democratically minded than those in other countries (foreigners are constantly amazed at the relaxed manner with which Scandinavian executives and labor leaders socialize), there is still a large fear of the unknown, especially when it involves modifying long-accepted authoritarian forms. For example, despite the considerable evidence now available showing the defects of traditional pyramidal management forms, a booklet published by the Swedish employers' group blandly states: "From the point of view of efficiency, the 'hierarchical' form of organization has so far shown its superiority over other ways of organizing work."[63]

Moreover, as Anker Jørgensen points out, democracy of the formal type—that is, representation on top-level boards—is a natural complement to lower-level direct democracy, each form acting to strengthen the other. Tor Halversen, an official of the Norwegian LO who is particularly occupied with industrial democracy, told me: "We want to create a complete, unified program to give workers influence at all levels. We know that the *bedriftsforsamling* will mean little to the man on the shop floor, but the point is that there must be bodies to solve problems at all levels."

Moreover, there is a widespread realization that none of these single steps in themselves constitute a conclusive answer to all the problems at hand. The government position on the Norwegian legislation emphasized that it was only "a first step on the way toward a wider democratization of Norwegian working life." What was important was not the technical content of any single proposal, but the goal—"that all people should have, to the degree possible, an influence on decisions that affect them."[64]

The significance of the Scandinavian experience is indeed not that it has revealed instant solutions to all problems. What it has done is to show, more clearly than in any other country, that industrial democracy is practical, that it works, that it is of benefit for all parties, and that all these facts can be coordinated politically. Thus many of the deep-seated, and long-lived, suspicions regarding the practicability of these ideas have been dealt with.

The Scandinavians are now trying to find workable methods of changing organizations in accordance with the discoveries made so far. The ferment of activity in governments and in companies will doubtless produce far-reaching changes in company organization, and many observers are convinced that the next few years will see radical transformations.

In the past, the Scandinavian nations have often proved to be ahead of other countries in attacking social problems; as writer Hudson Strode claimed in the case of Sweden, they have been "models for the world." That may again prove to be true in the case of industrial democracy. Georges Gurvitch, a French sociologist, has painted a picture of a future form of society—"pluralist decentralized collectivism"—today notably represented by the Scandinavian countries and Yugoslavia; this form of society is based on "the self-management of all workers and farmers."[65] Will worker-management be a central feature of the society of the future?

Some observers think so, and that Sweden will be especially instrumental in setting the pattern. But there is a clear realization that moves made up to now are only a beginning, that gigantic problems remain, and that solving them is the next task of the welfare state. Olof Palme, Swedish Prime Minister, has stated that his government's "principal preoccupation" is in this area: "The reforms we have achieved have meant great progress, but without touching people's daily working lives. . . . We must introduce democracy into enterprises. . . . It is necessary that workers be able to manage their own work. . . . In the 1970s and 1980s we are going to rebuild social life through democracy in work."[66]

XIV. WHAT IS TO BE DONE?

It is overwhelmingly apparent that industrial democracy is an idea whose time has come. Traditional authoritarian methods of managing enterprises are no longer adequate. Neither employees nor work organizations can stand the counterproductive management practices that have come to be accepted as necessary and unavoidable. The need for democratization of companies is neither an isolated phenomenon nor an abstraction invented by social thinkers looking for something new to complain about. Worker alienation is alarmingly manifest in every industrialized country and is arousing the concern of widely varying types of observers. A few quotations can be instructive:

"At the origin of these troubles, there is the depressing and irritating feeling that modern man experiences of being caught and dragged along in an economic and social machinery over which he has no control."[1]

"The worker's attitude towards his job was that of a wage-laborer and he was not directly interested in higher efficiency or better performance by his enterprise. He continued to be alienated from the means of production and could not change the conditions of production."[2]

"Finally . . . there are the needs for self-fulfillment. . . . The conditions of modern industrial life give only limited opportunity for these relatively dormant human needs to find expression."[3]

"Highly mechanized industries seldom give any scope for the individual's need for social fellowship, meaningful work and self-actualization. . . . Production is not only lower than necessary but the work in highly-rationalized processes carries with it the mutilation of the individual's personality and his opportunities for development."[4]

"Despite progressive advancement in social benefits, legislation and improved wage conditions, employees in large enterprises still feel dissatisfied. They now demand conditions which would enable them to derive satisfaction from their work, and seek to participate in management decision-making."[5]

The first of these statements is by General de Gaulle, in discussing his plans for bringing about wider participation in France; the second is by Marshal Tito, describing the conditions (under state socialism) the Yugoslav "self-management" system was designed to combat; the third is by American management expert Douglas McGregor, pinpointing a central management problem in modern industry; the fourth is by Swedish labor expert and socialist ideologist Lars Erik Karlsson; the fifth is by H. Darin-Drabkin, the Israeli kibbutz authority, in describing the problems the kibbutz helps solve.

These problems are not only apparent on the theoretical level. Employees are increasingly making known their distaste for traditional management methods and their desire to use their intelligence and initiative in their work—as is shown in more or less constant, widespread absenteeism, turnover, and sabotage, and in more spectacular displays of discontent, such as the events of May in France in 1968, the Upper Clyde Shipyard sit-in in Britain in 1971, and the Lordstown affair in the United States in 1972.

Although the most afflicted group of workers—blue-collar workers—is steadily shrinking in relative importance in the population, assembly-line techniques and "assembly-line blues" are being just as steadily applied in white-collar and other areas. Moreover, beyond the specific techniques involved in the scientific management principles—that is, the precise measurement of work stages, the exact planning of every move, the careful establishment of an elaborate, fixed routine for every job—the underlying philosophy of these methods is also increasingly taking hold: the belief that everyone needs to be told what to do, the reliance on strict authority, the downgrading of individual intelligence, the belief that "tightening up" on discipline will always improve results. Thus almost any work organization can be affected by this type of thinking. Louis Davis, the UCLA work psychologist, points out: "At present, almost 60 percent of the U.S. workforce is in the service sector, but service institutions seem to be using industrial models for organizations and jobs. As a result, there may now be more dehumanized jobs than there were a generation ago. This appears to indicate that the dominant influence on organizational form is not technology, but the values of society and its managers."[6] It is already apparent, however, that white-collar workers are no more happy to accept autocratic practices than are industrial workers, and there is thus no reason to expect that resistance to autocratic systems will diminish as the nature of the workforce shifts.

The fact is that there is a swift decline in the willingness of people to work under the antiquated conditions still characteristic of most work organizations, to leave their intelligence at Chauvey's "checkroom for ideas" and meekly to submit to the rigid discipline of the "papa knows best" system. People are no longer so impoverished that they feel compelled to put up with the prevalent structure, no longer so badly educated that they cannot see through the solemn sham that industrial-capitalist authoritarianism has become, and no longer so polite that they are willing to pretend they do not see the fakery of it all. If the system is to be preserved—if the assembly lines, the typist pools, the keypunch troops, the art departments, and the sales forces are to be kept functioning—it must be recognized that the situation is critical, and for a basic, simple reason. As Leonard Neal, British industrial relations expert, has put it: "The growth of affluence, the growth of education, has led to a shortage of morons."[7]

The problems—which have remained essentially unchanged since the very invention of industrial capitalism—are clear. For most of this book, we have been discussing various attempted solutions; how does this accumulation of experience provide us with clues to the future of industrial democracy?

Most importantly, it indicates that workers do very much want more influence over their work. Whether we look at opinion polls, studies by behavioral scientists, spontaneous comments by workers themselves, experience under virtually any democratic system that has been tried, or some of the more explosive manifestations of worker attitudes, the conclusion is much the same: The desire for democracy is overwhelmingly strong. A common occurrence in democratization procedures is a strong expression of worker hostility to the new methods and an agreement to cooperate only on condition that the old methods will be reinstated when the workers so demand. But when democratic methods are put into effect, employees are almost invariably enthusiastic, and a frequently voiced opinion is that "there is no road back." Sociologist Paul Blumberg notes: "There is hardly a study in the entire literature which fails to demonstrate that satisfaction in work is enhanced or that other generally acknowledged beneficial consequences accrue from a genuine increase in workers' decision-making power. Such consistency of findings, I submit, is rare in social research."[8]

The democratic spirit is not only virtually universally liked, but it also works. In surveying the variety of approaches, and despite the serious defects that afflict many of them, we see in almost every case the advantages outweigh the disadvantages. In the Israeli kibbutzim, the deep, direct involvement of each individual in the affairs of the group works out well in terms of both hard economic results and satisfaction for members. The Yugoslav self-management system suggests that even a rather poorly designed system, slowly improved by trial and error over the years, can result in rapid economic growth for the country and attract the widespread support of the populace. Both Yugoslav self-management and West German codetermination indicate that the direct transfer of power to worker representatives on top-level bodies in a company (although that may not be the best place to start a democratization process) does have its merits. Workers do have an interest in the matters that are discussed at these levels, and they do manage to acquire the competence to make contributions of value. The scientific studies of organizations carried out in Britain and the United States show not only that possession of decision-making power, autonomy, and control over a wide work span is a prime demand of individuals but that, when organizations find ways to meet these demands, one result is higher quality and better productivity. The experience of Scandinavia provides dramatic evidence that sound scientific methods can be used for the promotion of industrial democracy, in a clearly political context, with significant benefits for all concerned. Though the manifestations of the democratic spirit we have been examining display great differences, they are all part of the same basic picture. They show that the need for freedom, control, and opportunities for self-actualization is virtually universal in advanced societies; that democratization of work organizations can meet this need; and that this process is in the best interests of employees, organizations, and society as a whole.

As I know from many conversations on this subject, it will be objected that the evidence is meager, scattered, and inconclusive, and that where democratic methods do work, it is only because the organization in question is a "special case." I have had it pointed out to me that the kibbutzim in Israel are special because of ideology (or poverty, or because the country is at war); that Yugoslavia is special because it is Communist (or underdeveloped, or in conflict with the Soviet Union); that West Germany is special because of the unusual conditions under which codetermination was introduced; that Texas Instruments is special because it is a technologically advanced company; that Orrefors Glass is special because it is in a craft industry and thus technologically backward; that Procter & Gamble is special because it is a large company; that Nobø is special because it is a small company; that anyway the whole Scandinavian experience is special because everybody knows Scandinavians are "different"; that Monsanto is special because it is capital-intensive; that R. G. Barry is special because it is labor-intensive; and so on. To an extent, of course, any company is special, but such objections seem rather difficult to justify; managers in capital goods companies, say, do not ordinarily refuse to engage in marketing activities with the excuse that marketing is "special" and only of interest to consumer goods companies.

The fact is that democratic methods have worked under an astonishing variety of conditions—and with such varied groups as salesmen, scientists, ordinary production workers in process industries, ordinary production workers in mechanical, assembly-line plants, office workers, and people across the spectrum of education and skills. One of the most successful projects at Texas Instruments involved maintenance personnel with average below-fifth-grade education.

The very fact that uncannily similar situations have been worked out in widely varying contexts indicates that the underlying ideas are of wide validity. The "community" decision-making arrangement that has evolved at Procter & Gamble's Lima, Ohio, plant is strangely similar to the direct democracy practiced at kibbutzim in Israel. Rensis Likert's "linking-pin" concept—where interlocking circles of influence cut through the entire organization —bears a remarkable resemblance to the network of workers' councils and economic units in Yugoslavia, which, as Tito explains, comprise a basic "unity and interconnection of relationships, from the worker at his job, who is the first link in the chain, through the work organizations. . . ."[9] The basic ideas in either of these systems might be described as follows: "In the company, there is a hierarchisation, a restriction of information at every level. It can only be remedied by establishing a kind of pyramid of committees which would have the job of coordinating information coming from the bottom and the top and working out solutions to submit to workers at the bottom."[10] But this statement was actually made by a French worker during the events of May 1968, giving a "revolutionary" view of how companies should be managed. Take this description of work organization: "Nobody has one exclusive sphere of activity but each can become accomplished in any branch he wishes . . . to do one thing today and another tomorrow, to hunt in the morning, fish in the afternoon, rear cattle in the evening, criticize after dinner. . . ."[11] Despite the bucolic context, this is essentially a kind of job-enrichment program, and it is specifically aimed at combating work alienation, in principle much the same approach as that used by Frederick Herzberg—but this quotation is from Marx's description of life under communism. Another kind of job enrichment, though of an unusual kind, is represented in Communist China by the "May 7 Cadre" schools—where upper-level bureaucrats and executives get their lives enriched by carrying out menial jobs alongside peasants and workers. (Some observers feel that Western managers might derive great benefit from similar experiences; Ralph Nader, for example, has suggested, to "sensitize managers to real worker problems, they could usefully spend two or three weeks annually 'on the line.' "[12]) This description of how workers in China solved a tough technical problem in drilling a new oilfield might be a description of the merits of participative management (with a few key alterations): "The Taching workers . . . broke the assertion of capitalist technical authorities that when the oil-bearing structure is irregular it is impossible to get a clear picture. The workers' new theories provided a solid scientific ground for opening Taching. The Taching workers applied a principle from Chairman Mao. . . . The approach led to a whole set of new technologies in oilfield exploitation."[13] Now that America has taken steps toward solving its problems with China, observers have been increasingly intrigued with the Chinese theories of worker participation. One U.S. journalistic survey of life in China asserted: "China has made remarkable strides toward eliminating one of the major social ills faced by Western societies since the Industrial Revolution: the alienation of the worker."[14]

To be sure, it is not possible to manufacture one rigid recipe to precisely fit the needs of all countries. Some examples can be instructive. In West Germany, virtually all companies are required to include a quota of one-third worker representatives on company supervisory boards. But labor leaders insist that if they cannot get full equality of representation with capital, the system is decidedly unsatisfactory. In Norway, however, the unions are perfectly content with the third of the places allotted to workers on the newly created "company assembly," which is very similar to the German board. The moral is that Norwegians and Germans are different and that perhaps different solutions are suitable in different places. Cultural variances also show up in other ways. When the Harwood firm set up a plant in Puerto Rico and tried to introduce participative methods there, it was soon discovered that turnover was alarmingly high. Alfred Marrow wrote: "The workers had decided that if management were so 'ignorant' that it had to consult its employees, the company was badly managed and would soon fail. So they quit to look for jobs with 'well-managed' companies that did not consult their employees but told them what to do."[15] Syntex encountered somewhat similar problems in Mexico and other countries with strong "authority" traditions. Nevertheless, the company finds there is a "subculture" of receptivity to participative methods. Dale Miller of Syntex told me: "We have been able to export our methods because we have found that the 'subculture' is more powerful than the surface culture." Scott Myers of Texas Instruments, who has lived and worked in Iran and other countries, concurs. Though he cautions that "intercultural conflict" can cause problems, he nevertheless emphasizes that "principles of autonomy and delegation apply in the developing countries . . . no less than they do in America."[16]

Therefore, even though not every detail of every democratic arrangement is universally valid, there are common threads that point to the industrial democracy of the future. It has been amply demonstrated that industrial democracy works; the problem is to develop methodologies for putting the principles into practice.

The approaches to industrial democracy can be roughly divided into two categories. The first is indirect, or representative, democracy, in which workers are given decision-making power through the placing of representatives on high-level boards within companies. Included in this category are the Yugoslav workers' councils, which consist almost entirely of worker-members and which have full power; boards of directors in state-owned companies in various countries, where workers have a portion of the seats; the German *Mitbestimmung* system; and a few private companies that have voluntarily given workers seats. When one first thinks about transferring power, this is the method that springs to mind, since such bodies do possess legal control. The approach is sometimes known as "formal" democracy, since it is the form that is affected—not necessarily the reality.

The second category is direct, or participative, democracy, in which the individual has a direct and immediate effect on decisions. In a small organization—a kibbutz, or a small company— these decisions might be on all issues, including over-all management matters. In a larger company, worker decision-making might start in small subsections, where groups of ten to twenty workers manage the work with which they are concerned every day and that they know intimately. There seems to be something natural, comfortable, and workable about groups of this size, and they turn up in theory and practice in numerous contexts, from Dallas to Oslo and from Palo Alto to Peking. We have examined a variety of direct democracy examples, ranging from the kibbutzim in Israel to the advanced methods used at General Foods' plant and including the "autonomous group" techniques developed at the Tavistock Institute and widely applied in Scandinavia.

The aim of both direct and indirect democracy is to diffuse decision-making power throughout the organization. In direct democracy, decision-making is clearly and deliberately pushed down to the lowest possible level. Traditionally, information on which a decision is to be based must be passed up to the top, where the decision is made and then passed back down. In direct democracy, employees most familiar with the subject make the decisions themselves, thus eliminating much cumbersome shuffling of papers up and down the organization. Decisions are made where the information is.

This is merely a different way of describing a familiar concept: decentralization. In an age of enormous, clumsy, impersonal organizations, decentralization holds considerable appeal. Social critic Paul Goodman writes of discussions he has had with students: "If . . . I happen to mention that some function of society which is highly centralized could be much decentralized without loss of efficiency, or perhaps with a gain in efficiency, at once the students want to talk about nothing else. This insistence . . . used to surprise me, and I tested it experimentally by slipping in a decentralist remark during lectures on entirely different subjects. The students unerringly latched on to the remark. . . . From their tone, it is clear that in this subject something is at stake for their existence. They feel trapped in the present system of society that allows them so little say and initiative. . . ."[17] Journalist Anthony Lewis, discussing the remarkable persistence of neighborhood life in London and the repugnant "bigness" of modern institutions, observes: "Somehow we have to learn to make them smaller . . . by breaking large organizations down into parts encompassable by man."[18]

Of these two approaches, we can say direct democracy is the more "scientific." Behavioral scientists interested in industrial democracy favor this approach. Indeed, behavioral scientists with no interest whatever in industrial democracy favor this approach; to them, it is only a coincidence that giving workers autonomy, authority, and responsibility makes an organization work better.

Theoreticians often see a clear-cut dichotomy between direct democracy and representative democracy; those who favor one frequently dislike the other. The experts at the Tavistock Institute generally find representation on boards of directors highly uninteresting, and most German labor leaders have minimal interest in democracy at the work place. There is an assumption that it is an either-or thing: If you start at the top you cannot do anything at the bottom, and if you give workers more influence at the immediate workplace, that will absorb all their attention and prevent their reaching for more high-level influence.

But there is also the fear that the two may be connected. The possibility that workers might want to influence high-level decisions is worrisome to managers who hold high opinions of their own exclusive talents. Douglas McGregor wrote: "The usual fear is that if employees are given an opportunity to influence decisions affecting them, they will soon want to participate in matters which should be none of their concern." McGregor called this an "almost paranoid" attitude and said there was "little basis for anxiety over the issue of management prerogatives."[19]

Fortunately or unfortunately, McGregor is wrong. Many experts have theorized that possession of a bit of autonomy should logically lead to more. Chris Argyris writes: "Once an individual has achieved a level of aspiration that has led to psychological success, his tendency will be to define a new level of aspiration which is realistic and higher. Once this is achieved, still another goal which is realistic and higher will be defined. . . . We may infer that there is no inherent limit to man's psychological energy."[20] This principle has been repeatedly confirmed in real life. Swedish sociologist Bertil Gardell, who has studied worker attitudes in various situations, concludes: "In companies where employees believe they have . . . a great degree of influence on the company's operations, there is a relatively large group that wishes to influence larger management questions. . . . It is not true, as is often claimed, that self-management and influence over small areas will divert attention from the more important economic questions, it will rather create greater independence . . . and a more highly developed demand for participation in decision-making."[21] As we have seen, workers at Nobø in Norway have made aggressive suggestions to management on tying production more closely to marketing, and workers at Orrefors in Sweden have been demanding more influence over management issues. Expectations that influence on high-level decisions will evolve from democracy at the lower levels are common. Bengt Gustafsson, the full-time "industrial democrat" at Grängesberg, says: "Despite the defects in the 'representative' system, that's the only direction we can take. . . . But to create real democracy, you have to start at the bottom."[22] This has even occurred in the more advanced U.S. plants; workers at Procter & Gamble have been steadily moving into areas normally reserved to management.

If influence over lower-level decisions leads to a desire for influence over larger matters, the opposite can also hold true. The Yugoslav system, which began as a purely "representative" arrangement, has gradually evolved, with increasing amounts of influence being exercised by the economic units, and smaller workers' councils possessing limited jurisdiction over a relatively restricted area. Moreover, worker power at the top should be of immense value in overcoming whatever management objections there might be to the introduction of democracy at lower levels. In West Germany, some labor leaders are interested in this, and if they should decide to press the question, they can, through their representation on supervisory boards, apply direct pressure on managements.

The dichotomy between direct industrial democracy and representative industrial democracy is only a surface conflict. Rather than being two entirely different techniques, they might be more accurately described as merely two starting points to accomplish the same result: the democratization of work organizations.

If we consider, in isolation, apparently unrelated issues—such as whether workers would like to take over their companies, and whether managers think that might be a good idea—the principles of industrial democracy can sound far-fetched. But, by assembling all the evidence in proper order, we can see that there is a natural, step-by-step evolution at work:

If the present industrial system shows signs of collapsing under the resistance of workers to excessively autocratic methods (which seems indisputable); and if worker objections can be substantially reduced by creating organizations that include variety, autonomy, and opportunities for personal growth (which can be done); and if it is possible to do this while still meeting the objectives of the organizations (which is perfectly feasible); and if this makes for more efficient organizations (which is generally true); and if it stimulates workers to demand increasing amounts of influence (which it does); then we can conclude that—starting with the unarguably poor situation of industrialism today—we will inevitably arrive at full industrial democracy.

Indeed, the process is already in motion, as increasing numbers of companies are giving workers increased influence over their work. U.S. companies rarely call it democracy, but an evolution in that direction seems unavoidable. Some companies are consciously using an "open systems" approach, allowing for growth and development of the system. Others, which start with more limited aims, but noticing a natural tendency toward expanding employee influence, are finding this development to be a healthy one and are encouraging it. It is ever clearer that limited job-rearrangement techniques, in which jobs are enriched by managers who are deemed to know what employees want, are no longer adequate, that employees must be allowed to participate in successive expansions of their horizons. This vast expansion of employee influence in hitherto unexplored directions can seem a disturbing and frightening prospect for managers initiating participative programs to deal with what they may feel are only minor problems of worker morale. But it is difficult to see how the evolution can be stopped. There is every reason to believe it is something of a self-propelling process.

A few experts have explored the inevitability of democracy from other viewpoints. Warren Bennis and Philip Slater, respectively management consultant and social scientist, argue: "Democracy in industry is not an idealistic conception but a hard necessity in those areas in which change is ever-present and in which creative scientific enterprise must be nourished."[23] Obviously, corporations will be finding it difficult to demand creativity needed under modern competitive conditions, combined with submissiveness to authority customary in orthodox organizations. Seen in this light, democracy is strictly pragmatic: "Democracy seeks no stability, no end point, it is purposeless, save that it purports to ensure perpetual transition, constant alteration, ceaseless instability."[24] The issue is a whole new approach to business organization: "Adaptive, problem-solving, temporary systems of diverse specialists, linked together by coordinating and task-evaluating executive specialists in an organic flux—this is the organization form that will gradually replace bureaucracy as we know it."[25] This rapidity of change is also stressed by Donald Schon in his analysis of "the loss of the stable state" and its consequences: "Throughout our society we're experiencing the actual or threatened dissolution of stable organizations and institutions, anchors for personal identity and systems of values."[26] Constantly accelerating change places impossible demands on an organization in which authority is centralized and fixed. There must be flexibility, and democratization is a practicable answer.

Thus in the long run we can see that industrial democracy is—logically—inevitable. However, as everyone knows, the long run can be long indeed, and if we wait for the inevitable processes to work out, we may be in for an inordinately long wait. There is not a great deal of evidence that most managements are especially eager to democratize their companies, despite the benefits, and despite the social pressures. Many companies may in fact prefer an increasingly surly and uncooperative workforce—which is something they are at least used to—to the uncertainties of an open-system organization. Some managers want to solve the problems by avoiding anything genuinely radical, and when their half-hearted attempts fail, as is quite possible, they may conclude that reforming work is not possible and that the only solution is tighter discipline.

Therefore, it is probable that the movement toward industrial democracy will eventually have to be powered by legislation. And the most likely avenue is a requirement that workers be represented on high-level bodies within companies—boards of directors or other bodies such as the German *Aufsichtsrat* or the Norwegian *bedriftsforsamling*. Such representation is the fastest way to channel worker influence to the top levels, to press for more human working conditions, and to set forth demands for thorough-going democratization. It would be desirable that such bodies be specifically designed to promote democratization and humanization of the workplace, since that is the area of most interest to employees.

Admittedly, this is something of a contradiction. We have been emphasizing the importance of flexibility and adaptability and the shortcomings of any purely formal solution. Yet any pattern imposed through legislation must contain a measure of rigidity. Work psychologist Einar Thorsrud opposed the Norwegian legislation because, if only the form rather than the spirit is observed, it can become a "shell without content."

However, the value of this type of legislation is not that it solves all the problems, but that it can help to create further mechanisms that solve the problems. The ultimate objective is the creation of improved social and psychological relationships within work organizations by cutting through the bureaucratic and technological barriers, and the fact is that formal changes can help trigger the social changes desired. Just as some companies are "building in" a measure of democracy in designing drastically altered production systems, so can society as a whole "build in" a measure of democracy into *company organizational* systems, and the creation of a high-level board with worker membership would seem a good place to start. As has been frequently pointed out, such high-level bodies are defective in that they are remote from the ordinary employee and the matters discussed at those levels tend not to be those in which he is most interested or about which he has the most knowledge (though experience in Yugoslavia and West Germany indicates that workers do develop the capacity to make valuable contributions with time). Employees are far more interested in the democratization of their immediate workplaces and in gaining power over decisions that affect them and their work on a day-to-day basis. It is here that employees are most able to supply useful suggestions; it is here that a break-up of traditional power patterns is most valuable, both in fulfilling employee needs and in meeting company objectives; and it is the type of democratization that has shown (i.e., in Britain, Scandinavia, and the U.S.) the most spectacular results. Our present knowledge about democratization of the workplace therefore provides the vital link between the "worker democracy" ideologies of such thinkers as G. D. H. Cole and the everyday reality of functioning business organizations. Employees are not in constant need of the indirect power that representation on a high-level board gives in the same way they need power over their day-to-day activities. Nevertheless, the need is there, even though such a board can make its effect felt on the ordinary worker only occasionally, in the same way that a parliament only occasionally affects a citizen in a representative democracy. In particular, some kind of authority must exist in order to assure that the workplace-democratization process is carried out, and this can undoubtedly best be done by legislating company bodies into existence that possess that authority.

Legislation need not be confined to worker representation on top-level boards. The Swedish labor movement is demanding legislation on such points as worker involvement in long-range planning and budgeting, major capital investment programs, hiring and firing, accounting intricacies, shop-floor working conditions, and other matters. In the United States, at least one expert is trying to develop proposals to require companies to give workers a say over promotion, appointment of supervisors, compensation, work methods, recruiting, and production schedules. These are complicated matters, but if laws have been put in force in such complicated fields as safety, hiring practices, and union relations, it should be feasible to promote industrial democracy in the same way.

To an extent, *any* legislation on social problems might be considered a "second best" approach—it would be much preferable that the citizens solve all their problems voluntarily. It is clearly not possible to automatically bring about changes in, say, racial attitudes through legislation, but it has been possible to create conditions favorable to the growth of changed attitudes through changes in formal rules regarding jobs, housing, and educational opportunities. Not everybody likes these formal rules, just as not everybody can be expected to like formal rules regarding industrial democracy. But industrial democracy is a far less complicated and less emotional issue than are racial questions.

To sum up, a fully satisfactory system of industrial democracy will most likely have to include democracy at the immediate workplace (since that is where the worker is) as well as democracy at the highest levels in the company (since that is where the power is). And in order to put together this top-to-bottom democratization, legislation will probably, sooner or later, become necessary.

A principal argument of this book has been that the traditional money-instrumental view of work—that work is supplied only in exchange for money and has no further significance—is badly suited to our times. As we have seen, workers are intensely interested in such other aspects of their jobs as autonomy, variety, and personal involvement.

However, that does not mean that compensation is unimportant. Considerable confusion on this subject has been spread by some psychologists who have maintained, on rather weak evidence, that pay is of little importance and has little significance as a motivating element in work. Moreover, it is likely that many psychologists are more or less forced to neglect pay because they are relatively powerless figures in the companies where they work, and have no influence over compensation matters.

Pay is of particularly great importance in a discussion of industrial democracy, since higher profitability is an extremely frequent outcome of company democratization. It should be a matter of elementary justice that these higher profits are shared with workers— as they are, for example, at the Lima, Ohio, plant of Procter & Gamble, where the workers receive compensation in line with their contribution and far in excess of average company wages. Michael Beer of Corning Glass remarks, of the higher production achieved by highly motivated workers: "Pay and pay changes must catch up with psychological changes in involvement and motivation."[27] This is not always the case, however. A *Fortune* survey of participative techniques points out: "The most common theme of complaint heard in job-enriched plants is that there should be, but often is not, more pay for more responsibility and more production." A Texas Instruments worker is quoted: "I used to produce 8,000 parts a day, and now with the new machine I produce 15,000 a day, and they haven't changed the grade level."[28]

More importantly—to managers, at least—fair pay can be a key element in workers' motivation and thus their performance. Arthur Kornhauser looked at some of the nuances of the subject and warned against "loose overgeneralizations" to the effect that "pay is unimportant."[29] He adds: "Wages *can* loom very large indeed in working people's emotional reactions if their own pay appears unfair, sharply inadequate, or subject to arbitrary decisions according to their standards."[30] Scott Myers points out that money, in addition to its more obvious functions, can have great value to people as a "measure of status" and "a scorekeeping system."[31]

The idea that money is unimportant to any great number of people in modern society is so obvious an absurdity that it is surprising it has been discussed with such great seriousness. Edward Lawler, who has done extensive research on the subject and has sifted through virtually every piece of evidence available, concludes: "Money probably is important because of its association with a number of desired outcomes and . . . as long as these desired outcomes are valued, money will be valued."[32] Specifically, Lawler found that money can be a powerful motivator, but only if pay is closely related to performance and employees believe that performance will in fact be rewarded.[33] He further notes that this is most true in organizations where a "democratic approach to management" is practiced, since the necessary trust is best fostered in such organizations, and employees can be involved in job evaluation, goal-setting, and even establishing pay scales. By the same token, "the traditionally managed organization has difficulty in getting pay to work as a motivator because the conditions are not right for participative performance appraisal and joint goal setting."[34] We have seen that higher pay can be an extremely effective motivator—as well as a help in building a democratic system—in a number of cases, most dramatically at Lincoln Electric, where the extra wage costs are more than paid for by the vastly increased productivity.

Certainly, an equitable pay system that rewards superior performance would seem to be an integral part of any democratic system. In combating the idea that *only* pay is important in a job, let us not commit the equally grave error of assuming it is of *no* importance.

Any discussion of industrial democracy unavoidably has a rather anticapitalistic tone. Not surprisingly, many advocates of industrial democracy are aggressive socialists. Lars Erik Karlsson, a

Swedish authority, calls industrial democracy "a step on the road to socialism."[35] Ken Coates, a British ideologist, writes: "The workers' control strategy aims to stimulate people to aspirations which point towards the achievement of socialism."[36]

Are the two ideas inextricably interwoven?

Today, one need not, of course, be especially leftishly inclined to feel that capitalism is not succeeding. When everyone, even including prominent establishment figures, can openly complain about the chiseling of consumers by big business, the bland assumption by mismanaged corporations that they are entitled to welfare handouts, the squalid begging of political favors by corporations, the unfortunate record of the "military-industrial complex," and the cynicism of business leaders on their social responsibilities, one can suspect that the game is almost up. The idea that profit is and should be a corporation's only goal is no longer socially acceptable, and most businessmen avoid emphasizing the point in public. At the 1972 annual meeting of the Ford Motor Company, Henry Ford made headlines merely by unabashedly enunciating the traditional capitalist profit-comes-first principle.

Perhaps the most powerful influence in changing attitudes about the social role of business and the sanctity of private property has been concern over the environment. It has suddenly become apparent that "ownership"—and thus the independence of "owners" from social responsibility—is not as simple as had been thought. Businesses do not "own" the air, the water, or the beauty and tranquillity of nature that they deface with industrial processes. As far as the general public is concerned, therefore, curbing the "rights" of "owners" is scarcely any longer controversial.

This shift in attitudes should therefore facilitate the further incursion into private property rights that a transfer of power to employees must bring about. Just as governmental force has been used to promote pollution control, it will doubtless also have to be used to promote industrial democracy, and the public's receptivity to this use of governmental compulsion to attain socially desirable objectives will, it may be hoped, be as positive in the one case as in the other.

A shift of power to employees should not cause any great nervousness among those who now nominally possess power in corporations—the shareholders—since they have already happily ceded their power. In fact, John Kenneth Galbraith points out that it would not be especially helpful to the corporation if the shareholders should decide to use their power: "Exercise of such power on substantive questions requiring group decisions would be as damaging as any other. So the stockholder . . . must be excluded . . . he can vote but his vote is valueless."[37] At a "mock" General Electric meeting held in 1972 by a group of social activists focusing on the ills of big business, it was only a slight exaggeration of reality for the mock shareholders to be amiably advised by a mock executive: "We'll give you a taste of power. In just a moment we'll give you the opportunity to vote us back in office."[38] As Galbraith points out, real power is held by the corporate bureaucracy, including "all who bring specialized knowledge, talent or experience to group decision-making"—in his terminology, the "technostructure."[39] In the United States, a small band of eccentric agitators has enlivened many an annual meeting with its colorfully expressed demands for "corporate democracy," meaning more power to shareholders. These activities have had no perceptible effect on the average investor who, if he is dissatisfied with management, simply sells his shares. A simple proof of the worthlessness of the vote is seen in the case of convertible bonds which, unlike shares, carry no voting rights, but whose value is linked to the value of the same company's common stock. Investors evaluate the relative merits of convertible bonds and shares strictly on the basis of arithmetical formulas; any security analyst who recommended a share above a bond, in whole or in part because of the voting right attached to it, would have his intelligence seriously questioned by his fellow Wall Streeters. Some shares have no effective vote at all —either because (especially in Europe) they do not carry even a formal vote or because effective corporate control is held by a tight group of insiders—and nobody pays much attention to such peculiarities in evaluating the shares.

Therefore, transferring part or all of the formal power from shareholders, who neither want it or need it (and in fact do not even have it in any real sense), to the workers, who both want it and need it, should not disturb the shareholders. Indeed, if they should think about the matter at all, they should welcome such a development, since a group of apathetic and uninformed persons with no loyalty to or long-term interest in their company would be replaced by persons intensely and personally involved in the company's long-term progress. Decisions made at a company's upper levels have far-reaching effects on the lives of all employees, and it is difficult to justify the exclusion of these employees when the questions are discussed. Capitalist mythology holds that, since mismanaged companies become bankrupt and the suppliers of risk capital are thus punished, it is they who must make the decisions. But more attention needs to be given to the suppliers of risk labor, who are far more intimately involved and who are likely to be punished far more severely for the mistakes of management than are the shareholders. In 1971, General Motors stockholders received 948 million dollars in compensation for their contribution to the company's success, which compared with the 9.5 billion dollars received by employees. As the *Wall Street Journal* pointed out: "On a dollars-and-cents basis, the people on the payroll thus have ten times as much at stake in the corporation's affairs as those who receive the stock dividends."[40]

It is clear that the public repute of capitalism has declined drastically; that its advantages are beginning to be heavily balanced by grave defects; and that the whole system rests on a shareholder-power arrangement that is largely a fiction anyway. Surely the whole thing can be advantageously done away with?

Well, maybe so and maybe not, but there does not seem to be any direct connection between the need for industrial democracy and the need (if that's what it is) for socialism. There is not a shred of evidence that state-owned companies are any less alienating than privately owned companies. Two of the most autocratically managed companies in Europe are the French Renault auto works and the Swedish LKAB, both state-owned. Both are chronically plagued by labor disputes and both have been frequently and bitterly attacked for their backward personnel policies. To be sure, the democratization drive in the Norwegian Norsk Hydro (which is now, though it was not when the drive began, majority-state-owned) has shown great progress, but probably no more than the open-systems approach at the U.S. company Procter & Gamble.

Moreover, the introduction of democratic methods in a company does not seem to lead the employees to become particularly interested in socialism. To be sure, there is much evidence that they soon begin to question some of the traditional machinery of capitalism, but this has to do only with the authority structure, not with the system's economic underpinnings.

As a matter of fact, a capitalist system can well stimulate the growth of industrial democracy. Since there is good evidence that democratic methods are more productive, and therefore more profitable, than autocratic methods, managers can very likely be spurred to make greater efforts to democratize. If the "human resources accounting" work now under way at the Michigan Institute for Social Research produces hard data showing the financial advantages of democratic management methods and the feasibility of developing accounting techniques to measure such factors, it could have a powerful effect on capitalistic thinking about democracy. It is conceivable that progressive managements of the future will regularly report figures on human resources in the same way that progressive managements now report investments in research and development. Neither figure is audited and neither appears on the balance sheet, but both are of vital importance in evaluating the future of the corporation.

If there is no direct connection between industrial democracy and socialism, there may be an indirect one. If democratization of work organizations should become widespread, and if this should affect workers' attitudes off the job as well as on, then it is quite conceivable that drastic changes could occur in society's values—especially regarding the merits of high-pressure economic growth, unending emphasis on production, the profit motive as the only feasible prime mover, and so on. Over the long term, one result might be an option in favor of socialism, syndicalism, or simply a more human version of capitalism (even though that might mean a less prosperous economy).

However, this is a long-range speculation and of no significance in the present context. This book is based on present realities and present possibilities, and the realization of industrial democracy decidedly does not depend on the development of some future human being with values superior to (or different from) our own. And there is nothing in the present situation to suggest that capitalism need be harmed by industrial democracy nor that the introduction of democracy in work organizations would automatically have any fundamental effect on the structure of the economy.

One frequently voiced criticism of democratic organization—an objection often made against the Yugoslavian self-management system, for example—is the cumbersome and time-consuming nature of the decision-making process. Yet it is sometimes forgotten that the normal manner of making business decisions in Japan is to involve every single person who is affected in any way in making the decision—and few serious observers would question the outstanding performance of the Japanese economy. Peter Drucker notes: "Only when all of the people who will have to carry out the agreement have come together on the need to make a decision will the decision be made to go ahead."[41] The apparent inefficiency of such a system is deceptive; Egmund Henriksen, a Danish executive who spent some time in Japan, explains the hidden logic: "One of the weaknesses of the system is that the decision-making process is quite slow. But on the other hand, decisions that are taken can be executed extremely rapidly. In the West, we put great emphasis on dynamic, quick decisions, but the execution of the decisions can be quite slow."[42]

XV. THE FUTURE OF INDUSTRIAL
DEMOCRACY

In speaking of the future of industrial democracy in the United States, it is difficult not to notice that, so far, the degree of interest in the subject is just about zero.

In Europe, there is widespread interest among assorted social thinkers, psychologists, and groups ranging from (roughly) center to extreme left, either in "democracy" based on the scientific participative methods we have examined, or in more ideological notions of worker control, or both. In the United States, there is virtually no interest among any of these people in either. Neither unions, nor political parties, nor independent social philosophers, nor student groups, nor inflammatory periodicals are campaigning to give workers more freedom and power. Such control is exceedingly attractive to workers, at least when they become aware that gaining more control over their work is a practical and feasible alternative. How, then, can we explain this odd lack?

One reason is doubtless the free-enterprise ideology holding that the man at the top fought a hard battle to get there and is therefore qualified to tell those beneath him what to do—and the system is fair because everyone has an equal chance to engage in the battle. This picture has become more and more a myth, and the low-level worker without proper credentials finds the going increasingly tough as he tries to rise. Yet the folklore is accepted, and those who are left behind philosophically submit to fate, because according to the rules of the game, they could just as easily have won.

Another element is that the money-instrumental attitude—which we have been attacking as inadequate in an age of increasing prosperity—is still probably more valid in America than in other industrialized countries. Taylor's scientific management theories, based on money as the sole motivator, were well adapted to his times, since the worker's urgent need was indeed for money. Needs for autonomy and personal growth were far less pressing. In a sense, America is still astonishingly close to the Taylor era. Europeans are often struck by the brutality of economic life in America—the swiftness with which mass layoffs are carried out, the job insecurity that even high-level employees suffer from, and, relative to many European countries, the low level of assistance to those in need. Added to these rather special factors, there is the use (not confined to America) of unemployment as an instrument of economic policy. The coolness with which economic planners push unemployment up a few notches in order to combat inflation is a process of almost unbelievable cruelty, since the burden of the process is borne by those least able to do so. (It has been suggested that the economic thinkers automatically submit to a salary cut or in some other way "participate" actively every time they increase unemployment for policy reasons; the impact on policy might be striking.) In America, material circumstances seem overwhelmingly important because they *are* overwhelmingly important, and thoughts about psychological fulfillment do not tend to flourish under such circumstances. It is significant that demands for industrial democracy are most strong in Scandinavia, where full employment is a matter of government policy and anti-inflationary considerations are given lower priority. Compared with the United States, job insecurity is practically nonexistent. A somewhat similar situation arose in Switzerland, when new regulations limiting the import of foreign workers resulted in a drastic labor shortage. In order to lure new workers and retain those already in place, companies resorted to a variety of imaginative techniques, to a great extent aimed at increasing employees' freedom and standing. According to one 1971 account: "Knorr Food Products, Chocolat Tobier, and Sulzer Brothers, an industrial-goods producer, have introduced flexible work schedules. These require employees to work for a specified period of five or six hours a day, but allow them to put in the rest of their time whenever they please. The drug companies based in Basel have shifted hourly workers to monthly payrolls, which the workers consider more prestigious and more secure."[1]

To put it in terms of Maslow's hierarchy-of-needs theory, we can say that the Scandinavians and the Swiss are relatively free of worries on the lowest, physiological-need level, and can move up to the higher level of demanding opportunities for self-actualization. This type of escalation does not come quite so naturally under American conditions.

Probably the most formidable barrier to industrial democracy in the United States is our strange class structure, which, by blinding middle-class Americans to the situation of blue-collar workers, has also been blinding the middle-class workers to their own condition. The problems of work, though increasing at all levels, have been much more intense and easy to see (and thus to trace at other levels) in the case of blue-collar workers—if anybody is interested in looking. This class business is perhaps all the more dangerous in that it is not generally recognized. Edmund Dahlström, Professor of Sociology at the University of Gothenburg, remarked to me: "In America, there is much less emphasis on titles and everybody speaks in the same way—people have a much easier way of talking to each other. It is only on the surface, of course; in truth, the person with money always decides. But the ideology that there are no classes really means a lot to Americans." There is thus a strong, and generally unnoticed, barrier to understanding between classes, and this affects the commentaries of middle-class intellectuals on blue-collar workers. Galbraith, whose "technostructure" stops "at the outer perimeter" where it meets "the white- and blue-collar workers," cheerfully states, in reference to the United States: "In the richer country . . . there is little or no alienation."[2] A great many managers are also unaware of the changes taking place in the workforce and the increasing interest in freedom and self-control. Alfred Marrow, one top executive who does pay attention to the social forces, told me: "The heads of most organizations are much too remote from what goes on in their own plants." An extremely sophisticated lady working to increase participation in a major U.S. company explained to me that the top management in that company could never conceive of any social changes that could affect them: "Their feeling of power is reinforced in so many ways—their private dining rooms, their chauffeur-driven limousines, their executive airplanes—they don't think this power could ever change." When Michael Harrington, in the early 1960s, began documenting the poverty of a huge minority of Americans—poverty that was "hidden . . . socially invisible to the rest of us"—much of the public was astonished to learn the facts.[3] Similarly today, everyone knows the blue-collar worker exists, but few people recognize the extent of his—and his white-collar cousins'—problems. It is only quite recently that some attention is being devoted to problems of work in America, but the full extent of the problems has yet to be discussed widely, and there is virtually no discussion of far-reaching solutions that attack the basic troubles.

During World War II, because of the unusual sense of unity, workers often displayed unusual enthusiasm, willingness to learn, and ability to perform at a high level—and many companies learned to encourage such behavior. Just after the war, there was considerable interest in investigating this spirit further and extending it to peacetime conditions. Alexander Heron, president of a large company, wrote a thoughtful book on the subject, in which he announced that a new era was opening up for managers: "They may be on the way to a new, dynamic relationship in which workers will take an interest in jobs they understand, jobs which they themselves will 'manage.' "[4] That was in 1948. In 1950, writing in *Fortune* about the Scanlon Plan, Russel Davenport argued that it "could have repercussions around the civilized world" and added: "The average employer has little conception of the wealth and imagination and ingenuity lying untapped in the heads of the workmen."[5] Was anybody listening? Just twenty years later, Judson Gooding, again in *Fortune*, wrote: "America's factory workers . . . can do more, and do it better, and contribute a flood of valuable ideas. . . . They know more about their jobs than anyone else— they spend forty hours a week doing nothing else—and hardly any of their suggestions for improving methods are impractical."[6]

The suspicion arises that perhaps these methods are not so wonderful after all. What do the opponents of democratic management say?

Actually, there are not many. There are numerous people, especially businessmen and union officials, who disbelieve in the capacity of ordinary employees to carry greater responsibility and exercise more control, but there are few expert observers who have examined the evidence objectively and found it wanting.

One who has is Milton Derber, Professor of Industrial Relations at the University of Illinois. He wrote: "A few years ago in the United States, optimistic theories like those of McGregor and Likert regarding workers' needs and desires for self-actualization seemed to be sweeping the field; today they are regarded as psychologically inadequate and faulty."[7] Derber told me that, while he favored the "idea of worker participation," his observations convinced him that it was "more talked about than achieved" and that the very lack of adoption was poor testimony to its effectiveness. Moreover, he pointed out that many of the most popular theories—e.g., those of McGregor and Maslow—have not been empirically confirmed. All of this is true, but not, I think, conclusive. In the history of any new set of ideas, there always must be a period during which they are not making much progress. The lack of rigorous scientific grounding is a fact, as was pointed out by Maslow: "If we wait for conventionally reliable data, we should have to wait forever."[8] To say that theories have not been proven is surely not to say they have been disproven.

Another skeptic is sociologist Daniel Bell of Harvard, who, in a study first published in 1956, examined the problems of work, long before they attracted general attention. He recognized that "the revolt against work is widespread and takes many forms," but concluded: "By and large the sociologist . . . has written off any effort to readjust the work process; the worker, like the mythical figure of Ixion, is chained forever to the endlessly revolving wheel."[9] This pessimistic view is anchored, Bell said, in the conflict between goals: "the satisfactions of the immediate work group" and productivity. He added: "Short of pressure from the workers themselves, there is no action which would force modern enterprise to reorder the flow of work."[10]

Though Bell wrote this some years ago, he has retained his pessimism. He told me that, though Lordstown had made discontent with work a fashionable issue for the moment, it had no long-term significance since "the time span of these things is very short."

Thanks to the steady decline in the percentage of the workforce engaged in manufacturing, he did not feel such problems to be of critical importance, especially in view of the virtual impossibility of persuading either managers or workers to accept economic sacrifices to get more meaningful work. He thought that thoroughgoing job reform could only function for "companies in protected markets." As for evidence that democratic methods might be more profitable than conventional methods, he said such claims were "hogwash" and that any superior results that might turn up would be only the result of a "Hawthorne effect" (a temporary surge of enthusiasm when workers know they are the object of a scientific investigation).

Though the evidence we have been examining conflicts rather sharply with these conclusions, experts such as Derber and Bell have a point: It is quite possible that the successful examples of participative management are due only to special circumstances in each case and that they cannot be applied on a broad scale. This viewpoint does not, however, take into consideration the rising antiwork feelings in society, which may force managements to develop methods (if the present ones are indeed ineffective) that will meet the shift in mood. Some experts harbor the suspicion that manifestations of antiwork feelings will be increasing. Thomas Jeswold, a personnel specialist at the Ford Motor Company, has said: "In the near future the workforce may take more direct and severe action. Some knowledgeable people even feel that this may take the form of employee sit-in demonstrations in corporate executive suits on a scale to rival any seen on college campuses."[11] The choice of *whether* to act may shortly become transformed into a choice of *how* to take action. Michael Beer has pointed out: "Does it make sense to spend inordinate effort in determining whether participative and open management systems are valid for a given organization when the social changes around us clearly indicate that if they are not now, they will be in the near future?"[12] Robert Coles, the Harvard psychiatrist, observed, in reference to the writings of Simone Weil: "No doubt today what she (and over the decades many, many workers) wanted done inside those factories can still seem impractical. But that word 'impractical' is one that history has taught us to think twice about. One generation's impracticality has a way of becoming another's urgent necessity."[13]

In any case, the workability of democratic management methods is not the only factor determining their popularity. One factor is simply that they are out of step with conventional management techniques.

In organizations, there is a kind of homeostasis—the tendency of subsystems to remain in equilibrium with each other. When the equilibrium is disturbed, some reaction must take place that restores the equilibrium. In a completely open-systems approach, provision is made for allowing a new arrangement in one subsystem to develop in that subsystem and to spread to others surrounding it, thereby preserving a balanced development. Attempts to "bottle up" the effects only lead to trouble. This was illustrated some years ago when an assembly line in a toy factory was reorganized and operators were given considerable autonomy in deciding upon speed, operating methods, and other working conditions. It worked well, but production was so high that it created numerous problems with the environments, that is, the rest of the plant. Most seriously, the operators, who were compensated on a piece-rate basis, were earning considerably more than anticipated—since, with their new freedom, they worked with much greater efficiency. Management was unprepared for such an eventuality and did not wish to meet the challenge of reordering the entire plant or otherwise countering the friction that arose. It chose instead to cancel the change and revert to the old methods. As the consultants involved pointed out, it was "an experiment that failed because it succeeded too well."[14]

More serious is the conflict with managers' accepted ideas of how businesses should be run. These ideas are, of course, closely connected with managers' assumptions about people. Management consultant Raymond Miles, in studying management attitudes, found that a surprisingly large percentage of managers felt their subordinates to be basically different from themselves—less able, less responsible, and less ambitious: "Managers in every group to date have rated their subordinates well below themselves, particularly on such important managerial traits as *responsibility*, *judgment*, and *initiative*."[15] Many of the principles of the modern theorists are extremely well known, especially McGregor's concepts of Theory X and Theory Y (autocratic and democratic thinking patterns). Mason Haire, a professor at MIT, explained to me: "Almost all managers talk in Theory Y terms but act in Theory X terms. In America, you couldn't possibly say you run a centralized operation—it would be like asking for a sweet martini. But in fact that's what they're doing." He points to one underlying reason: "There is a lack of faith in the other person. Any type of democracy—whether Jeffersonian or what—basically depends on faith in other people." In a multicountry study of management attitudes, of which Haire was a co-author, it was pointed out that managers have "a relatively low opinion of the capabilities of the average person"—and that held true for all of the fourteen countries studied.[16] It is thus understandable that democratic methods enjoy rather poor acceptance and helps explain why, as we have seen, those working to develop democracy in companies often must do so without the support of top management. One solution, Rensis Likert reports, is for managers using democratic methods to lie to their superiors: "We have seen some corporate staffs and divisional presidents . . . withhold from their top corporate officers results of measurements which would correct the faulty impressions held by those top officers."[17]

Much of the apprehension about democratic methods revolves around the issue of power. British industrial psychologist J. A. C. Brown wrote: "There are good reasons why self-centered and power-loving individuals should not be placed in positions of responsibility; for the power-loving man is a sick man who seeks to compensate for his own inadequacies by gaining control over others."[18] Nevertheless, power-loving men are often in charge, and more democratically minded methods are naturally disfavored. James Richard, a former personnel director at Polaroid Corporation who is now a professor at Boston College, wrote: "Some men get real satisfaction from manipulating, controlling, and guiding people. For some men there is challenge and excitement in the game of company politics. This game is looked upon as the way to get ahead. . . . And the whole traditional program of management rewards and status is constructed to reinforce this set of attitudes and motivations."[19] Charles Hughes at Texas Instruments told me he thought such discouraging management attitudes as exist today are closely connected with the political mood in America: "The political climate in the United States has gone very reactionary, and this is private enterprise's way of expressing the political climate. Right-wing political viewpoints correlate with right-wing management viewpoints."

Managers to whom power means much are not eager to share that power with lower-level employees, even though fears on this point are not entirely rational. Employees are already carrying out much of the day-to-day management of companies and thus already possess considerable power. In some cases, their primary opportunity to exercise it is negative (through sabotage, apathy, and slowdowns), but the power nevertheless exists. Kenneth Walker, head of the International Industrial Relations Association, points out: "The question is not whether information and power should be shared, because information and power are already being shared."[20] The point is whether the sharing is to be done constructively.

Many managers fear that a sharing of power must mean a loss of control. This is based on the assumption that there is a fixed amount of control in all organizations that can be sliced up like a pie, so that more for one party means less for the others. This is a fallacy. Arnold Tannenbaum of the Institute for Social Research in Michigan has studied the question carefully, and concludes: "Increases in the control which persons exercise in organizations may sometimes be accompanied by increases in the extent to which these persons *are* controlled in the organization. Paradoxically, one of the costs to the influential organization member for the influence he exercises may be the increased control to which he is subject. The loyalty and identification which he feels for the organization may lead him to . . . conform to organizational norms which he otherwise might not do."[21] Tannenbaum told me: "If management has complete power it may take lots of decisions, but it has little control if the decisions are not carried out. But if the management can arouse workers' commitment and involvement, its own control can also be increased. In fact, I think we have evidence that management can increase its power by giving more power to workers." An extreme case is seen in some European countries marked by severe class conflict. "Workers in America have more control than in Italy," Tannenbaum told me, "but American managers also have more power. In Italy, they approach the model of nobody having control."

That these fears can have a decided impact can be seen in an incident at Polaroid Corporation some years ago.

Polaroid has acquired considerable fame not only for its stunning technological and financial successes, but also for the humane views of its founder, Dr. Edwin Land. It was once said of Land that he wished "Polaroid to be known as the first manufacturer in the world that recognized the human dignity of every employee all day long."[22] And the company has done much to deliver on that ambition. A major program is an "employees' committee" with some thirty elected members (none from management), which serves as a pipeline for grievances, demands, and general worker feelings to top management. Though it has no formal power, it has great informal power, and a company spokesman told me he could not recall any request it had ever made being refused. Employees also often form spontaneous ad hoc committees to deal with special large-scale complaints. One was a committee of blacks protesting against the overly white-oriented workers' committee; the blacks' committee was listened to, given official status, and subsidized by the company. When it received satisfaction, it voluntarily disbanded. Another ad hoc committee was formed to look into alleged differences between pay scales of blacks and whites; it discovered that there were such differences, so they were eliminated and the committee dissolved itself. When I visited Polaroid the current strong ad hoc committee was pushing for more women's opportunities in traditional male jobs—carpentry, plumbing, and so on. The company operates weekend "intercultural workshops," intended primarily to bring minority groups together with whites to promote understanding, help employees understand themselves better, and help them to function more effectively in groups. The company is quite proud of its job-posting system. Every job is openly advertised, and any employee can bid on any job. Free vocational training is provided, as is also free training for underqualified candidates (those with meager skills in reading, mathematics, and so on) to be able to qualify for the vocational training courses.

All this has generated an unusually healthy climate. Bill Lytle, organization development consultant, told me: "There is a feeling that you can influence top management." One example was the celebrated demand in 1971 that Polaroid stop selling its products in South Africa, especially for the purpose of making the identification cards blacks must carry. Although the company says that most of the agitation was by outside groups and that few employees were involved (no ad hoc group was formed), Polaroid nevertheless sent an interracial committee to South Africa to study the situation and promised to follow its recommendation (which was to stay in South Africa, but not to collaborate in making the identification cards, and to upgrade employment opportunities for blacks in the local distributor's organization). Another show of democratic feeling was in mid-1970, when some layoffs were announced. Immediately, an ad hoc committee proposed that a fund for voluntary employee contributions be set up; the laid-off workers would then perform work assigned by the local municipality, but would receive money from the fund instead of wages. The company accepted and even volunteered to match all employee contributions. (The Internal Revenue Service then stepped in to question the legality of the deal, and while it was thinking it over, the workers were called back to work. Some fifteen thousand dollars was collected.)

But the introduction of democracy directly on the job caused impossible problems at Polaroid. In the early 1960s, there was a project in which a group of some 120 machine operators were put on an unusual routine. Instead of spending all day at the machine, they spent one hour in special training, two doing coordinating work, and five running the machine, thus gaining an unusually intimate understanding of what they were doing. This was done in preparation of the introduction of film packs in August 1962, which called for high-quality operation of complex machinery to meet a pressing deadline for the new product. Lytle says: "The film was brought into production on time by this group, and most people think we would never have gotten it out otherwise. The worker used more than just his hands—he also used his head. When something went wrong he didn't just scream for the supervisor." Well, if the program was so successful, what was the problem? Ray Ferris, training director, told me: "It was *too* successful. What were we going to do with the supervisors—the managers?

We didn't need them any more. Management decided it just didn't want operators that qualified. We tried twice to reinstitute the program but had to give it up. The man who started the program quit the company." The employees' newly revealed ability to carry more responsibility was too great a threat to the established way of doing things and to established power patterns. Rather than try to deal with the threats, management chose to liquidate the whole thing. This has created a considerable amount of cynicism regarding Dr. Land's grandiose comments about "human dignity." James Richard, former personnel director at Polaroid, told me the reason for the company's failure to live up to Land's expressed ideals was simply the pressures of ordinary business life: "I saw things going in the opposite direction, the environment being tightened up, and the willingness to commit the corporation diminishing. It's not because people are basically bad—it's that the system is so powerful."

If democratic management at Polaroid is dead, it is not forgotten. Ferris remarked: "The operators are still talking longingly about it."

Although American managers have been only moderately interested in democratic management techniques, labor leaders have been almost completely uninterested, and indeed very few of them are even aware that such things exist. Again, the situation is sharply different in Europe, where many unions have radically modified their programs in recent years to demand more participation for workers. That U.S. unions have not been more vigorous in defending their members' interests can seem surprising, but unionists argue that some special features of U.S. labor contracts—emphasis on local bargaining, elaborate grievance procedures, and extremely detailed contracts—make any further freedom unnecessary. John Crispo, a labor expert at the University of Toronto, writes: "Neither co-determination, nor works councils, nor anything else European Industrial Relations systems have thus far produced protects the workers as much as a local can in North America, given the more sophisticated nature of our collective agreements and our grievance and arbitration procedures."[23] Nat Goldfinger, research director of the AFL-CIO, explained to me that industrial democracy was not needed in America: "The issue is irrelevant here. I would suspect that most of the issues that are bugging Europeans are taken care of here in the collective bargaining process."

There are also some basic practical objections. One is the hostility that some unionists feel for, not only management, but other labor leaders. Regarding the idea of putting union representatives on boards of directors, Abe Morgenstern of the International Union of Electrical Workers remarked to me: "Take Meany and his crowd—they are practically on the boards already. What would they do that's any different from what's being done now? I believe I would lose sleep if there were something like *Mitbestimmung* in, say, the construction industry. Labor and management would just gouge the public together." Another fear is that of compromising the union position. Bill Webb, of the Communications Workers of America, pointed out: "We want management to make the decision so we can be free to start a grievance about it. Otherwise we could be accused of helping make bad decisions. So we have always left the decisions up to management."

And there is virtually no interest in questions of alienation. One union official who has had opinions on such subjects is Paul Schrade, formerly West Coast regional director for the United Auto Workers. The central problem is obvious, he told me: "The work lacks satisfaction. The worker has to find methods of getting satisfaction outside the job—by using 'do-it-yourself' three- and four-day work weeks." Workers should help decide "the work schedule, the work pace, the speed of the assembly line." And Schrade wants to go farther: "Workers should have a say in all kinds of decisions. It is the managements who are responsible for pollution and unsafe cars. If workers were involved in the decision-making process at GM the company would probably produce better cars at lower cost. I think there's a whole new movement that could be built around these ideas within the unions." Schrade concedes his viewpoint has not gotten very far: "We are not supposed to talk about these things before they have been discussed with the international board, and they never get cleared with the board because they won't discuss them." Schrade, a social activist of wide-ranging interests, has been called "one of the leading spiritual preservers" of the socially oriented approach of Walter Reuther, but, on factory reorganization and other sensitive issues, he was badly out of phase with union leadership and apparently especially with Leonard Woodcock, head of the UAW. "None of this sat very well with Mr. Woodcock," ran one press report on Schrade's fight with the union leaders.[24] He was defeated for re-election to his post in 1972, largely, he thinks, because of Woodcock's dislike for attacking matters like promoting worker decision-making. (The UAW says it was because of Schrade's devotion to other social causes, which left him little time for union business.)

For the most part, U.S. labor has enthusiastically accepted the principle that man works only for money. Bargaining has thus been confined to a relatively narrow range of issues. Goldfinger told me: "A union demand is a negotiable demand which, if not satisfied, can be met by a strike. How do you talk about these other questions in terms of a negotiable demand and a possible strike?"

It is interesting to note that not even independent labor experts are much interested in such issues as combating worker alienation, in sharp contrast to the numbers of independent management experts who are constantly urging managers to be more democratic. A. H. Raskin, the leading U.S. labor writer, published an article in 1970 in which he pleaded that "the labor movement must start moving." Noting that the "pathetically sluggish movement" was afflicted with "frozen leadership, stale ideas, and a front fragmented by organizational and personal rivalries," Raskin suggested that the leaders turn their attention to questions such as a switch from hourly to weekly wages, civil rights, and environmental issues.[25] But surely it would seem that the very center of the worker's life—the nature of his work—could get equal billing.

To be sure, there is some realization that workers' psychological problems exist. An AFL-CIO pamphlet published in 1969 pointed out: "Work methods are not rigidly determined by technological factors. Employers have a range of choice in the organization of work. They can do much to fit jobs to the physiological, psychological and social needs of their workers. . . . Giving the worker the opportunity to share in the process of revising work methods when technological changes occur can increase job interest and worker morale."[26] But there has been no action on this declaration of principles. Goldfinger, conceding that "we've been a little backward on this job satisfaction thing," told me one reason was a suspicion of the methods being used: "Behavioral scientists are manipulating the organization for the benefit of management. Where is the benefit to the workers? There is a good healthy suspicion of people who are working for management."

This should present a golden opportunity for unions to get the behavioral scientists lined up on *their* side—or at least into a neutral position—as is being done in some European countries, to prevent the use of participative methods to manipulate employees or to undermine the union, and to ensure that workers who produce more through greater use of their abilities get a just share of the material benefits. Some companies are already using participative methods solely to combat union organization, and this trend can be expected to continue if unions do not take counteroffensive action. Up to now, managements have felt that unions are not only ignorant of democratic management methods but quite hostile, and most of the progress has been made in nonunion plants. Some studies indicate that workers in the most alienating jobs tend to be the most loyal to their unions, and it is conceivable that the unions might regard attacks on alienation as a threat to union power. But, as Robert Blauner has pointed out, the retention of the nonalienating characteristics of traditional crafts, in the printing industry, is in large part attributable to a strong union. And there are a number of examples of harmonious blending of unions and democratic organization.

The potential for real democratization of American work places might seem far from bright, and some sophisticated observers take a gloomy view. Arne Derefeldt, a Swedish personnel specialist, wrote after a trip through America in 1970: "It would greatly surprise me if the concept of industrial democracy should be given much serious attention in the U.S. during the 1970's. But if it doesn't, then one can see, rather pessimistically, great risks for disturbances in American working life, at the latest toward the end of the decade."[27]

Nevertheless, it is possible to detect some positive signs.

For one thing, there has been a vast surge of interest in the problems of work—particularly following Lordstown—and this interest is inevitably leading to an interest in industrial democracy.

A most significant factor has been a beginning of a change in some labor leaders' thinking. A few years ago, Charles Hughes of Texas Instruments remarked to me: "I can see the unions bargaining for more satisfying job content as the mental health aspects of work become more apparent, just as they now bargain for wages." David Anderson of the Communications Workers of America made this prophecy to me: "I believe American labor unions are going to change in the next decade—and change radically. We'll be involved much more in the worker's life, and we'll be getting away from the idea that we can bargain only for wages."

These visions have not yet been fulfilled, but there are signs of a new direction, and in at least one union—the UAW—there is a strong feeling that new tactics may be in order. When I visited UAW headquarters in 1970, I found virtually no interest in alienation, assembly-line boredom, or other such ills. To the extent that such phenomena were problems, they had been resolved some years earlier, I was assured, by extra relief pauses obtained through bargaining. One staff member told me: "This concept of deadly monotony on the job is an intellectual middle-class concept—*we* couldn't stand it—but for the worker it is acceptable because he doesn't have to think about what he's doing." Since that time, attitudes have begun to shift. Sam Fishman, UAW Michigan coordinator, notes that the nature of the struggle has altered: "It's a desire on the part of the worker of democratize the workplace. He wants to have more of a say over the conditions that exist."[28] And Irving Bluestone, head of the UAW's GM department, noted in a speech in early 1972 that workers "question traditional authoritarian managerial prerogatives" and recommended "workers' direct participation in the decision-making process." He further specified: "It will evidence itself initially in the area of 'managing the workers' job'; then . . . it will spread to aspects of 'managing the enterprise.'"[29] Bluestone told me that discussions on the point had just started, and that he did not know how the union might proceed. "We might put it in the form of a bargaining point," he said, but he thought that then it would no doubt be looked at suspiciously by management. He was therefore thinking of a different approach: "I feel that the companies and the

unions should join in cooperative efforts to study this question."
He had been impressed by the joint union-management industrial
democracy projects in Norway and Sweden, and believed they
might serve as a useful model. He was further examining modern
democratic management techniques, and was carrying on some
discussions with Scott Myers of Texas Instruments and Eric Trist
of the Wharton School to study ways in which the union might
take an initiative in using them for the workers' benefit.

The U.S. government has also taken more interest in problems
of worker alienation. A beginning was a paper prepared by Assistant Secretary of Labor Jerome Rosow in mid-1970, calling attention to the "insecurity and alienation" of blue-collar workers in
"oppressively tedious, noisy, and mind-numbing" jobs who "feel
blocked from further opportunity." The paper's suggested remedies were a rather weak mix of better educational opportunities,
housing aid, and "public relations" to "enhance the status of blue-
collar work."[30] But it was a start.

Since then, other government agencies have been contributing
to the discussion. Neal Herrick, a deputy administrator in the Employment Standards Division of the Labor Department, has been
organizing seminars and conferences on "the humanization of
work" and is considering ways of pursuing that end through policy
measures, perhaps through legislation. The Department of Health,
Education, and Welfare has launched a "Work in America" study
project to learn what, if anything, should be done to alleviate the
problems of work. The deterioration of the U.S. trade balance has
focused attention on low gains in industrial productivity in recent
years, and some observers have concluded that the low involvement of workers in their work is a prime culprit. Notably, President
Nixon was reported to be "very much concerned," especially over
the fact that younger workers "lack dedication to their work, and
that the resultant absenteeism, sloppiness and general lack of
craftsmanship threatens to prolong inflation, hold back domestic
economic growth and damage the U.S. in world trade."[31] Senator
Charles Percy of Illinois also notices a troublesome trend that he
asserts needs attention: "The idea is taking root that work must be
a fulfilling, personally rewarding experience."[32]

Attitudes among the U.S. public are developing in ways that
should create an increasingly receptive attitude to industrial democ-

racy. A 1971 survey designed to discover how these attitudes might be related to work improvement, carried out by Neal Herrick (at the time a fellow of the W. E. Upjohn Institute for Employment Research), turned up some startling results. When asked whether improvement was needed in "the chance to participate in management decisions," no less than 28 percent of blue-collar workers, 31 percent of union officials, and 47 percent of white-collar workers put the need in the "very much category," and 19 percent of employers agreed. When asked their opinions on the possible "introduction of a work-fulfillment bill before the U. S. Congress containing all feasible elements of a comprehensive program," 12 percent of managers, 36 percent of union officials, and 60 percent of shop stewards (workers were not asked on this point) expressed themselves as "for."

Though admittedly a "shoestring survey" and possibly containing some ambiguity, the poll nevertheless shows that opinions are changing. Herrick comments: "Workers are demanding more than 'just a job' and their behavior when they don't get it is forcing management to sit up and take notice." He theorizes that this situation is relatively new: "I am inclined to think that—as recently as five years ago—very few respondents to such a survey would have thought it a matter of serious concern that jobs be changed to allow more opportunity for the worker to achieve and grow."[33]

The Ford Foundation has also become attracted to the problems of work and, in 1972, it awarded two grants totaling some three hundred thousand dollars for research and the dissemination of information regarding past research. Such projects should help direct public attention to work problems.

In August 1972, a bill was introduced in the Senate (by Senators Kennedy, Javits, Nelson, and Stevenson) designed to seek "solutions to the problem of alienation among American workers" in order to combat "absenteeism, high turnover, poor quality work . . . and lessened productivity" as well as "poor mental health, poor motivation, alcoholism, drug abuse, and social dissatisfaction among workers."[34] The bill called for the provision of $10 million in fiscal 1973 and a like amount in fiscal 1974 to carry out various educational and research projects aimed at the maximization of "potentials for democracy, security, equity, and craftsmanship." The bill accurately notes that "promising efforts to deal with the problems of alienation carried out in this country and abroad are not widely known," and expresses the hope that this lack of awareness can be remedied. This is the first time the recently awakened concern about workers and their problems has been given expression in any legislative proposal and would seem to be an excellent step.

Progress toward industrial democracy will nevertheless doubtless be slow until there exists a conscious and articulated feeling that it is desirable and necessary. As Louis Davis has pointed out: "These questions have to be raised to the level of public debate. The quality of working life is too important to be left to managements and unions alone."[35] Yet what discussion exists of these issues is largely in rather arid and opaque terms that do much to obscure, and little to illuminate, the real significance. There is practically no openly expressed interest in "industrial democracy" (or any similarly ideological term) as such. The recent wave of interest in job reform as a method of attacking low productivity appears to be based on the belief that a bit of superficial rearrangement of jobs can solve the problems while leaving untouched existing intra-company power structures. The people who are promoting really advanced techniques—and who are in a real sense promoting industrial democracy—tend to avoid the word "democracy" and instead speak of job enrichment, job design, goal-setting, the humanization of work, open systems, socio-technical systems, work simplification, System 1-System 4, Theory X-Theory Y, autonomous groups, integration of goals, and so on. No doubt any advance of knowledge must be accompanied by a new jargon, but in this case it would be more helpful if more of the experts on the subject were a bit less reticent about what it is they are trying to achieve and what point their work has for society as a whole. One management consultant of my acquaintance who believes strongly in industrial democracy—not only as a method of organizing work but also in terms of demolishing such things as undeserved management "class" privileges—invariably and studiously avoids speaking of "democracy." If there is a latent broad-based sentiment that favors genuine industrial democracy, which it seems there is, certainly the experts in the field would be performing a valuable social service by injecting some clarity into the public discussion.

If any great portion of Americans should learn that democracy on the job is not only possible and desirable but that it could mean a whole new way of life, some interesting developments might ensue. Interest is low in America partly because the real possibility of democratically organized companies has never been presented to most Americans. In the comparative study of worker attitudes in Yugoslavia and America discussed earlier, we saw that while control tended, in both places, to be concentrated at the top, the workers in Yugoslavia described the "ideal" situation as one in which more control was exercised at lower levels, while Americans viewed the "ideal" as very close to the actual. The discrepancy was attributed to the "new social values emerging in contemporary Yugoslavia."[36] But it is conceivable that such "new social values" could emerge in the United States as well, and if that should happen, it would create strong pressures for company democratization.

The attention of intellectuals, social critics, and other opinion leaders has not yet been intensely focused on the problems of work, but that will no doubt come in the United States. One of the few discussions of this type was a note in the *New York Times* by Robert Dahl, a professor of political science at Yale. He pointed to the "puzzling lack of challenge to authoritarian management traditions in corporations," an anomaly in an age when every other institution was being attacked. Referring to the Yugoslav self-management system as a possible model for combating the "powerlessness of the ordinary American employee," Dahl concludes: "It seems obvious that if we place much value on democracy at the work place, the present arrangement is ludicrously far from desirable."[37]

In some ways, the prospects for industrial democracy are brighter in America than elsewhere, for America has one outstanding advantage: a vast capacity for accommodating change. The lack of stable institutions in America is often regarded as a crippling handicap, but it can be an enormous help in bringing about social change. The rigid bureaucracies in many European countries, seen in their most extreme form in France and Italy, help preserve stability under the threat of mild crisis, but they cannot cope well with great internal strains. When faced by such threats, either the entire structure must be altered, or it breaks down completely; the latter in fact happens all too frequently. This problem is much less severe in America. French leftist ideologist Jean-François Revel argues in his book *Ni Marx Ni Jésus*: "The revolution of the twentieth century will take place in the United States. It can only take place there. It has already begun. It will occur in the rest of the world only if it first succeeds in North America."[38] Although Revel's vision of a worldwide socialist revolution led by the United States may be a trifle extreme, he is correct in pointing out that the most revolutionary waves of the past decade have begun in America—the student revolt, civil rights activism, and other mass movements. The Europeans have been left behind: "The European dissidents . . . are the disciples of the American dissidents."[39]

Revel's view of America may not be so far-fetched as it sounds. In the mid-1960s, I was interviewing a Swedish economist who was occupied with the fight for women's social and economic equality, which at the time had become a lively social issue in Sweden. He mentioned that he had just been in the United States and had inquired about the status of the women's rights discussion in that country; of course there was no debate of this kind at the moment, and people only laughed at him for thinking the subject was even worth mentioning, so he stopped mentioning it. Only a few years later, the "Women's Lib" movement exploded in America, the subject became, almost overnight, a fervently discussed question, and the Americans were soon providing leadership and ideas for their sisters in other countries—including Sweden. More recently, I happened to be speaking to another Swedish economist, this one specializing in industrial democracy, which is a lively social issue in Sweden. As it happened, he had just returned from the United States, where he had been visiting factories and other business establishments, and had on occasion inquired about the industrial democracy situation in America. His American friends thought this was so peculiar a subject to be interested in that he became almost ashamed to bring it up, so he soon stopped talking about it.

At the moment, America is well behind European countries in thinking on this subject, and for the time being it would seem necessary and useful for America to borrow ideas on basic ideology from European countries. As noted, the ideology has found expression in legislation, first in West Germany and more recently in Sweden, Norway, and The Netherlands. Unions in France, Denmark, Norway, and Sweden have become increasingly interested in industrial democracy. And unions in Belgium and Italy have also been turning their attention to such matters. Guy Desolre, of the Sociological Institute of the Free University of Brussels, notes: "Everything indicates that the theme of worker control will play an increasing role in the labor movement during the years to come."[40] One leading Italian union has begun to focus attention on making jobs more meaningful and acquiring for workers a voice in designing factory processes.[41] In the Fiat strike in 1971, some modest victories in these areas were in fact registered. A poll in Switzerland showed that 22 percent of workers queried placed "participation" at the top of their list of wants.[42] The draft company law for the European Common Market, drawn up in 1970, provides for worker representation on boards of directors.

The United States may be well behind Europe and "underdeveloped" at the moment, but when things begin to happen in America they often happen quickly, and it is by no means impossible that America will one day be catching up and perhaps even supplying Europe with ideas in industrial democracy.

In the foregoing pages, the question of industrial democracy may seem rather complicated. But the essential point is that the wants and needs of man in his working life are the same as in life as a whole. More than merely the reworking of tasks, industrial democracy is the fundamental enrichment of life through freedom. It is the kind of freedom—liberating yet demanding—that psychiatrist C. R. Rogers wrote about: "The permissiveness which is being described is not softness or indulgence or encouragement. It is permission to be *free*, which also means that one is responsible. The individual is as free to be afraid of a new venture as to be eager for it; free to bear the consequences of his mistakes as well as of his achievements. It is this type of freedom responsibly to be oneself which fosters the development of a secure locus of evaluation within oneself, and hence tends to bring about the inner conditions of constructive creativity."[43]

To break down the over-all message of this book into its component parts, we can say that half of it is the problem of work created by overly autocratic work environments, and the other half is the will to find solutions. The existence of the problem is inescapably obvious. But, happily, solutions—practical and of demonstrable effectiveness—are readily available. Freedom is within reach.

NOTES

CHAPTER I

1. Adam Smith, *The Wealth of Nations*. London: Dent, 1970, Vol. 2, p. 264.
2. G. D. H. Cole, "Collectivism, Syndicalism, and Guilds." In Ken Coates and Tony Topham (eds.), *Workers' Control*. London: Panther Modern Society, 1970, p. 47.

CHAPTER II

1. Michael Harrington, *The Accidental Century*. London: Penguin Books, 1967, p. 87.
2. Armas Lappalainen, "Marxism under 60-Talet." *Dagens Nyheter*, July 28, 1970.
3. Daniel and Gabriel Cohn-Bendit, *Obsolete Communism: The Left-Wing Alternative*. London: Penguin Books, 1969, p. 48.
4. Irving Howe, "New Styles in 'Leftism.'" In Irving Howe (ed.), *Beyond the New Left*. New York: McCall, 1970, p. 20.
5. Betty Werther, "Higher Education in France and the U.S." *International Herald Tribune*, May 14, 1971.
6. Aaron Levenstein, *Why People Work*. New York: Crowell-Collier, 1962, p. 40.
7. *Newsweek*, April 24, 1972.
8. *Newsweek*, February 7, 1972.
9. *Wall Street Journal*, May 2, 1972.
10. *L'Express*, January 18, 1971.
11. *Dagens Nyheter*, April 21, 1971.
12. *Sunday Times*, July 4, 1971.
13. *The Economist*, January 9, 1971.
14. *New York Times*, June 21, 1971.
15. Staughton Lynd, "Again—Don't Treat on Me." *Newsweek*, July 6, 1970.
16. W. N. Penzer, "Managing Motivated Employees." *Personnel Journal*, May 1971.

17. Brendan Sexton, "'Middle-Class' Workers and the New Politics." In Irving Howe (ed.), *Beyond the New Left*. New York: McCall, 1970, p. 200.

18. Herbert Marcuse, *One Dimensional Man*. London: Sphere Books Ltd., 1968, p. 197.

19. Theodore Roszak, *The Making of a Counter Culture*. Garden City, N.Y.: Anchor Books, 1969, p. 35.

20. Leonard Silk, "Blue-Collar Blues in the United States." *International Herald Tribune*, September 4, 1970.

21. Abraham Ribicoff, "The Alienation of the American Worker," *Saturday Review*, April 22, 1972.

22. Charles R. Walker, and Robert H. Guest, *The Man on the Assembly Line*. Cambridge: Harvard University Press, 1952, p. 6.

23. Harold Hodgkinson, *Institutions in Transition: A Study of Change in Higher Education*. Berkeley: Carnegie Commission on Higher Education, 1970. Cited by Joseph Kraft, "Elite in Trouble of Own Making," *International Herald Tribune*, July 29, 1970.

24. Mark Gerzon, *The Whole World Is Watching*. New York: Paperback Library, 1969, p. 9.

25. Roszak, op. cit., p. xii.

26. Gerzon, op. cit., p. 297.

27. Cohn-Bendit, op. cit., p. 47.

28. C. Wright Mills, *White Collar*. New York: Oxford University Press, 1951, p. 229.

29. William H. Whyte, Jr., *The Organization Man*. New York: Simon & Schuster, 1956, p. 3.

30. W. H. Auden, "The Poet and the City." In James Scully (ed.), *Modern Poets on Modern Poetry*. London: Collins-Fontana, 1966, p. 176.

31. Frank Lloyd Wright, *The Future of Architecture*. New York: The Horizon Press, 1953, p. 90.

32. Sigmund Freud, *Civilization and Its Discontents*. London: The Hogarth Press Ltd., 1930, p. 68.

33. Ibid., p. 34.

CHAPTER III

1. Walter S. Neff, *Work and Human Behavior*. New York: The Atherton Press, 1968, p. 51.

2. Claude Mossé, *The Ancient World at Work*. London: Chatto & Windus, 1969, p. 1.

3. Ibid., pp. 27–28.

4. Ibid., p. 25.

5. II Thessalonians 3:10.

6. C. Wright Mills, *White Collar*. New York: Oxford University Press, 1951, p. 217.

7. Ronald Fraser (ed.), *Work*. London: Penguin Books, 1968, pp. 11–12.

8. Max Weber, *Protestantism and the Spirit of Capitalism*. London: Unwin University Books, 1930, p. 75.

9. R. H. Tawney, *Religion and the Rise of Capitalism.* London: Penguin Books, 1938, p. 36.

10. Luke 6:24.

11. Tawney, op. cit., p. 122.

12. II Thessalonians 3:11.

13. I Thessalonians 4:11, 3.

14. Tawney, op. cit., p. 114.

15. Weber, op. cit., p. 157.

16. Ibid., p. 158.

17. Ibid., p. 162.

18. Ibid., p. 53.

19. Phyllis Deane, *The Industrial Revolution in England 1700–1914.* London: Fontana, 1969, pp. 18–20.

20. Adam Smith, *The Wealth of Nations.* London: Dent, 1970, Vol. I, p. 5.

21. Deane, op. cit., p. 73.

22. Smith, op. cit., Vol. II, pp. 264–65.

23. Ibid., Vol. I, p. 13.

24. Ibid., Vol. I, p. 73.

25. Jean-Luc Godard, "La Vie Moderne." *Le Nouvel Observateur,* October 12, 1966.

26. Reinhard Bendix, *Work and Authority in Industry.* New York: John Wiley & Sons, 1956, pp. 41–42.

27. Frederick W. Taylor, *The Principles of Scientific Management,* 1911. Included in Taylor, *Scientific Management.* New York: Harper & Row, 1947, p. 20.

28. Frederick Taylor, *Shop Management,* 1903. Included in Taylor, *Scientific Management,* p. 44.

29. Taylor, op. cit., 1911, p. 32.

30. Ibid., p. 34.

31. Ibid., pp. 64–66.

32. Ibid., pp. 42–46.

33. Ibid., p. 59.

34. Ibid., pp. 61–62.

35. Taylor, op. cit., 1903, pp. 54–55.

36. Taylor, op. cit., 1911, p. 83.

37. Taylor, op. cit., 1903, pp. 98–99.

38. Frederick Taylor, *Testimony Before the Special House Committee,* 1912. Included in Taylor, *Scientific Management,* p. 262.

39. Taylor, op. cit., 1911, p. 40.

40. Taylor, op. cit., 1912, p. 86.

41. Ibid., p. 49.

42. Taylor, op. cit., 1903, p. 176.

43. Gustav Janouch, *Gespräche mit Kafka.* Frankfurt: S. Fischer Verlag, 1951, p. 68.

44. Taylor, op. cit., 1903, p. 132.

45. Ibid., p. 126.

46. Ibid., p. 69.

47. *Time*, November 9, 1970.

48. Deane, op. cit., p. 78.

49. Max Weber, "The Ideal Bureaucracy." In Gerald D. Bell, *Organizations and Human Behavior*. Englewood Cliffs, N.J., 1967, pp. 86–89.

50. Bendix, op. cit., pp. 293–94.

51. Ibid., p. 309.

52. Elton Mayo, *The Human Problems of an Industrial Civilization*. Boston: Harvard University, Graduate School of Business Administration, 1946, p. 173.

53. Adolf Sturmthal, "Workers' Participation in Management: A Review of United States Experience." *International Institute for Labor Studies Bulletin*, June 1969.

CHAPTER IV

1. Karl Marx, *Economic and Philosophical Manuscripts of 1844*. London: Lawrence & Wishart Ltd., 1970, pp. 110–11, 114.

2. Ibid., p. 118.

3. Robert Freedman (ed.), *Marx on Economics*. London: Penguin Books, 1962, p. 235.

4. Marx, op. cit., pp. 117–18.

5. Robert Blauner, *Alienation and Freedom*. Chicago: University of Chicago Press, 1964, pp. 15–32.

6. Georges Friedmann, *Le Travail en Miettes*. Paris: Gallimard, 1964.

7. Marx, op. cit., p. 110.

8. Friedmann, op. cit., p. 50.

9. Charles R. Walker and Robert H. Guest, *The Man on the Assembly Line*. Cambridge: Harvard University Press, 1952, p. 53.

10. Ibid., pp. 54–55.

11. Ibid., pp. 113.

12. Ibid., p. 88.

13. Ibid., p. 160.

14. Simone Weil, *L'Enracinement*. Paris: Gallimard, 1949, p. 75.

15. Friedmann, op. cit., p. 117.

16. Bertil Gardell and Gunnela Westlander, *Om Industriarbete och Mental Hälsa*. Stockholm: Personaladministrativa Rådet, 1968, p. 16.

17. Arthur Kornhauser, *Mental Health of the Industrial Worker*. New York: John Wiley & Sons, 1965, p. 25.

18. Ibid., pp. 56–57.

19. Ibid., pp. 196–97.

20. Ibid., p. 50.

21. Friedmann, op. cit., p. 189.

22. Stanley Parker, *The Future of Work and Leisure*. London: MacGibbon & Klee, 1971, p. 85.

23. Kornhauser, op. cit., pp. 212, 234.

24. Ibid., p. 100.

25. Ibid., p. 263.

26. R. D. Laing, *The Divided Self*. London: Penguin Books, 1965, pp. 78–79.

27. Ibid., p. 90.

28. E. Kapustin, "Soviet Workers' Participation in Management." Paper presented at Second World Congress of International Industrial Relations Association, September 1–4, 1970, Geneva.

29. Barry Richman, *Management Development and Education in the Soviet Union*. East Lansing: Michigan State University Press, 1967, p. 46.

30. Adolf Sturmthal, *Workers Councils*. Cambridge, Mass.: Harvard University Press, 1964, p. 22.

31. Olga A. Narkiewicz, *The Making of the Soviet State Apparatus*, Manchester: Manchester University Press, 1970, p. 10.

32. Ibid., p. 57.

33. V. I. Lenin, "The Immediate Tasks of the Soviet Government," *Pravda* No. 83, April 28, 1918. Reprinted in V. I. Lenin, *Questions of the Socialist Organization of the Economy*. Moscow: Progress Publishers, undated.

34. Richman, op. cit., p. 46.

35. Friedmann, op. cit., p. 165.

36. G. V. Osipov (ed.), *Industry and Labour in the U.S.S.R.* London: Tavistock Publications, 1966, pp. 119–22.

37. Ibid., p. 257.

38. *The Economist*, November 22, 1969.

39. Reinhard Bendix, *Work and Authority in Industry*. New York: John Wiley & Sons, 1956, p. 362.

40. "Fundamental Legislation of the Union of Soviet Socialist Republics and Union Republics on Labor." *Moscow News*, No. 31, 1970.

41. Blauner, op. cit., p. 53.

42. Ibid., p. 81.

43. Ibid., pp. 167, 181.

44. Paul Blumberg, *Industrial Democracy: The Sociology of Participation*. London: Constable, 1968, p. 57.

45. C. Wright Mills, *White Collar*. New York: Oxford University Press, 1951, p. 227.

46. Theodore Roethke, "Dolor." In *The Awakening*. New York: Doubleday, 1953, p. 51.

47. Bertil Gardell and Edmund Dahlström, "Teorier om Anpassning och Motivation." In Edmund Dahlström et al., *Teknisk Förändring och Arbetsanpassning*. Stockholm: Prisma, 1966, pp. 133–34.

48. James C. Hyatt, "Productivity Push." *Wall Street Journal*, April 25, 1972.

49. Neal Q. Herrick, "Who's Unhappy at Work and Why." *Manpower*, January 1972.

50. P. C. Jersild, "Vem Ska Man Dressera—Människan eller Maskinen?" *Dagens Nyheter*, August 5, 1970.

51. Erich Fromm, *The Revolution of Hope*. New York: Bantam Books, 1968, p. 33.

52. Alfred T. DeMaria, Dale Tarnowieski, and Richard Gurman, *Manager Unions?* New York: American Management Association, 1972.

53. Blauner, op. cit., p. 29.

54. Ibid., pp. 29, 83–87.

55. *The Economist*, March 16, 1968.

56. Sigmund Freud, *Civilization and Its Discontents*. London: The Hogarth Press Ltd., 1930, p. 33.

57. Peter Drucker, *The Concept of the Corporation*. New York: Harper, 1946, pp. 140–41.

58. Sula Benet, "Why They Live to be 100, or Even Older, in Abkhasia." *New York Times Magazine*, December 26, 1971.

59. Antoine de St.-Exupéry, *Terre des Hommes*. Paris: Gallimard, 1939, p. 7.

60. Adam Smith, *The Wealth of Nations*. London: Dent, 1970, Vol. II, p. 264.

61. Edward E. Lawler III and J. Richard Hackman, "Corporate Profits and Employee Satisfaction: Must They Be in Conflict?" *California Management Review*, Fall, 1971.

62. Parker, op. cit., p. 12.

63. Erik H. Erikson, *Childhood and Society*. London: Penguin Books, 1965, p. 251.

64. Johan Huizinga, *Homo Ludens*. London: Paladin, 1970, p. 29.

65. M. Scott Myers, *Every Employee a Manager*. New York: McGraw-Hill, 1970, p. 65.

66. *The Observer*, June 15, 1969.

67. Bertrand Russell, *Autobiography*, Vol. I. London: George Allen & Unwin, Ltd., 1967, p. 152.

68. J. A. C. Brown, *The Social Psychology of Industry*. London: Penguin Books, 1954, p. 140.

69. Barbara Garson, "Luddites in Lordstown." *Harper's Magazine*, June 1972.

70. Cited in Blumberg, op. cit., p. 51.

71. Sophocles, *Oedipus at Colonus*. In Whitney J. Oates and Eugene O'Neill, Jr. (eds.), *The Complete Greek Drama*. New York: Random House, 1938, Vol. I, p. 654.

72. Kornhauser, op. cit., p. 290.

73. Jean-Jacques Rousseau, *Du Contrat Social*. Paris: Union Générale des Éditions, 1963, pp. 50–52.

74. Erich Fromm, *Escape from Freedom*. New York: Avon Books, 1965, p. 53.

75. Ibid., p. 163.

76. Ibid., p. 173.

77. Ibid., p. 173.

78. Ibid., p. 186.

79. Ibid., p. xiv.

80. Thomas Jefferson, *Basic Writings*. Garden City: Halcyon House, 1950, p. 807.

81. G. D. H. Cole, "Collectivism, Syndicalism, and Guilds." In Ken Coates and Tony Topham (eds.), *Workers' Control*. London: Panther Modern Society, 1970, p. 47.

82. Carole Pateman, *Participation and Democratic Theory*. London: Cambridge University Press, 1970, p. 43.

83. Ibid., p. 105.

CHAPTER V

1. Stowe Persons, "Christian Communitarianism in America." In Donald Drew Egbert and Stowe Persons (eds.), *Socialism and American Life*. Princeton, N.J.: Princeton University Press, 1952, Vol. I, p. 138.

2. Albert Fried, *Socialism in America: From the Shakers to the Third International*. Garden City, N.Y.: Doubleday, 1970, p. 66.

3. Ibid., pp. 69–70.

4. Ibid., pp. 76–77.

5. Ibid., p. 140.

6. Edmund Wilson, *To the Finland Station*. Garden City, N.Y.: Doubleday, 1940, p. 90.

7. Fried, op. cit., p. 80.

8. Ibid., p. 56.

9. Stewart H. Holbrook, *Dreamers of the American Dream*. Garden City, N.Y.: Doubleday, 1957, p. 51.

10. Wilson, op. cit., p. 90.

11. Robert Freedman (ed.), *Marx on Economics*. London: Penguin Books, 1962, p. 9.

12. Adolf Sturmthal, *Workers Councils*. Cambridge: Harvard University Press, 1964, p. 40.

13. Ibid., p. 43.

14. P. J. D. Drenth, "The Works' Councils in the Netherlands." In P. H. van Gorkum et al., *Industrial Democracy in the Netherlands*. Meppel: J. A. Boom en Zoom, 1969, p. 39.

15. Sturmthal, op. cit., p. 68.

16. W. Schwartz, "Cogestion et Participation dans la République Fédérale d'Allemagne." In Paul Frize et al., *La Participation dans L'Entreprise*. Paris: Centre National d'Information pour la Productivité des Entreprises, 1969, p. 100.

17. Sturmthal, op. cit., p. 125.

18. Ibid., p. 138.

19. Z. Rybicki, "Workers' Participation in Management in Poland." *International Institute for Labour Studies Bulletin*, November 1968.

20. *Le Monde*, January 31, 1971.

21. *New Statesman*, February 5, 1971.

22. F. J. Stendenbach, "Industrial Democracy—A Contemporary Need."

Paper presented at Participation and Manpower Policy seminar sponsored by OECD, Paris, September 10–12, 1969.

CHAPTER VI

1. Melford E. Spiro, *Kibbutz: Venture in Utopia*. New York: Schocken Books, 1963, pp. 11–13.
2. Moshe Kerem, *The Kibbutz*. Jerusalem: Israel Digest, 1965, p. 5.
3. Spiro, op. cit., p. 84.
4. Bjørg Aase Sørensen, *Når Arbeiderne Styrer Bedriften*. Oslo: Pax Forlag, 1970, p. 47.
5. Ibid., p. 54.
6. Joseph E. Shatil, "Criteria for Socio-Economic Efficiency of the Kibbutz." Proceedings of the Second World Congress for Rural Sociology, Enschede, The Netherlands, August 1968. Tel Aviv: Centre International de Recherches sur les Communautés Rurales.
7. Sørensen, op. cit., p. 48.
8. Ibid., p. 101.
9. Ibid., p. 104.
10. Ibid., p. 82.
11. Ibid., p. 83.
12. Seymour Melman, "Industrial Efficiency under Managerial vs. Cooperative Decision-Making." Report published by Hakibutz Ha'artzi Hashomer Hatzair, Tel Aviv, undated.
13. Figures supplied by Kibbutz Industries Association.
14. Sørensen, op. cit., p. 11.
15. Naphtali Golomb, "Managing without Sanctions or Rewards." *Management of Personnel Quarterly*, Summer 1968.
16. Menachem Rosner, "Principles, Types and Problems of Direct Democracy in the Kibbutz." In *The Kibbutz as a Way of Life in Modern Society*. Southfield, Michigan: College of Jewish Studies, 1970, pp. 13–15.
17. Sørensen, op. cit., p. 15.
18. Ibid., p. 134.
19. Bruno Bettelheim, *The Children of the Dream*. New York: Avon Books, 1970, p. 306.
20. Naphtali Golomb and Daniel Katz, *The Kibbutzim as Open Social Systems*. Tel Aviv: Ruppin Institute, undated, p. 59.
21. Bettelheim, op. cit., p. 318.
22. Sørensen, op. cit., p. 138.
23. Joseph Klatzmann, *Les Enseignements de L'Experience Israélienne*. Paris: Presses Universitaires de France, 1963, p. 9.
24. Yehuda Yudin, "Workers' Participation in Management in Israel." Paper presented at Participation and Manpower Policy seminar sponsored by OECD, September 10–12, 1969, Paris.
25. J. Y. Tabb, "Workers' Participation in Management in Israel." *International Institute for Labour Studies Bulletin*, June 1970.
26. Ibid.

27. John R. P. French, Jr., and Naphtali Golomb, "A Report to the American Council for the Behavioral Sciences." Ann Arbor, Mich.: The Institute for Social Research, 1968.

CHAPTER VII

1. Dušan Bilandžić, *Some Aspects of the Yugoslav System of Self-Management and Worker Management*. Belgrade: Medunarodna Politika, 1968, p. 11.

2. Ibid., p. 14.

3. Ibid., p. 18.

4. Josip Broz Tito, "The Speech of the President." Delivered at the Sixth Congress of the Confederation of Trade Unions of Yugoslavia, Belgrade, 1968. Belgrade: CTUY, 1968, p. 95.

5. Najdan Pašić, *Dictatorship by the Proletariat or over the Proletariat*. Belgrade: Stipe Dužević, 1968, p. 8.

6. Bilandžić, op. cit., p. 30.

7. Josip Broz Tito, "Report." Paper delivered at the Ninth Congress of the League of Communists of Yugoslavia, 1969. Belgrade: Aktuelna Pitanja Socijalizma, 1969, p. 76.

8. Albert Meister, *Où Va L'Autogestion Yougoslave?* Paris: Éditions Anthropos, 1970, p. 65.

9. Economic and Development Review Committee, OECD, *Yugoslavia*. Paris: OECD, 1970, p. 19–21.

10. Ibid., p. 21.

11. Josip Broz Tito, "Power Must Remain in the Hands of the Working Class." In *Reorganization of the LCY*. Belgrade: Aktuelna Pitanja Socijalizma, 1967, p. 23.

12. Ibid., p. 60.

13. Ibid., p. 73.

14. Ibid., p. 35.

15. Ibid., p. 39.

16. Ibid., p. 75.

17. Ibid., p. 96.

18. Tito (1969), op. cit., p. 39.

19. Peter Neersø, *Den Jugoslaviske Arbejderselvforvaltning*. Copenhagen: Arbejdsministeriets Udvalg Vedrørende Forholdene på Arbejdspladserne m.v., 1969, p. 23.

20. Bilandžić, op. cit., p. 41.

21. Ibid., p. 53.

22. Meister, op. cit., p. 66.

23. Economic and Development Review Committee, OECD, op. cit., p. 18.

24. Adolf Sturmthal, *Workers Councils*. Cambridge, Mass.: Harvard University Press, 1964, p. 18.

25. Jiri Kolaja, *Workers' Councils: The Yugoslav Experience*. London: Tavistock Publications, 1965, p. 60.

26. Josip Županov and Arnold S. Tannenbaum, "The Distribution of Control in Some Yugoslav Industrial Organizations." In Tannenbaum (ed.), *Control in Organizations.* New York: McGraw-Hill, 1968, p. 109.

27. Miša D. Jezernik, "Changes in the Hierarchy of Motivational Factors and Social Values in Slovenian Industry." *Journal of Social Issues*, April 1968.

28. Gilbert Burck, "A Socialist Enterprise that Acts Like a Fierce Capitalist Competitor." *Fortune*, January 1972.

29. Ichak Adizes, *Industrial Democracy: Yugoslav Style.* New York: The Free Press, 1971, p. 246–47.

30. Ibid., p. 250.

31. Jakov Sirotković, "The Influence of Self-Management on the Development of Yugoslav Economics." *Ekonomist* (English issue), 1969.

32. Stane Mozina, Janez Jerovsek, Arnold S. Tannenbaum, and Rensis Likert, "Testing a Management Style." *European Business*, Autumn, 1970.

33. Mitja Kamušič, "Economic Efficiency and Workers' Self-Management." In M. J. Broekmeyer (ed.), *Yugoslav Workers' Self-Management.* Dordrecht, Holland: D. Reidel Publishing Company, 1970, pp. 112–13.

34. Carole Pateman, *Participation and Democratic Theory.* London: Cambridge University Press, 1970, p. 97.

35. Chris Cviic, "Another Way," *The Economist*, August 21, 1971.

36. Nebojša Popov, "Strajkovi u Savremenon Jugoslovenskom Društvu." *Sociologija*, No. 4, 1969.

37. Adizes, op. cit., p. 221.

38. Economic and Development Review Committee, OECD, op. cit., p. 53.

39. Kolaja, op. cit., p. 76.

40. Meister, op. cit., p. 365.

41. Adizes, op. cit., p. 222.

42. Jan Tinbergen, "Does Self-Management Approach the Optimum Order?" In M. J. Broekmeyer (ed.), *Yugoslav Workers' Self-Management.* Dordrecht, Holland: D. Reidel Publishing Company, 1970, pp. 119–20.

43. Kamušič, op. cit., p. 113.

44. Tito (1968), op. cit., p. 36.

CHAPTER VIII

1. Bent Akjær *Medbestemmelseretten i Den Tyske Forbundsrepublik.* Copenhagen: Arbejdsministeriets Udvalg Vedrørende Forholdene på Arbejdspladserne m.v., 1969, p. 12.

2. Ibid., p. 13.

3. DGB, *Cogestion: Une Revendication de Notre Temps.* Düsseldorf: Deutscher Gewerkschaftsbund, 1966, pp. 30–31.

4. Ernst-Gerhard Erdmann, "Der Mythos von der Mitbestimmung." *Der Arbeitgeber,* July 20, 1966.

5. Figures supplied by DGB.

6. Friederich Fürstenberg, "Workers' Participation in the Federal Republic of Germany." *International Institute for Labour Studies Bulletin*, June 1969.

7. Kurt Hans Biedenkopf et al., *Mitbestimmung im Unternehmen* (Parliamentary Report). Bonn: Bonner Universitäts-Buchdruckerei, 1970, p. 35.

8. Philip Lynch, "*Mitbestimmung*: Socializing the Losses?" *Dun's Review*, July 1969.

9. Bundesvereinigung der Deutschen Arbeitgeberverbände, "This Kind of Co-Determination." Cologne: Bundesvereinigung der Deutschen Arbeitgeberverbände, undated.

10. SAF, *Direct and Total Wage Costs for Workers, International Surveys*. Stockholm: Svenska Arbetsgivareföreningen, 1964–71.

11. Heiner Radzio (ed.), *Warum Mitbestimmung—und Wie?* Düsseldorf: Econ Verlag, 1970, pp. 49–51.

12. Eric Jacobs, "Going Capitalist with the Law on Their Side." *Sunday Times*, April 30, 1972.

13. Fürstenberg, ibid.

CHAPTER IX

1. Chronologies of the events are contained in special issues of *Connaissance de L'Histoire*, No. 56 bis, 1968; *Syndicalisme*, No. 1191, June 10, 1968; *Le Peuple*, Nos. 799, 800, 801 (combined issue), May 15–June 30, 1968.

2. Alain Touraine, *Le Mouvement de Mai ou le Communisme Utopique*. Paris: Éditions du Seuil, 1968, p. 290.

3. Alfred Willener, *L'Image-Action de la Société*. Paris: Éditions du Seuil, 1970, p. 41.

4. Ibid., p. 183.

5. Touraine, op. cit., p. 203.

6. Michel Crozier, *Le Phénomène Bureaucratique*. Paris: Éditions du Seuil, 1963, p. 356.

7. Ibid., p. 319.

8. Ibid., p. 319.

9. Club Jean Moulin, *Que Faire de la Révolution de Mai?* Paris: Éditions du Seuil, 1968, p. 39.

10. Lucien Rioux, "Un Colosse Écartelé." *Le Nouvel Observateur*, April 27, 1970.

11. Roger Priouret, *La France et le Management*. Paris: Denoël, 1968, p. 18.

12. Rioux, op. cit.

13. Henri Krasucki, *Syndicats et Lutte de Classes*. Paris: Éditions Sociales, 1969, pp. 106–7.

14. Crozier, op. cit., p. 319.

15. Ibid., p. 375.

16. Ibid., p. 387.

17. Serge Mallet, *La Nouvelle Classe Ouvrière*. Paris: Éditions du Seuil, 1969, p. 94.

18. André Gorz, *Réforme et Révolution*. Paris: Éditions du Seuil, 1969, p. 98.

19. Ibid., pp. 106–7.

20. Ibid., p. 115.

21. Ibid., p. 116.

22. François Bloch-Lainé, *Pour une Réforme de l'Entreprise*. Paris: Éditions du Seuil, 1963, p. 184.

23. Ibid., p. 30.

24. Gorz, op. cit., p. 61.

25. Bloch-Lainé, op. cit., p. 29.

26. Touraine, op. cit., pp. 10–11.

27. Willener, op. cit., p. 31.

28. Touraine, op. cit., p. 177.

29. Ibid., p. 54.

30. Ibid., p. 30.

31. Josette Blancherie et al., *Cent Entreprises*. Paris: Centre National d'Information pour la Productivité des Entreprises, 1968, p. 13.

32. Ibid., p. 25.

33. Ibid., pp. 34–35.

34. Ibid., p. 28.

35. *Le Monde*, June 28, 1968.

36. *Formation*, March–April 1969.

37. Blancherie et al., op. cit., p. 41.

38. Ibid., p. 72.

39. *Le Monde*, June 26, 1968.

40. Alain Peyrefitte (ed.), *Qu'est-ce Que la Participation?* Paris: Plon, 1969, p. 122.

41. Ibid., p. 118.

42. Ibid., p. 145.

43. Ibid., p. 148.

44. Ibid., p. 149.

45. Ibid., pp. 217–18.

46. Krasucki, op. cit., p. 31.

47. *Le Monde*, January 28, 1971.

48. *Le Monde*, July 1, 1968.

49. *Le Monde*, January 2, 1969.

50. *Le Monde*, May 18–19, 1969.

51. *Entreprise*, April 25, 1970.

52. Peyrefitte, op. cit., p. 126.

53. *Syndicalisme*, March 26, 1970.

54. Edmond Maire, *Pour un Socialisme Démocratique*. Paris: E.P.I., 1971, pp. 56–58.

55. Marcel Loichot, *La Mutation ou L'aurore du Pancapitalisme*. Paris: Tchou, 1970, pp. 70, 72.

56. *Dirigeant*, May 1969.

57. Jean-Jacques Servan-Schreiber, *Ciel et Terre*. Paris: Denoël, 1970, p. 115.

58. Marcel Demonque et J. Y. Eichenberger, *La Participation*. Paris: Éditions France-Empire, 1968.

59. Daniel Chauvey, *Autogestion*. Paris: Éditions du Seuil, 1970, p. 74.

60. Ibid., p. 107.

61. *Syndicalisme,* June 10, 1968.

62. *Le Figaro,* March 30, 1971.

CHAPTER X

1. Chris Argyris, *Personality and Organization.* New York: Harper & Row, 1957.

2. Abraham Maslow, *Motivation and Personality.* New York: Harper & Row, 1970, p. xv.

3. Ibid., p. 37.

4. Ibid., p. 46.

5. Ibid., p. 49.

6. Ibid., p. xiii.

7. Ibid., p. 7.

8. Daniel Katz and Robert L. Kahn, *The Social Psychology of Organizations.* New York: John Wiley & Sons, 1966, p. 80.

9. Douglas McGregor, *The Human Side of Enterprise.* New York: McGraw-Hill, 1960, pp. 33–34.

10. Ibid., p. 40.

11. Ibid., pp. 47–48.

12. Ibid., p. 61.

13. Ibid., p. 67.

14. Ibid., p. 139.

15. Robert Townsend, *Up the Organization.* Greenwich: Fawcett, 1970, p. 123.

16. Ibid., p. 122.

17. Ibid., p. 27.

18. McGregor, op. cit., p. 75.

19. Harold M. F. Rush, *Behavioral Science—Concepts and Management Application.* New York: National Industrial Conference Board, 1970, p. 8.

20. Chris Argyris, *Integrating the Individual and the Organization.* New York: John Wiley & Sons, 1964, p. 58.

21. Ibid., p. 115.

22. Ibid., p. 201.

23. Edgar H. Schein, *Organizational Psychology.* Englewood Cliffs, N.J.: Prentice-Hall, 1965, p. 80.

24. Raymond E. Miles, "Human Relations or Human Resources?" *Harvard Business Review,* July–August 1965.

25. Frederick Herzberg, Bernard Mausner, and Barbara Bloch Snyderman, *The Motivation to Work.* New York: John Wiley & Sons, 1959, p. 132.

26. Victor Vroom, *Work and Motivation.* New York: John Wiley & Sons, 1964, pp. 127–29.

27. Edward E. Lawler III, *Pay and Organizational Effectiveness: A Psychological View.* New York: McGraw-Hill, 1971, pp. 32–33, 38–42.

28. Herzberg et al., op. cit., p. 136.

29. Per Sørensen, "Lighedspunkter og Forskelle." *Ledelse og Udvikling*, June 1971.

30. Frederick Herzberg, *Work and the Nature of Man*. London: Staples Press, 1968, p. 178.

31. Robert Ford, "The Obstinate Employee." *Public Opinion Quarterly*, Fall 1969.

32. *Sunday Times*, January 31, 1971.

33. Rensis Likert, *New Patterns of Management*. New York: McGraw-Hill, 1961, p. 103.

34. Ibid., p. 110.

35. Ibid., p. 38.

36. Ibid., p. 100.

37. Ibid., pp. 39–43.

38. Ibid., p. 27.

39. Ibid., p. 182.

40. Rensis Likert, *The Human Organization*. New York: McGraw-Hill, 1967, pp. 13–29.

41. Ibid., p. 46.

42. Ibid., p. 182.

43. Ibid., p. 108.

44. Ibid., p. 51.

45. Ibid., p. 123.

46. Dennis F. Thompson, *The Democratic Citizen*. London: Cambridge University Press, 1970, p. 13.

CHAPTER XI

1. Eliot Jaques, *The Changing Culture of a Factory*. London: Routledge & Kegan Paul, 1951, p. 36.

2. Ibid., p. 105.

3. Ibid., p. 263.

4. Ibid., p. 316.

5. Ibid., p. 263.

6. F. E. Emery and E. L. Trist, "Socio-Technical Systems." In F. E. Emery (ed.), *Systems Thinking*. London: Penguin Books, 1969, p. 286.

7. E. L. Trist, G. W. Higgin, H. Murray, and A. B. Pollock, *Organizational Choice*. London: Tavistock Publications, 1963, p. xi.

8. Ibid., p. xiii.

9. Ibid., p. 294.

10. Daniel Katz and Robert Kahn, *The Social Psychology of Organizations*. New York: John Wiley & Sons, 1966, p. 442.

11. Stephen Aris, "Happy Workmen Go Well for Shell." *Sunday Times*, December 5, 1971.

12. William B. Paul, Jr., Keith B. Robertson, and Frederick Herzberg, "Job Enrichment Pays Off." *Harvard Business Review*, March–April 1969.

13. G. D. H. Cole, "Collectivism, Syndicalism, and Guilds." In Ken Coates and Tony Topham (eds.), *Workers' Control*. London: Panther Modern Society, 1970, p. 49.

14. Jack Jones, "A Plan for a Break-Through in Production." *Tribune*, February 11, 1966.

15. John Goldthorpe et al., *The Affluent Worker*. London: Cambridge University Press, 1968, Vol. 1, pp. 108–9.

16. Ibid., 1970, Vol. 3, p. 28.

17. Ibid., p. 193–94.

18. *The Times*, May 28, 1971.

19. *The Observer*, August 1, 1971.

20. Anthony Sampson, "The Middle-Class Monopoly," *Sunday Times*, August 22, 1971.

CHAPTER XII

1. Alfred J. Marrow, David G. Bowers, and Stanley E. Seashore, *Management by Participation*. New York: Harper & Row, 1967, p. 26.

2. Ibid., p. 131.

3. Ibid., p. 121.

4. Stanley E. Seashore and David G. Bowers, "Durability of Organizational Change." *American Psychologist*, March 1970.

5. M. Scott Myers, "Conditions for Manager Motivation." *Harvard Business Review*, January–February 1966.

6. M. Scott Myers, "Every Employee a Manager." *California Management Review*, Spring 1968.

7. M. Scott Myers, "Increasing Employee Motivation." In Harold M. F. Rush (ed.), *Managing Change*. New York: The National Industrial Conference Board, 1970.

8. M. Scott Myers (1966), op. cit.

9. M. Scott Myers and Earl R. Gomersall, "Breakthrough in On-the-Job Training." *Harvard Business Review*, July–August 1966.

10. M. Scott Myers (1968), op. cit.

11. M. Scott Myers (1970), op. cit.

12. Michael Beer and Edgar Huse, "Improving Organizational Effectiveness Through Planned Change and Development." Unpublished report, undated.

13. Agis Salpukas, "Workers Increasingly Rebel Against Boredom on Assembly Line." *New York Times*, April 2, 1972.

14. D. L. Landen and H. C. Carlson, "Rough Draft of Chapter of a New Book Being Edited by Alfred J. Marrow." To be published by the American Management Association.

15. *GM Personnel Development Bulletin*, February 23, 1972.

16. Agis Salpukas, "Auto Workers Are Given a Voice on Assembly Line." *New York Times*, June 19, 1972.

17. Harold M. F. Rush, *Job Design for Motivation*. New York: The Conference Board, 1971, p. 76.

18. Harold M. F. Rush, *Behavioral Science—Concepts and Managerial Applications*. New York: National Industrial Conference Board, 1970, p. 87.

19. Ibid., p. 90.

20. Ibid., p. 95.

21. Harold M. F. Rush (1971), op. cit., p. 34.

22. Ibid., p. 35.

23. Ibid., p. 37.

24. "A Happy Factory that Pays Off," *The Executive Voice* (tape cassette subscription service), May 1972.

25. James F. Lincoln, *Incentive Management*. Cleveland: The Lincoln Electric Company, 1951, p. 55.

26. Ibid., p. 62.

27. Ibid., pp. 58–60.

28. Ibid., p. 220.

29. Mitchell Fein, *Motivation for Work*. New York: American Institute of Industrial Engineers, 1971, p. 56.

30. *Fortune*, June 1972.

31. James F. Lincoln, op. cit., p. 12.

32. Charles P. McCormick, *The Power of People*. New York: Harper & Brothers, 1949, p. 6.

33. Ibid., p. 87.

34. Ibid., p. 9.

35. Frederick G. Lesieur, *The Scanlon Plan*. Cambridge, Mass.: M.I.T. Press, 1958, p. 39.

36. Ibid., p. 90.

37. Frederick G. Lesieur and Elbridge S. Puckett, "The Scanlon Plan Has Proved Itself." *Harvard Business Review*, September–October 1969.

38. Bill Paul, "Overnite Success." *Wall Street Journal*, February 22, 1972.

39. Lyman D. Ketchum, paper presented at Humanizing of Work symposium at the American Association for the Advancement of Science annual meeting, Philadelphia, Pa., December 27, 1971.

40. Ibid.

41. Daniel Katz and Robert L. Kahn, *The Social Psychology of Organizations*. New York: John Wiley & Sons, 1966, p. 463.

42. Rensis Likert, "The Relationship Between Management Behavior and Social Structure." Talk given at CIOS conference, Tokyo, 1969.

43. Rensis Likert, *New Patterns of Management*. New York: McGraw-Hill, 1961, pp. 61–74.

44. Rensis Likert, *The Human Organization*. New York: McGraw-Hill, 1967, p. 114.

45. Nancy Belliveau, "Is the Financial Man a Leadership Cripple?" *Corporate Financing*, January–February 1971.

46. Robert Freedman (ed.), *Marx on Economics*. London: Penguin Books, 1962, p. 74.

47. Benjamin Graham and David L. Dodd, *Security Analysis* (Third Edition). New York: McGraw-Hill, 1951, pp. 479–80.

48. Bernard Baruch, *My Own Story*. New York: Holt, 1957, p. 256.

49. R. Lee Brummet, Eric G. Flamholtz, and William C. Pyle, "Human

Resources Measurement: A Challenge for Accountants." *The Accounting Review*, April 1968.

50. William C. Pyle, "Monitoring Human Resources—'On Line.' " *Michigan Business Review*, July 1970.

51. Edward Stan, "Human Resources Accounting and Financial Management." In R. Lee Brummet et al., *Human Resource Accounting*. Ann Arbor, Mich.: Foundation on Human Behavior, 1968.

52. Richard E. Walton, "Alienation and Innovation in the Work Place." Paper prepared for the Work in America Project, sponsored by the Secretary of the Department of Health, Education and Welfare, 1972.

,3. Will McWhinney with James Elden, "Not Industrial Democracy, but a Reticular Society." Paper presented at the Center for Study of Democratic Institutions, Santa Barbara, California, October 1971.

54. Louis Davis, "The Coming Crisis for Production Management: Technology and Organization." *International Journal of Production Research*. No. 1, 1971.

55. George A. Miller, "Psychology as a Means of Promoting Human Welfare." Presidential address delivered at a meeting of the American Psychological Association, Washington, D.C., September 1969.

CHAPTER XIII

1. Einar Thorsrud and Fred Emery, *Industrielt Demokrati*. Oslo: Universitetsforlaget, 1964, p. 17.

2. Harriet Holter, "Øket Medvirkning—De Ansattes Ønsker og Muligheter." *Tidskrift for Samfunnsforskning*, No. 1, 1964.

3. Thorsrud and Emery, op. cit., p. 115.

4. Einar Thorsrud and Fred Emery, *Mot en Ny Bedriftsorganisasjon*. Oslo: Tanum, 1969, p. 116.

5. Ibid., p. 131.

6. *Veckans Affärer*, February 6, 1969.

7. Ulrik Qvale, "The Industrial Democracy Project in Norway." Paper presented at International Industrial Relations Association Second World Congress, Geneva, September 1–4, 1970.

8. Thorsrud and Emery (1969), op. cit., p. 137.

9. Ibid., p. 161.

10. Ibid., p. 166.

11. *Veckans Affärer*, February 20, 1969.

12. Ernst Wigforss, *Materialistisk Historieuppfattning—Industriell Demokrati*. Stockholm: Tidens Förlag, 1970, p. 115.

13. Ibid., p. 120.

14. Ibid., p. 148.

15. Ibid., p. 149.

16. Ernst Wigforss, *Ur Mina Minnen*. Stockholm: Bokförlaget Prisma, 1964, p. 234.

17. LO, *Fackföreningsrörelsen och Företagsdemokrati*. Stockholm: Landsorganisationen i Sverige, 1961.

344 NOTES

18. **T. L.** Johnston, *Collective Bargaining in Sweden.* London: George Allen & Unwin, 1962, p. 216.

19. Eric Rhenman, *Företagsdemokrati och Företagsorganisation.* Stockholm: Pan/Norstedts, 1967, p. 155.

20. *Veckans Affärer,* October 9, 1969.

21. *Industriförbundets Tidskrift,* No. 7, 1969.

22. *Dagens Nyheter,* November 10, 1971.

23. Inge Janérus et al., *Inflytande i Förtagen.* Stockholm: Tidens Förlag, 1971, p. 22.

24. Erik Bolinder and Bo Ohlström, *Stress på Svenska Arbetsplatser.* Stockholm: Prisma, 1971.

25. LO, *Demokrati i Företagen.* Stockholm: Prisma, 1971.

26. Modig, Karl-Erik et al., *Demokratisering av Arbetslivet.* Stockholm: Tjänstemännens Centralorganisation, 1970.

27. Lena Svanberg, "Hur Ge Mening åt Jobbet vid Maskinen?" *Industria,* April 1971.

28. Christina Hultgren, "En Fräsare till Företagsdemokrat." *Vår Industri,* No. 4, 1971.

29. *Arbetsgivaren,* March 3, 1972.

30. *Svenska Dagbladet,* March 22, 1971.

31. Lena Svanberg, "Ingen Väg Tillbaka." *Industria,* March 1971.

32. Mats Hallgren, "Gruppjobb Ersätter Löpande Bandet." *Dagens Nyheter,* September 12, 1972.

33. *Veckans Affärer,* October 29, 1970.

34. *Svenska Dagbladet,* January 10, 1971.

35. *Svenska Dagbladet,* September 4, 1971.

36. *Svenska Dagbladet,* June 20, 1972.

37. *Veckans Affärer,* May 6, 1971.

38. *Berlingske Tidende,* April 9, 1972.

39. *Svenska Dagbladet,* March 26, 1971.

40. *Svenska Dagbladet,* January 29, 1972.

41. Edmund Dahlström, *Fördjupad Företagsdemokrati.* Stockholm: Prisma, 1969, p. 28.

42. *Veckans Affärer,* May 6, 1970.

43. *Veckans Affärer,* May 13, 1971.

44. *Veckans Affärer,* June 11, 1970.

45. Lennart Lennerlöf, "Personaladministrationen i Framtidens Företag." Talk given at conference organized by the Development Council, April 23, 1970.

46. *Berlingske Tidende,* January 31, 1971.

47. *Arbeidsgiveren,* April 22, 1971.

48. *Politiken,* January 2, 1969.

49. Torben Agersnap et al., *Samarbejde på Arbejdspladsen.* Copenhagen: Arbejdsministeriets Udvalg Vedrørende Forholdene på Arbejdspladserne m.v., 1971.

50. *Politiken,* April 28, 1972.

51. *Politiken,* May 4, 1971.

52. *Børsen*, November 10, 1969.
53. *Berlingske Aftenavis Weekend*, May 10, 1969.
54. *Politiken*, September 23, 1971.
55. *Politiken*, August 24, 1972.
56. *Børsen*, October 27, 1972.
57. *Berlingske Tidende*, November 12, 1972.
58. Anker Jørgensen, speech given at the DASF Congress, September 9, 1971, Copenhagen.
59. DASF, *Motivation og Selvstyrende Grupper*. Copenhagen: Dansk Arbejdsmands- og Specialarbejder Forbund, 1971, p. 26.
60. E. F. Eckhoff, *Innstilling om Demokrati i Bedriftslivet* (parliamentary report). Oslo: Engers Boktrykkeri, 1971.
61. *Norges Industri*, No. 10, 1971.
62. *Arbetsgivaren*, No. 21, 1972.
63. SAF, *Om Samarbetet i Företagen*. Stockholm: Svenska Arbetsgivareföreningen, 1971, p. 6.
64. *Arbeidsgiveren*, April 13, 1972.
65. Georges Gurvitch, *Les Cadres Sociaux de la Connaissance*. Paris: Presses Universitaires de France, 1966, p. 230.
66. *Le Monde*, July 19, 1972.

CHAPTER XIV

1. *Le Monde*, January 2, 1969.
2. Josip Broz Tito, "Report." Paper delivered at Ninth Congress of the League of Communists of Yugoslavia, 1969. Belgrade: Aktuelna Pitanja Socijalizma, 1969, p. 95.
3. Douglas McGregor, *The Human Side of Enterprise*. New York: McGraw-Hill, 1960.
4. Lars Erik Karlsson, *Demokrati på Arbetsplatsen*. Stockholm: Prisma, 1969, p. 98.
5. H. Darin-Drabkin, "The Nature of Direct Democracy in the Kibbutz and Its Implications for Other Social Conditions." Tel Aviv: International Research Center on Rural Cooperative Communities. Mimeographed. Undated.
6. Louis Davis, "Enhancing the Quality of Working Life." Program statement for research project. Center for Organizational Studies, Graduate School of Management, UCLA, 1972.
7. *The Listener*, December 24, 1970.
8. Paul Blumberg, *Industrial Democracy: The Sociology of Participation*. London: Constable, 1968, p. 123.
9. Josip Broz Tito, "Power Must Remain in the Hands of the Working Class." In *Reorganization of the LCY*. Belgrade: Aktuelna Pitanja Socijalizma 1969, p. 100.
10. Sylvain Segal, *Les Idées de Mai*. Paris: Gallimard, 1968, p. 44.
11. Robert Freedman (ed.), *Marx on Economics*. London: Penguin Books, 1962, pp. 234-35.

12. *Wall Street Journal*, April 26, 1972.

13. *China Reconstructs*, June 1971.

14. *Newsweek*, February 21, 1972.

15. Alfred J. Marrow, David G. Bowers, and Stanley E. Seashore, *Management by Participation*. New York: Harper & Row, 1967, p. 70.

16. M. Scott Myers, *Every Employee a Manager*. New York: McGraw-Hill, 1970, p. 129.

17. Paul Goodman, *People or Personnel and Like a Conquered Province*. New York: Vintage Books, 1968, pp. 4–5.

18. Anthony Lewis, "Down in the Village," *International Herald Tribune*, December 25, 1971.

19. McGregor, op. cit., pp. 129–30.

20. Chris Argyris, *Integrating the Individual and the Organization*. New York: John Wiley & Sons, 1964, p. 29.

21. Bertil Gardell, "Produktionsteknik och Människovärde." *Fackföreningsrörelsen*, November 19, 1970.

22. Christina Hultgren, "En Fräsare till Företagsdemokrat." *Vår Industri*, No. 4, 1971.

23. Warren G. Bennis and Philip E. Slater, *The Temporary Society*. New York: Harper & Row, 1968, p. 7.

24. Ibid., p. 12.

25. Ibid., p. 74.

26. Donald Schon, "Change and Industrial Society." *The Listener*, November 19, 26, December 3, 10, 17, 24, 1970.

27. Michael Beer, "A Systems Approach to Organizational Development." Paper presented at American Psychological Association Convention, September 3, 1969.

28. Judson Gooding, "It Pays to Wake up the Blue-Collar Worker." *Fortune*, September 1970.

29. Arthur Kornhauser, *Mental Health of the Industrial Worker*. New York: John Wiley & Sons, 1965, p. 252.

30. Ibid., p. 97.

31. Myers (1970), op. cit., p. 170.

32. Edward E. Lawler III, *Pay and Psychological Effectiveness*. New York: McGraw-Hill, 1971, p. 23.

33. Ibid., p. 157.

34. Ibid., pp. 276–77.

35. Karlsson, op. cit., p. 191.

36. Ken Coates and Tony Topham (eds.), *Workers' Control*. London: Panther Modern Society, 1970, p. 406.

37. John Kenneth Galbraith, *The New Industrial State* (Revised Edition). Boston: Houghton Mifflin, 1971, pp. 77–80.

38. *Wall Street Journal*, May 26, 1972.

39. Galbraith, op. cit., p. 71.

40. *Wall Street Journal*, April 17, 1972.

41. Peter Drucker, "What We Can Learn from Japanese Management." *Harvard Business Review*, March–April 1971.

42. *Politiken*, October 29, 1972.

CHAPTER XV

1. *Fortune*, July 1971.
2. John Kenneth Galbraith, *The New Industrial State* (Revised Edition.) Boston: Houghton Mifflin, 1971, p. 137.
3. Michael Harrington, *The Other America*. London: Penguin Books, 1963, p. 6.
4. Alexander Heron, *Why Men Work*. Palo Alto: Stanford University Press, 1948, p. 78.
5. Russel W. Davenport, "Enterprise for Everyman." *Fortune*, January 1950.
6. Judson Gooding, "It Pays to Wake Up the Blue-Collar Worker." *Fortune*, September 1970.
7. Milton Derber, "Crosscurrents in Worker Participation." *Industrial Relations*, February 1970.
8. Abraham Maslow, *Motivation and Personality*. New York: Harper & Row, 1970, p. 149.
9. Daniel Bell, *Work and Its Discontents*. New York: League for Industrial Democracy, 1970, p. 23.
10. Ibid., p. 44.
11. Thomas A. Jeswold, "Job Enrichment for Employee Motivation." Paper presented at a meeting of the National Association of Accountants, Indianapolis, Indiana, April 1972.
12. Michael Beer, "A Systems Approach to Organizational Development." Paper presented at American Psychological Association Convention, September 3, 1969.
13. Robert Coles, "On the Meaning of Work." *The Atlantic*, October 1971.
14. Alex Bavelas and George Strauss, "Group Dynamics and Intergroup Relations." In Gerald D. Bell (ed.), *Organizations and Human Behavior*. Englewood Cliffs, N.J.: Prentice-Hall, 1967, p. 151.
15. Raymond E. Miles, "Human Relations or Human Resources?" *Harvard Business Review*, July–August 1965.
16. Mason Haire, Edwin E. Ghiselli, and Lyman W. Porter, *Managerial Thinking: An International Study*. New York: John Wiley & Sons, 1966, p.21.
17. Rensis Likert, *The Human Organization*. New York: McGraw-Hill, 1967, p. 110.
18. J. A. C. Brown, *The Social Psychology of Industry*. London: Penguin Books, 1954, p. 239.
19. James E. Richard, "A President's Experience with Democratic Management." The A. G. Bush Library of Management, University of Chicago, Occasional Paper No. 18, 1959.
20. Kenneth F. Walker, "Workers' Participation in Management." Paper delivered at Second World Congress of International Industrial Relations Association, Geneva, September 1–4, 1970.
21. Arnold S. Tannenbaum, "Individual Adjustment and Organizational

Performance." In Arnold S. Tannenbaum (ed.), *Control in Organizations*. New York: McGraw-Hill, 1968, p. 311.

22. Francis Bello, "The Magic That Made Polaroid," *Fortune*, April 1959.

23. John Crispo, "Worker and Union Participation in Decision-Making." *Proceedings*, Industrial Relations Research Association, winter meeting, New York City, December 29–30, 1969.

24. Norman Pearlstine, "UAW: 'Causes' vs. Bread and Butter." *Wall Street Journal*, April 25, 1972.

25. A. H. Raskin, "The Labor Movement Must Start Moving." *Harvard Business Review*, January–February 1970.

26. AFL-CIO, *Labor Looks at Automation*. Washington, D.C.: American Federation of Labor and Congress of Industrial Organizations, 1969, pp. 34–35.

27. Arne Derefeldt, "Personaladministration i USA," mimeographed report. Malmö, Sweden: Personaladministrativa Rådet, 1970.

28. Charlton R. Price, *New Directions in the World of Work—A Conference Report*. Washington, D.C.: The W. E. Upjohn Institute for Employment Research, 1971, p. 9.

29. Irving Bluestone, "The Next Step Toward Industrial Democracy." Speech at The Conference Board Meeting, New York City, January 21, 1972.

30. Jerome M. Rosow, "The Problems of the Blue-Collar Worker." Memorandum prepared for the Secretary of Labor, Washington, D.C., April 1970.

31. *Wall Street Journal*, April 17, 1972.

32. Charles H. Percy, "How Good Is the News about Productivity?" *Fortune*, May 1972.

33. Neal Q. Herrick, "Institutional Attitudes toward Human Fulfillment through Work." Unpublished paper, 1971.

34. S. 3916, 92nd Congress, 2nd Session, proposal for "Worker Alienation Research and Technical Assistance Act of 1972."

35. Price, op. cit., p. 35.

36. Josip Županov and Arnold S. Tannenbaum, "The Distribution of Control in Some Yugoslav Industrial Organizations." In Arnold S. Tannenbaum (ed.), *Control in Organizations*. New York: McGraw-Hill, 1968, p. 109.

37. Robert Dahl, "Citizens of the Corporation." *New York Times*, March 17, 1971.

38. Jean-François Revel, *Ni Marx Ni Jésus*. Paris: Robert Laffont, 1970, p. 9.

39. Ibid., p. 14.

40. Guy Desolre, "The Belgian Trade Union Movement and the Problem of 'Workers' Control.'" Paper presented at the Second World Congress of the International Industrial Relations Association, Geneva, September 1–4, 1970.

41. *Sunday Times*, March 7, 1971.

42. *La Tribune de Genève*, May 3, 1971.

43. C. R. Rogers, "Towards a Theory of Creativity." In P. E. Vernon (ed.), *Creativity*. London: Penguin Books, 1970, p. 149.

BIBLIOGRAPHY

Adizes, Ichak, *Industrial Democracy: Yugoslav Style*. New York: The Free Press, 1971.

AFL-CIO, *Labor Looks at Automation*. Washington, D.C.: American Federation of Labor and Congress of Industrial Organizations, 1969.

Agersnap, Torben et al., *Samarbejde på Arbejdspladsen*. Copenhagen: Arbejdsministeriets Udvalg Vedrørende Forholdene på Arbejdspladserne m.v., 1971.

Akjær, Bent, *Medbestemmelseretten i Den Tyske Forbundsrepublik*. Copenhagen: Arbejdsministeriets Ulvalg Vedrørende Forholdene på Arbejdspladserne m.v., 1969.

Argyris, Chris, *Integrating the Individual and the Organization*. New York: John Wiley & Sons, 1964.

———, *Personality and Organization*. New York: Harper & Row, 1957.

Aris, Stephen, "Happy Workers Go Well for Shell." *Sunday Times*, December 5, 1971.

Auden, W. H., "The Poet and the City." In Scully, James (ed.), *Modern Poets on Modern Poetry*. London: Collins-Fontana, 1966.

Baruch, Bernard, *My Own Story*. New York: Holt, 1957.

Bavelas, Alex, and Strauss, George, "Group Dynamics and Intergroup Relations." In Gerald D. Bell (ed.), *Organizations and Human Behavior*. Englewood Cliffs, N.J.: Prentice-Hall, 1967, p. 151.

Beer, Michael, "A Systems Approach to Organizational Development." Paper presented at American Psychological Association Convention, September 3, 1969.

Beer, Michael, and Huse, Edgar, "Improving Organizational Effectiveness Through Planned Change and development." Unpublished report, undated.

Bell, Daniel, *Work and Its Discontents*. New York: League for Industrial Democracy, 1970.

Belliveau, Nancy, "Is the Financial Man a Leadership Cripple?" *Corporate Financing*, January–February 1971.

Bendix, Reinhard, *Work and Authority in Industry*. New York: John Wiley & Sons, 1956.

Benet, Sula, "Why They Live to be 100, or Even Older, in Abkhasia." *New York Times Magazine*, December 26, 1971.

Bennis, Warren G., and Slater, Philip E., *The Temporary Society*. New York: Harper & Row, 1968.

Bettelheim, Bruno, *The Children of the Dream*. New York: Avon Books, 1970.

Biedenkopf, Kurt Hans et al., *Mitbestimmung im Unternehmen* (parliamentary report). Bonn: Bonner Universitäts-Buchdruckerei, 1970.

Bilandžić, Dušan, *Some Aspects of the Yugoslav System of Self-Government and Worker Management*. Belgrade: Medunarodna Politika, 1968.

Blancherie, Josette et al., *Cent Entreprises*. Paris, Centre National d'Information pour la Productivité des Entreprises, 1968.

Blauner, Robert, *Alienation and Freedom*. Chicago: University of Chicago Press, 1964.

Bloch-Lainé, François, *Pour une Réforme de l'Entreprise*. Paris: Éditions du Seuil, 1963.

Bluestone, Irving, "The Next Step Toward Industrial Democracy." Talk given at The Conference Board meeting, New York City, January 21, 1972.

Blumberg, Paul, *Industrial Democracy: The Sociology of Participation*. London: Constable, 1968.

Bolinder, Erik, and Ohlström, Bo, *Stress på Svenska Arbetsplatser*. Stockholm: Prisma, 1971.

Brown, J. A. C., *The Social Psychology of Industry*. London: Penguin Books, 1954.

Brummet, R. Lee, Flamholtz, Eric G., and Pyle, William C., "Human Resources Measurement: A Challenge for Accountants." *The Accounting Review*, April 1968.

Bundesvereinigung der Deutschen Arbeitgeberverbände, *This Kind of Co-Determination*. Cologne: Bundesvereinigung der Deutschen Arbeitgeberverbände, undated.

Burck, Gilbert, "A Socialist Enterprise that Acts Like a Fierce Capitalist Competitor." *Fortune*, January 1972.

Chauvey, Daniel, *Autogestion*. Paris: Éditions du Seuil, 1970.

Club Jean Moulin, *Que Faire de la Révolution de Mai?* Paris: Éditions du Seuil, 1968.

Coates, Ken, and Topham, Tony (eds.), *Workers' Control*. London: Panther Modern Society, 1970.

Cohn-Bendit, Daniel and Gabriel, *Obsolete Communism: The Left-Wing Alternative*. London: Penguin Books, 1969.

Cole, G. D. H., "Collectivism, Syndicalism, and Guilds." In Ken Coates and Tony Topham (eds.), *Workers' Control*. London: Panther Modern Society, 1970.

Coles, Robert, "On the Meaning of Work." *The Atlantic*, October 1971.

Crispo, John, "Worker and Union Participation in Decision-Making." *Proceedings*, Industrial Relations Research Association winter meeting, New York City, December 29–30, 1969.

Crozier, Michel, *Le Phénomène Bureaucratique*. Paris: Éditions du Seuil, 1963.

Cviic, Chris, "Another Way." *The Economist*, August 12, 1971.

Dahl, Robert, "Citizens of the Corporation." *New York Times*, March 17, 1971.

Dahlström, Edmund, *Fördjupad Företagsdemokrati*. Stockholm: Prisma, 1969.

Darin-Drabkin, H., "The Nature of Direct Democracy in the Kibbutz and Its Implications for Other Social Conditions." Tel Aviv: International Research Center on Rural Cooperative Communities, mimeographed report, undated.

Davenport, Russel, "Enterprise for Everyman." *Fortune*, January 1950.

DASF, *Motivation og Selvstyrende Grupper*. Copenhagen: Dansk Arbejdsmands- og Specialarbejder Forbund, 1971.

Davis, Louis, "Enhancing the Quality of Working Life." Program Statement for Research Project. Center for Organizational Studies, Graduate School of Management, UCLA, 1972.

————, "The Coming Crisis for Production Management: Technology and Organization." *International Journal of Production Research*, No. 1, 1970.

Deane, Phyllis, *The Industrial Revolution in England 1700–1914*. London: Fontana, 1969.

DeMaria, Alfred T.; Tarnowieski, Dale; and Gurman, Richard, *Manager Unions?* New York: American Management Association, 1972.

Demonque, Marcel, and Eichenberger, J. Y., *La Participation*. Paris: Éditions France-Empire, 1968.

Derber, Milton, "Crosscurrents in Worker Participation." *Industrial Relations*, February 1970.

Derefeldt, Arne, "Personaladministration i USA." Mimeographed report, 1970.

Desolre, Guy, "The Belgian Trade Union Movement and the Problem of 'Workers' Control.'" Paper presented at the Second World Congress of the International Industrial Relations Association, Geneva, September 1–4, 1970.

Deutscher Gewerkschaftsbund, *Cogestion: Une Revendication de Notre Temps*. Düsseldorf: Deutscher Gewerkschaftsbund, 1966.

Drenth, P. J. D., "The Works' Councils in the Netherlands." In P. H. van Gorkum et al., *Industrial Democracy in the Netherlands*. Meppel: J. A. Boom en Zoom, 1969.

Drucker, Peter, *Concept of the Corporation*. New York: Harper, 1946.

————, "What We Can Learn from Japanese Management." *Harvard Business Review*, March–April 1971.

Eckhoff, E. F., *Innstilling om Demokrati i Bedriftslivet* (parliamentary report). Oslo: Engers Boktrykkeri, 1971.

Economic and Development Review Committee, OECD, *Yugoslavia*. Paris: OECD, 1970.

Emery, F. E., and Trist, E. L., "Socio-Technical Systems." In F. E. Emery (ed.), *Systems Thinking*. London: Penguin Books, 1969.

Erdmann, Ernst-Gerhard, "Der Mythos von der Mitbestimmung." *Der Arbeitgeber*, July 20, 1966.

Erikson, Erik H., *Childhood and Society*. London: Penguin Books, 1965.

The Executive Voice, "A Happy Factory that Pays Off." *The Executive Voice* (tape cassette subscription service), May 1972.

Fein, Mitchell, *Motivation for Work*. New York: American Institute of Industrial Engineers, 1971.

Ford, Robert, "The Obstinate Employee." *Public Opinion Quarterly*, Fall 1969.

Fraser, Ronald (ed.), *Work*. London: Penguin Books, 1968.

Freedman, Robert (ed.), *Marx on Economics*. London: Penguin Books, 1962.

French, John R. P., Jr., and Golomb, Naphtali, "A Report to the American Council for the Behavioral Sciences." Ann Arbor, Mich.: The Institute for Social Research, 1968.

Freud, Sigmund, *Civilization and Its Discontents*. London: The Hogarth Press Ltd., 1930.

Fried, Albert, *Socialism in America: From the Shakers to the Third International*. Garden City, N.Y.: Doubleday, 1970.

Friedmann, Georges, *Le Travail en Miettes*. Paris: Gallimard, 1964.

Fromm, Erich, *Escape from Freedom*. New York: Avon Books, 1965.

————, *The Revolution of Hope*. New York: Bantam Books, 1968.

Fürstenberg, Friederich, "Workers' Participation in the Federal Republic of Germany." *International Institute for Labour Studies Bulletin*, June 1969.

Galbraith, John Kenneth, *The New Industrial State* (Revised Edition). Boston: Houghton, Mifflin, 1971.

Gardell, Bertil, "Produktionsteknik och Människovärde." *Fackföreningsrörelsen*, November 19, 1970.

————, and Dahlström, Edmund, "Teorier om Anpassning och Motivation." In Edmund Dahlström et al., *Teknisk Förändring och Arbetsanpassning*. Stockholm: Prisma, 1965.

————, and Westlander, Gunnela, *Om Industriarbete och Mental Hälsa*. Stockholm: Personaladministrativa Rådet, 1968.

Garson, Barbara, "Luddites in Lordstown." *Harper's Magazine*, June 1972.

Gerzon, Mark, *The Whole World Is Watching*. New York: Paperback Library, 1969.

Godard, Jean-Luc, "La Vie Moderne," *Le Nouvel Observateur*, October 12, 1966.

Goldthorpe, John H., et al., *The Affluent Worker*. London: Cambridge University Press, Vols. I–II, 1968; Vol. III, 1969.

Golomb, Naphtali, "Managing without Sanctions or Rewards." *Management of Personnel Quarterly*, Summer 1968.

————, and Katz, Daniel, *The Kibbutzim as Open Social Systems*. Tel Aviv: Ruppin Institute, undated.

Gooding, Judson, "It Pays to Wake up the Blue-Collar Worker." *Fortune*, September 1970.

Goodman, Paul, *People or Personnel and Like a Conquered Province.* New York: Vintage Books, 1968.

Gorz, André, *Réforme et Révolution.* Paris: Éditions du Seuil, 1969.

Graham, Benjamin, and Dodd, David L., *Security Analysis* (Third Edition). New York: McGraw-Hill, 1951.

Gurvitch, Georges, *Les Cadres Sociaux de la Connaissance.* Paris: Presses Universitaires de France, 1966.

Haire, Mason, Ghiselli, Edwin E., and Porter, Lyman L., *Managerial Thinking: An International Study.* New York: John Wiley & Sons, 1966.

Hallgren, Mats, "Gruppjobb Ersätter Löpande Bandet." *Dagens Nyheter,* September 12, 1972.

Harrington, Michael, *The Accidental Century.* London: Penguin Books, 1967.

————, *The Other America.* London: Penguin Books, 1963.

Heron, Alexander, *Why Men Work.* Palo Alto: Stanford University Press, 1948.

Herrick, Neal Q., "Institutional Attitudes toward Human Fulfillment through Work." Unpublished paper, 1971.

————, "Who's Unhappy at Work and Why." *Manpower,* January 1972.

Herzberg, Frederick, *Work and the Nature of Man.* London: Staples Press, 1968.

————, Mauser, Bernard, and Snyderman, Barbara Bloch, *The Motivation to Work.* New York: John Wiley & Sons, 1959.

Hodgkinson, Harold, *Institutions in Transition: A Study of Change in Higher Education.* Berkeley: Carnegie Commission on Higher Education, 1970. Cited in Joseph Kraft, "Elite in Trouble of Own Making." *International Herald Tribune,* July 29, 1970.

Holbrook, Stewart H., *Dreamers of the American Dream.* Garden City, N.Y.: Doubleday, 1957.

Holter, Harriet, "Øket Medvirkning—De Ansattes Ønsker og Muligheter." *Tidskrift for Samfunnsforskning,* No. 1, 1964.

Howe, Irving, "New Styles in 'Leftism.'" In Irving Howe (ed.), *Beyond the New Left.* New York: McCall, 1970.

Huizinga, Johan, *Homo Ludens.* London: Paladin, 1970.

Hultgren, Christina, "En Fräsare till Företagsdemokrat." *Vår Industri,* No. 4, 1971.

Hyatt, James C., "Productivity Push." *Wall Street Journal,* April 25, 1972.

Jacobs, Eric, "Going Capitalist with the Law on Their Side." *Sunday Times,* April 30, 1972.

Janérus, Inge et al., *Inflytande i Företagen.* Stockholm: Tidens Förlag, 1971.

Janouch, Gustav, *Gespräche mit Kafka.* Frankfurt: S. Fischer Verlag, 1951.

Jaques, Eliot, *The Changing Culture of a Factory.* London: Routledge & Kegan Paul, 1951.

Jefferson, Thomas, *Basic Writings.* Garden City, N.Y.: Halcyon House, 1950.

Jersild, P. C., "Vem Ska Man Dressera—Människan eller Maskinen?" *Dagens Nyheter*, August 5, 1970.

Jeswold, Thomas A., "Job Enrichment for Employee Motivation." Paper presented at National Association of Accountants meeting, Indianapolis, April 1972.

Jezernik, Miša D., "Changes in the Hierarchy of Motivational Factors and Social Values in Slovenian Industry." *Journal of Social Issues*, April 1968.

Johnston, T. L., *Collective Bargaining in Sweden*. London: George Allen & Unwin, 1962.

Jones, Jack, "A Plan for a Break-Through in Production." *Tribune*, February 11, 1966.

Jørgensen, Anker, speech given at DASF Congress, September 9, 1971, Copenhagen.

Kapustin, E., "Soviet Workers' Participation in Management." Paper presented at Second World Congress of International Industrial Relations Association, September 1–4, 1970, Geneva.

Kamušič, Mitja, "Economic Efficiency and Workers' Self-Management." In M. J. Broekmeyer (ed.), *Yugoslav Workers' Self-Management*. Dordrecht, Holland: D. Reidel Publishing Company, 1970.

Karlsson, Lars Erik, *Demokrati på Arbetsplatsen*. Stockholm: Prisma, 1969.

Katz, Daniel, and Kahn, Robert L., *The Social Psychology of Organizations*. New York: John Wiley & Sons, 1966.

Kerem, Moshe, *The Kibbutz*. Jerusalem: Israel Digest, 1965.

Ketchum, Lyman D., paper presented at Humanizing of Work symposium at the American Association for the Advancement of Science annual meeting, Philadelphia, Pa., December 27, 1971.

Klatzmann, Joseph, *Les Enseignements de l'Experience Israélienne*. Presses Universitaires de France, 1963.

Kley, Gilbert, *Replies to the DGB's Demands*. Cologne: Bundsvereinigung der Deutsche Arbeitgeberverbände, 1969.

Kolaja, Kiri, *Workers' Councils: The Yugoslav Experience*. London: Tavistock Publications, 1965.

Kornhauser, Arthur, *Mental Health of the Industrial Worker*. New York: John Wiley & Sons, 1965.

Krasucki, Henri, *Syndicates et Lutte de Classes*. Paris: Editions Sociales, 1969.

Laing, R. D., *The Divided Self*. London: Penguin Books, 1965.

Landen, D. L., and Carlson, H. C., "Rough draft of chapter of a new book being edited by Alfred J. Marrow." To be published by the American Management Association.

Lappalainen, Armas, "Marxism under 60-Talet." *Dagens Nyheter*, July 28, 1970.

Lawler, Edward E., III, *Pay and Organizational Effectiveness*. New York: McGraw-Hill, 1971.

———, and Hackman, J. Richard, "Corporate Profits and Employee Satisfaction: Must They Be in Conflict?" *California Management Review*, Fall 1971.

Lenin, V. I., "The Immediate Tasks of the Soviet Government." *Pravda*, No. 83, April 28, 1918. Reported in Lenin, *Questions of the Socialist Organization of the Economy*. Moscow: Progress Publishers, undated.

Lennerlöf, Lennart, "*Personaladministration i Framtidens Företag*." Talk given at conference organized by the Development Council, April 23, 1970.

Lesieur, Frederick G., *The Scanlon Plan*. Cambridge, Mass.: M.I.T. Press, 1958.

———, and Puckett, Elbridge S., "The Scanlon Plan Has Proved Itself." *Harvard Business Review*, September–October 1969.

Levenstein, Aaron, *Why People Work*. New York: Crowell-Collier, 1962.

Lewis, Anthony, "Down in the Village." *International Herald Tribune*, December 25, 1971.

Likert, Rensis, *New Patterns of Management*. New York: McGraw-Hill, 1961.

———, *The Human Organization*. New York: McGraw-Hill, 1967.

———, "The Relationship between Management Behavior and Social Structure." Talk given at CIOS conference, 1969, Tokyo.

Lincoln, James F., *Incentive Management*. Cleveland: The Lincoln Electric Company, 1951.

LO, *Demokrati i Företagen*. Stockholm: Prisma, 1971.

———, *Fackföreningsrörelsen och Företagsdemokrati*. Stockholm: Landsorganisationen i Sverige, 1961.

Loichot, Marcel, *La Mutation ou L'Aurore du Pancapitalisme*. Paris: Tchou, 1970.

Lynch, Philip, "*Mitbestimmung*: Socializing the Losses?" *Dun's Review*, July 1969.

Lynd, Staughton, "Again—Don't Tread on Me." *Newsweek*, July 6, 1970.

Maire, Edmond, *Pour un Socialisme Démocratique*. Paris: E.P.I., 1971.

Mallet, Serge, *La Nouvelle Classe Ouvrière*. Paris: Éditions du Seuil, 1969.

Marcuse, Herbert, *One Dimensional Man*. London: Sphere Books Ltd., 1968.

Marrow, Alfred J., Bowers, David G., and Seashore, Stanley E., *Management by Participation*. New York: Harper & Row, 1967.

Marx, Karl, *Economic and Philosophical Manuscripts of 1844*. London: Lawrence & Wishart Ltd., 1970.

Maslow, Abraham, *Motivation and Personality*. New York: Harper & Row, 1970.

Mayo, Elton, *The Human Problems of an Industrial Civilization*. Boston: Harvard University, Graduate School of Business Administration, 1946.

McCormick, Charles P., *The Power of People*. New York: Harper & Brothers, 1949.

McGregor, Douglas, *The Human Side of Enterprise*. New York: McGraw-Hill, 1960.

McWhinney, Will, with Élden, James, "Not Industrial Democracy, but a Reticular Society." Paper presented at the Center for Study of Democratic Institutions, Santa Barbara, California, October 1971.

Meister, Albert, Où Va l'Autogestion Yougoslave? Paris: Éditions Anthropos, 1970.

Melman, Seymour, "Industrial Efficiency under Managerial vs. Cooperative Decision-Making." Mimeographed report published by Hakibutz Ha'artzi Hashomer Hatzair, Tel Aviv, undated.

Miles, Raymond E., "Human Relations or Human Resources?" Harvard Business Review, July–August 1965.

Miller, George A., "Psychology as a means of Promoting Human Welfare." American Psychologist, October 1969.

Mills, C. Wright, White Collar. New York: Oxford University Press, 1951.

Modig, Karl-Erik et al., Demokratisering av Arbetslivet. Stockholm: TCO, 1970.

Moscow News, "Fundamental Legislation of the Union of Soviet Socialist Republics and Union Republics on Labor." Moscow News, No. 31, 1970.

Mossé, Claude, The Ancient World at Work. London: Chatto & Windus, 1969.

Mozina, Stane; Jerovsek, Janez; Tannenbaum, Arnold S., and Likert, Rensis, "Testing a Management Style." European Business, Autumn 1970.

Myers, M. Scott, "Conditions for Manager Motivation." Harvard Business Review, January–February 1966.

———, "Every Employee a Manager." California Management Review, Spring 1968.

———, Every Employee a Manager. New York: McGraw-Hill, 1970.

———, "Increasing Manager Motivation." In Harold M. F. Rush (ed.), Managing Change. New York: National Industrial Conference Board, 1970.

———, and Gommersall, Earl D., "Breakthrough in On-the-Job Training." Harvard Business Review, July–August 1966.

Narkiewicz, Olga A., The Making of the Soviet State Apparatus. Manchester: Manchester University Press, 1970.

Neersø, Peter, Den Jugoslaviske Arbejderselvforvaltning. Copenhagen: Arbejdsministeriets Udvalg Vedrørende Forholdene på Arbejdspladserne m.v., 1969.

Neff, Walter, Work and Human Behavior. New York: Atherton Press, 1968.

Osipov, G. V. (ed.), Industry and Labour in the U.S.S.R. London: Tavistock Publications, 1966.

Parker, Stanley, The Future of Work and Leisure. London: MacGibbon & Klee, 1971.

Pašić, Najdan, Dictatorship by the Proletariat or over the Proletariat. Belgrade: Stipe Duževič, 1968.

Pateman, Carole, Participation and Democratic Theory. London: Cambridge University Press, 1970.

Paul, Bill, "Overnite Success." Wall Street Journal, February 22, 1972.

Paul, William B., Jr.; Robertson, Keith B., and Herzberg, Frederick, "Job Enrichment Pays Off." Harvard Business Review, March–April 1969.

Pearlstine, Norman, "UAW: 'Causes' vs. Bread and Butter." Wall Street Journal, April 25, 1972.

Penzer, W. N., "Managing Motivated Employees." *Personnel Journal,* May 1971.

Percy, Charles H., "How Good Is the News about Productivity?" *Fortune,* May 1972.

Persons, Stowe, "Christian Communitarianism in America." In Donald Drew and Stowe Persons (eds.), *Socialism and American Life,* Vol. I. Princeton, N.J.: Princeton University Press, 1952.

Peyrefitte, Alain (ed.), *Qu'est-ce Que la Participation?* Paris: Plon, 1969.

Popov, Nebojša, "*Strajkovi u Savremenom Jugoslovenskom Društvu.*" *Sociologija,* No. 4, 1969.

Price, Charlton R., *New Directions in the World of Work—A Conference Report.* Washington, D.C.: The W. E. Upjohn Institute for Employment Research, 1971.

Priouret, Roger, *La France et le Management.* Paris: Denoël, 1968.

Pyle, William C., "Monitoring Human Resources—'On Line.'" *Michigan Business Review,* July 1970.

Qvale, Ulrik, "The Industrial Democracy Project in Norway." Paper presented at International Industrial Relations Association Second World Congress, Geneva, September 1–4, 1970.

Radzio, Heiner (ed.), *Warum Mitbestimmung—und Wie?* Düsseldorf: Econ Verlag, 1970.

Raskin, A. H., "The Labor Movement Must Start Moving." *Harvard Business Review,* January–February 1970.

Revel, Jean-François, *Ni Marx Ni Jésus.* Paris: Robert Laffont, 1970.

Rhenman, Eric, *Företagsdemokrati och Företagsorganisation.* Stockholm: Pan/Norstedts, 1967.

Ribicoff, Abraham, "The Alienation of the American Worker." *The Saturday Review,* April 22, 1972.

Richard, James E., "A President's Experience with Democratic Management." The A. G. Bush Library of Management, University of Chicago, Occasional Paper No. 18, 1959.

Richman, Barry, *Management Development and Education in the Soviet Union.* East Lansing, Mich.: Michigan State University Press, 1967.

Rioux, Lucien, "Un Colosse Écartelé." *Le Nouvel Observateur,* April 27, 1970.

Roethke, Theodore, "Dolor." In *The Awakening.* Garden City, N.Y.: Doubleday, 1953.

Rogers, C. R., "Towards a Theory of Creativity." In P. E. Vernon (ed.), *Creativity.* London: Penguin Books, 1970.

Rosner, Menachem, "Principles, Types and Problems of Direct Democracy in the Kibbutz." In *The Kibbutz as a Way of Life in Modern Society.* Southfield, Mich.: College of Jewish Studies, 1970.

Rosow, Jerome N., "The Problems of the Blue-Collar Worker." Memorandum prepared for the Secretary of Labor, Washington, D.C., April 1970.

Roszak, Theodore, *The Making of a Counter Culture.* New York: Anchor Books, 1969.

Rousseau, Jean-Jacques, *Du Contrat Social*. Paris: Union Générale des Éditions, 1963.

Rush, Harold M. F., *Behavioral Science—Concepts and Management Application*. New York: National Industrial Conference Board, 1970.

————, *Job Design for Motivation*. New York: The Conference Board, 1971.

Russell, Bertrand, *Autobiography*, Vol. I. London: George Allen & Unwin, 1967.

Rybicki, Z., "Workers' Participation in Management in Poland." *International Institute for Labour Studies Bulletin*, November 1968.

SAF, *Direct and Total Wage Costs for Workers, International Surveys*. Stockholm: Svenska Arbetsgivareföreningen, 1964–71.

————, *Om Samarbetet i Företagen*. Stockholm: Svenska Arbetsgivareföreningen, 1971.

Salpukas, Agis, "Auto Workers Are Given a Voice on Assembly Line." *New York Times*, June 19, 1972.

————, "Workers Increasingly Rebel Against Boredom on Assembly Line." *New York Times*, April 2, 1972.

Sampson, Anthony, "The Middle-Class Monopoly." *Sunday Times*, August 22, 1971.

Schein, Edgar H., *Organizational Psychology*. Englewood Cliffs, N.J.: Prentice-Hall, 1965.

Schon, Donald, "Change and Industrial Society." *The Listener*, November 19, 26, December 3, 10, 17, 24, 1970.

Schwartz, W., "*Cogestion et Participation dans la République Fédérale d'Allemagne*." In Paul Frize et al., *La Participation dans l'Entreprise*. Paris: Centre National d'Information pour la Productivité des Entreprises, 1969.

Seashore, Stanley E., and Bowers, David E., "Durability of Organizational Change." *American Psychologist*, March 1970.

Segel, Sylvain, *Les Idées de Mai*. Paris: Gallimard, 1968, p. 44.

Servan-Shreiber, Jean-Jacques, *Ciel et Terre*. Paris: Denoël, 1970.

Sexton, Brendan, "'Middle-Class' Workers and the New Politics" in Irving Howe (ed.), *Beyond the New Left*. New York: McCall, 1970.

Shatil, Joseph E., "Criteria for Socio-Economic Efficiency of the Kibbutz." Proceedings of the Second World Congress for Rural Sociology, Enschede, The Netherlands, August 1968. Tel Aviv: Centre International de Recherces sur les Communautés Rurales.

Silk, Leonard, "Blue-Collar Blues in the United States." *International Herald Tribune*, September 4, 1970.

Sirotković, Jakov, "The Influence of Self-Management on the Development of Yugoslav Economics." *Ekonomist*, 1969.

Smith, Adam, *The Wealth of Nations*. London: Dent, 1970.

Sophocles, "Oedipus at Colonus" in Whitney J. Oates and Eugene O'Neill, Jr. (eds.), *The Complete Greek Drama*, Vol. I. New York: Random House, 1938.

Sørensen, Bjørg Aase, *Når Arbeiderne Styrer Bedriften*. Oslo: Pax Forlag, 1970.

Sørensen, Per, "Lighedspunkter og Forskelle." *Ledelse og Udvikling*, June 1971.

Spiro, Melford E., *Kibbutz: Venture in Utopia*. New York: Schocken Books, 1963.

Stan, Edward, "Human Resource Accounting and Financial Management." In R. Lee Brummet et al., *Human Resource Accounting*. Ann Arbor, Mich.: Foundation for Research on Human Behavior, 1968.

Stendenbach, F. J., "Industrial Democracy—A Contemporary Need." Paper presented at Participation and Manpower Policy seminar sponsored by OECD, Paris, September 10–12, 1969.

Sturmthal, Adolf, *Workers Councils*, Cambridge, Mass.: Harvard University Press, 1964.

———, "Workers' Participation in Management: A Review of United States Experience." *International Institute for Labour Studies Bulletin*, June 1969.

Svanberg, Lena, "Hur Ge Mening åt Jobbet vid Maskinen?" *Industria*, April 1971.

———, "Ingen Väg Tillbaka." *Industria*, March 1971.

Tabb, J. Y., "Workers' Participation in Management in Israel." *International Institute for Labour Studies Bulletin*, June 1970.

Tannenbaum, Arnold S., "Individual Adjustment and Organizational Performance." In Arnold S. Tannenbaum (ed.), *Control in Organizations*. New York: McGraw-Hill, 1968.

Tawney, R. H., *Religion and the Rise of Capitalism*. London: Penguin Books, 1938.

Taylor, Frederick Winslow, *Scientific Management*. New York: Harper & Row, 1947.

Thompson, Dennis F., *The Democratic Citizen*. London: Cambridge University Press, 1970.

Thorsrud, Einar and Emery, Fred, *Industrielt Demokrati*. Oslo: Universitetsforlaget, 1964.

———, *Mot en Ny Bedriftsorganisasjon*. Oslo: Tanum, 1969.

Tinbergen, Jan, "Does Self-Management Approach the Optimum Order?" In M. J. Broekmeyer (ed.), *Yugoslav Workers' Self-Management*. Dordrecht, Holland: D. Reidel Publishing Company, 1970.

Tito, Josip Broz, "Power Must Remain in the Hands of the Working Class." In *Reorganization of the LCY*. Belgrade: Aktuelna Pitanja Socijalizma, 1967.

———, "Report." Paper delivered at Ninth Congress of the League of Communists of Yugoslavia, 1969. Belgrade: Aktuelna Pitanja Socijalizma, 1969.

———, "The Speech of the President." Delivered at the Sixth Congress of the Confederation of Trade Unions of Yugoslavia, 1968. Belgrade: CTUY, 1968.

Touraine, Alain, *Le Mouvement de Mai ou le Communisme Utopique*. Paris: Éditions du Seuil, 1968.

Townsend, Robert, *Up the Organization*. Greenwich: Fawcett, 1970.

Trist, E. L.; Higgin, G. W.; Murray, H., and Pollock, A. B., *Organizational Choice*. London: Tavistock Publications, 1963.

Vroom, Victor H., *Work and Motivation*. New York: John Wiley & Sons, 1964.

Walker, Charles R., and Guest, Robert H., *The Man on the Assembly Line*. Cambridge, Mass.: Harvard University Press, 1952.

Walker, Kenneth F., "Workers' Participation in Management." Paper presented at Second World Congress of International Industrial Relations Association, Geneva, September 1–4, 1970.

Walton, Richard E., "Alienation and Innovation in the Work Place." Paper prepared for the Work in America Project, sponsored by the Secretary of the Department of Health, Education and Welfare, 1972.

Weber, Max, *Protestantism and the Spirit of Capitalism*. London: Unwin University Books, 1930.

———, "The Ideal Bureaucracy." In Gerald D. Bell, *Organizations and Human Behavior*. Englewood Cliffs, N.J.: Prentice-Hall, 1967.

Weil, Simone, *L'Enracinement*. Paris: Gallimard, 1949.

Werther, Betty, "Higher Education in France and the U.S." *International Herald Tribune*, May 14, 1971.

Whyte, William H., Jr., *The Organization Man*. New York: Simon & Schuster, 1956.

Wigforss, Ernst, *Materialistisk Historieuppfattning—Industriell Demokrati*. Stockholm: Tidens Förlag, 1970.

———, *Ur Mina Minnen*. Stockholm: Bokförlaget Prisma, 1964.

Willener, Alfred, *L'Image-Action de la Société*. Paris: Éditions du Seuil, 1970.

Wilson, Edmund, *To the Finland Station*. Garden City, N.Y.: Doubleday, 1940.

Woodward, Joan, "Management and Technology," in Tom Burns (ed.), *Industrial Man*. London: Penguin Books, 1969.

Wright, Frank Lloyd, *The Future of Architecture*. New York: The Horizon Press, 1953.

Yudin, Yehuda, "Workers' Participation in Management in Israel." Paper presented at Participation and Manpower Policy seminar sponsored by OECD, Paris, September 10–12, 1969.

Županov, Josip, and Tannenbaum, Arnold S., "The Distribution of Control in Some Yugoslav Industrial Organizations." In Arnold S. Tannenbaum (ed.), *Control in Organizations*. New York: McGraw-Hill, 1968.